Lecture Notes in Computer Science 2549

Edited by G. Goos, J. Hartmanis, and J. van Leeuwen

Springer
Berlin
Heidelberg
New York
Barcelona
Hong Kong
London
Milan
Paris
Tokyo

Jordi Cortadella   Alex Yakovlev
Grzegorz Rozenberg (Eds.)

Concurrency and Hardware Design

Advances in Petri Nets

Springer

Series Editors

Gerhard Goos, Karlsruhe University, Germany
Juris Hartmanis, Cornell University, NY, USA
Jan van Leeuwen, Utrecht University, The Netherlands

Volume Editors

Jordi Cortadella
Technical University of Catalonia, Department of Software
Campus Nord, Mòdul C5, Jordi Girona Salgado 1-3, 08034 Barcelona, Spain
E-mail: jordic@lsi.upc.es

Alex Yakovlev
University of Newcastle, School of Electrical, Electronic and Computer Engineering
Newcastle upon Tyne, NE1 7RU, UK
E-mail: alex.yakovlev@ncl.ac.uk

Grzegorz Rozenberg
Leiden University, Center for Natural Computing
Niels Bohrweg 1, 2333 CA Leiden, The Netherlands
E-mail: rozenber@liacs.nl

Cataloging-in-Publication Data applied for

A catalog record for this book is available from the Library of Congress.

Bibliographic information published by Die Deutsche Bibliothek
Die Deutsche Bibliothek lists this publication in the Deutsche Nationalbibliografie;
detailed bibliographic data is available in the Internet at <http://dnb.ddb.de>.

CR Subject Classification (1998): B, C, D.2.4, F.1, F.4

ISSN 0938-5894
ISBN 3-540-00199-9 Springer-Verlag Berlin Heidelberg New York

Springer-Verlag Berlin Heidelberg New York
a member of BertelsmannSpringer Science+Business Media GmbH

http://www.springer.de

© Springer-Verlag Berlin Heidelberg 2002
Printed in Germany

Typesetting: Camera-ready by author, data conversion by DA-TeX Gerd Blumenstein
Printed on acid-free paper   SPIN: 10871699   06/3142   5 4 3 2 1 0

Preface

As CMOS semiconductor technology strides towards billions of transistors on a single die new problems arise on the way. They are concerned with the diminishing fabrication process features, which affect for example the gate-to-wire delay ratio. They manifest themselves in greater variations of size and operating parameters of devices, which put the overall reliability of systems at risk. And, most of all, they have tremendous impact on design productivity, where the costs of utilizing the growing silicon 'real estate' rocket to billions of dollars that have to be spent on design, verification, and testing. All such problems call for new design approaches and models for digital systems. Furthermore, new developments in non-CMOS technologies, such as single-electron transistors, rapid single-flux-quantum devices, quantum dot cells, molecular devices, etc., add extra demand for new research in system design methodologies.

What kind of models and design methodologies will be required to build systems in all these new technologies? Answering this question, even for each particular type of new technology generation, is not easy, especially because sometimes it is not even clear what kind of elementary devices are feasible there. This problem is of an interdisciplinary nature. It requires an bridges between different scientific communities. The bridges must be built very quickly, and be maximally flexible to accommodate changes taking place in a logarithmic timescale. On one side of such a bridge lies the nature (physics, chemistry, or biology) of the elementary devices that can be built in the chosen technology. On the other side are the functional properties of the desired computational operators. The recent developments in the area of DNA computing serve as a very good example of interdisciplinary bridge construction.

This book is, however, not about front-end nanotechnologies and novel computational mechanisms made possible on their basis. It is about one, relatively old and well-known behavioral paradigm in computing, called concurrency, and the ways concurrency is exhibited or can be exploited in relatively standard, digital hardware devices. Nevertheless, our hope is that the book will contribute to the series of publications aimed to be interdisciplinary. The above-mentioned bridge here should not be too challenging to construct as the 'banks of the river' are not too far apart. They can be roughly termed theoretical computer science and electronic system engineering. Understanding of most of this book by the representatives of both communities should not require additional background reading. So, thanks to this gap being not too wide, it seems possible to keep this material to a highly technical level, which should hopefully enable and encourage researchers standing on either side to start, or continue, thinking about new models, applications, design methods, algorithms, or software tools.

The book is aimed at inviting computer scientists working in the area of concurrency to look in the direction of hardware technology, of what is practically implementable regardless of theoretical bounds and restrictions. Remember Sean

Connery's saying in one of his numerious action movies: "It is impossible ... but it's doable!" This is exactly what engineers and practitioners often have in mind, when theoreticians tell them about computationally intractable problems or exponential growths.

On the other hand, computer scientists often go for solutions to real-world problems that are far too abstract and require layers of intermediate software packages to implement. A hardware engineer (not perhaps with a soldering iron these days!) can come up with an elegant and simple solution that can be realized in a handful of logic gates or transistors. For example, controlling concurrent processes and asynchronous interactions is relatively easy to implement in circuits. Yet, complicated mechanisms are required to be built on top of operating system kernels in software to support concurrency between different execution threads. In the end, what is clear and transparent mathematically becomes obscure and unpredicatble in realization.

This book also aims to give some messages to theoreticians, often relying on abstract computational models that are far from physical reality. As an example, many of us attended courses on data structures and algorithms, where we learnt that a quick sort is much faster than a bubble sort ($O(n \log n)$ vs. $O(n^2)$). That analysis was done under the assumption that moving one element from one location of the array to another location takes a constant time. However, a circuit designer implementing such algorithms in hardware would immediately disagree with such a complexity analysis. Today, wire delays are comparable to gate delays, and moving data across a chip takes a time proportional to the length of the move. For this reason, hardware designers would probably choose bubble sort as the best approach to sort an array stored in a one-dimensional space, since all moves are local (i.e., take a constant time). Instead, moves in a quick sort are global, thus taking time $O(n)$, and resulting in an overall complexity of $O(n^2 \log n)$. The question is, at which level of abstraction is a quick sort better than a bubble sort? Definitely not at the physical level.

For many years, practical digital circuits were built using global clocking. Although the clock was often not needed to perform the system's main function (barring, perhaps, hard real-time systems, but the real-time clock is another issue!), using the clock to pulse time explicitly, at the very-high-frequency (up to hundreds of megahertz) level, helped to construct complex circuits without worrying about races and hazards in gates and flip-flops. The age of global clocking is however coming to an end, whether designers welcome this fact or not. There are fundamental problems with distributing the signal of the gigahertz clock uniformly and reliably to every part of several-square-centimeter silicon die with devices of less than 100 nanometers. The irony of the situation is that while the clock used to be the bodyguard against hazards and unpredictable asynchrony, it now becomes its first enemy! With the increasing clock frequency the effects of parametric jitter, due to thermal fluctuations for example, that may cause synchronization failures, become unavoidable. New ways of building hardware, using distributed clocking, are being sought. One such paradigm is called Globally Asynchronous Locally Synchronous (GALS) systems. It is based on the idea of a compromise between two contradictory issues. One is the fact that at the chip level communications have to be asynchronous and not rely on one central timing engine. The other is the fact that the productivity crisis forces designers to maximize the reuse of existing hardware solutions, the so-called intellectual property (IP) cores. Since the latter have been typically designed for clocked systems, they are deemed to remain intact and thus, when placed in the 'hostile' asynchronous surrounding, must be protected by using special wrappers. Whether this GALS paradigm, somewhat of a half-measure, is here to stay with us for another decade or longer does not really matter, but there is a clear meassage from the semiconductor technology people that 'serious climatic changes on the face of the die' have approached us already.

It is worth emphasizing here, particularly for the computer science audience, that temperature is one of the biggest threats to system design these days. Part of this problem boomerangs back on the same old designer's friend, the clock. The clock is responsible for radiating at least 40 % of the thermal energy on modern microprocessor chips.

The problems with variations of temperature and other parameters, such as switching thresholds of transistors, either in operation or at fabrication, add to the motivation for searching for ways of living without the clock at all. And here we come back to the subject of this book. Indeed, we must now look at self-timed or asynchronous circuit design, which is often associated with the real, physical world of concurrency. The history of research in asynchronous hardware design has traditionally been a fertile field for research on concurrency and Petri nets. Many new ideas about modeling and the analysis of concurrent systems, and Petri nets in particular, grew out of the theory of asynchronous digital circuits. For example, the theory of speed-independent circuits by D.E. Muller and W.C. Bartky laid the foundation for the important concepts of feasible sequences, cumulative states, finite equivalence classes, confluence, semimodularity, and so on. Similarly, the theory and practice of digital hardware design have always been watchful to the appearance of new results in concurrency models and analytic tools, including Petri nets, CSP, CCS, BDD and symbolic traversal, partial-order reductions, etc. Likewise, with clocked hardware, the sequential model of a finite state machine played the role of the 'theoretical mentor' to keep logic design well-disciplined.

The subject of concurrency and hardware design brings to our mind the question of what is specific about this relation and how it is different, if at all, from the use of concurrency in software engineering. One, perhaps, controversial idea is the following, which is based on the notion of computation distribution.

Hardware, especially when clockless, is distributed by its nature. So, in hardware design, the original concept of the system specification gradually becomes more distributed and concurrent as it evolves from the specification to its implementation. Thus the hardware synthesis is the problem of distributing a global system's state between a set of local states, the states of registers and flip-flops. In software design the process is somewhat reversed. One often starts with a possibly ambitious object-oriented and highly concurrent model. In the end everything must eventually be run on a single processor, or even a set of parallel processors, where the computations are sequential by definition (unless and until they become concurrent again at the microcode level thanks to superscalar and asynchronous hardware!). The design process, seen as solving a synthesis problem, must therefore schedule concurrent actions in a sequential time line, collecting the local states into the global state of the C or machine-level program. Both of these views are closely related, especially in the world of embedded systems, increasingly implemented as Systems-on-a-Chip (SoCs), where the traditional understanding of the boundary between hardware and software becomes very blurred. Because of that, it is most natural to consider the area of designing embedded systems also within the scope of interest of this volume.

In the last four years we have been involved in several attempts to bring the theory of concurrency and Petri nets closer to hardware design applications. These included two special workshops (1998, Lisbon, and 1999, Williamsburg) and one advanced tutorial (2000, Aarhus) held within the annual International Conference on Applications and Theory of Petri Nets. Two conferences on the Application of Concurrency to System Design have been held (1998, Auzu, Japan, and 2002, Newcastle, UK). One collective monograph, *Hardware Design and Petri Nets*, was published in 2000.

The papers collected in this book cover the scope of applications of concurrency techniques in hardware design. They are organized into four parts. Part I deals with formal models of digital circuits using process-based and net-based descriptions, and demonstrates their interrelationship. The three contributions here cover the problem of process composition satisfying certain safety and progress properties, the problem of the decomposition of signal transition graphs for more efficient synthesis of asynchronous circuits, and finally the method of translating delay-insensitive process algebra specification to Petri nets for their subsequent synthesis into circuits. Part II introduces approaches to designing asynchronous circuits. One of them is based on the idea of distributed clocking of arrays of processing elements, which nicely complements the micropipeline approach. The other presents new methods for the synthesis of asynchronous circuits using structural approximations and interface-preserving transformations on signal transition graphs. The papers in Part III deal with design support for embedded systems. One of them presents the functional model, the system architecture, and the mapping between functional blocks and architectural elements within VCC, a widely used tool for system-level design. The other paper looks at the design methodology for highly heterogenous embedded systems that is currently implemented in the new-generation tool Metropolis. Finally, Part IV addresses the problems of timed verification and performance analysis of hardware using symbolic techniques. The first contribution introduces a methodology for analyzing timed systems symbolically, from a formula characterizing sets of timed states, and applies it to timed guarded command models of circuits. The second paper presents a symbolic approach to analyzing the performance of asynchronous circuits using discrete-time Markov chains, and shows a method for battling the state-space explosion problem.

Acknowledgements. We are very much indebted to all the authors contributing to this book, and to David Kinniment, Alex Kondratyev, Maciej Koutny, Oded Maler, and Fei Xia, who acted as external referees (note that the papers were also cross-refereed internally), for their constructive criticism. Finally, we would like to mention the excellent cooperation with Springer-Verlag during the preparation of this volume.

September 2002   Jordi Cortadella
                                                        Alex Yakovlev
                                                    Grzegorz Rozenberg

Table of Contents

Composing Snippets

Igor Benko[1] and Jo Ebergen[2]

[1] University of Waterloo, Waterloo, ON N2L3G1, Canada
[2] Sun Microsystems Laboratories, Palo Alto, CA 94303, USA

Abstract. We introduce a simple formal framework for specifying and implementing concurrent systems. The framework enables the specification of safety and progress properties and is based on Enhanced Characteristic Functions. The use of Enhanced Characteristic Functions leads to simple definitions of operations such as hiding and various process compositions. We discuss two compositions: the network composition for building networks of processes and the specification composition for building specifications of processes. A central notion in our framework is the notion of a snippet. A snippet represents a part behavior of a process satisfying one specific constraint. A specification of a concurrent process satisfying all constraints is expressed by means of a specification composition of snippets. We present various properties of the specification and network compositions that can be helpful in the specification and implementation of concurrent systems. We illustrate our design approach with the design of some asynchronous circuits.

1 Introduction

The first step in building software or hardware is producing a specification. This step can present major challenges, especially when one is faced with specifying a system that involves a significant degree of concurrency. One challenge is to choose a formalism that is simple, yet expressive enough to capture the intended properties of a design.

We propose a simple formal framework for the specification and implementation of concurrent systems. The formalism makes use of Enhanced Characteristic Functions (ECFs), which are due to Verhoeff [20]. Enhanced Characteristic functions assign a safety and progress property to each sequence of communication events. Enhanced Characteristic Functions also lead to simple definitions of operations such as hiding and various process compositions. We discuss two compositions: the network composition for building networks of processes and the specification composition for building specifications of processes.

A central notion in our framework is the notion of a snippet. A snippet represents a part behavior of a process satisfying one specific constraint. We build a specification of a concurrent process by means of a specification composition of snippets, possibly hiding some internal symbols. Such specifications can then be used to verify or derive an implementation. We present various properties of the specification and network compositions, which may be helpful in the specification and implementation of concurrent systems. Besides presenting a simple

J. Cortadella et al. (Eds.): Concurrency and Hardware Design, LNCS 2549, pp. 1–33, 2002.

formalism, our main contributions are a constraint-based approach to building specifications and a part-wise refinement method that allows us to avoid state explosions in the verification of an implementations.

Although our design method can be applied to the design of various concurrent systems, we illustrate our method with the design of some asynchronous circuits. An asynchronous circuit consists of a network of components, each operating at its own speed, without a global synchronization signal, commonly called the clock. Global synchronization performed by the clock is replaced by local synchronization between components, typically achieved by means of some request/acknowledge handshaking. Designing circuits without a clock has been studied since the 1940's [17], but it has only been since the late 1980's that asynchronous circuits have been receiving a growing attention [16], because of their potential for quick design turnaround, low power, speed, or reduced electromagnetic radiation [18].

A number of formalisms have been applied to asynchronous circuit design; see [4, 7] for an overview. ECF processes belong to the family of formalisms called trace theory [9, 10, 19, 20]. ECF functions are introduced by Tom Verhoeff in [20] to describe his XDI model of processes. Willem Mallon et al. expanded this model to the X^2DI model in [12]. The basic features of our model are similar to the models of Verhoeff and Mallon. There are, however, some differences. Most notably, we consider a domain of processes that is larger than the domain of delay-insensitive processes captured by the XDI and X^2DI models. Although our larger domain of processes has its limitations when implementing processes as asynchronous circuits [5], we believe the larger domain leads to a simpler formalism. Because of the larger domain of processes, our model has a different definition for the composition of processes.

Our progress criteria are closely related to finalization in Process Spaces from [14]. The Process Spaces model, however, requires a separate specification of a process for each correctness condition that is addressed. ECF processes, on the other hand, capture safety and progress concerns at the same time.

Several formalisms propose a constraint-based approach to building specifications, which can be useful when behaviors involve a large degree of concurrency.

In [3] the authors discuss how a constraint-based approach to specifications is supported in LOTOS. In [10] the use of the "weave" operation is advocated for building specifications from constraints. The usage of the weave in [11] and [2] demonstrates how combining behavioral constraints can lead to concise specifications of non-trivial behaviors. In [15], a constraint-based specification takes advantage of chain constraints to introduce timing requirements into specifications.

2   Overview

For the convenience of the reader, here is a brief overview of the rest of the sections with a brief explanation what is in each section.

Section 3: ECF Processes. This section defines an ECF process: a process defined by means of an Enhanced Characteristic Function (ECF). An ECF process can be represented by a state machine, where each state is labeled with one of five state labels. The label in each state indicates the safety and progress conditions of the process in that state. Safety conditions indicate whether the process can cause a failure, for example. Progress conditions indicate whether the process must proceed or may stop, for example.

Section 4: Safety and Progress Violations. Some processes may violate general safety and progress requirements. This section explains what constitutes a safety violation and what constitutes a progress violation. The definitions of the violations make use of the state transitions of the state machine and the extra state information present in an ECF process.

Section 5: Refinement. What does it mean that one process implements another process? This section formalizes the implementation conditions by defining a refinement relation such that the statement "P refines Q" is the same as saying "P implements Q." The refinement relation is a partial ordering relation among processes.

Section 6: Product. The most important operation on processes is the product. We use the product of processes to define the two process compositions, namely network composition and specification composition. This section gives the mathematical definition of process product and states some of its properties. A subsection explains the network composition and illustrates this composition with an example.

Section 7: Reflection. A specification prescribes the behavior of a process and its environment. The reflection operation switches the roles of process and environment. This section defines the reflection and presents some of its properties.

Section 8: Refinement and Correctness Conditions. This section combines the results of the previous four sections. We explain how the refinement ordering of Section 5 relates to the safety and progress conditions of Section 4. The relationship makes use of the product of processes defined in Section 6 and the reflection of a process defined in Section 7.

Section 9: Hiding. The hiding operation is our second most important operation on processes. As the name suggests, hiding allows us to abstract away local symbols. This section defines the hiding operation on ECF processes and gives a number of useful properties of hiding.

Section 10: Two Design Theorems. The process operations, such as the product and hiding operations, are only useful if they allow us to find or verify process refinements in a convenient way. Two theorems that are crucial in finding and verifying refinements are the Substitution Theorem and the Factorization Theorem. We explain and illustrate both theorems in this section.

Section 11: Specification Composition. The second composition also derived from the process product is the specification composition. The specification composition is convenient for building specifications of a process by composing what we call "snippets." This section presents the definition of specification composition, snippets, and gives many properties of the specification composition.

Section 12: Commands. In order to represent processes in a convenient textual form, we define commands. Commands are similar to regular expressions.

Section 13: Part-Wise Design Method. This section brings all previous sections together. It explains a part-wise design method and illustrates the part-wise design method by specifying and verifying a hardware implementation of the famous dining philosopher's problem.

Section 14. Conclusions. We conclude with a brief summary and some remarks.

For the sake of brevity, we omitted most of the proofs. The missing proofs and additional information can be found in [1].

3   ECF Processes

An ECF process P is a triple $\langle \mathbf{i}.P, \mathbf{o}.P, \mathbf{f}.P \rangle$, where $\mathbf{i}.P$ is an input alphabet, $\mathbf{o}.P$ is an output alphabet. The input and output alphabet of a process contain all input and output actions that can occur for that process. We stipulate that $\mathbf{i}.P$ and $\mathbf{o}.P$ are disjoint. The alphabet of process P, denoted by $\mathbf{a}.P$ is $\mathbf{i}.P \cup \mathbf{o}.P$. A sequence of actions from an alphabet is called a trace. An enhanced characteristic function (ECF) is a function $\mathbf{f}.P : (\mathbf{a}.P)^* \to \Lambda$, which maps traces over alphabet $\mathbf{a}.P$ to a set of labels Λ. By attaching a label to a trace we specify the progress and safety properties of a process after having executed the sequence of communication events represented by the trace. We borrow the set of labels from [20]:

$$\Lambda = \{\perp, \Delta, \square, \nabla, \top\}$$

The labels $\perp$, Δ, $\square$, ∇, and $\top$ are pronounced as "bottom," "delta," "box," "nabla," and "top," respectively. The interpretation of labels specifies the requirements and guarantees that pertain to either a process or to its environment. After a process has executed a trace labeled with ∇, the process guarantees progress by eventually producing an output. In other words, a trace labeled with ∇ puts a process in a *transient* state. Traces labeled with ∇ are called transient traces. In a transient state, a process may be capable of receiving an input. Notice that ∇ resembles a triangle standing on a single corner, which is an unstable or "transient" state.

A trace labeled with $\square$ brings the process in an *indifferent* state. Such a trace is called an indifferent trace. After having executed an indifferent trace, a process does not guarantee to produce an output, neither does the process demand an input from its environment.

A trace labeled with Δ is called a *demanding* trace and brings a process to a demanding state. In a demanding state, a process demands an input but does not guarantee to produce an output, although producing an output may be possible.

A trace labeled with $\bot$ is a *failure* trace and brings a process to a failure state. An output ending in a failure state indicates that the process can cause a failure by producing that output. An input ending in a failure state indicates that the environment causes a failure if it provides that input. When we want to specify that in a certain state a process cannot receive particular input, because that would lead to a failure, then we specify that the next state after that input is a failure state.

A trace labeled with $\top$ is a *miracle* trace and brings a process to a miracle state. An input ending in a miracle state indicates that the environment can cause a miracle by producing that input. An output ending in a miracle state indicates that the process can cause a miracle by producing that output. Miracles, however, cannot be performed by a process. Accordingly, when we want to specify that in a certain state a process cannot produce a particular output, we specify that the next state after that output is a miracle state. Thus, $\bot$ and $\top$ provide a way to specify that an input or output may not or cannot occur in a particular state: an input may not occur if it leads to a $\bot$ state and an output cannot occur if it leads to a $\top$ state.

Traces labeled with either $\square$, Δ, or ∇ are called *legal* traces, and traces labeled with either $\bot$ or $\top$ are called *illegal* traces. The set of legal traces for process P is denoted by $l.P$. Illegal traces define the behaviors of a process where a failure or miracle has occurred. We require that all extensions of illegal traces are also illegal. More formally, an ECF for a process must be $\bot$-persistent and $\top$-persistent:

$$\mathbf{f}.P.t = \bot \;\; \Rightarrow \;\; (\forall u : u \in (\mathbf{a}.P)^* : \mathbf{f}.P.tu = \bot) \tag{1}$$

$$\mathbf{f}.P.t = \top \;\; \Rightarrow \;\; (\forall u : u \in (\mathbf{a}.P)^* : \mathbf{f}.P.tu = \top) \tag{2}$$

We write $\mathcal{PROC}(I, O)$ to denote the domain of processes with input alphabet I and output alphabet O. In $\mathcal{PROC}(I, O)$ there are two special processes, MIRACLE(I, O) and ABORT(I, O). All traces in MIRACLE(I, O) are labeled with $\top$, and all traces in ABORT(I, O) are labeled with $\bot$. MIRACLE can be interpreted as "the best possible process" and ABORT can be seen as "the worst possible process".

We often depict ECF processes by means of state graphs. We start by creating an initial state, which is labeled with $\mathbf{f}.P.\varepsilon$. Next we create a distinct state for each one-symbol trace a and label the state with $\mathbf{f}.P.a$. We also create a transition for each symbol a, such that the transition leads from the initial state to the state corresponding to one-symbol trace a. Input symbols are postfixed with a question mark and output symbols are postfixed with an exclamation mark. We continue this process inductively, creating an infinite state graph, which contains a distinct state for each trace. This state graph can be reduced in the usual way: When the sets of traces, including the labels, stemming from two states are the same, the two states are equivalent. Equivalent states in a state graph may be merged into one state, thus reducing the size of the state graph.

For example, all states of a process labeled with $\bot$ are equivalent, because of the requirement that each process $\bot$ persistent. For that reason, all transitions leaving states labeled with ⊥ are self loops. A similar argument holds for ⊤ states. In order to reduce clutter, we omit the self loops on ⊤ and ⊥ states when we depict processes with state graphs.

Similar to the definition of legal and illegal traces, we call states labeled with either □, △, or ▽ *legal* states and states labeled with either ⊥ or ⊤ *illegal* states.

3.1 Example

Figure 1b shows the state graph corresponding to a process that specifies a WIRE with input a and output b. The sign > points at the initial state of the state graph. Notice that the WIRE is initially in a □ state. That is, neither the WIRE nor its environment have any obligation for producing a communication action. Furthermore, in the initial state the WIRE cannot produce output b, because that leads to a ⊤ state, and may receive input a. After the WIRE has received an input a, the WIRE is in a ▽ state, where it is obliged to produce output b. Moreover, in the ▽ state the WIRE may not receive input a, because that leads to a ⊥ state. The reason for disallowing two inputs a in a row is to guarantee proper behavior of a physical wire, where every voltage transition at the input of the wire leads to a single voltage transition at the output of the wire.

In order to reduce clutter, we may omit the states labeled with ⊥ and ⊤, which results in the state graph of Figure 1c. When the ⊤ and the ⊥ state are not shown, we stipulate that all missing transitions on output symbols lead to the ⊤ state, which means these outputs cannot be produced by the process, and all missing transitions on input symbols lead to the ⊥ state, which means these inputs may not be produced by the environment.

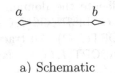

a) Schematic

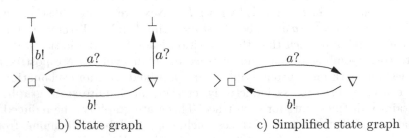

b) State graph   c) Simplified state graph

Fig. 1. A specification of a WIRE as an ECF process

4   Safety and Progress Violations

Safety and progress violations can both be present in a process. A safety violation manifests itself by the presence of a failure state that can be reached by an output from a legal state. If a process can reach such a state, then the process may cause a failure by producing that output. Figure 2 shows a safety violation.

A progress violation manifests itself by the presence of so-called *unhealthy states*. In an unhealthy state progress is required but cannot be satisfied. For example, a ∇ state requires progress by the process, but no output can be produced, because all outputs lead to the $\top$ state. Such a state is shown in Figure 3a. Following [12], we call traces leading to such a state ∇-*unhealthy traces*, and we call a process that contains a ∇-unhealthy trace a ∇-*unhealthy* process.

A similar observation can be made for Δ states where progress is required from the environment but the environment cannot provide an input. A trace leading to such a state is called a Δ-*unhealthy trace* and a process containing a Δ-unhealthy trace is a Δ-unhealthy process. Figure 3b shows a Δ-unhealthy state. A process is unhealthy if it is either ∇ or Δ-unhealthy.

Safety and progress violations can arise in various ways: as a result of composing healthy processes or as a result of hiding output symbols from a healthy process. We have chosen to include processes with safety and progress violations in our domain of ECF processes. The other choice would be to exclude unhealthy processes from our process domain and require that the process domain be closed under composition and hiding. Because the latter choice results in more complicated definitions of composition and hiding, we decided to include unhealthy processes in the domain of ECF processes. For similar reasons, [12] also includes unhealthy processes in the X^{2}DI domain. The XDI model [20] does not include unhealthy processes.

5   Refinement

The refinement relation defines whether one process implements another. If process Q refines process P, denoted by $P \sqsubseteq Q$, we can also say that process Q implements process P. When $P \sqsubseteq Q$, then process Q is at least as safe as process P. Furthermore, process Q makes at least as many progress guarantees

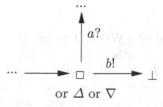

Fig. 2. A safety violation: a failure state can be reached by an output from a legal state

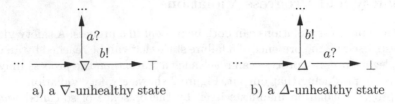

a) a ∇-unhealthy state   b) a Δ-unhealthy state

Fig. 3. A progress violation manifests itself by a legal, unhealthy state

as process P and process Q makes at most as many progress demands on its environment as process P.

The refinement relation is based on the order among trace labels from [20]:

$$\bot \sqsubseteq \Delta \sqsubseteq \Box \sqsubseteq \nabla \sqsubseteq \top \tag{3}$$

A justification for the order on labels is as follows: A failure trace is worse than a trace that does not fail. For that reason, $\bot$ is the least element in the total order on labels. A trace that demands an input but does not guarantee an output is worse than a trace that does not demand an input, so $\Delta \sqsubseteq \Box$. A trace that makes no progress requirements is worse than a trace that guarantees progress, hence $\Box \sqsubseteq \nabla$. Finally, producing a miracle is always better than anything else, thus $\top$ is the greatest of all the labels.

Refinement of processes is defined by the trace-wise extension of refinement of labels. There is one important restriction of refinement: the refinement between two processes is only defined when they have the same input and output alphabet.

Definition 1 (Refinement). *Let P and Q be processes, such that $\mathbf{i}.P = \mathbf{i}.Q$ and $\mathbf{o}.P = \mathbf{o}.Q$. P is refined by Q, denoted by $P \sqsubseteq Q$, iff*

$$P \sqsubseteq Q \;\equiv\; \left(\forall t : t \in (\mathbf{a}.P)^* : \mathbf{f}.P.t \sqsubseteq \mathbf{f}.Q.t \right) \tag{4}$$

Theorem 1 (Properties of refinement). *The refinement relation $\sqsubseteq$ is a partial order on $\mathcal{PROC}(I,O)$. Furthermore, $(\mathcal{PROC}(I,O), \sqsubseteq)$ is a complete lattice.*

5.1   Example

Figure 4 shows a refinement of a WIRE. Process Q in Figure 4 specifies a "reliable" WIRE. Process P, on the other hand, specifies a "demanding lazy" WIRE. In the initial state, process P demands from its environment an input on port a. After having received an input on port a, process P makes no progress guarantees. That is, process P may or may not produce an output on port b. Process Q implements process P, because in the initial state process Q does not demand an input from the environment. That is, process Q makes fewer progress demands

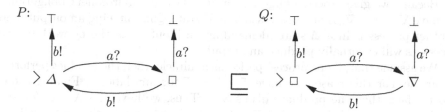

Fig. 4. An example of refinement

on the environment than process P. Furthermore, after having received an input on port a, process Q guarantees that an output on port b is produced. This means that process Q guarantees progress where process P does not. Finally, we notice that the same traces that lead to the $\bot$ state in process P also lead to the $\bot$ state in process Q. Similarly, the same traces that lead to the $\top$ state in process P also lead to the $\top$ state in process Q. Hence, process Q refines process P.

6 Product

Process product is an operation that allows us to compose processes. Our definition of process product is based on the product of trace labels, defined in Table 1. The product table comes from Chapter 7 of [20].

The product of labels captures interaction between two processes. Consider, for example, the table entry $\Delta \times \square = \Delta$. This entry describes a state in an interaction between two processes where one process demands an input and another process has no progress requirements or obligations. The result of the label product tells us that the network of two processes also demands an input from its environment. A similar argument explains why $\nabla \times \square = \nabla$: if one process guarantees progress and the other process has no progress requirements and guarantees, then the network of these two processes guarantees progress.

Table 1. Product table

$\times$	$\bot$	Δ	$\square$	∇	$\top$
$\bot$	$\bot$	$\bot$	$\bot$	$\bot$	$\top$
Δ	$\bot$	Δ	Δ	∇	$\top$
$\square$	$\bot$	Δ	$\square$	∇	$\top$
∇	$\bot$	∇	∇	∇	$\top$
$\top$	$\top$	$\top$	$\top$	$\top$	$\top$

Because we give process obligations a priority over environment obligations, we have $\nabla \times \Delta = \nabla$. If one process is in a ∇ state, guaranteeing an output, and another process is in a Δ state, demanding an input, then the network of two processes will eventually produce an output.

We assume that, if one process performs a miracle, then the product performs a miracle. For this reason we have $\top \times \lambda = \top$ for any label λ. Finally, if one process fails, then the product fails as well. Thus, we have $\bot \times \lambda = \bot$ for any label λ other than $\top$. Notice that $\top \times \bot = \top$. That is, a miracle cures a failure.

The process product $P \times Q$ is defined by means of the trace-wise product of the traces in P and Q, unless the $\top$ or the $\bot$ state has been reached. Once the product reaches the $\top$ or the $\bot$ state, the product stays in that state. This property guarantees that the product of two processes is again $\top$ and $\bot$ persistent.

Definition 2 (Product). *The product of processes P and Q, denoted by $P \times Q$, is defined as*

$$\mathbf{i}.(P \times Q) = (\mathbf{i}.P \cup \mathbf{i}.Q) - (\mathbf{o}.P \cup \mathbf{o}.Q)$$

$$\mathbf{o}.(P \times Q) = \mathbf{o}.P \cup \mathbf{o}.Q$$

$$\mathbf{f}.(P \times Q).\varepsilon = \mathbf{f}.P.\varepsilon \times \mathbf{f}.Q.\varepsilon$$

$$\mathbf{f}.(P \times Q).ta = \begin{cases} \mathbf{f}.P.(ta \downarrow \mathbf{a}.P) \times \mathbf{f}.Q.(ta \downarrow \mathbf{a}.Q) & \text{if } \mathbf{f}.(P \times Q).t \notin \{\top, \bot\} \\ \mathbf{f}.(P \times Q).t & \text{otherwise} \end{cases}$$

The notation $s \downarrow A$ denotes trace s projected on alphabet A.

Notice that the definition of product stipulates that an output of a process is an output of the product and an input of a process is an input of the product, except when the input appears as an output in one of the processes. When a symbol appears as an input in one process and as an output in the other process, the symbol is an output of the product.

Theorem 2 (Product properties). *The product of processes is associative, commutative, and idempotent. Moreover, the product is monotonic with respect to refinement:*

$$P \sqsubseteq Q \;\Rightarrow\; P \times R \sqsubseteq Q \times R \tag{5}$$

6.1   Network Composition

We use the product of processes to describe two closely related compositions: network composition and specification composition. A network composition computes the joint behavior of a set of devices that form a network. For example, processes P and Q from Figure 5 each represent a physical device. Ports of P and Q with the same name are connected, meaning that communication between P and Q may take place. The network composition of P and Q, denoted by $P \parallel Q$, is a process that models the joint operation of processes P and Q. Formally, the network composition is nothing but the product of processes with one restriction: no connections between outputs may occur. The motivation for

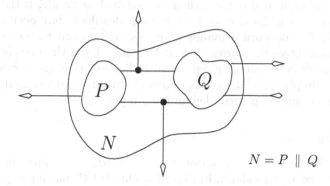

$$N = P \parallel Q$$

Fig. 5. The network composition

this restriction on outputs stems from electrical circuits, where connecting outputs of circuit components must be avoided. As a consequence of this restriction, each output in a network of processes is produced by exactly one process.

Unlike a network composition, which describes the joint behavior of a network consisting of multiple devices, the specification composition describes the behavior of a single device by composing partial behaviors referred to as "snippets." Snippets may share outputs, but must satisfy other alphabet restrictions. We define the specification composition and snippets in Section 11. In this section we explain only the network composition.

Definition 3 (Network composition).
The network composition *of P and Q, denoted by P $\parallel$ Q, applies when* **o**.$P \cap$ **o**.$Q = \emptyset$, *and is equal to P $\times$ Q.*

Although the results of $P \parallel Q$ and $P \times Q$ are the same, we use the notation $\parallel$ to indicate explicitly that the alphabet condition for the network condition is satisfied.

Notice that we make no restrictions on connections between inputs, unlike [20]. That is, we can connect any number of input ports in order to create a "composite" input port of the network. If we are concerned about multiple input connections, we can connect input ports via explicit fork components.

Furthermore, unlike [12, 20], we leave internal network connections visible. More precisely, a connection between an input port and an output port within a network is seen as an output port of the network. An internal connection between two input ports is seen as an input port of the network. If we wish to make any of the output ports of the network invisible, we can apply the hiding operator. This approach separates the operations of network composition and hiding and gives us the freedom to apply each of these two operations at the most appropriate point in the design process.

Because a process may contain both safety and progress violations, a network composition can tell us if the network satisfies all safety and progress properties. For example, if the network composition contains a legal trace that leads to a failure after an additional output, then the network is unsafe. If the network composition contains a Δ-unhealthy state, then deadlock may occur, because some process in the network demands progress, but no other process nor the environment guarantees that progress will be made. Even the presence of a $\square$ state in a network composition gives us an indication that the network may, at some point, simply stop. Recall that in a $\square$ state no process guarantees to provide an output and no process demands an input.

6.2   Example

Let us apply the network composition to two WIREs. Consider the network composition of two WIREs shown in Figure 6. One WIRE has input port a and output port m, and another has input port m and output port b.

Let us see what the labels are of traces am and $amam$ in the network composition. The label for trace am with respect to the first WIRE is $\square$. The label for trace am with respect to the second WIRE is the label for trace m, which is ∇. According to Table 1, the label of trace am in the network composition is ∇, which corresponds with the label in the state graph of the network composition. The label for trace $amam$ in the first WIRE is $\square$. The label for trace $amam$ with respect to the second WIRE is the label for trace mm, which is $\perp$. According

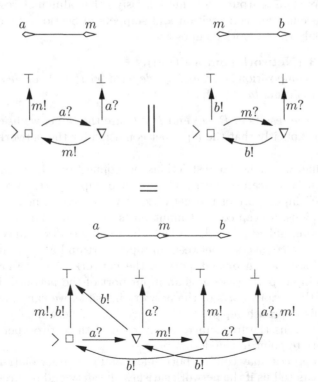

Fig. 6. The network composition of two WIREs

to Table 1, the label of trace *amam* in the network composition is $\perp$, which corresponds with the label in the state graph of the network composition.

The network of two WIREs contains a safety failure. If the first wire receives an input on port a before the second WIRE has produced an output on port b, the network may fail. In the state graph of Figure 6, we can see this failure, because the trace *amam* leads to the $\perp$-state. That is, the last symbol in trace *amam* is an output symbol that leads from a legal state to the $\perp$ state. This illustrates that we can detect potential safety violations by checking whether there is an output transition from a legal state to the $\perp$-state.

The state labels in the graphs of Figure 6 also contain information about progress properties of a network of two WIREs. For example, after the first WIRE has received an input on port a and has produced an output on port m, the product ends up in a state labeled with ∇, because the second WIRE guarantees that it will produce an output on port b.

7   Reflection

Each specification describes the behavior of a process and its environment. The process produces the outputs according to the specification, and the environment produces the inputs according to the specification. Thus, each specification describes the interplay between process and environment. When designing implementations, it is useful to consider the environment of a process the as just another process in a network. Reflection is the operation that swaps the roles of a process and its environment [10]. In Section 8 we show that any implementation of process P must operate correctly in the environment determined by the reflection of process P.

When we reflect a process we swap the input and the output alphabet of a process, and for each label we calculate its reflection according to Table 2 [20].

Definition 4 (Reflection).
Reflection of process P, denoted by $\sim P$, is defined as

$$\mathbf{i}.\sim P = \mathbf{o}.P \qquad \mathbf{o}.\sim P = \mathbf{i}.P \qquad \mathbf{f}.\sim P.t = \sim(\mathbf{f}.P.t)$$

Let us illustrate how the reflection swaps the roles of a process and its environment. Consider, for example, the reflection of ∇. Recall that ∇ denotes a state of a process in which it guarantees to produce an output. The environment of such a process can demand an input in that state, thus $\sim\nabla = \Delta$.

Table 2. Reflection on labels

λ	$\perp$	Δ	$\square$	∇	$\top$
$\sim\lambda$	$\top$	∇	$\square$	Δ	$\perp$

Theorem 3 (Properties of reflection). *The reflection on processes is its own inverse and it reverses the partial order:*

$$\sim\sim P = P \qquad\qquad P \sqsubseteq Q \;\Rightarrow\; \sim Q \sqsubseteq \sim P$$

Notice that $\mathsf{MIRACLE}(I, O)$ and $\mathsf{ABORT}(O, I)$ are reflections of each other.

8   Refinement and Correctness Conditions

In this section we define our safety and progress conditions and we show how these two conditions are related to process refinement. That is, we show that, for processes P and Q

$$P \sqsubseteq Q \;\Leftrightarrow\; \mathbf{safe}.(\sim P \times Q) \wedge \mathbf{prog}_\Delta.(\sim P \times Q)$$

where $\mathbf{safe}.S$ denotes that process S is safe and $\mathbf{prog}_\Delta.S$ denotes that process S satisfies the progress condition. We introduce the need for both conditions through examples.

We demonstrated in Figure 6 that we can detect safety problems by identifying output transitions from a legal state to the $\perp$ state. A process is also unsafe if its initial state is a failure state. This approach is formalized in the safety condition defined below.

Definition 5 (Safety).
We say that process P is safe, denoted by $\mathbf{safe}.P$, if the following holds:

$$\mathbf{safe}.P \equiv \Big(\forall t : t \in (\mathbf{l}.P)(\mathbf{o}.P) \cup \{\varepsilon\} : \mathbf{f}.P.(t) \neq \perp\Big) \qquad\qquad (6)$$

Without proof we mention that refinement implies the following safety property.

$$P \sqsubseteq Q \;\Rightarrow\; \mathbf{safe}.(\sim P \times Q)$$

This property indicates that the refinement relation may be characterized by correctness criteria that must hold for $\sim P \times Q$, the network consisting of the implementation Q and of the reflection $\sim P$ of the specification [10]. That is, we are looking for a correctness condition, for which we have $P \sqsubseteq Q \Leftrightarrow \mathbf{correct}.(\sim P \times Q)$.

Figure 7 demonstrates that the safety condition alone is insufficient for our correctness condition. One can check that $\mathbf{safe}.(\sim P \times Q)$ holds, but $P \not\sqsubseteq Q$, because $\mathbf{f}.P.a = \nabla$ and $\mathbf{f}.Q.a = \square$.

What went wrong in the example above? Notice that process P, after having received an input on port a, guarantees progress, while process Q does not. That is, the prospective "implementation" Q does not guarantee progress whereas the specification P does guarantee progress.

How is such a violation of progress requirements reflected in the product $\sim P \times Q$? Notice that $\sim P \times Q$, shown in Figure 7, has an empty set of input symbols, which means that the network is *closed*. On the other hand, $\sim P \times Q$,

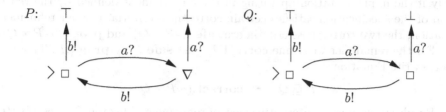

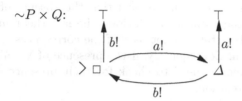

Fig. 7. Refinement requires more than safety

has a state labeled with Δ, which indicates that the network demands an input from its environment, but there is no input transition out of this state. That is, process $\sim P \times Q$ is Δ-unhealthy, demanding progress from its environment while no environment can satisfy such a demand, because the network has no inputs.

The example above leads to our progress condition: the closed network may not have any Δ-unhealthy states. Because the network $\sim P \times Q$ is a closed network and therefore has no inputs, this progress condition amounts to the condition that there may be no traces labeled with Δ in the closed network. This last condition is the same as the progress condition from [20].

Definition 6 (Progress).
Process P satisfies the Δ-progress requirement, denoted by $\textbf{prog}_\Delta.P$, if P does not contain any Δ-unhealthy states.

The example of Figure 7 demonstrated that the safety condition alone does not suffice for an alternative characterization of the refinement relation. The Δ-progress condition alone is insufficient as well. The conjunction of the safety and the Δ-progress condition, on the other hand, do characterize our refinement relation:

Theorem 4 (Refinement characterization). *For processes P and Q we have*

$$P \sqsubseteq Q \iff \textbf{safe}.(\sim P \times Q) \wedge \textbf{prog}_\Delta.(\sim P \times Q) \tag{7}$$

Theorem 4 provides an alternative view of the refinement relation that is similar to the one introduced in [10]: an implementation refines a specification if and only if the implementation operating in the environment defined by the reflection of the specification satisfies certain correctness criteria. For our refinement relation, the two correctness criteria are **safe**.$(\sim P \times Q)$ and **prog**$_\triangle.(\sim P \times Q)$.

For the remainder we define **correct**.$P \equiv$ **safe**.$P \wedge$ **prog**$_\triangle.P$. Thus, we can rewrite Equation 7 as

$$P \sqsubseteq Q \iff \mathbf{correct}.(\sim P \times Q) \tag{8}$$

Besides providing an alternative view of refinement, Theorem 4 gives a better understanding of which correctness criteria are included and which are excluded in the refinement relation. Because the presence of a ∇-unhealthy state can be seen as a progress violation, one would expect that the absence of this progress violation be covered by the refinement relation. The last theorem tells us that the absence of ∇-unhealthy states is not part of the correctness criteria covered by the refinement relation. Consequently, if the presence of ∇-unhealthy states may cause a problem then we need to check for their presence separate from checking the refinement relation.

9   Hiding

Hiding conceals output ports of a process. Recall that our refinement relation requires that an implementation has the same input and output ports as a specification. This alphabet restriction may cause a problem if an implementation is expressed as a product of processes, where "internal" connections between these processes appear as output ports in the product. The output alphabet of the specification does not include internal ports of the implementation, thus we cannot compare the implementation and the specification. By means of hiding we can hide the internal ports and then verify whether the refinement holds.

The result of hiding is a process that tells us what kind of behavior the environment can expect from process P when ports in set A are concealed. Suppose that the environment of P has observed the trace of communication actions given by t. Let

$$X(t) = \{s : s \in (\mathbf{a}.P)^* \wedge s \downarrow (\mathbf{a}.P - A) = t : s\}$$

$X(t)$ is the set of all traces that process P may execute in order for the environment to observe communication actions that amount to trace t. The environment does not know which trace from set $X(t)$ process P executes. For this reason, after observing trace t, the environment does not know in what kind of a state process P is: a failure, demanding, indifferent, transient, or miracle state. In order for the environment to be able to cope with the worst possible outcome of events, the environment must assume that the state of process P is represented by the least label of all traces in $X(t)$.

Definition 7 (Hiding). *Let P be a process and let $A \subseteq \mathbf{o}.P$. The hiding of symbols from A in process P is denoted by $\|[A :: P]\|$ and defined by*

$$\mathbf{i}.\|[A :: P]\| = \mathbf{i}.P$$
$$\mathbf{o}.\|[A :: P]\| = \mathbf{o}.P - A \tag{9}$$
$$\mathbf{f}.\|[A :: P]\|.t = \left(\sqcap s : s \in (\mathbf{a}.P)^* \wedge s \downarrow (\mathbf{a}.P - A) = t : \mathbf{f}.P.s\right)$$

The notation ⊓ denotes the greatest lower bound. Because our labels obey a total order, taking the greatest lower bound of a set is the same as taking the smallest element of the set. The idea for this definition of hiding was introduced to us by Willem Mallon [13].

Theorem 5 (Properties of hiding and product). *Processes are closed under hiding. Hiding is monotonic, and hiding distributes over product. In formula, for processes P and Q and subset A of $\mathbf{o}.P$,*

$$P \sqsubseteq Q \;\Rightarrow\; |[\,A :: P\,]| \sqsubseteq |[\,A :: Q\,]| \tag{10}$$

$$|[\,A :: P\,]| \times Q \;=\; |[\,A :: P \times Q\,]| \;\text{ if }\; A \cap \mathbf{a}.Q = \emptyset \tag{11}$$

For process P, such that $\mathbf{i}.P = \emptyset$, and set $A \subseteq \mathbf{o}.P$, we have

$$correct.P \;\Leftrightarrow\; correct.|[\,A :: P\,]| \tag{12}$$

9.1   Example

Hiding takes into account progress and safety properties of a process. For example, consider the network composition of two WIREs shown as process P and Q in Figure 8.

The result of hiding output m in process P is the specification of a WIRE, shown as process Q in Figure 8b. For example, take trace $t = aa$. Some traces in $X(aa)$ are aa, ama, and $amam$. Their corresponding labels in process P are $\mathbf{f}.P.aa = \bot$, $\mathbf{f}.P.ama = \nabla$, $\mathbf{f}.P.amam = \bot$. Because $\bot$ is the smallest of these labels, we have by definition of hiding $\mathbf{f}.|[\,m :: P\,]|.aa = \bot$, which agrees with $\mathbf{f}.Q.aa = \bot$. Because we interpret any input that leads to a $\bot$ state as an input that may not be produced by the environment, the result of hiding forbids the environment to provide inputs that may cause an internal safety failure of a process.

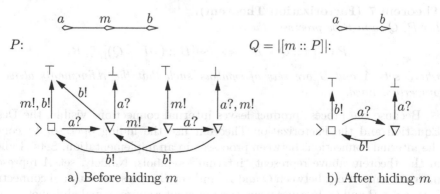

a) Before hiding m b) After hiding m

Fig. 8. Hiding a connection between two WIREs

10   Two Design Theorems

In this section we present two design theorems that hold for ECF processes. The Substitution theorem is the cornerstone of hierarchical refinement, because it allows us to substitute a process in a network with an implementation of that process without violating any correctness conditions.

Theorem 6 (Substitution Theorem).
Let P, Q, R, and S be processes. If $P \sqsubseteq |[A :: Q \times R]|$ and $R \sqsubseteq S$, then

$$P \sqsubseteq |[A :: Q \times S]|$$

Proof.

$\quad R \quad \sqsubseteq \quad S$
$\Rightarrow \quad \{$ Equation 5 — monotonicity of $\times$ $\}$
$\quad Q \times R \quad \sqsubseteq \quad Q \times S$
$\Rightarrow \quad \{$ Equation 10 — monotonicity of hiding $\}$
$\quad |[A :: Q \times R]| \quad \sqsubseteq \quad |[A :: Q \times S]|$
$\Rightarrow \quad \{$ $P \sqsubseteq |[A :: Q \times R]|$, Theorem 1 — transitivity of $\sqsubseteq$ $\}$
$\quad P \sqsubseteq |[A :: Q \times S]|$

$\square$

The second design theorem, the Factorization Theorem, allows us to apply ECF processes to the following design problem from [20]: When we are looking for an implementation of a given specification P, we can often guess at least one process, call it Q, that could be a part of an implementation. The question is, given specification P and process Q, can we find a process R that defines the rest of the implementation such that

$$P \sqsubseteq |[A :: Q \times R]| \tag{13}$$

This inequality, illustrated in Figure 9, is known as the Design Equation [20, 12]. The Factorization Theorem gives a lower bound for process R, or alternatively an upper bound for process $\sim P$ as illustrated in Figure 9.

Theorem 7 (Factorization Theorem).
Let P, Q, and R be processes then

$$P \sqsubseteq |[A :: Q \times R]| \quad \Leftrightarrow \quad \sim|[B :: (\sim P \times Q)]| \sqsubseteq R$$

where sets A and B are sets of symbols such that the refinements above are properly defined.

Because the process product leaves internal connections visible, the Design Equation and the Factorization Theorem use the hiding operator to conceal the internal connections between processes in an implementation. Sets A and B in the theorem above represent "internal" symbols. Namely, set A represents internal connections between Q and R, and set B represents internal connections between $\sim P$ and Q. Because process refinement requires equal alphabets, sets A and B are defined implicitly. That is, set A is defined by $A = (\mathbf{o}.Q \cup \mathbf{o}.R) - \mathbf{o}.P$ and B is defined by $B = (\mathbf{i}.P \cup \mathbf{o}.Q) - \mathbf{i}.R$.

Design Equation:

Bound for R:

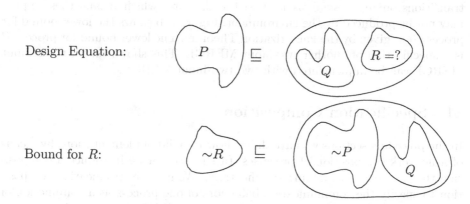

Fig. 9. Factorization Theorem

Proof.

$P \sqsubseteq |[A :: Q \times R]|$
$\Leftrightarrow$ { Equation 8 — refinement characterization }
  correct.$(\sim P \times |[A :: Q \times R]|)$
$\Leftrightarrow$ { $A \cap \mathbf{a}.P = \emptyset$, Equation 11 — distributivity of hiding }
  correct.$|[A :: \sim P \times Q \times R]|$
$\Leftrightarrow$ { $\sim P \times Q \times R$ is closed, Equation 12 — hiding preserves correctness }
  correct.$(\sim P \times Q \times R)$
$\Leftrightarrow$ { $\sim P \times Q \times R$ is closed, Equation 12 — hiding preserves correctness }
  correct.$|[B :: \sim P \times Q \times R]|$
$\Leftrightarrow$ { $B \cap \mathbf{a}.R = \emptyset$, Equation 11 — distributivity of hiding }
  correct.$(|[B :: \sim P \times Q]| \times R)$
$\Leftrightarrow$ { Equation 8 — refinement characterization }
  $\sim|[B :: \sim P \times Q]| \sqsubseteq R$

$\square$

Let us illustrate an application of the Factorization theorem with an example. Figure 10a shows process P, which is a specification of a three-input MERGE. A MERGE is a standard component in asynchronous circuits which merges any of a number of input signals into one output signal. One could characterize a MERGE as an OR component for events: An event on any input port of a MERGE will cause the MERGE to produce an event on its output port.

Process Q of Figure 10b is a specification of a two-input MERGE. We would like to implement a three-input MERGE with the two-input MERGE, and we need to find a process R that completes the implementation.

The Factorization Theorem tells us that we need to compute the process $\sim|[B :: \sim P \times Q]|$, where $B = \{a, b\}$. Figure 11a shows the result of computing $\sim P \times Q$. In order to reduce clutter, the state graph for $\sim P \times Q$ is a simplified state graph, where all missing transitions on output symbols lead to the $\top$ state, which means these outputs cannot be produced by the process, and all missing transitions on input symbols lead to the $\bot$ state, which means these inputs may not be produced by the environment. Figure 11b shows the lower bound for process R as given by the Factorization Theorem. The lower bound for process R is a specification of another two-input MERGE. This shows that a three-input MERGE can be implemented with two two-input MERGEs.

11   Specification Composition

In the preceding sections we have shown how to build implementations by means of a network composition of processes. In this section we introduce a composition that is useful for building specifications. We use the specification composition to specify the communication behaviors of one process as a conjunction of constraints. Such specifications are called constraint-based specifications. A constraint can be seen as a partial view of the communication behavior of the process pertaining only to a subset of its ports. Constraints are expressed by special processes called *snippets*. Once we have collected a complete set of constraints, we combine their snippets with the specification composition. The result is the complete specification of the process.

In order to present the definition and some properties of the specification composition we introduce the definitions of rounded product, snippet, and output-persistent refinement. We first start with the definition of the *rounded product* of processes. By rounding we transform a potentially unhealthy process into a healthy one. More precisely, if $\mathbf{u}.P$ denotes the set of *unhealthy* traces of process P, then by rounding we transform each unhealthy trace in $\mathbf{u}.P$ into an indifferent trace. Notice that an indifferent trace is always a healthy trace.

Definition 8 (Rounding). *Let P be a process. Rounding of process P is denoted by $[P]$ and is defined as follows:* $\mathbf{i}.[P] = \mathbf{i}.P$, $\mathbf{o}.[P] = \mathbf{o}.P$, *and*

$$\mathbf{f}.[P].t = \begin{cases} \mathbf{f}.P.t & \text{if } t \notin \mathbf{u}.P \\ \Box & \text{if } t \in \mathbf{u}.P \end{cases} \tag{14}$$

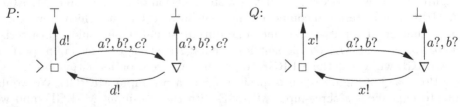

a) A three-input MERGE

b) Can this two-input MERGE
    be part of an implementation for P?

Fig. 10. The MERGE

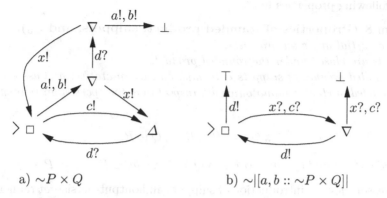

a) $\sim P \times Q$ b) $\sim\lVert [a, b :: \sim P \times Q] \rVert$

Fig. 11. The Factorization Theorem tells us what the rest of the implementation is: another two-input MERGE

For processes P and Q we write $P \otimes Q$ to denote their rounded product $[P \times Q]$.

Our second definition concerns *snippets*. Informally, a snippet is a special process that makes the most guarantees and the least demands. The most guarantees means that the process always guarantees progress, if an output is possible. The least demands means that the process never demands an input and the environment never produces a miracle. Formally, we have

Definition 9 (Snippet). *Process P is called a* snippet *if*

1. *Process P guarantees progress iff an output is possible: for every legal trace t we have $(\mathbf{f}.P.t = \nabla) \Leftrightarrow (\exists a : a \in \mathbf{o}.P : \mathbf{f}.P.ta \neq \top)$*
2. *The environment of P never guarantees progress and never performs a miracle: for all legal traces t we have $\mathbf{f}.P.t \neq \Delta$, $\mathbf{f}.P.\varepsilon \neq \top$ and $(\forall b : b \in (\mathbf{i}.P) : \mathbf{f}.P.tb \neq \top)$*

From the definition of a snippet it follows that a snippet is a healthy process.

Our third definition pertains to the *output-persistent* refinement denoted by $\sqsubseteq_o$. If $P \sqsubseteq_o Q$, then, on top of the standard refinement, implementation Q must be capable of producing every output that can be produced by the specification P.

Definition 10 (Output-persistent refinement). *The output-persistent refinement of snippet P by snippet Q is denoted by $P \sqsubseteq_o Q$ and is defined as*

$$P \sqsubseteq_o Q \;\equiv\; P \sqsubseteq Q \wedge P \preceq_o Q \tag{15}$$

where $P \preceq_o Q$ stands for process Q being output-persistent with respect to process P:

$$P \preceq_o Q \;\equiv\; (\forall t, a : t \in \mathbf{l}.P \wedge a \in \mathbf{o}.P : (\mathbf{f}.P.ta \neq \top \Rightarrow \mathbf{f}.Q.ta \neq \top)) \tag{16}$$

The following properties hold.

Theorem 8 (Properties of rounded product, snippets, and $\sqsubseteq_o$).
1. $\sqsubseteq_o$ is a partial order on processes.
2. Snippets are closed under the rounded product.
3. The rounded product of snippets is idempotent, commutative, and associative.
4. The rounded product is monotonic with respect to output-persistent refinement, i.e.,

$$P \sqsubseteq_o Q \;\Rightarrow\; P \otimes R \sqsubseteq_o Q \otimes R$$

5. For snippets P and Q where $\mathbf{o}.P \cap \mathbf{o}.Q = \emptyset$, we have $P \otimes Q = P \times Q$.

The reasons for the introduction of snippets and output-persistent refinement is that some properties above do not hold for processes and refinement in general. For example, the rounded product applied to processes is not associative in general and is also not monotonic with respect to refinement.

Our definition of the specification composition is based on the rounded product:

Definition 11 (Specification composition). *The* specification composition *of P and Q applies when P and Q are snippets and when $\mathbf{o}.P \cap \mathbf{i}.Q = \emptyset$, and $\mathbf{o}.Q \cap \mathbf{i}.P = \emptyset$. The specification composition of P and Q is denoted by $P \,\&\, Q$, is pronounced as "P and Q," and is defined by $P \otimes Q$.*

Although the results of $P \,\&\, Q$ and $P \otimes Q$ are the same, we use the notation $\&$ to indicate explicitly that the alphabet condition for the specification composition is satisfied.

There are two important differences between network composition and specification composition. The first difference concerns the alphabet restrictions. In a network composition, an output in one process may be an input in the other process and *vice versa*. The two processes, however, may have no outputs in common. In a specification composition, it is almost exactly the opposite. An output in one process cannot be an input in the other process and *vice versa*. Each symbol that the two processes have in common is either an input or an output in both processes. In other words, in a specification composition an input remains an input and an output remains an output.

The second and main difference between network composition and specification composition lies in the handling of progress requirements. The network composition requires progress if and only if at least one of the processes requires progress. The specification composition requires progress if and only if at least one of the snippets requires progress *and* if the progress requirements can be satisfied. If the progress requirements cannot be satisfied in a particular state, that state becomes an indifferent state.

Although snippets are closed under the specification composition, they are not closed under hiding. We often build specifications by composing a number of snippets, where we introduce "auxiliary internal" symbols that serve as internal synchronization points. After we have composed the snippets, we hide these internal symbols. Because snippets are not closed under hiding, the final specification may not be a snippet, but it certainly is a process. For this reason, hiding is often the last step in obtaining a specification of a process.

11.1   Examples

Many basic components in asynchronous circuit design can be expressed as a specification composition of snippets. Two families of such components are JOINs, or Muller C-elements, and SEQUENCERs.

We first give a specification of a two-input JOIN. Figure 12a shows a schematic of a two-input JOIN. It has two inputs a and b and one output c. The operation of the JOIN is an alternation of the receipt of both inputs followed by the production of output c. Initially and each time after output c is produced, the environment may provide inputs a and b concurrently, but the environment is not obliged to provide those inputs. After inputs a and b have been received, the JOIN must produce output c. The complete state graph for the JOIN appears in Figure 12c. A simplified state graph for the JOIN appears in Figure 12b. Recall that in a simplified state graph all missing input transitions lead to the $\perp$ state and all missing output transitions lead to the $\top$ state.

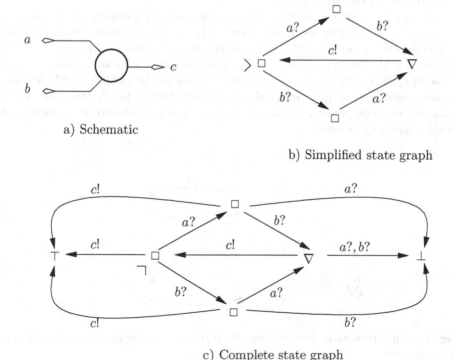

a) Schematic

b) Simplified state graph

c) Complete state graph

Fig. 12. A specification of a JOIN

We can specify the JOIN as a specification composition of two snippets. Figure 13 shows the alternative specification of the JOIN. One snippet specifies the alternation of input a and output c, and the other snippet specifies the alternation of input b and output c. The specification composition of these snippets yields the state graph of Figure 12c. Notice that after receipt of input a only, one snippet is in a ∇ state and the other snippet is a $\square$ state. The product of these labels is ∇. But, because in the specification composition no output can be produced after trace a, the label is rounded down to $\square$. This corresponds with the label in the complete state graph after trace a.

A different basic component is an initialized SEQUENCER. An initialized SEQUENCER is an arbiter that arbitrates among requests that can arrive concurrently from a number of different sources. The arbiter ensures that only one pending request is granted at any time.

In Figure 14 we show three snippets that capture the behavior of the SEQUENCER. For each snippet we give a simplified state graph. The first snippet specifies that requests r_0 and grants g_0 must alternate and that, after receiving request r_0, the arbiter guarantees progress. The second snippet is similar to the first, except that it addresses the alternation of r_1 and g_1. Finally, the third snippet expresses the mutual exclusion between grants g_0 and g_1. This snippet also states that a grant and done signal must alternate. Moreover, by labeling the initial state of this snippet with ∇ we require that the SEQUENCER must proceed when it can issue a grant.

Figure 15b shows the result of the specification composition of the snippets of Figure 14. Notice that the initial state of the graph of Figure 15b carries label $\square$, whereas the product of the labels of the initial states of the snippets from Figure 14 is ∇. This means that the label of the initial state of the specification of the SEQUENCER is rounded down to $\square$, because the SEQUENCER initially cannot produce an output. Notice also that the arbiter is in a ∇ state only when it has received one or two requests *and* a done signal d. Initially, we assume that signal d has been received.

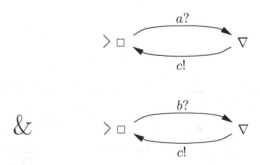

Fig. 13. An alternative specification of a JOIN as a specification composition of two snippets

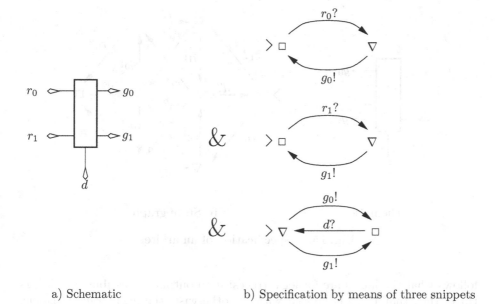

a) Schematic   b) Specification by means of three snippets

Fig. 14. Snippets for the SEQUENCER

The specification of the SEQUENCER involves a significant amount of concurrency. Requests r_0 and r_1 can arrive independently of each other, which contributes to sequences of events that may not be easy to envision if we were to generate the state graph directly rather than by computing the specification composition of snippets. Thinking in terms of snippets allows us to focus on a few aspects of the behavior of the SEQUENCER, which combined lead to the final specification. It also allows us to give a concise specification: an n input SEQUENCER requires only $n + 1$ small snippets, whereas the complete state graph quickly becomes prohibitively large.

12   Commands

We use a textual notation called *commands* to represent snippets. A command is a regular expression for the legal trace set of a snippet. The basic building blocks are $a?$ and $a!$ denoting an input and an output action, respectively. If E and F are commands, then $E; F$ denotes their *concatenation*, $E \mid F$ denotes the *union*, and $*[E]$ denotes the unbounded repetition of E.

The safety and progress properties of the traces of a command are defined as follows. First we stipulate that commands always express safe snippets. Thus, every illegal trace obtained from a legal trace by adding an output symbol is labeled with $\top$, and every illegal trace obtained from a legal trace by adding an input symbol is labeled with $\bot$. Secondly, from the definition of a snippet, it

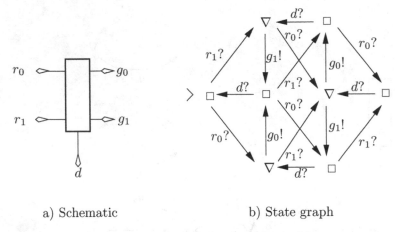

a) Schematic   b) State graph

Fig. 15. A specification of an arbiter

follows what the labels are for legal traces: if an output is possible after a legal trace, then that trace is labeled with ∇; otherwise, the legal trace is labeled with $\square$.

Because a command defines a snippet and a snippet is a process, we can use commands to specify processes. For example, a specification for a WIRE by means of a command is

$$\text{WIRE} = *[\,a?;b!\,]$$

A specification for a two-input JOIN as a command is

$$\begin{aligned}\text{JOIN} = \quad &*[\,a?;c!\,]\\ \&\ &*[\,b?;c!\,]\end{aligned}$$

A specification for an initialized SEQUENCER as a command is

$$\begin{aligned}\text{SEQUENCER} = \quad &*[\,r_0?;g_0!\,]\\ \&\ &*[\,r_1?;g_1!\,]\\ \&\ &*[\,(g_0!\,|\,g_1!);d?\,]\end{aligned}$$

13   Part-Wise Design Method

In this section we outline the part-wise design method that applies to situations where specification S is expressed as a specification composition of snippets,

$$S = |[\,A :: P \ \& \ Q\,]|$$

The set A represents "auxiliary internal" symbols, which are hidden. Notice that process S may not be a snippet, because snippets are not closed under hiding.

Our goal is to obtain a refinement for specification S in a part-wise manner. The first step is to seek output-persistent refinements for each of the snippets P

and Q in isolation. Then we combine components of the output-persistent refinements for snippets P and Q and arrive at a refinement for specification S.

Assume that snippet P can be refined by the network composition of snippets P_0 and P_1, and that snippet Q can be refined by the network composition of snippets Q_0 and Q_1. Assume, furthermore, that these refinements are output-persistent refinements:

$$P \sqsubseteq_o P_0 \parallel P_1$$
$$Q \sqsubseteq_o Q_0 \parallel Q_1$$

Recall that the network composition $P_0 \parallel P_1$ represents the product of $P_0 \times P_1$, where P_0 and P_1 have no outputs in common. By Theorem 8 (5), the product of P_0 and P_1 then is equal to the rounded product of P_0 and P_1: $P_0 \parallel P_1 = P_0 \otimes P_1$. A similar reasoning applies to the network composition of Q_0 and Q_1. Thus we have

$$P \sqsubseteq_o P_0 \otimes P_1$$
$$Q \sqsubseteq_o Q_0 \otimes Q_1$$

Recall that snippets are closed under rounded product. Thus, $P_0 \otimes P_1$ and $Q_0 \otimes Q_1$ are snippets. Hence, we can apply monotonicity of rounded product with respect to output-persistent refinement and transitivity of output-persistent refinement, which leads to

$$P \otimes Q \sqsubseteq_o P_0 \otimes P_1 \otimes Q_0 \otimes Q_1$$

Next, in order to replace the rounded product $\otimes$ by $\&$ or $\parallel$, we group snippets that have outputs or inputs in common, but not symbols that are an input in one process and an output in the other process. For example, assume that snippets P_0 and Q_0 have only outputs in common. Thus, we can write $P_0 \otimes Q_0 = P_0 \& Q_0$. From our specification we know that $P \otimes Q = P \& Q$. Hence, we get

$$P \& Q \sqsubseteq_o (P_0 \& Q_0) \otimes P_1 \otimes Q_1$$

Finally, if the processes $P_0 \& Q_0$, P_1, and Q_1 have no outputs in common, then by Theorem 8 (5), the rounded product of these processes is equal to their network composition:

$$P \& Q \sqsubseteq_o (P_0 \& Q_0) \parallel P_1 \parallel Q_1$$

Thus we have derived that the specification composition of snippets P and Q can be refined by a network of three processes, where each process is a specification composition of one or more snippets from the part refinements.

The last step in obtaining a refinement for S is the inclusion of hiding. Recall that the output-persistent refinement implies the standard refinement. Furthermore, hiding is monotonic with respect to refinement. Thus, we get our final refinement for S

$$|[A :: P \& Q]| \sqsubseteq |[A :: (P_0 \& Q_0) \parallel P_1 \parallel Q_1]|$$

Let us summarize the part-wise design method. In order to obtain a refinement of a specification composition of snippets, we first look at refinements of the individual snippets in isolation. Then, we group those snippets that have symbols in common such that each common symbol is an output in all snippets or an input in all snippets. If any group of snippets has no outputs in common with any other group of snippets, then the specification composition of the snippets in each group represents a process in an implementation of the original specification.

We emphasize that verifying output-persistent refinements of P and Q in isolation and then combining the results using part-wise refinement tends to be significantly less complex than performing a "flat" verification of a refinement of specification S. Notice that the verification work is proportional to the number of states in a specification, and the number of states in $P \& Q$ can be of the order of the product of the number of states of P and Q. Thus, by looking at snippets P and Q in isolation, we may avoid a state explosion.

13.1   Dining Philosophers: Specification

We illustrate an application of the part-wise design method to the problem of the dining philosophers. The dining philosophers is a canonical synchronization problem that was originally stated by Dijkstra [8]:

> N philosophers, numbered from 0 through $N-1$ are living in a house where the table is laid for them, each philosopher having her own place at the table. Their only problem – besides those of philosophy – is that the dish served is a very difficult kind of spaghetti, that has to be eaten with two forks. There are two forks at each plate, so that presents no difficulty, but as a consequence, however, no two neighbors can be eating simultaneously.

To keep the example simple, we consider the case with only three philosophers using the table shown in Figure 16a. We would like to design a device that schedules the meals for the philosophers. Each philosopher is engaged in an

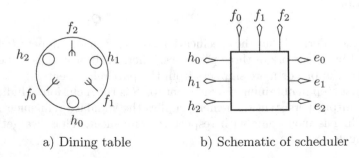

a) Dining table   b) Schematic of scheduler

Fig. 16. Three dining philosophers

unbounded cycle of thinking followed by eating. When philosopher i gets hungry, she sends signal h_i to the scheduler, shown in Figure 16b. If both forks f_i and f_{i+1} are free, the scheduler sends signal e_i to philosopher i to inform her that she can eat, where additions are modulo 3. When philosopher i has finished a meal, she releases the forks. This release eventually leads to signals f_i and f_{i+1} to the scheduler, meaning that forks i and $i + 1$ are no longer in use.

Let us demonstrated how to arrive at a specification of a non-trivial component such as the scheduler for dining philosophers by using a specification composition of snippets. First we specify that, if a philosopher becomes hungry, she will eventually eat. That is, input h_i must be followed by output e_i. This observation leads to the following snippets for $i = 0, 1, 2$

$$*[\, h_i?; e_i! \,]$$

Next we turn to the use of the forks. Each fork can be accessed by two philosophers, but only one philosopher may use it at any time. Thus, for fork i, signal f_i must be followed by either signal e_i or e_{i-1}. We assume that initially all forks are on the table. These observations lead to the following snippet that describes the usage of fork i:

$$*[\, (e_i! \mid e_{i-1}!); f_i? \,]$$

The specification of the meal scheduler simply is the specification composition of the six snippets introduced above:

$$
\begin{aligned}
\text{SCH} = \quad & *[\, h_0?; e_0! \,] \\
\& \;\; & *[\, h_1?; e_1! \,] \\
\& \;\; & *[\, h_2?; e_2! \,] \\
\& \;\; & *[\, (e_0! \mid e_2!); f_0? \,] \\
\& \;\; & *[\, (e_0! \mid e_1!); f_1? \,] \\
\& \;\; & *[\, (e_1! \mid e_2!); f_2? \,]
\end{aligned}
$$

The complete state graph for this specification contains 64 states and would be hard to find without the using the specification composition.

13.2   Dining Philosophers: Implementation

Figure 17 shows an implementation of the meal scheduler consisting of three SEQUENCERs. This implementation closely follows Dijkstra's solution [8]. Each SEQUENCER corresponds to a semaphore guarding the usage of a fork. The connections between the SEQUENCERs implicitly force an order in the assignment of forks to philosophers. This particular implementation stipulates that philosophers 0 and 1 first get assigned their left-hand forks and then their right-hand forks. Notice that, for philosopher 0 for example, signal h_0 first must propagate through the SEQUENCER with input f_0 and then through the SEQUENCER with input f_1 before the implementation produces output e_0. Philosopher 2, on the other hand, first gets assigned her right-hand fork and then her left-hand fork. This approach follows Dijkstra's solution [8] of the dining philosophers

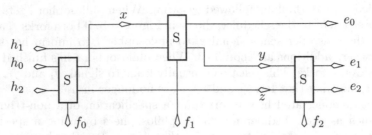

Fig. 17. A solution to the dining philosophers problem

problem, where such an asymmetry in the sequence of acquiring forks guarantees the absence of deadlock.

We verify this implementation in a few steps using the part-wise refinement. We first introduce the internal symbols x, y, and z in the specification of the scheduler and name the resulting specification SCH_0:

$$\begin{aligned}
SCH_0 = \quad & *[\, h_0?; x!; e_0! \,] \\
& \&\ *[\, h_1?; y!; e_1! \,] \\
& \&\ *[\, h_2?; z!; e_2! \,] \\
& \&\ *[\, (x!; e_0! \mid z!; e_2!); f_0? \,] \\
& \&\ *[\, (e_0! \mid y!; e_1!); f_1? \,] \\
& \&\ *[\, (e_1! \mid e_2!); f_2? \,]
\end{aligned}$$

The introduction of symbols x, y and z is based on the schematic of the implementation in Figure 17. Without proof we mention that

$$SCH \ = \ |[\, x, y, z :: SCH_0 \,]| \tag{17}$$

The snippets that form SCH_0 have the following simple refinements:

$$\begin{aligned}
*[\, h_0?; x!; e_0! \,] && \sqsubseteq_o *[\, h_0?; x! \,] \ \& \ *[\, x!; e_0! \,] \\
*[\, h_1?; y!; e_1! \,] && \sqsubseteq_o *[\, h_1?; y! \,] \ \& \ *[\, y!; e_1! \,] \\
*[\, h_2?; z!; e_2! \,] && \sqsubseteq_o *[\, h_2?; z! \,] \ \& \ *[\, z!; e_2! \,] \\
*[\, (x!; e_0! \mid z!; e_2!); f_0? \,] && \sqsubseteq_o *[\, (x! \mid z!); f_0? \,] \ \& \ *[\, x!; e_0! \,] \ \& \ *[\, z!; e_2! \,] \\
*[\, (e_0! \mid y!; e_1!); f_1? \,] && \sqsubseteq_o *[\, (e_0! \mid y!); f_1? \,] \ \& \ *[\, y!; e_1! \,] \\
*[\, (e_1! \mid e_2!); f_2? \,] && \sqsubseteq_o *[\, (e_1! \mid e_2!); f_2? \,]
\end{aligned}$$

According to our part-wise refinement method we must group snippets with common output symbols and take their specification composition. The network composition of these groupings forms a refinement of the scheduler. We consider three groups: one group of snippets that have outputs $x!$ and $z!$ in common; one group of snippets that have outputs $y!$ and $e_0!$ in common; and one group of snippets that have outputs $e_1!$ and $e_2!$ in common. Thus, we get

$$
\begin{aligned}
&\text{SCH} \\
&\sqsubseteq \,|[\,x,y,z\,:: \\
&\quad (\,*[\,h_0?;x!\,]\ \&\ *[\,h_2?;z!\,]\ \&\ *[\,(x!\mid z!);f_0?\,]\,) && \text{(SEQUENCER)} \\
&\quad \|\ (\,*[\,h_1?;y!\,]\ \&\ *[\,x?;e_0!\,]\ \&\ *[\,(e_0!\mid y!);f_1?\,]\,) && \text{(SEQUENCER)} \\
&\quad \|\ (\,*[\,y?;e_1!\,]\ \&\ *[\,z?;e_2!\,]\ \&\ *[\,(e_1!\mid e_2!);f_2?\,]\,) && \text{(SEQUENCER)} \\
&\,]|
\end{aligned}
$$

Consequently, the implementation of SCH consists of three SEQUENCERs connected as shown in Figure 17.

If an implementation assigns the forks of each philosopher in the same order, then, as demonstrated in [8], the resulting "solution" has a possibility of deadlock. Our refinement relation detects such deadlocks as progress violations.

The solution can easily be generalized to any number of philosophers. A flat verification of such an implementation quickly becomes impossible, even for a machine, because of the state explosion. Using part-wise refinement, however, our proof obligations increase only slightly and can simply be done by hand.

14 Conclusions

We have presented a formalism for the specification and implementation of processes, with some applications to the design of asynchronous circuits. Three aspects of of this formalism deserve a special mention: the network composition, the specification composition, and the part-wise refinement method.

The network composition models the joint behavior of a network of devices, where each device is represented by a process. The specification composition, on the other hand, models the behavior of just one device as a combination of snippets, where each snippet represents an aspect of the device's behavior. The usefulness of the specification composition becomes apparent when we specify complex behaviors that involve a large degree of concurrency. State graphs for such specifications tend to grow quickly and may become difficult to keep track of. It has been our experience that individual snippets tend to remain small in size, and a list of snippets tends to be smaller and easier to keep track of than the state graph that represents the complete behavior. Furthermore, focusing on small individual aspects of a complex behavior allows us to gain a better insight into the operation of a device.

The part-wise refinement method allow us to avoid a state explosion in the verification: Instead of verifying a complete implementation, the part-wise refinement method allows us to verify the refinements of just the snippets of a process. The part-wise refinement can be used in combination with a stepwise refinement, also called hierarchical verification. Together they form powerful tools in any verification.

Snippets play a central role in our formalism. We try to specify a process by means of a specification composition of snippets and we express an implementation of a process by means of a network composition of processes, where each process often is also a snippet. Thus specifying and implementing a process both amount to composing snippets.

Acknowledgment

Acknowledgments are due to Graham Birtwistle and John Brzozowski for their comments on previous drafts of this paper. Sun Microsystems Laboratories is gratefully acknowledged for their financial support.

References

[1] Igor Benko. *ECF Processes and Asynchronous Circuit Design*. PhD thesis, University of Waterloo, Department of Computer Science, `file://plg.uwaterloo.ca/pub/maveric/reports/All-reports/IB_Thesis.pdf`, 1999. 4

[2] Igor Benko and Jo Ebergen. Delay-insensitive solutions to the committee problem. In *Proc. International Symposium on Advanced Research in Asynchronous Circuits and Systems*, pages 228–237. IEEE Computer Society Press, November 1994. 2

[3] Tomaso Bolognesi and Ed Brinksma. Introduction to the ISO specification language LOTOS. *Computer Networks and ISDN Systems*, 14:25–59, 1987. 2

[4] Janusz A. Brzozowski, Scott Hauck, and Carl-Johan H. Seger. Design of asynchronous circuits. In Brzozowski, J. A. and Seger, C.-J. H. *Asynchronous Circuits, Chapter 15*. Springer-Verlag, 1995. 2

[5] M. E. Bush and M. B. Josephs. Some limitations to speed-independence in asynchronous circuits. In *Proc. International Symposium on Advanced Research in Asynchronous Circuits and Systems*. IEEE Computer Society Press, March 1996. 2

[6] B. A. Davey and H. A. Priestley. *Introduction to Lattices and Order*. Cambridge University Press, 1990.

[7] Al Davis and Steven M. Nowick. Asynchronous circuit design: Motivation, background, and methods. In Graham Birtwistle and Al Davis, editors, *Asynchronous Digital Circuit Design*, Workshops in Computing, pages 1–49. Springer-Verlag, 1995. 2

[8] Edsger W. Dijkstra. Hierarchical ordering of sequential processes. *Acta Informatica*, 1:115–138, 1971. 28, 29, 31

[9] David L. Dill. *Trace Theory for Automatic Hierachical Verification of Speed-Independent Circuits*. ACM Distinguished Dissertations. MIT Press, 1989. 2

[10] Jo C. Ebergen. A Formal Approach to Designing Delay-Insensitive Circuits. *Distributed Computing*, 5(3):107–119, 1991. 2, 13, 14, 15

[11] Jo C. Ebergen. Arbiters: an exercise in specifying and decomposing asynchronously communicating components. *Science of Computer Programming*, 18(3):223–245, June 1992. 2

[12] W. C. Mallon, J. T. Udding, and T. Verhoeff. Analysis and applications of the XDI model. In *Proc. International Symposium on Advanced Research in Asynchronous Circuits and Systems*, pages 231–242, April 1999. 2, 7, 11, 18

[13] Willem Mallon. Personal communication, 1997. 17

[14] Radu Negulescu. *Process Spaces and Formal Verification of Asynchronous Circuits*. PhD thesis, Dept. of Computer Science, Univ. of Waterloo, Canada, August 1998. 2

[15] Radu Negulescu and Ad Peeters. Verification of speed-dependences in single-rail handshake circuits. In *Proc. International Symposium on Advanced Research in Asynchronous Circuits and Systems*, pages 159–170, 1998. 2

[16] Ivan E. Sutherland. Micropipelines. *Communications of the ACM*, 32(6):720–738, January 1989. 2

[17] Alan Turing. Lecture to the London Mathematical Society on 20 February 1947. In *Charles Babbage Institute Reprint Series for the History of Computing, Vol. 10, 1986*. MIT Press, 1947. 2

[18] C. H. (Kees) van Berkel, Mark B. Josephs, and Steven M. Nowick. Scanning the technology: Applications of asynchronous circuits. *Proceedings of the IEEE*, 87(2):223–233, February 1999. 2

[19] Jan L. A. van de Snepscheut. *Trace Theory and VLSI Design*. Springer-Verlag, Heidelberg, 1985. 2

[20] Tom Verhoeff. *A Theory of Delay-Insensitive Systems*. PhD thesis, Eindhoven University of Techology, 1994. 1, 2, 4, 7, 8, 9, 11, 13, 15, 18

[21] Tom Verhoeff. Analyzing specifications for delay-insensitive circuits. In *Proc. International Symposium on Advanced Research in Asynchronous Circuits and Systems*, pages 172–183, 1998.

A Programming Approach to the Design of Asynchronous Logic Blocks

Mark B. Josephs and Dennis P. Furey

Centre for Concurrent Systems and Very Large Scale Integration
School of Computing, Information Systems and Mathematics
South Bank University
103 Borough Road, London SE1 0AA, UK
{josephmb,fureyd}@sbu.ac.uk

Abstract. Delay-Insensitive Sequential Processes is a structured, parallel programming language. It facilitates the clear, succinct and precise specification of the way an asynchronous logic block is to interact with its environment. Using the tool `di2pn`, such a specification can be automatically translated into a Petri net. Using the tool `petrify`, the net can be automatically validated (for freedom from deadlock and interference, and for implementability as a speed-independent circuit) and asynchronous logic can be automatically synthesised.

1 Introduction

The semiconductor industry is beginning to appreciate the opportunities (such as low power dissipation, low electro-magnetic emission, and heterogeneous timing) for application of asynchronous circuit technology [24]. Exploitation will require appropriate methods and tools to be available to the digital logic designer.

We suggest that the language of Delay-Insensitive Sequential Processes (DISP), a variant of Communicating Sequential Processes [9] and of DI-Algebra [11], may be attractive to designers of asynchronous logic blocks, particularly for controllers that use request and acknowledge signals. DISP is a structured, parallel programming language, but without program variables and assignment. Instead, input/output-bursts (as in Burst-Mode specifications [19]) serve as primitive statements, where inputs and outputs are to be interpreted as signal transitions (from logic-0 to logic-1, or vice versa).

Programming in DISP is convenient for exploring a variety of handshaking protocols, an important aspect of asynchronous design. Small changes to the order in which signal transitions occur in a program (known as "reshuffling" [15]) can have a significant impact on area and performance when the program is implemented as an asynchronous circuit. Such changes may inadvertantly introduce deadlock or affect the complexity of logic synthesis.

J. Cortadella et al. (Eds.): Concurrency and Hardware Design, LNCS 2549, pp. 34–60, 2002.

1.1 Syntax of DISP

In presenting the syntax of DISP, we assume a set *sig* of signal names and a set *var* of process variables. We let X range over *var* and let N range over the set *num* of natural numbers.

The BNF syntax of a list of signal names is

siglist ::= - | *sig* { , *sig* }

That is, a dash indicates an empty list and signal names are separated by commas in a non-empty list. It is implicit that repetition of signal names is not allowed in a list. We let $xs, ys, \ldots$ range over *siglist*.

The BNF syntax of an input/output-burst is

burst ::= *siglist*/*siglist*

The BNF syntax of a process and of a set of alternatives are

proc ::= *var* | **stop** | **skip** | **error**
   | *burst* | **pushback** *siglist*
   | **forever** do *proc* **end** | **for** *num* **do** *proc* **end**
   | *proc* ; *proc* | *proc* **or** *proc* | *proc* **par** *proc*
   | **select** *alt-set* **end**
alt-set ::= [*burst* [**then** *proc*] { **alt** *burst* [**then** *proc*] }]

We let $P, Q, \ldots$ range over *proc*.

The process **stop** does nothing. It cannot terminate successfully and so never becomes ready to hand over control to a successor. In contrast, the process **skip** terminates successfully and the process **error** might do anything whatsoever.

The process xs/ys waits for all of the specified inputs (i.e., transitions by signals in xs), then generates the specified set of outputs (i.e., transitions by signals in ys), and finally terminates successfully.

The process **pushback** xs terminates successfully with the specified set of inputs made available to its successor, cf. the **unread** method of the **Pushback-InputStream** class in the Java programming language [8].

The processes **forever** do P **end** and **for** N **do** P **end** perform infinite repetition and N-fold repetition, respectively, of the process P.

The process $P; Q$ first behaves like P and, if this terminates successfully, then behaves like Q. The process P **or** Q behaves like P or like Q. The process P **par** Q is the parallel composition of P and Q, in which outputs of one may be communicated as inputs to the other, signals used for this purpose being local to the process; it terminates successfully only when both P and Q have done so.

The process **select** xs_0/ys_0 **then** P_0 **alt** ... **alt** xs_n/ys_n **then** P_n **end** waits until it is able to select an alternative for which all the specified inputs xs_i are available. It then generates the specified set of outputs ys_i and behaves like the guarded-process P_i (or terminates successfully if the guarded-process has been omitted).

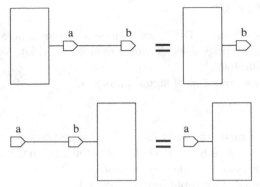

Fig. 1. Signal renaming with the Wire element

The above primitive and compound processes enjoy a rich set of algebraic properties. The reader is referred to Appendix A for examples of the "laws of programming" for DISP.

A DISP program consists of a main process preceded by the declaration of any process variables to which it refers.[1] In modelling an asynchronous logic block, it would not make sense for the program to terminate successfully; therefore the main process usually takes the form P ; `forever do` Q `end`, where P describes the initial behaviour (if any) of the block before it starts to behave in a cyclic manner. On the other hand, in the absence of information about the environment, there is always the danger of deadlock or interference.

The processes that make up a program should use signals in a consistent way, either for input from the environment or for output to the environment, or for local communication in a parallel composition. For example, a/b `par` b/c is permitted, but a/b ; b/c is not. Furthermore, processes composed in parallel should not share input signals or output signals, e.g., a/b `par` a/c and a/c `par` b/c are both illegal.

To illustrate programming in DISP, we describe several well-known building blocks for delay-insensitive systems.

Wire has one input signal, a, and one output signal, b. It propagates transitions from the former to the latter. This behaviour is expressed by the following program:

`forever do a/b end`

A program P that has b as an output signal, but does not use the signal a, can be decomposed into a Wire element in parallel with a transformed version of P

---

[1] By disallowing recursion, we limit the expressivity of our language to "finite-state" processes. The reason for doing so is to ensure that every process can be effectively translated into a Petri net fragment; an implementation in asynchronous logic will in any case be finite-state.

in which b is replaced by a. A similar decomposition is also possible if P has a as an input signal, but does not use the signal b, in which case a is replaced by b. Conversely, the Wire element acts as a renaming operator on programs, which are otherwise unaffected by adding delays to inputs and outputs, Fig. 1.

Other programs that describe the Wire element, equivalent to that above, are

```
forever do a/b ; a/b end

a/b ; forever do a/b end

forever do a/- ; -/b end

a/- ; forever do -/b ; a/- end

forever do a/- ; pushback a~; a/b end

forever do a/- ;
            select -/b
                alt a/- then error
            end
end
```

In particular, the last program can be explained by the fact that, if the environment provides a second transition on a before the first has been acknowledged (on b), then the two transitions may interfere with each other, which is considered to be unsafe.

Join has two input signals, a and b, and an output signal, c. It repeatedly waits for a transition of each input signal, acknowledging them both with a single output transition.

```
forever do a,b/c end
```

A program P that never has one of a and b occurring in an input-burst without the other, i.e., always waiting for both together, can be decomposed into a Join element in parallel with a transformed version of P in which a,b is replaced by c, provided that the signal c is not already used. For example, a three-input Join element can be decomposed into two two-input Join elements:

```
forever do a,b,d/e end =    forever do a,b/c end
                        par forever do c,d/e end
```

One-Hot Join behaves like the Join element above, except that input is already available on a.

```
pushback a~; forever do a,b/c end
```

An equivalent program for One-Hot Join is

```
select a/- then error
    alt b/c then forever do a,b/c end
end
```

Fork has one input signal, c, and two output signals, a and b. It repeatedly waits for a transition of its input signal, propagating it to both its output signals.

```
forever do c/a,b end
```

A program P that never has one of a and b occurring in an output-burst without the other, i.e., always transmitting both together, can be decomposed into a Fork element in parallel with a transformed version of P in which a,b is replaced by c, provided that the signal c is not already used.

Merge has two input signals, a and b, and an output signal, c. It repeatedly waits for a transition of an input signal and propagates it.

```
forever do select a/c
             alt b/c
          end
end
```

Inputs a and b are mutually exclusive here. This is implied only because, if both were available, each would in turn give rise to an output on c, and these transitions might interfere with each other. An equivalent description of the Merge element which makes this explicit is

```
forever do select a/c
             alt b/c
             alt a,b/- then error
          end
end
```

Mutex has two ports, 0 and 1, but is prepared to engage in a four-phase handshake on only one of them at a time.

```
forever do select r0/a0 then r0/a0
             alt r1/a1 then r1/a1
          end
end
```

In this case, requests r0 and r1 may both be available, but an acknowledgement will only be generated for one of them. Not until a release (using the same signal as the request) has been received, can the other request be acknowledged.

$m \times n$ **Decision-Wait** is a generalization of a Join element to m mutually-exclusive "row" inputs and n mutually-exclusive "column" inputs. A 2×1 Decision-Wait is described as follows:

```
forever do select r0,c/e0
             alt r1,c/e1
             alt r0,r1/- then error
          end
end
```

Note that in any program the occurrence of an alternative xs/- then error indicates that it is unsafe for all of the inputs specified in xs to be available. This is a constraint on the environment. In the sequel we shall have no need to include such alternatives because the behavour of the environment will be described in a separate program.

1.2   DISP versus Other Languages/Notations

DISP is similar to "handshaking expansions" (HSE) [15, 14], but more uniform in its treatment of signals: DISP simply uses the name of a signal (both for input signals and for output signals) to designate a transition (both for rising transitions and for falling transitions); HSE uses the name of an input signal to denote its logic level (i.e. as a literal in a Boolean expression) and the decorated name of an output signal to designate a rising or falling transition. For example, the synchronization of four-phase handshakes on two passive ports L and R might be written as forever do rL,rR/aL,aR ; rL,rR/aL,aR end in DISP and forever do wait(rL and rR) ; aL+,aR+ ; wait(rL' and rR') ; aL-,aR- end in HSE, where we have adopted a user-friendly concrete syntax in which to express both DISP and HSE. An advantage of DISP is that a more compact description is sometimes possible, forever do rL,rR/aL,aR end in this example, since forever do S ; S end is semantically equivalent to forever do S end, as one would expect in any structured programming language.

Besides HSE, Signal Transition Graphs (STG's) [2, 21] (i.e. interpreted Petri nets) and Burst-Mode (BM) specifications, are the most popular notations for describing asynchronous controllers. Logic synthesis tools (such as petrify [3] and minimalist [4]) are available that take STG's and Burst-Mode specifications as input. These notations lack the structure of DISP and so can be considered low level, in the same way that assembly programming is low level compared with C. Note that STG's allow the expression of causal relationships between input transitions and between output transitions, but this generality is not required when specifying delay-insensitive systems. Note also that parallel activity (as might be expressed in DISP by rL/aL par rR/aR) cannot be directly described in a BM specification. Assuming that no other inputs are allowed, the corresponding BM specification would have to replace the parallel composition by choice, depicting an initial state offering three alternatives, each converging to the same termination state (something that could be expressed in DISP as select rL/aL then rR/aR alt rR/aR then rL/aL alt rL,rR/aL,aR end).

DISP grew out of DI-Algebra. In DI-Algebra, sequential behaviour is described by prefixing processes with signal transitions (rather than by composing arbitrary processes in sequence). Although this is adequate if one only needs to express the parallel composition of sequential behaviour, the sequential composition of parallel behaviour cannot be described directly. Another deficiency of DI-Algebra is that recursion has to be used instead of iteration. DISP was therefore developed in order to support sequential composition, iteration and distributed termination (i.e., a parallel composition of processes terminates once each process has done so). For example, in DISP (rL/aL par rR/aR) ; P is a process that must handshake on both L and R before it is prepared to behave like P, whereas in DI-Algebra the less compact expression select rL/aL then rR/aR ; P alt rR/aR then rL/aL ; P end would have to be used.

1.3   DISP and CAD Tools

A DISP specification consists of a pair of programs, one describing the behaviour of the logic block and the other describing the behaviour of the environment in which it will operate. Publicly available at http://www.sbu.ac.uk/~fureyd/di2pn/ and http://www.lsi.upc.es/~jordic/petrify/, the CAD tools di2pn and petrify can be used to automatically validate a DISP specification and to automatically synthesise asynchronous logic from it. di2pn is used at the front end, translating the specification into a Petri net. It uses the same text-file format as petrify, an enhanced version of the ASTG format devised for SIS [23]. It is petrify that does the actual validation and logic synthesis, interpreting the Petri net as an STG.

di2pn is most closely related in function to the digg tool [13], which translates terms in DI-Algebra into state-graphs rather than Petri net fragments. An alpha release of di2pn adopted the same input format as digg. Compatibility with digg was abandoned in the beta release [10] because it was considered desirable to adopt input/output-bursts in place of the individual signal transitions of DI-Algebra. The current release of di2pn accepts DISP rather than DI-Algebra. It also now performs peep-hole optimisations. Consequently, the Petri nets it produces are simpler, making them more readable and requiring less work to be performed by petrify.

1.4   Summary

In the body of this chapter, we apply the DISP programming language to the design of a number of interesting aynchronous logic blocks that can be found in the literature. This includes two small, but real-world, design examples: (1) asynchronous controllers for a micropipeline stage, of the kind used in the ARM-compatible asynchronous processor core of the AMULET2e embedded system chip [6]; (2) a self-timed adder cell of the kind used in the arithmetic units of the Caltech asynchronous microprocessors [17, 18] and in the dual-rail cell library of the Tangram silicon compiler [12] (which is used for product design by Philips Semiconductors). The other examples are asynchronous controllers for an analog-to-digital (A/D) converter and for a token ring. The translation by di2pn of our designs into Petri nets, and their validatation and logic synthesis by petrify, are also illustrated.

To give a deeper insight into DISP, we present some of its algebraic properties in Appendix A and the translation algorithm implemented in di2pn in Appendix B. After translation, di2pn applies certain peephole optimisations, but these are not discussed in this chapter.

2   Designing with DISP, di2pn and petrify

The language, DISP, has been expressed in a concrete syntax that should make the meaning of programs reasonably self-evident. It is used here to describe the behaviour of asynchronous logic blocks and their environments in terms of input/output-bursts of signal transitions. Programs do not express the direction (+ or -) of each transition, since this is not required for their translation by di2pn into Petri net fragments, but instead use "toggle-transitions". The decision as to whether to initialise the signals of a logic block to logic-0 or logic-1 has to be taken prior to logic synthesis, of course.[2]

In the examples that follow, logic blocks interact with their environments by means of request and acknowledge signals on communication ports. We adopt the following naming convention: rX for the request signal and aX for the acknowledgement signal on port X. (In one example, double-rail encoded bits are communicated using signals tX and fX.) A toggle-transition of a signal s will simply be written s, rather than $s\tilde{\ }$ or $s*$, as are sometimes used.

In each example, we write a pair of DISP programs:

- one program describes the behaviour of the environment (i.e., repeated hand-shaking on each port);
- the other program describes the behaviour of the asynchronous logic block.

The asynchronous logic block and its environment are assumed to be connected by wires of arbitrary delay, which are grouped together to form channels. By convention, the same signal (port) name is used to identify each end of the wire (channel). Moreover, we shall sometimes use the port name when referring to the channel and when referring to a process that handshakes on that port.

di2pn automatically translates the pair of programs into a Petri net[3] and simplifies the net by performing peep-hole optimisations. petrify can then be used in various ways:

1. petrify -no simply checks that the specification is free from deadlock and interference. If the specification is not free from interference, the Petri net will not be 1-safe and this will be reported, e.g.,

   FATAL ERROR: (Boundedness): marking exceeds
   the capacity for place p39+

   If the specification is not free from deadlock, then this will be reported either as

   FATAL ERROR: No initial marking has been defined

---

[2] By default, petrify assumes that all signals are initially 0. The directive .initial state a b ... should be inserted into the text-file representation of the Petri net for those signals, a, b, etcetera, that are initially 1.

[3] It translates each program into a Petri net fragment – see Appendix B for details – and combines the two fragments into a Petri net that models the closed system.

or by giving a trace, e.g.,

```
Error: There are deadlock states in the system.
Trace of events to a~deadlock state:
  b a~t54
```

The -no option tells `petrify` that a (transformed) Petri net is not required.

2. `petrify -untog` interprets the Petri net as an STG and transforms it so that toggle-transitions are replaced by rising (+) and falling (-) transitions. This gives the designer the opportunity to re-examine the specification at a lower level of abstraction.

3. `petrify -no -csc` checks that the transition system represented by the STG has a "complete state coding"(csc), a condition that must be met before logic minimisation can be used to synthesise a speed-independent circuit implementation. In most cases, the STG will not, but `petrify` can be used to try to solve for csc.

4. `petrify -no -cg` or `-gc` attempts to solve for csc (if necessary) and to perform logic minimisation, targetting a speed-independent circuit implementation using complex gates or generalised C elements, respectively.

In fact there are many other options available for `petrify`, including logic decomposition and synthesis of circuits that make relative timing assumptions.

It should be stressed that the designer does not have to be concerned with Petri nets: there is no need to examine the output of `di2pn` before feeding it into `petrify` for validation and logic synthesis!

In the first two of the four examples that follow, we show the Petri net that is output by `di2pn` and the net into which it can be transformed by `petrify`. The net output by `petrify` gives the causal relationships between rising and falling transitions. In other words, we end up with an STG that would traditionally be written by hand. For logic synthesis, `petrify` can either be applied to the Petri net output by `di2pn` or to its transformed version.

In the third example, we use `petrify` to validate deadlock-freedom and, in the fourth example, we use `petrify` to validate csc.

On a technical note, the reader may wonder why we need to write a program describing the behaviour of the environment at all. The practical reason for this is that `di2pn` translates an individual program into a Petri net fragment which captures causal relationships between input transitions and output transitions, but not between output transitions and input transitions; `petrify` would misinterpet such a fragment, as it is designed to take a Petri net that captures all relevant causal relationships and translate it into a transition system. Alternatively, however, one could translate a program into a transition system, either by assuming that it is designed to operate in the "weakest" safe environment (the approach implemented in the `digg` tool) or by requiring that the program always makes explicit those input bursts that are allowed (the approach taken in BM specification).

2.1   Controller for an A/D Converter

In order to compare various strategies for the synthesis of asynchronous logic from STG's, Carmona et al. [1] used a suite of eight benchmarks. Their first benchmark, adfast, specified an "analog-to-digital fast converter" with three input signals and three output signals[4]. They reported that the tool petrify could synthesise asynchronous logic from their STG specification. In this sub-section, we write a pair of programs that specify adfast and show how they can be translated automatically into the original STG.

The input and output signals of the controller correspond to request and acknowledge signals on (somewhat unusually) three active ports, L, Z and D. That is, the controller is responsible for outputting the request transitions, rL, rZ and rD, which are input by its environment. The corresponding acknowledge transitions, aL, aZ and aD, are output by the environment and input by the controller.

The following program describes the behaviour of the environment, as the parallel composition of three sub-programs (processes), one per channel:

```
L = forever do rL/aL end

Z = forever do rZ/aZ end

D = forever do rD/aD end

L par Z par D
```

The following program, named ADFAST, describes the behaviour of the controller:

```
pushback aL ;
forever do
  aL/rL,rD,rZ ;
  aD/- ;
  ( aL/rD par aZ/rZ );
  aD,aZ/rL
end
```

Note that pushback aL means that an acknowledgement on L is initially available to the controller, so it is able to start by issuing requests on all three ports.

---

[4] This benchmark appears to based on one of the earliest examples of STG specification and synthesis, a successive approximation A/D converter [2]. The signal rZ is the control input to a comparator which senses the difference between an input voltage and a reference voltage. The signal aZ indicates that the comparator has reached a decision – the smaller the voltage difference the longer the time it takes for the comparator to decide. The other signals are concerned with a latch and combinational logic, which form a finite state machine. Data are latched on one edge of rL, which is acknowledged on aL. The combined delay of the combinational logic and a digital-to-analog converter are matched by a delay circuit from rD to aD.

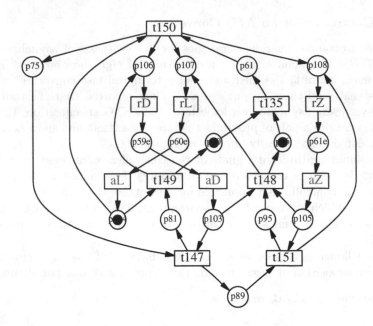

INPUTS: aZ,aL,aD
OUTPUTS: rZ,rL,rD
DUMMY: t135,t147,t149,t148,t151,t150

Fig. 2. Petri net output by `di2pn` for controlling A/D converter

The pair of programs are written in a text-file and input to `di2pn`, which will create the file `ADFAST.pn`. Fig. 2 shows the result of drawing `ADFAST.pn` using the tool, `draw_astg`, which is packaged with `petrify`. Fig. 3 shows the result of transforming `ADFAST.pn` using `petrify` and the options `-untog` and `-bisim`, and drawing it using `draw_astg`. Fig. 3 is identical to the STG benchmark in [1].

Another way to express `ADFAST` in DISP is as follows:

```
pushback aL ;
forever do
  aL/rL,rD,rZ ;
  select aD,aL/rD then aZ/rZ
     alt aD,aZ/rZ then aL/rD
  end ;
  aD,aZ/rL
end
```

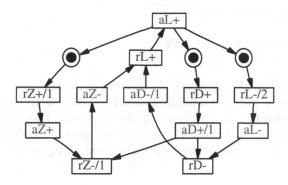

INPUTS: aZ,aL,aD
OUTPUTS: rZ,rL,rD

Fig. 3. STG output by `petrify` after resynthesis of the Petri net in Fig. 2, having inserted the directive `.initial state aL rL` into the file `ADFAST.pn`

2.2   Controller for a Micropipeline Stage

In [5], Furber and Day showed how they used STG's to explore various ways of controlling a micropipeline stage. They specified simple, semi-decoupled and fully-decoupled controllers and implemented them using generalised C elements. In this subsection we show how it is possible to specify the behaviour of these controllers in DISP.

The controller for a micropipeline stage communicates with a producer on passive port `IN` and with a consumer on active port `OUT`. The controller is also responsible for closing and re-opening an array of transparent latches on the data path. Furber and Day point out that the signal that operates the latches "must have reasonable drive buffering". Indeed their implementations include a buffer, the output of which controls the latches. We shall consider the buffer to be part of the environment and model it with the process `LT`.

The following program describes the behaviour of the environment:

```
IN = pushback aIN ;
     forever do aIN/rIN end

OUT = forever do rOUT/aOUT end

LT = forever do rLT/aLT end

IN par OUT par LT
```

Note that, by including `pushback aIN`, we have enabled the environment to start by making a request on port `IN`.

A program that specifies a *simple* controller is given by

```
pushback aOUT ;
forever do
  rIN,aOUT/rLT,rOUT ; aLT/aIN
end
```

The compactness of this specification reflects symmetry in the behaviour of the controller between rising and falling transitions. Although iterations of the loop alternate between closing and opening the latches and so differ in effect, they are indistiguishable in the way in which they sequence toggle-transitions.

Of course, we can unfold the loop and obtain an equivalent program:

```
pushback aOUT ;
forever do
  rIN,aOUT/rLT,rOUT ; aLT/aIN ;
  rIN,aOUT/rLT,rOUT ; aLT/aIN
end
```

Now, in each iteration, a complete four-phase handshake takes place on each channel and the latches will be closed and re-opened.

In the first half of each iteration, it may be acceptable to relax the requirement that transition aOUT is input before transitions rLT and aIN are output. The result is a *semi-decoupled* controller:

```
pushback aOUT ;
forever do
  rIN/rLT ;
  ( aLT/aIN par aOUT/rOUT );
  rIN,aOUT/rLT,rOUT ; aLT/aIN
end
```

The same dependency can be removed from the second half of each iteration, yielding a *full-decoupled* controller:

```
pushback aOUT ;
forever do
  rIN/rLT ;
  ( aLT/aIN par aOUT/rOUT );
  rIN/rLT ;
  ( aLT/aIN par aOUT/rOUT )
end
```

This simplifies to

```
pushback aOUT ;
forever do
  rIN/rLT ;
  ( aLT/aIN par aOUT/rOUT )
end
```

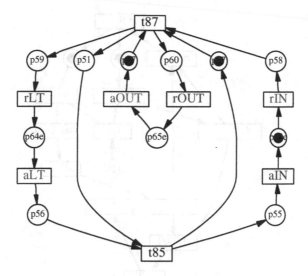

INPUTS: rIN,aOUT,aLT
OUTPUTS: rOUT,rLT,aIN
DUMMY: t85,t87

Fig. 4. Petri net output by `di2pn` for simple controller of micropipeline stage

Figs. 4 and 5 show the Petri nets output by `di2pn` and `petrify`, respectively, in the case of a simple controller. Asynchronous logic, similar to that in [5], can then be synthesised by invoking `petrify` with the options `-gc -eqn`.

2.3   Controller for a Stage in a Token Ring

To illustrate the problem of deadlock being introduced by reshuffling of hand-shaking expansions, Manohar [14] considers the example of a ring of three processes containing a single token. Process I, the initiator, forwards the token along channel R to process B, which in turn forwards the token along channel S to process A. Process A returns the token to process I along channel F.

Given the following programs for I and A, our task is to find a suitable program for B:

```
I = pushback aR ;
    aR/rR ; aR/rR ;
    forever do aR,rF/rR,aF end

A~= pushback aF ;
    forever do aF/rS ; aS/rF end
```

Manohar considers the following program for B, but his analysis reveals that the ring would deadlock:

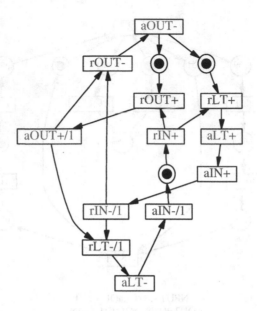

INPUTS: rIN,aOUT,aLT
OUTPUTS: rOUT,rLT,aIN

Fig. 5. STG output by `petrify` after resynthesis of the Petri net in Fig. 4

```
forever do rR,rS/aR,aS end
```

We can detect this automatically by running `di2pn` and `petrify`:

```
Error: There are deadlock states in the system.
Trace of events to a~deadlock state:
 t143e rS t145e rR t55 aR t144e rR aS t148e
```

The dummy transitions in this trace are only meaningful if we examine the Petri net output by `di2pn`, Fig. 6.

We might try instead the following program:

```
forever do
  rR,rS/aR,aS ;
  rR/aR par rS/aS
end
```

This time `petrify` detects a trace of 21 transitions (9 on channels R and S) leading to a deadlock state.

The following program is successfully validated as deadlock-free by `petrify`:

```
rR,rS/aR,aS ;
forever do
  rR/aR par rS/aS
end
```

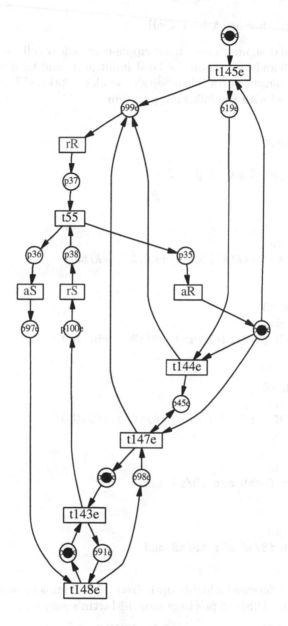

INPUTS: rS,rR
OUTPUTS: aS,aR
DUMMY: t55,t148e,t145e,t144e,t147e,t143e

Fig. 6. Petri net output by `di2pn` from first attempt at program for B

Once this is established, `petrify` can also easily synthesise a speed-independent circuit implementation.

2.4   Datapath for an Adder Cell

The problem of designing a self-timed ripple-carry adder cell was first introduced in [22]. Let A, B and C (carry-in) be 1-bit input ports and let D (carry-out) and S (sum) be 1-bit output ports. Then Seitz's "weak conditions" for the environment can be expressed with the following program:

```
forever do
   aD,aS/rA,rB,rC
end
par A~par B par C par D par S
```

where

```
A~= pushback rA ;
     forever do
        ( rA/fA ; rA/fA ) or ( rA/tA ; rA/tA )
     end

B = pushback rB ;
     forever do
        ( rB/fB ; rB/fB ) or ( rB/tB ; rB/tB )
     end

C = pushback rC ;
     forever do
        ( rC/fC ; rC/fC ) or ( rC/tC ; rC/tC )
     end

D = forever do
        select fD/aD alt tD/aD end
     end

S = forever do
        select fS/aS alt tS/aS end
     end
```

Martin [16] designed a highly-optimised CMOS implementation of the adder cell. We can use DISP to precisely model Martin's solution.

```
forever do
   select fA,fB/fD then
             select fC/fS then ( fA,fB/fD par fC/fS )
                alt tC/tS then ( fA,fB/fD par tC/tS )
             end
      alt fB,fC/fD then
             select fA/fS then ( fA,fB/fD par fC/fS )
                alt tA/tS then ( tA,fB/fD par fC/tS )
```

```
                 end
         alt fC,fA/fD then
                 select fB/fS then ( fA,fB/fD par fC/fS )
                     alt tB/tS then ( fA,tB/fD par fC/tS )
                 end
         alt tA,tB/tD then
                 select fC/fS then ( tA,tB/tD par fC/fS )
                     alt tC/tS then ( tA,tB/tD par tC/tS )
                 end
         alt tB,tC/tD then
                 select fA/fS then ( fA,tB/tD par tC/fS )
                     alt tA/tS then ( tA,tB/tD par tC/tS )
                 end
         alt tC,tA/tD then
                 select fB/fS then ( tA,fB/tD par tC/fS )
                     alt tB/tS then ( tA,tB/tD par tC/tS )
                 end
     end
end
```

By running di2pn and petrify we are able to validate that the underlying
transition system has a complete state coding. Logic minimisation (using the
-gc option for a generalised C element implementation) then determines that

- the set condition for both tS' and fS' is fC' tC', i.e., two p-type transistors
  in series (with inputs fC and tC) in each case;
- the set condition for both tD' and fD' is fB' tB' fA' tA', i.e., four p-type
  transistors in series in each case;
- the reset condition for tS' is tC (fB fA + tB tA) + fC (tB fA + fB tA)
  and that for fS' is tC (tB fA + fB tA) + fC (fB fA + tB tA), i.e., two
  networks of 10 n-type transistors each;
- the reset condition for tD' is tA (tB + tC) + tC tB and that for fD' is fA
  (fB + fC) + fC fB, i.e., two networks of 5 n-type transistors each.

Note that 8 transistors can be saved by sharing the subnetworks implementing
fB fA + tB tA and tB fA + fB tA, as Martin has observed, so the transistor
count per cell is 34, or 42 if one includes an inverter for each output signal.

Furthermore, the program can be modified by making subtle changes to the
causality relationships in the return-to-zero phase. As a result, we are able to
obtain an improved implementation that avoids the undesirable situation of having 4 p-type transistors in series. The modified program for the adder cell is as
follows:

```
forever do
  select fA,fB/fD then
            select fC/fS then fA,fB,fC/fD,fS
                 alt tC/tS then ( fA,fB/fD par tC/tS )
```

```
            end
    alt fB,fC/fD then
            select fA/fS then fA,fB,fC/fD,fS
                alt tA/tS then ( fB,fC/fD par tA/tS )
            end
    alt fC,fA/fD then
            select fB/fS then fA,fB,fC/fD,fS
                alt tB/tS then ( fC,fA/fD par tB/tS )
            end
    alt tA,tB/tD then
            select fC/fS then ( tA,tB/tD par fC/fS )
                alt tC/tS then tA,tB,tC/tD,tS
            end
    alt tB,tC/tD then
            select fA/fS then ( tB,tC/tD par fA/fS )
                alt tA/tS then tA,tB,tC/tD,tS
            end
    alt tC,tA/tD then
            select fB/fS then ( tC,tA/tD par fB/fS )
                alt tB/tS then tA,tB,tC/tD,tS
            end
    end
end
```

In obtaining this solution, and rejecting others, we found it useful to be able to automatically validate the csc property. This time, logic minimisation determines that the set condition for both tS' and tD' is tB' tC' tA' and that for both fS' and fD' is fB' fC' fA', with the reset conditions as previously, so the transistor count per cell is unchanged. This implementation is depicted in Fig. 7.

3 Conclusion

petrify is a powerful tool for the analysis and transformation of Petri nets and for the synthesis of asynchronous logic. Using di2pn as a front-end to petrify allows designs to be conveniently entered as DISP programs rather than as Petri nets. This combination of tools offers an innovative methodology for the design of (relatively small) asynchronous logic blocks. The examples in this chapter provide evidence that the methdology has potential for application to real-world design problems.

Acknowledgement

DISP has evolved out of work undertaken by the first author on DI-Algebra in collaboration with Jan Tijmen Udding and his students. The tool di2pn was developed with financial support from the UK Engineering and Physical Sciences

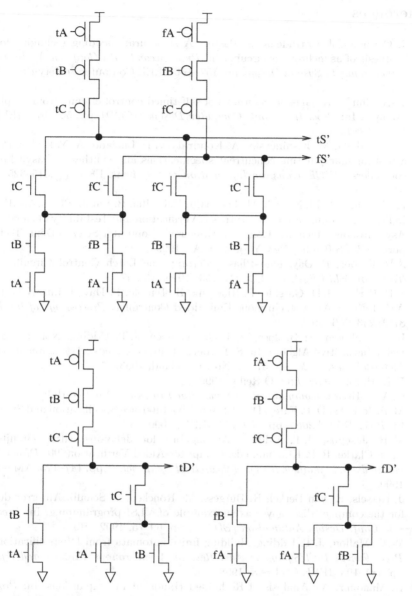

Fig. 7. Improved transistor-level implementation of a self-timed adder cell

Research Council under grant number GR/M51567. Early dissemination of this work has been facilitated by the support of the European Commission for the Working Group on Asynchronous Circuit Design (ACiD-WG).

References

[1] J. Carmona, J. Cortadella, E. Pastor. A structural encoding technique for the synthesis of asynchronous circuits. In: *Proc. Second Int'l Conf. on Application of Concurrency to System Design,* pp. 157–166, IEEE Computer Society Press, 2001. 43, 44

[2] T.-A. Chu, L. A. Glasser. Synthesis of self-timed control circuits from graphs: an example. In: *Proc. Int'l Conf. Computer Design (ICCD),* pp. 565–571, IEEE CS Press, 1986. 39, 43

[3] J. Cortadella, M. Kishinevsky, A. Kondratyev, L. Luciano, A. Yakovlev. Petrify: a tool for manipulating concurrent specifications and synthesis of asynchronous controllers. *IEICE Trans. on Information and Systems,* E80-D(3):315–325, 1997. 39

[4] R. M. Fuhrer, S. M. Nowick, M. Theobald, N. K. Jha, B. Lin, L. Plana. MIMIMAL-IST: An environment for the Synthesis, Verification and Testability of Burst-Mode Asynchronous Machines. Columbia University Computer Science Dept. Tech. Report #CUCS-020-99, New York, U. S. A., 1999. 39

[5] S. B. Furber, P. Day. Four-Phase Micropipeline Latch Control Circuits. *IEEE Trans. on VLSI Systems,* 4(2):247–253, 1996. 45, 47

[6] S. B. Furber, J. D. Garside, P. Riocreux, S. Temple, P. Day, J. Liu, N. C. Paver. AMULET2e: An Asynchronous Embedded Controller. *Proceedings of the IEEE,* 87(2):243–256, 1999. 40

[7] R. Groenboom, M. B. Josephs, P. G. Lucassen, J. T. Udding. Normal Form in Delay-Insensitive Algebra. In: S. Furber, M. Edwards, eds. *Asynchronous Design Methodologies, A-28,* pp. 57–70, North-Holland, 1993. 55

[8] E. R. Harold. *Java I/O.* O'Reilly, 1999. 35

[9] C. A. R. Hoare. *Communicating Sequential Processes.* Prentice-Hall, 1985. 34

[10] M. B. Josephs, D. P. Furey. Delay-Insensitive Interface Specification and Synthesis. In: *Proc. DATE 2000,* pp. 169–173, IEEE, 2000. 40

[11] M. B. Josephs, J. T. Udding. An algebra for delay-insensitive circuits. In: E. M. Clarke, R. P. Kurshan, eds. Computer-Aided Verification '90. *DIMACS Series in discrete mathematics and theoretical comp. sci. 3,* pp. 147–175, AMS-ACM, 1990. 34

[12] J. Kessels, K. van Berkel, R. Burgess, M. Roncken, F. Schalij. An error decoder for the compact disc player as an example of VLSI programming. In: *Proc. Europ. Conf. Design Automation (EDAC),* pp. 69–75, 1992. 40

[13] W. C. Mallon, J. T. Udding. Building finite automata from DI specifications. In: *Proc. Fourth Int'l Symp. on Adv. Res. in Asynchronous Circuits and Systems,* pp. 184–193, IEEE CS Press, 1998. 40

[14] R. Manohar. An Analysis of Reshuffled Handshaking Expansions. In: *Proc. 7th Int'l Symp. on Asynchronous Circuits and Systems,* pp. 96–105, IEEE Computer Society Press, 2001. 39, 47

[15] A. J. Martin. Compiling Communicating Processes into Delay-Insensitive VLSI Circuits. *Distributed Computing,* 1:226-234, 1986. 34, 39

[16] A. J. Martin. Asynchronous Datapaths and the Design of an Asynchronous Adder. *Formal Methods in System Design,* 1:117-137, 1992. 50

[17] A. J. Martin, S. M. Burns, T. K. Lee, D. Borkovic, P. J. Hazewindus. The design of an asynchronous microprocessor. In: *Proc. Decennial Caltech Conference on VLSI,* pp. 351–373, MIT Press, 1999. 40

[18] A. J. Martin, A. Lines, R. Manohar, M. Nystrom, P. Penzes, R. Southworth, U. V. Cummings, T. K. Lee. The design of an asynchronous MIPS R3000. In: *Proc. Seventeenth Conf. on Adv. Res. in VLSI,* pp. 164–181, 1997. 40

[19] S. M. Nowick, D. L. Dill. Synthesis of asynchronous state machines using a local clock. In: *Proc. Int'l Conf. Computer-Aided Design ICCAD,* pp. 192–197, 1991. 34

[20] A. W. Roscoe. *The Theory and Practice of Concurrency.* Prentice-Hall, 1998. 55

[21] L. Y. Rosenblum, A. V. Yakovlev. Signal graphs: from self-timed to time dones. In: *Proc. Int'l Workshop on Timed Petri Nets,* pp. 197-207, IEEE CS Press, 1985. 39

[22] C. L. Seitz. System Timing. Chapter 7 in *Introduction to VLSI Systems* by C. Mead and L. Conway, Addison-Wesley, 1980. 50

[23] E. M. Sentovich, K. J. Singh, L. Lavagno, C. Moon, R. Murgai, A. Saldanha, H. Savoj, P. R. Stephan, R. K. Brayton, A. Sangiovanno-Vincentelli. SIS: A System for Sequential Circuit Synthesis. Electronics Research Lab. Memo. No. UCB/ERL M92/41, Dept. of EECS, Univ. of California, Berkeley, U. S. A., 1992. 40

[24] C. H. van Berkel, M. B. Josephs, S. M. Nowick. Applications of Asynchronous Circuits. *Proceedings of the IEEE,* 87(2):223–233, 1999. 34

A   Algebraic Laws

In this appendix, we provide a number of algebraic laws that give us a deeper understanding of the DISP language. These laws are written as equalities between processes, it being postulated that the processes are indistinguishable to an observer[5]. The significance of delay-insensitivity is that input/output-bursts can only be observed from the ends of wires.

With a *complete* set of laws one can reduce processes to "normal form". This is a highly restricted syntax in which equivalent processes are syntactically identical, or perhaps differ in a well-defined and trivial way (such as the order in which alternatives appear in a **select** statement). Normalizing (in CSP) is discussed further in [20] and a complete set of laws for DI-Algebra can be found in [7], for example. Algebraic manipulation is also sometimes undertaken in order to prove the correctness of a particular decomposition of a process. This involves the re-expression of all parallel activity in terms of selection between alternatives by applying an "expansion theorem".

Let us first consider some laws concerning sequential composition. This is an associative operator

$$(P;Q);R = P;(Q;R)$$

which means that we can drop the parentheses without causing ambiguity. It also has two left-zeros, **stop** and **error**, i.e.,

---

[5] Alternatively, these laws could be obtained as theorems by showing that the left-hand and right-hand expressions denote the same set of behaviours in an appropriately defined trace-theoretic model. This could be done directly (by giving a denotational semantics) or indirectly (by abstracting from the non-observable features of an operational semantics, such as the Petri net semantics given in Appendix B).

$$\texttt{stop};P \;=\; \texttt{stop} \qquad \texttt{error};P \;=\; \texttt{error}$$

and a (left and right) unit, `skip`, i.e.,

$$\texttt{skip};P \;=\; P \;=\; P;\texttt{skip}$$

It distributes through nondeterministic choice, both in its left argument and in its right argument, i.e.,

$$(P \texttt{ or } Q);R \;=\; (P;R) \texttt{ or } (Q;R)$$
$$P;(Q \texttt{ or } R) \;=\; (P;Q) \texttt{ or } (P;R)$$

Note that the difference between `stop` and `error` is revealed by the fact that parallel composition only has `error` as a zero.

Next we consider some laws concerning input/output-bursts. `skip` can be thought of as a special case, viz.,

$$\texttt{skip} = \texttt{-/-}$$

An input/output-burst can be decomposed into an input-burst followed by an output-burst, i.e.,

$$xs/ys \;=\; xs/\texttt{-} \;\texttt{;}\; \texttt{-}/ys$$

An input-burst consists of parallel activity, but cannot terminate until all inputs have arrived, i.e.,

$$xs,ys/\texttt{-} \;=\; xs/\texttt{-} \texttt{ par } ys/\texttt{-} \;=\; xs/\texttt{-} \;\texttt{;}\; ys/\texttt{-}$$

where xs and ys are disjoint. Similarly, an output-burst consists of parallel activity, and can terminate as soon as all outputs have been transmitted, i.e.,

$$\texttt{-}/xs,ys \;=\; \texttt{-}/xs \texttt{ par } \texttt{-}/ys \;=\; \texttt{-}/xs \;\texttt{;}\; \texttt{-}/ys$$

where xs and ys are disjoint. On the other hand, if xs is a non-empty list,

$$xs/\texttt{-} \;\texttt{;}\; xs/\texttt{-} \;=\; \texttt{stop}$$
$$\texttt{-}/xs \;\texttt{;}\; \texttt{-}/xs \;=\; \texttt{error}$$

It follows that `stop` acts as a right-zero for input-bursts, since $xs/\texttt{-};\texttt{stop} \;=\; \texttt{skip};\texttt{stop} \;=\; \texttt{stop}$, if xs is the empty list, and $xs/\texttt{-};\texttt{stop} \;=\; xs/\texttt{-};(xs/\texttt{-}; xs/\texttt{-}) \;=\; (xs/\texttt{-};xs/\texttt{-}); xs/\texttt{-} \;=\; \texttt{stop}; xs/\texttt{-} \;=\; \texttt{stop}$, otherwise. Similarly, `error` acts as a right-zero for output-bursts.

Finally, we illustrate the expansion of parallel composition:

$$(\; xs_0/ys_0 \;\texttt{;}\; P \;) \texttt{ par } (\; xs_1/ys_1 \;\texttt{;}\; Q \;) =$$

$$\left\{ \begin{array}{ll}
\texttt{stop} & \text{, if both } xs_0 \text{ and } xs_1 \text{ include signals local to the parallel composition} \\
xs_1/\texttt{-} \;\texttt{;}\; (\; (\; xs_0/ys_0 \;\texttt{;}\; P \;) \texttt{ par } (\; \texttt{-}/ys_1 \;\texttt{;}\; Q \;) \;) & \text{, if only } xs_0 \text{ does} \\
xs_0/\texttt{-} \;\texttt{;}\; (\; (\; \texttt{-}/ys_0 \;\texttt{;}\; P \;) \texttt{ par } (\; xs_1/ys_1 \;\texttt{;}\; Q \;) \;) & \text{, if only } xs_1 \text{ does} \\
\texttt{select } xs_0/\texttt{-} \texttt{ then } (\; (\; \texttt{-}/ys_0 \;\texttt{;}\; P \;) \texttt{ par } (\; xs_1/ys_1 \;\texttt{;}\; Q \;) \;) & \\
\quad \texttt{alt } xs_1/\texttt{-} \texttt{ then } (\; (\; xs_0/ys_0 \;\texttt{;}\; P \;) \texttt{ par } (\; \texttt{-}/ys_1 \;\texttt{;}\; Q \;) \;) & \\
\texttt{end} & \text{, if neither does}
\end{array} \right.$$

Furthermore, an output-burst can be distributed and buffered up:
(-/ys ; P) par Q = pushback ys_0; (P par (pushback ys_1 ; Q)),
where ys_0 and ys_1 partition ys, the former consisting of non-local signals and
the latter consisting of local signals to the parallel composition.

Of course, there are many more laws that could have been stated.

B   An Algorithm for Translating Programs into Petri Net Fragments

The input/output behaviour of a logic block and of its environment are specified
by a pair of programs. Each is translated into a Petri net fragment, as described
below, and the two fragments are combined to form a Petri net. If the logic block
can safely operate in that environment, then the Petri net will be 1-safe, i.e., no
place will ever be occupied by more than one token.

Our translation algorithm operates upon two data structures, a list L and
a Petri net fragment N. The list consists of tuples of the form (α, ω, Φ), where
α and ω are places in N, and Φ is either a process, or a set of alternatives,
that has yet to be translated. When the list is empty, the algorithm terminates,
returning N.

A convenient way to picture L and N is to draw a graph consisting of directed
arcs, places, boxes and clouds. There should be a cloud labelled Φ with pre-set
α and post-set ω, for each tuple (α, ω, Φ) in L. Thus the translation algorithm
terminates when there are no clouds remaining.

Given a program P, the data structures are initialised as follows: L contains
a single tuple $(0, 1, P)$, whilst N consists of

- a marked place 0 and an unmarked place 1,
- a transition (labelled x) with an empty pre-set and a post-set consisting of
  a single unmarked place (also labelled x) for each input signal x of P,
- a transition (labelled x) with an empty post-set and a pre-set consisting of
  a single unmarked place (also labelled x) for each output signal x of P,
- a single unmarked place (labelled x) for each local signal x of P.[6]

While L is non-empty, any tuple is removed from the list and an expansion rule is applied to it. The algorithm terminates because each expansion rule
strictly reduces the sum over each tuple in L of the size of its third component.
We now give the rules for each of the language constructs.

B.1   Expansion Rules for Tuples

(α, ω, X): add tuple (α, ω, P) given the declaration $X = P$.

$(\alpha, \omega, \text{stop})$: do nothing.

---

[6] For simplicity, we are assuming that different names are given to signals that are
local to different parallel compositions.

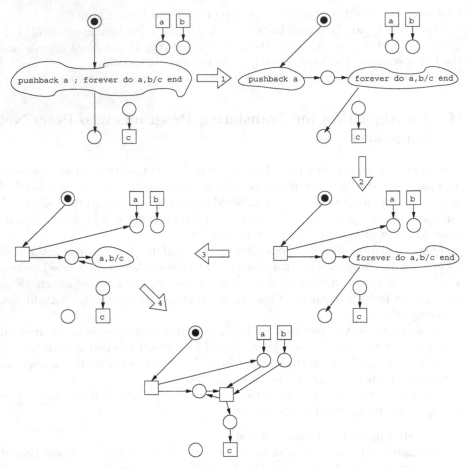

Fig. 8. Step-by-step translation from One-Hot Join program to Petri net fragment

$(\alpha, \omega, \texttt{skip})$: add dummy transition to N with pre-set α and post-set ω.

$(\alpha, \omega, \texttt{error})$: add token to place α in N.

$(\alpha, \omega, xs/ys)$: add dummy transition to N with pre-set α, xs and post-set ω, ys.

$(\alpha, \omega, \texttt{pushback } xs)$: add dummy transition to N with pre-set α and post-set ω, xs.

$(\alpha, \omega, \texttt{forever do } P \texttt{ end})$: add tuple (α, α, P) to L.

$(\alpha, \omega, \texttt{for } 0 \texttt{ do } P \texttt{ end})$: same as for skip.

$(\alpha, \omega, \texttt{for } n+1 \texttt{ do } P \texttt{ end})$: add place β to N and tuples (α, β, P) and $(\beta, \omega, \texttt{for } n \texttt{ do } P \texttt{ end})$ to L.

$(\alpha, \omega, P; Q)$: add place β to N and tuples (α, β, P) and (β, ω, Q) to L.

$(\alpha, \omega, P \texttt{ or } Q)$: add one dummy transition to N with pre-set α and post-set α_0 (for new place α_0), another dummy transition to N with pre-set α and post-set α_1 (for new place α_1) and the tuples (α_0, ω, P) and (α_1, ω, Q) to L.

$(\alpha, \omega, P \texttt{ par } Q)$: add one dummy transition to N with pre-set α and post-set α_0, α_1 (for new places α_0, α_1), another dummy transition to N with pre-set ω_0, ω_1 and post-set ω (for new places ω_0, ω_1) and the tuples (α_0, ω_0, P) and (α_1, ω_1, Q) to L.

$(\alpha, \omega, \texttt{select } \varPhi \texttt{ end})$: add tuple $(\alpha, \omega, \varPhi)$ to L.

$(\alpha, \omega, xs/ys \texttt{ then } P)$: add place β to N and tuples $(\alpha, \beta, xs/ys)$ and (β, ω, P) to L.

$(\alpha, \omega, \varPhi \texttt{ alt } \varPsi)$: add tuples $(\alpha, \omega, \varPhi)$ and $(\alpha, \omega, \varPsi)$ to L.

B.2   Example

Consider the One-Hot Join element of section 1.1. L is initialised to

$$(0, 1, \texttt{pushback a ; forever do a,b/c end})$$

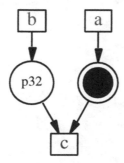

Fig. 9. Petri net fragment for One-Hot Join automatically generated by di2pn

and N consists of 5 places (labelled 0, 1, a, b and c) and 3 transitions (labelled a, b and c), with transitions a and b connected to places a and b, respectively, and place c connected to transition c. Place 0 is marked.

The algorithm may then proceed as shown in Fig. 8. That is:

1. The single tuple in L is replaced by two, namely, $(0, 2, \texttt{pushback a})$ and $(2, 1, \texttt{forever do a,b/c end})$ and a place labelled 2 is added to N.
2. The tuple $(0, 2, \texttt{pushback a})$ is removed and a transition t is added to N, with place 0 connected to t and transition t connected to places 2 and a.
3. The tuple $(2, 1, \texttt{forever do a,b/c end})$ is replaced by $(2, 2, \texttt{a,b/c})$.
4. The tuple $(2, 2, \texttt{a,b/c})$ is removed and a transition u is added to N, with places 2, a and b connected to u and transition u connected to places 2 and c.

L is now empty and N can be returned. Fig. 9 shows the Petri net fragment returned by di2pn after it has simplified N by applying various peephole optimizations.

GALA (Globally Asynchronous – Locally Arbitrary) Design

Victor Varshavsky[1] and Vyacheslav Marakhovsky[2]

[1] Neural Network Technologies Ltd.
3, Ha'Hashmonaim, Bnei-Brak, 51264, Israel
`victor12@netvision.net.il`
[2] The University of Aizu, Hardware Department
Aizu-Wakamatsu City, 965-8580 Japan
`marak@u-aizu.ac.jp`

Abstract. The problem of organizing the temporal behavior of digital systems is discussed. This problem is mainly associated with providing the interface between physical (natural) and logical (artificial) time. The most common method of interfacing is based on a system clock that removes physical time from the behavior models A number of algorithms that can be easily formulated in logical time present a great difficulty in the asynchronous case. The suggested GALA (Globally Asynchronous – Locally Arbitrary) design methodology is based on decomposing the system to a Processors Stratum and a Synchro-Stratum. The synchro-stratum acts as a distributed asynchronous clock that produces local synchro-signals for the processor stratum, which is basically a synchronous prototype. A synchro-stratum, like any asynchronous circuit, interacts with the external devices, including the processor stratum, by handshake. Every local device produces an acknowledgment signal and sends it to the synchro-stratum. The designer can use a wide range of methods to implement this signal (Locally Arbitrary): from a self-timed design to a built-in parallel delay. For various disciplines of prototype clocking, corresponding synchro-stratum implementations are suggested. The GALA methodology is illustrated on several design examples, such as a counter with constant response time, one-two-one track FiFo, arbitration-free counterflow processor architecture.

> *"Problems are divided into unsolvable and trivial ones."*
> *Mathematical folklore.*

1   Introduction

Synchronization is one of the most important problems for digital systems. Experts in hardware and software treat it and solve it in different ways at different levels of the system hierarchy.

The term *synchronization* assumes the coordination of events (signals, operations or processes) in time. The coordination of events reflects cause-and-effect

J. Cortadella et al. (Eds.): Concurrency and Hardware Design, LNCS 2549, pp. 61–107, 2002.

relationships between them and is usually determined by the partial order on the set of events extracted in the system. Note that this definition of synchronization is close to the concept of *logical time* whose flow is marked by events. At the same time, any system functions in continuous *physical time* which is represented by an independent variable and discretized by clock signals.

When people say some events occur synchronously, they usually mean that these events are the consequence of the same set of causes. Such a notion of synchrony is good for both logical and physical times. However, when we talk about a synchronous system, we usually imply that all events in the system can only occur on the ticks of an external clock, i.e. they are additionally synchronized by physical time marks. Such a notion of synchrony is only relevant for the level of system hardware.

The complexity of solving the external clocking problem can be explained, at least, by two reasons:

- The events in the external clock have no cause-and-effect relation to the events in the system. This may result in disrupting the general casual semantics of system behavior.
- The clock signal delivery system is a physical object with a certain precision of functioning. It can only function correctly if its precision corresponds to the required accuracy of synchronization.

Similarly, the term *asynchrony* is often treated differently by software and hardware experts. Programmers usually treat asynchrony as dependence of the number of steps necessary for obtaining the results from the initial data. Such a consideration is useful only for the estimation of program efficiency. Parallel programming implies that the algorithm steps can proceed concurrently. In this case, program specification uses casual-effect relations between the operations and their partial order relation. This is equivalent to incorporating logical time into the algorithm.

At the hardware level, the flow of logical time is usually measured by physical time units (cycles) generated by the common clock. Using *wait* operation and well-known synchro-primitives along with the common clock allows one to solve the problems of time behavior in a parallel system, although the processes within it can be locally asynchronous. We call such systems "systems with *synchronous concurrency.*"

When we give up using a common clock, we arrive at systems which are asynchronous in physical time. There are approaches to designing asynchronous hardware which eliminate the common clock from the event coordination process. However, all of them, including self-timing, produce solutions of high complexity and require hardware behavior to be re-specified and, hence, re-designed.

There are four ways of organizing time behavior in hardware:

FS — fully synchronous (synchronization from a common clock);

FA — fully asynchronous (e.g. self-timing);

LAGS — locally asynchronous, globally synchronous;

GALS — globally asynchronous, locally synchronous.

FS and LAGS require a clock signal delivery system, the shortcomings of which we have already discussed. FA systems have a number of significant advantages but they are very complicated and break the continuity of hardware development. GALS systems are most attractive as they combine the advantages of both synchronous and asynchronous approaches.

We suggest an idea of designing GALA systems (globally asynchronous, locally arbitrary) which are an extension of GALS systems. In such systems, two types of time coexist: physical time in which physical components of the system operate and logical time that represent the causal semantics. In physical time, asynchrony is treated as unpredictable variations in durations of physical transient processes. In logical time, asynchrony is treated as variations in the quantity of discrete steps in processes. Physical time can be transformed into logical time by incorporating a common clock or using self-timing. We will speak about *global* logical time, if the functioning of structural system blocks is coordinated in logical time. *Local* logical time flows inside a structural block.

As we demonstrated in [1–4], an asynchronous system can be decomposed into the synchronization subsystem (Synchro-Stratum) and synchronized subsystem (for example, Processor Stratum). This approach allows one to use synchronous prototypes when constructing an asynchronous system, providing continuity and evolution of hardware. The synchro-stratum acts as a distributed asynchronous clock globally synchronizing the system blocks. It can be built in accordance with the prototype clocking system.

The absence of an external clock requires that the synchro-stratum asynchronously interacts with the system blocks. This can be organized as a handshake, which needs signals from the blocks to report the completion of transient processes in them. This task can be solved in many ways, depending on the block type and structure, its size, possible variation of the transient process duration, etc. For example, the completion signal can be produced by a delay incorporated in parallel with the block, by self-timed design or by a start-stop local clock controlled by a synchro-signal counter. It is also possible to use synchro-strata of second and higher hierarchy levels.

Hereafter, we will ignore the internal structure of the system blocks. Only the signals of transient process initiation and completion are important. In this work, we develop the ways of transforming a prototype clock system to the specification of the synchro-stratum which globally synchronizes the system blocks. Another problem tackled here is that of building new, more efficient synchro-strata implementations.

2 Logical and Physical Time. A Didactic Example

When talking about *synchronization* or *synchronous/asynchronous* behavior, we inevitably have to discuss the basic concept of *time*. Not claiming to be in the rank of great researchers of time from Aristotle to Prigozhin, we still find it necessary to discuss some fairly general problems relevant to our tasks.

First of all, we should realize that, whenever we talk about synchronous or asynchronous devices, we actually mean the way of *synchronizing* the device's behavior. The problem is to organize the *temporal* behavior of the device or, in other words, to incorporate time into the model of the device. Obviously, we have to clearly define what we mean by the word "time".

Modern science says that time has diadic nature, just like substance. On the one hand, starting from ancient Greeks, time was treated as number (Plato & Aristotle) or as moment (Corpus Hermeticum). It was treated as a reflection of cause-and-effect relationship between events that determines their order. Aristotle is known to have said: "If nothing happens, no time." The Greek tradition was continued by Leibniz who treated time as relation. From this standpoint, time is defined as partial order of events determined by cause-and-effect relationship between them. Note that the McGraw-Hill Encyclopedia of Science & Technology defines synchronization as "the process of maintaining one operation in step of another."[1] Time here is considered discrete; hereafter we will call it logical or discrete time.

The concept of analog time, time as substance, is associated with the name of Isaac Newton who continued and developed the ancient Indo-European conceptualization of time as stretch. Time treated as a continual independent physical variable will be called hereafter physical time. Note that all available definitions of physical time are in some way associated with the procedure of time measurement which can be performed only with a certain degree of accuracy. The measuring procedure provides the link between physical and logical time. The basic measuring tool for this is a clock; it compares the temporal interval between two discrete events in the measured process with the number of also discrete events in the reference process. The correlation of two events is closely associated with the concept of *simultaneity* which can be treated only as a logical abstraction, attained also with a certain degree of accuracy.[2]

All the steps of design, from formulating the initial specification to physical development, are in some way concerned with organizing the temporal behavior of the device. We are thus entitled to interpret the design of a synchronization system as creation of the system time.

In spite of the fact that our devices are physical objects functioning in the real physical time, the experts and designers of different profile deal with different types of time and treat differently the system time, as well as the terms "synchronous" and "asynchronous" associated with it.

---

[1] 7th Ed., p.662.

[2] The uncertainty of the concept of simultaneity is the source of electronic arbitration. With some speculation, we can say that temporal discretization is determined by the uncertainty expression in the form of time $\tau = \hbar/\Delta E$, where τ is the average time of transition from one quantum state to another with the difference of energetic levels ΔE and $\hbar$ is Planck's constant. When $\Delta E = 1FJ \approx 600eV$ (characteristic energy for advanced micro-electronic device switching), $\tau \approx 10^{-3}ps$. Practically the same value ($\tau \approx 2 \cdot 10^{-3}ps$) is given by calculation of the average switching time of a quantum device when taking up one photon with $\lambda \approx 900nm$ (normal frequency for a fiber line). These values can be treated as approximate digits for a time quantum.

Algorithm and architecture experts deal with logical time. They treat time as a number of a step in a process with discrete states (the number of transitions from one discrete state to another). Asynchronism is treated as variations (for example, data-dependency) of the number of steps in the process (algorithm) from its initialization to obtaining the result. For example, non-restoring division is a synchronous process, while restoring division is an asynchronous one. Other examples are synchronous and asynchronous "pseudo-division" algorithms for calculating elementary functions using "digit-by-digit" methods.

Microelectronics and computer engineering experts deal with physical processes that flow in physical devices and, hence, with analog physical time. Asynchrony for them is associated with uncontrolled variations of time necessary to go from one discrete state to another. The factors crucial to such variations can either be permanent (like, for example, dispersion of technological parameters) or variable (like changes in the operation conditions: temperature, voltage, etc.), as well as data-dependent (for example, length of carry in adders).

Synchronization problems are centered around the interface between physical and logical time. The simplest and most conventional way of providing this interface in a synchronous system is by means of a system clock. The sequence of events in the clock (cycles, synchro-signals, etc.) determines the steps of logical time in the system. The physical time interval between two events must be long enough to mask all the possible variations of the transient process durations. This completely excludes physical time from the consideration and the device model contains only logical time. This is the major advantage of the synchronous approach with a common clock.

In spite of all its advantages, the synchronous approach has a number of shortcomings that become more and more obvious as technology increases performance and integration scale. Most crucial are the difficulties in providing the system of delivering the synchro-signals to the points of their consumption.

An alternative to the synchronous approach is a fully asynchronous model (self-timed, speed-independent, delay-insensitive). The system time is determined by partial order imposed on discrete events in the system. Time is introduced by specifying the cause-and-effect relationship between the events; the interface between physical and logical times is provided by certain mechanisms of detecting the completion of transient processes in the system components.

Putting aside the well-known positive and negative aspects of synchronous and asynchronous models, often cited in the literature, we will focus our attention on the main methodological difference between the two approaches.

In the synchronous approach, the mechanisms that provide the system time are completely separated from the system behavior model.

In the asynchronous approach, the mechanisms that provide the system time are incorporated into the system behavior model and should be designed together with creation of the initial behavioral specification.

Asynchronous design is considered difficult mainly due to the fact that the behavioral algorithms are usually formulated as synchronous. Translating a synchronous algorithm to an asynchronous one is a fairly complicated task requiring

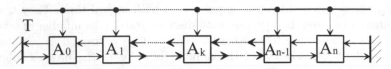

Fig. 1. Synchronous 1D automata array

a lot of ingenuity. A brilliant example of such an ingenuity is the delay-insensitive counter with constant response time suggested by Christian D.Nielsen [5].[3]

Before going further, let us consider an instructive example. Its didactic value, at least to the authors, is not only a chance to illustrate the relationship between logical time in synchronous and asynchronous models. We used this example in the report submitted to Asynch-94. This example was the main target for criticism in the review which declined the report. In order to avoid another fiasco, we will try to discuss this example more carefully.[4]

Starting from, probably, Hennie, homogeneous automata arrays (or cellular automata arrays) are considered as an excellent model object for studying the features of systems and algorithms. Among the studied models, wave propagation processes in such arrays are of special interest, both practical and theoretical.

Figure 1 shows a synchronous one-dimensional (1D) array of automata. All the automata are similar, being Moore automata whose outputs coincide with their internal states. Usually, for the considered model examples, the complexity of automata and their transition functions do not depend on the number of automata in the array. An automaton's state transition is determined by a function that depends on the previous state of the automaton and the states of its two neighbors:

$$S_k(t+1) = F[S_{k-1}(t), S_k(t), S_{k+1}(t)], \quad k = (1, n-1). \tag{1}$$

The transition functions for the automata that are located on each end of the array are also determined by an external signal or the signal of the array border.

For the sake of being definite, let us consider the automaton to be built using a *master-slave* register. When $T = 1$, its state is copied from the slave register (S) to the master register (M). When $T = 0$, a new state is formed in the slave register, as a function of the master register states [5], i.e.

$$S_k(t+1) = F[M_{k-1}(t), M_k(t), M_{k+1}(t)],$$
$$M_k(t+1) = S_k(t), \quad k = (1, n-1). \tag{2}$$

---

[3] Below we will demonstrate how this task is solved automatically in our proposed GALA methodology.

[4] Note however that the report declined at Asynch-94 was later accepted as a keynote address at the First International Conference on Massively Parallel Computing Systems [1] (May, 1994, Ischia, Italy).

[5] For master registers, the time steps are marked by $T = 1$, for slave registers by $T = 0$. Actually, the next state can be formed in every phase of T changing, doubling the array performance.

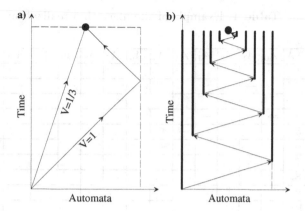

Fig. 2. Two ways of search for the middle of an array: by signals with different speeds of propagation (a); by shift of the reflecting boundary (b)

Let us now discuss the problem of finding the middle of the array in the shortest possible time. For simplicity, consider an array with an odd number of automata so that there is only one automaton in the middle. Passing to the general case will not be too difficult.

If the search process is initiated in one of the end automata, one of the signals that propagate through the array with the speed of 1 unit (one automaton per cycle) must at least pass through the entire array and get back to the middle. Hence, when there are $n = 2m + 1$ automata, the minimum time to find the middle is $t_{min} = 3m + 2$ that determines the algorithm (fig. 2,a):

After one of the end automata is initiated, two signals start to propagate through the array: one with speed 1 (one automaton per cycle) and the other with speed 1/3 (one automaton per three cycles). The first signal is reflected from the opposite end of the array and goes back with the same speed. It is easy to see that the reflected signal will meet the signal that goes with speed 1/3 exactly in the middle of the array.

An example of the algorithm realization is given in Table 1. The automaton has 7 states. An empty cell in the table corresponds to a passive state. Table 1 directly produces the rules of changing the automaton states, for example: $F(\Rightarrow$, $,\leftarrow) = \bullet$ or $F(,\Downarrow,) = \Rightarrow$, etc.

We will not discuss in detail the automaton transition function. It should be obvious that such an automaton can be built and its synchronous implementation is not concerned with any difficulties.

Now let us turn to the asynchronous model in its classical version. While in the synchronous model the automaton changes its state after the clock signal has switched, in the asynchronous model the automaton state changes after the state (states) of its neighbor (neighbors) does. The signal ($\rightarrow$) initiated by the end automaton propagates through the array with some speed. This speed is determined by the local physical parameters of the automata and, generally

Table 1. Example of the algorithm realization

T\A	A_0	A_1	A_2	A_3	A_4	A_5	A_6	A_7	A_8	A_9	A_{10}	A_{11}	A_{12}
1	→												
2	↓	→											
3	⇓		→										
4	⇒			→									
5		↓			→								
6		⇓				→							
7		⇒					→						
8			↓					→					
9			⇓						→				
10			⇒							→			
11				↓							→		
12				⇓								→	
13				⇒									→
14					↓								←
15					⇓							←	
16					⇒						←		
17						↓				←			
18						⇓			←				
19						⇒		←					
20							●						

speaking is different for different points (automata) of the array. In this situation, using an algorithm based on comparing the speeds of signal propagation makes no sense. A natural question arises: "Can any wave propagation algorithm be implemented in an asynchronous array? And, if yes, then how?"

First of all, note that we are interested in a general solution. This is why our example uses an algorithm based on comparing the speeds. Such algorithms are most difficult for asynchronous realization. The middle of the array can be found by a wave propagation algorithm that does not use the concept of signal propagation speed. The realization of such an algorithm is clear from fig. 2,b.

The signal initiated at one of the ends is propagated with maximum (physical) speed and after reaching the opposite end is reflected, setting the end automaton into a reflecting state. Then, as the signal bounces between the automata that are already in the reflecting states, the working area of the array gradually shrinks until it contains only one (middle) automaton. Such a method provides an asynchronous solution to the problem. However, one of the aims is not met by this solution, which achieving the shortest possible time of the search. In this algorithm, the time grows quadratically with the number of automata in the array.

We are sure that this problem does have an asynchronous solution with minimum time. Of course, some bright student will manage to find such a solution.

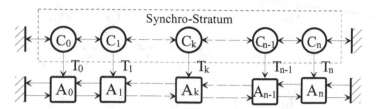

Fig. 3. Representing an automata array as a composition of Synchro-Stratum and Automata Stratum

But where can we find a bright student for every possible problem? The goal of this paper is to present a method of translating between synchronous and asynchronous implementations, and we want to start with illustrating this method by the example of searching the middle of an automata array.

Table 1 represents sequences of the array automata states unfolded in logical time. The leftmost column contains the numbers of the logical time steps. In the structure of fig. 1, we have the common time signal T for all of the array automata. Now let us designate the synchro-signal for automaton A_k as T_k.[6] Then the transition function should be written as

$$S_k(T_k + 1) = F[S_{k-1}(T_{k-1}), S_k(T_k), S_{k+1}(T_{k+1})], \quad k = (1, n - 1). \tag{3}$$

For the correct functioning of the algorithm, it is necessary and sufficient that during the change of A_k state the values of logical times T_{k-1}, T_k, and T_{k+1} are equal.[7] For the behavior of A_k, it does not matter what the values of T_j are at the inputs of the automata that are not adjacent to A_k. Hence, in order to mimic the synchronous behavior, the "hard-wired synchro-signal delivery system" (fig. 1) should be replaced by an active asynchronous environment that will coordinate the local synchro-signals (fig. 3). We will call such an environment "Synchro-Stratum".

Figure 4 shows a fragment of an unfolding of the signal graph for T_j where Y_j is an auxiliary variable that is needed for the signal graph to be correct [6]. The vertices of the graph designate rising and falling transitions of appropriate signals, arcs correspond to causal relations, and a vertex fires when all its input conditions are true.

As we have mentioned above, we consider a master-slave implementation of the automata. Hence, a change in T_j must initiate changes in the enabling signals for the master and slave registers. In the graph of fig. 4, let us refine the signals $\pm T_j$ and $\pm Y_j$ by the following sequences:

$$+T_j = -EnS_j \rightarrow +EnM_j,$$
$$-T_j = -EnM_j \rightarrow +EnS_j,$$
$$+Y_j = -a_j \rightarrow +b_j,$$

---

[6] In the synchronous model, $T_k = T$ for all k.
[7] Here T_j is the positive integer number (the number of logical time step).

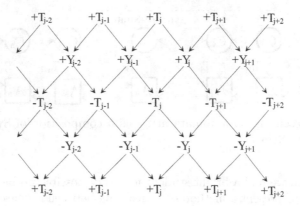

Fig. 4. A fragment of the signal graph unfolding around the local synchronization signal of the j-th automaton

$$-Y_j = -b_j \rightarrow +a_j$$

where $EnS_j = 1$ and $EnM_j = 1$ enable writing the slave and master registers, respectively, and a_j and b_j are auxiliary signals introduced for the implementability of the signal graph by a logic circuit [6]. From the refined graph, the implementation of a synchro-stratum can be derived as follows:

$$EnM_j = \overline{EnS_j + b_{j-1} \cdot b_j}; \quad EnS_j = \overline{EnM_j + a_{j-1} \cdot a_j};$$
$$a_j = \overline{b_j + EnM_j \cdot EnM_{j+1}}; \quad b_j = \overline{a_j + EnS_j \cdot EnS_{j+1}}. \tag{4}$$

The system of logical equations (4) defines an autonomous[8] asynchronous synchro-stratum. To get an asynchronous implementation of the automata array, we should provide a handshake interface between the synchro-stratum and the automata stratum. Let $AckM_j$ ($AckS_j$) be the completion signal for writing the master (slave) register of the j-th automaton[9]. Then substituting corresponding acknowledgment signals for their enable signals in (4) we derive:

$$EnM_j = \overline{AckS_j + b_{j-1} \cdot b_j}; \quad EnS_j = \overline{AckM_j + a_{j-1} \cdot a_j};$$
$$a_j = \overline{b_j + AckM_j \cdot AckM_{j+1}}; \quad b_j = \overline{a_j + AckS_j \cdot AckS_{j+1}}. \tag{5}$$

The respective circuit is shown in fig. 5.

The obtained synchro-stratum together with the asynchronous (handshaked) implementation of the automata provides the solution of our problem in the following sense. After the synchro-stratum cell which generates the local synchro-signal for the middle automaton in the array switches $3m + 2$ times (minimum time), this automaton goes to the marked state ($\bullet$).

In conclusion, let us make one important note. Decomposition as such does not provide any new possibilities. The composition of the automaton and local

---

[8] When the indexes change by modulo n.
[9] Here we are not interested how these signals are obtained.

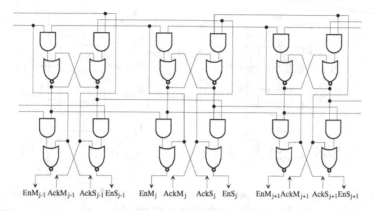

EnM$_{j-1}$ AckM$_{j-1}$ AckS$_{j-1}$ EnS$_{j-1}$ EnM$_j$ AckM$_j$ AckS$_j$ EnS$_j$ EnM$_{j+1}$AckM$_{j+1}$ AckS$_{j+1}$EnS$_{j+1}$

Fig. 5. Fragment of the synchro-stratum circuit for the problem

synchro-stratum cell can have considerably simpler implementation than the decomposed solution. However, the suggested way of decomposition allows us to formally pass from a synchronous specification to its asynchronous implementation. The reverse composition opens up possibilities for using formal methods of minimization.

3 Distributed Timing Specifications and Synchro-Stratum Implementations

3.1 Strategies of Clocking

The main idea of synchronization by means of signals coming from a clock is associated, in one way or another, with organizing the master-slave behavior of circuit components. As a model for synchronization strategy, we will consider cellular arrays in which cells are finite Moore automata built as two-register master-slave circuits (see fig. 6). At one value of the clock signal T, the automaton changes its current state by writing a new state to the master register (the new state is a function of the previous state and the states of the automaton's neighbors in the array). On the opposite value of T, the newly adopted current state does not change, it is copied to the slave register. This is a two-phase functioning with dual-polarity control.[10] Other synchronization methods can be reduced to the general scheme described above.

To synchronize arrays, various synchro-systems are used, depending on the ways of signaling between the cells and the logic basis of cell implementation. The simplest case is single-track 2-phase synchronization with dual-polarity control (fig. 6,a). Let $R_{1,i}$ ($R_{2,i}$) be the state of the first (second) register of the i-th automaton and let $S_i(t) = F_i[S_{i-1}(t-1), S_i(t-1), S_{i+1}(t-1)]$ be the automaton

---

[10] Block arrows labeled $R_{1,i}$ in fig. 6 are used as it will be shown later in other synchronization methods.

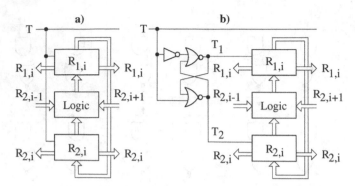

Fig. 6. Two-register automaton structure with 2-phase synchronization: with dual-polarity control (a); with unipolar control (b)

state at time t, which is determined by the transition function F_i. Then the synchro-behavior of the automaton can be represented as:

if $T = 1$, then $R_{1,i} := F_i(R_{2,i-1}, R_{2,i}, R_{2,i+1})$,

if $T = 0$, then $R_{2,i} := R_{1,i}$.

Note that a circuit for an automaton with two-phase synchro-signal control functions works in a stable way only when the variation in the delays of the wires of T is negligible, so that T changes its value at the inputs of both the registers at exactly the same time. To eliminate the influence of delays in wires, a 2-phase 2-track synchronization must be used with unipolar control over the registers using different signals and the discipline of synchro-signal change is $\ldots \rightarrow +T_1 \rightarrow -T_1 \rightarrow +T_2 \rightarrow -T_2 \rightarrow +T_1 \rightarrow \ldots$. In this case, the synchro-behavior of the automaton is defined as:

if $T_1 = 1$, then $R_{1,i} := F_i(R_{2,i-1}, R_{2,i}, R_{2,i+1})$,

if $T_2 = 1$, then $R_{2,i} := R_{1,i}$.

Synchro-sequence T can be transformed into a couple of synchro-sequences T_1 and T_2 with a special circuit realizing the signal graph $\ldots \rightarrow +T \rightarrow -T_1 \rightarrow +T_2 \rightarrow -T \rightarrow -T_2 \rightarrow +T_1 \rightarrow \ldots$, for example, as shown in fig. 6,b. Hereafter, without loss of generality, we will assume that only one synchronizing sequence T arrives to every cellular automaton. At the same time, the automata in the cellular array can be synchronized by different synchro-sequences.

Depending on the interconnection structure between automata and accepted protocols of interaction, various multi-track systems of synchro-signals can be used for array synchronization. The timing diagram of the most common 2-track 2-phase synchronization system is shown in fig. 7,a. There are also 3-track (fig. 7,b) and 4-track (fig. 7,c) schemes. The arrows show the directions and the moments of information exchange between the automata during synchronization.

An example of 2-track 2-phase synchronization for a one-dimensional cellular array is given in fig. 8,a. Signals T_1 synchronize the odd automata; T_2 synchronize

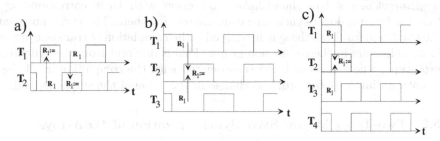

Fig. 7. Timing diagrams for multi-track synchro-signals: 2-track (a); 3-track (b); 4-track (c)

the even ones. With the accepted two-phase discipline of automata functioning, they have the following synchro-behavior:

   if $T = 1$, then $R_{1,i} := F_i(R_{1,i-1}, R_{2,i}, R_{1,i+1})$,

   if $T = 0$, then $R_{2,i} := R_{1,i}$

and the output signal of every automaton is the state of its register R_1. When this register changes its state, registers R_1 of the two adjacent automata keep their states. In such an array, information flows can be transferred in both directions and processes can be initiated via the free ports of both end automata without causing unwanted collisions. In other words, any wave-propagation algorithm can be implemented, as the clock signals T_1 and T_2 provide correct interaction between adjacent automata.

   An example of a one-dimensional cellular array implemented asynchronously with a separate synchro-stratum is given in fig. 8,b. The interconnection structure synchro-stratum is isomorphic to that of the automata array. Synchro-

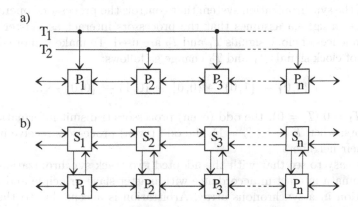

Fig. 8. One-dimensional processor array: synchronous two-track two-phase implementation (a); asynchronous implementation with a separate synchro-stratum (b)

stratum elements have handshake interaction with their corresponding automata, forming local synchronization signals for them. For every automaton, the condition for firing the synchro-signal is the completion of transient processes in its neighbors in the connection graph. This is different from the synchronous prototype, where this condition is associated with the completion in all the automata initiated by the previous change in the value of the sinchro-signal.

3.2   Two-Track Master-Slave Synchronization of 1D Arrays

Suppose that the processor array in fig. 8,a consists of Mealy automata and the array is built to perform a certain algorithm. The algorithm is defined as a sequence of steps, i.e. in logical time. At every instant t in this time, all the processors of the array should execute the step number t of the algorithm. When the algorithm is being executed, the internal state $S_i(t)$ of every i-th processor and the states of its right $X_i(t)$ and left $Y_i(t)$ outputs at time t are determined by its internal state at the previous moment, $t-1$, and by the information received at time t from its left and right neighbors. Thus, the behavior of the i-th processor is described by a system of automaton equations:

$$S_i(t) = F_i[X_{i-1}(t), S_i(t-1), Y_{i+1}(t)],$$
$$X_i(t) = f_{i_1}[X_{i-1}(t), S_i(t-1), Y_{i+1}(t)], \qquad (6)$$
$$Y_i(t) = f_{i_2}[X_{i-1}(t), S_i(t-1), Y_{i+1}(t)].$$

We are now interested neither in the structure nor in the contents of this equation. The only important thing is that, if some algorithm is put into the array, the equation system (6) is fully defined. Since we are interested only in time invariants of the behavior, then at the model level it is sufficient to consider the problem of synchronizing a cellular automata array.

Synchronous implementation of the processor array requires further refinement of the synchronization system that controls the processors' operations. The structure in fig. 8,a assumes that the processors interact as master and slave. Two sequences of clock signals T_1 and T_2 are used. To make it more definite, let the set of clock signals T_1 and T_2 change as follows:

$$\{0,0\} \rightarrow \{1,0\} \rightarrow \{0,0\} \rightarrow \{0,1\} \rightarrow \{0,0\} \rightarrow ... \qquad (7)$$

When $T_1 = 0$ ($T_2 = 0$), the odd (even) processors transmit information to their neighbors; when $T_1 = 1$ ($T_2 = 1$), the odd (even) processors receive information from their neighbors.

It is easy to see that with the adopted two-track synchronization discipline (7) automata interact in accordance with master-slave principle and there is no arbitration in a synchronous array. Arbitration is absent due to the following fact: at the moment when automaton P_i receives data from its neighbors and changes its state, the neighbors do not react to the change of its output signals and do not change their own output signals. In fact, this is the only condition to be satisfied when designing an asynchronous synchronizer (synchro-stratum).

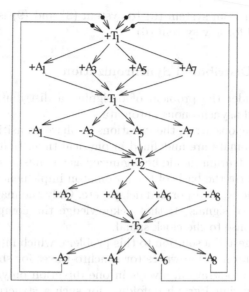

Fig. 9. Signal graph of parallel two-track two-phase synchronization of an 8-automata one-dimensional array

Note that in the synchronization structure mentioned above, every step k in logical time consists of two consecutive steps in physical time. This kind of structuring of logical time may lead to a change in system (6) that describes the behavior of every automaton.

Figure 9 presents the signal graph of parallel two-track two-phase synchronization in physical time for an 8-automaton one-dimensional array with the synchronization discipline (7). In this graph, signals $\pm T_1$ and $\pm T_2$ represent the transitions of clock signals T_1 and T_2; events $+A_i$ and $-A_i$ have the meaning of transition processes of limited duration in automata P_i. Synchronization at the graph nodes is provided by extra time (nodes $-T_1$, $+T_2$ wait transient process completion signals from all odd automata and $-T_2$, $+T_1$ from all even automata). The graph shows that, at step k of the so structured logical time, the behavior of the even automata is described by an equation system that is similar to (6):

$$S_i(k) = F_i[X_{i-1}(k), S_i(k-1), Y_{i+1}(k)],$$
$$X_i(k) = f_{i_1}[X_{i-1}(k), S_i(k-1), Y_{i+1}(k)], \qquad (8)$$
$$Y_i(k) = f_{i_2}[X_{i-1}(k), S_i(k-1), Y_{i+1}(k)].$$

For the odd automata, the equations look as follows:

$$S_i(k) = F_i[X_{i-1}(k-1), S_i(k-1), Y_{i+1}(k-1)],$$
$$X_i(k) = f_{i_1}[X_{i-1}(k-1), S_i(k-1), Y_{i+1}(k-1)], \qquad (9)$$
$$Y_i(k) = f_{i_2}[X_{i-1}(k-1), S_i(k-1), Y_{i+1}(k-1)].$$

The transition from system (6) to system (8) and (9) is purely formal and can be performed for any system (6).

3.3   Globally Distributed Synchronization

Let us now consider the problem of designing a distributed synchronizer for arrays of matched asynchronous automata.

In an asynchronous array, the durations of phase transitions (transition processes) in the automata are undefined in physical time. Hence, their interaction with the synchro-stratum should be organized as a handshake. It does not matter what principles form the basis of the automaton implementation — self-timing, start-stop local clock, incorporated delays, etc. Only the matching is important, i.e. the presence of signals A_i that acknowledge the completion of transition processes in response to the clock signal.

In [1], we suggested a solution to this problem, which introduced a system of logical time synchronization waves (or synchro-waves for short) that propagate through the synchro-stratum, always in one direction only. Figure 10 presents a fragment of the signal graph unfolding for such a structure (see fig. 8,b). In this graph, $\pm T_{ij}(k)$ denotes an event that consists in the k-th transition of the

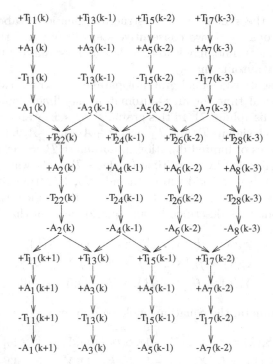

Fig. 10. A fragment of the unfolding of the signal graph describing wave logical synchronization of a one-dimensional array

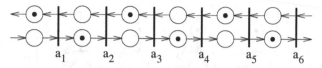

Fig. 11. Labeled Petri net describing pipeline interaction of the automata in a one-dimensional array

clock signal T_i, $i \in \{1,2\}$ (logical time step k) that comes to the j-th automaton of the array. The equation system (6) becomes as follows:

$$S_i(k) = F_i[X_{i-1}(k), S_i(k-1), Y_{i+1}(k-1)],$$
$$X_i(k) = f_{i_1}[X_{i-1}(k), S_i(k-1), Y_{i+1}(k-1)], \qquad (10)$$
$$Y_i(k) = f_{i_2}[X_{i-1}(k), S_i(k-1), Y_{i+1}(k-1)].$$

Incidentally, it is easy to see from the graph in fig. 10 that the same logical time in the array exists in different automata at different physical times, and at the same physical time there are different logical times.

Figure 10 depicts only general relationship between the signals; it is an initial specification for synchro-stratum design. The implementation requires extra variables and extra design. One of the possible solutions [1] is as follows.

Let a_j be an event that corresponds to a full cycle of the j-th automaton, i.e. $a_j = +T_{ij} \rightarrow +A_j \rightarrow -T_{ij} \rightarrow -A_j$. Then, proceeding from the graph in fig. 10, the necessary event coordination is described by a labeled Petri net (see fig. 11). It is easy to see that this is a specification of a simple pipeline. A direct translation of the specification to the implementation using simple distributor cells [7-9] provides a sufficiently simple synchro-stratum circuit shown in fig. 12. This translation is possible because, unlike the situation in a C-element pipeline, in a distributor cell pipeline the output signal of every j-th cell makes the full cycle on a_j and after that the next, $(j+1)$-th cell begins to change its output signal. However, this solution has a drawback, low speed, since the pipeline of fig. 12 attains its maximum speed when filled at $1/3$ and adding buffer distributor cells to the synchro-stratum to increase the speed is fraught with incorrect interaction of the automata.

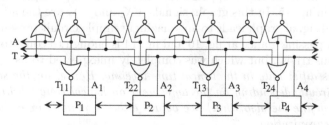

Fig. 12. Synchro-stratum on distributor cells

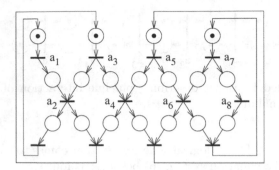

Fig. 13. Another variant of the specification of one-dimensional array automata interaction

The signal graph unfolding shown in fig. 10 allows one to derive a Petri net of another kind, which is presented in fig. 13. From this net, again with the help of direct translation [7,8], a synchro-stratum can be built which uses three distributor cells per two automata (correct operation of a circuit based on distributors requires that every cycle has no less than three cells)[11].

The described solutions are based on the standard pipeline methodology – organizing a pipelined distribution of logical time synchro-waves. This methodology prevails at the architecture level in modern self-timed and asynchronous system design. It was this stereotype of thinking that prompted us to look in this direction and resulted in the solution presented in [1]. Let us now try to overcome it and look at the problem of array synchronization without referring to any pipeline structures.

Figure 14 shows a fragment of a signal graph unfolding that defines parallel, rather than wave-based, synchronization. Unlike fig. 10, all the parallel clock signals (clock signals of the same unfolding tier) correspond to the same, rather than consecutive, moments in logical time. Note that for a sufficiently large array (i.e. sufficiently wide signal graph) different logical time can exist at the same moment of physical time. Note also that in the case of parallel synchronization the algorithm is represented by equations (8) and (9).

To synthesize a circuit of the synchro-stratum, one should derive a correct signal graph adding extra variables that resolve the state coding conflicts in the initial specification. It appears that there is a surprisingly simple solution presented in fig. 15. In this graph, signals $\pm X_i$ and $\pm Y_i$ are the additional ones. The refined signal graph leads to an amazingly simple circuit presented in fig. 16.

Even a passing glance at fig. 10 and fig. 14 is enough to come to a conclusion which seems trivial, but which was completely unexpected to us:
The graphs differ only in the logical time labeling. Hence, for the same synchrostratum circuit, depending on the agreement on logical time labeling (i.e. which equations define the algorithm), we obtain either a parallel or a wave system of global synchronization.

---

[11] The circuit from two distributor cells connected in cycle has a deadlock [8].

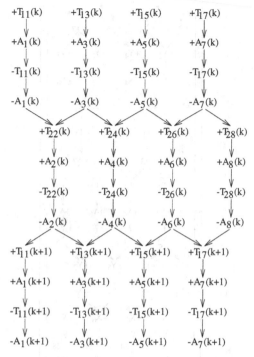

Fig. 14. Signal graph unfolding fragment describing parallel synchronization of a 1D array

Now let us consider a synchro-stratum for a system of automata placed at the vertices of an arbitrary graph, the arcs of which correspond to the connections between the automata. With the accepted synchronization discipline, i.e. two synchronization systems T_{1j} and T_{2j}, the connection graph should be a König graph (i.e. bipartite) [10].

The reduction of an arbitrary interconnection graph to a König graph is trivial; for example, it can be done by inserting buffer registers into all interconnections. Note that this should not affect the overall synchronization strategy since, as mentioned above, the synchronization strategy itself is invariant to the semantics of the synchronized automaton behavior. The insertion of buffer registers may be useful irrespective of the type of graph interconnection, especially if the cycle of the processor operation is significantly longer than the write cycle of the buffer registers. In such a case signals $T_{1j} = 1$ initiate the activity of the processors and signals $T_{2j} = 1$ initiate the write cycle of the buffer registers. A more sophisticated internal organization of the processors can be used to achieve greater concurrency. However, these problems are to do with the strategy of forming the acknowledgment signals and the methods of internal processor synchronization, and so are beyond the scope of this paper. We would like to repeat that the approach we have chosen, i.e. decomposing a system into the

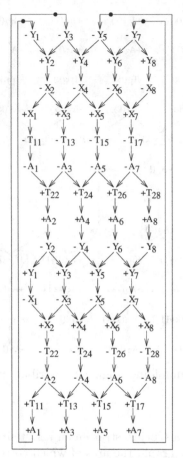

Fig. 15. Correct signal graph for parallel synchronization of a 1D array

processor and synchronization strata, allows us to separate out the problem of global synchronization and that of processor behavior.

Let us return to fig. 16. What local properties of the circuit guarantee the correctness of the synchro-stratum behavior?

Firstly, in the layer of gates, the outputs of which are signals T_{1j} and T_{2j}, the connections between neighboring gates (through automata A_j) cause the transition of the output of a gate from state 0 to state 1 iff the outputs of all the neighbor gates are equal to 0.

Secondly, the transition of a gate with output T_{ij} from state 0 to state 1 should be deterministic. Therefore, memory is needed to hold information about the previous state; this is performed by two layers of gates with outputs X_j and Y_j. For these outputs to appear no sooner than the neighbor lateral gates have switched to 0, gates X_j and Y_j are connected similarly to those between gates T_{ij}.

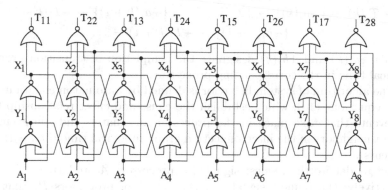

Fig. 16. Synchro-stratum for parallel synchronization of an 8-automata one-dimensional array

Similar requirements on local interaction, augmented with the interaction with all the neighbors in the graph, allow one to build a cell of the synchro-stratum for an arbitrary König graph (fig. 17). Depending on the degree of graph vertices, the required number of inputs per gate may exceed the gate fanin bounds. Of course, in this case the cell circuit will have to change somewhat, but that can be done by standard methods of self-timed design, for example, using intermediate C-elements.

3.4   More Precise Definition of Global Synchronization

Until now, we have assumed that the concept of global synchronization is intuitive. Now we shall try to define it more clearly. As an initial specification, we have a synchronous implementation with a two-track two-phase master-slave synchronization system which consists of two clock signal sequences T_1 and T_2 with a discipline defined by (7). Such a synchronization system breaks down the set of the processors into two subsets: processors $\{A_i\}$ clocked by T_1 and $\{B_i\}$ clocked by T_2. For a synchronous implementation, the unfolding of a signal graph similar to the one displayed in fig. 9 is as follows:

$$+T_1(k) \to \{+a_i(k)\} \to -T_1(k) \to \{-a_i(k)\} \to +T_2(k) \to \{+b_j(k)\} \to$$

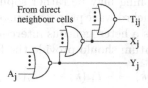

Fig. 17. A cell to built a synchro-stratum for an arbitrary König interconnection graph

$$-T_2(k) \rightarrow \{-b_j(k)\} \rightarrow +T_1(k+1) \rightarrow \{+a_i(k+1)\} \rightarrow -T_1(k+1) \rightarrow$$
$$\{-a_i(k+1)\} \rightarrow +T_2(k+1) \rightarrow \dots . \tag{11}$$

Signals $\pm a_i(k)$ and $\pm b_j(k)$ designate the completion of transition processes in physical time in the corresponding processors.

The algorithm of system behavior is defined by automaton equations (8), (9) or by equations (10), which establish the cause-and-effect relationship between the events that take place in the processor automaton and the events in its nearest neighbors in the interconnection graph in logical time (i.e., partial order of events).

Let us denote the request signals for processors A_i and B_j as T_{1i} and T_{2j}, respectively; the request signals for the subset of processors B_j that are the nearest neighbors of processor A_i in the interconnection graph as $\{T_{2j}[A_i]\}$; the request signals for the subset of processors A_i that are the nearest neighbors of processor B_j as $\{T_{1i}[B_j]\}$. Also, let a_i and b_j be the acknowledgment signals of processors A_i and B_j respectively. We say that the signal graph of synchro-stratum behavior specifies the global parallel synchronization of an asynchronous system that corresponds to the synchronous prototype if the following two conditions are satisfied: *(i) the signal graph of the synchronous prototype is homomorphic to the signal graph of the synchro-stratum with respect to the mapping* $\{\pm T_{lj}(k)\} \rightarrow \pm T_l(k), l \in \{1,2\}$, *and (ii) the signal graph of the synchro-stratum conforms to the relation of precedence between the events in every processor and its closest neighbors as defined by automata systems (8) and (9):*

$$+T_{1i}(k) \rightarrow +a_i(k) \rightarrow -T_{1i}(k) \rightarrow -a_i(k) \rightarrow \{+T_{2j}[A_i](k)\},$$
$$+T_{2j}(k) \rightarrow +b_j(k) \rightarrow -T_{2j}(k) \rightarrow -b_j(k) \rightarrow \{+T_{1i}[B_j](k+1)\}. \tag{12}$$

For the wave synchronization defined by system (10), the direction of synchro-wave propagation should be given for every point in the synchro-stratum. To do this, for every processor (A_i and B_j), the set of its nearest neighbors in the interconnection graph should be broken down into two subsets – the sources of the synchro-wave front ($Bs_j(A_i)$ and $As_i(B_j)$) and its receivers ($Br_j(A_i)$ and $Ar_i(B_j)$). Besides, some vertex in the synchro-stratum should be appointed as a rhythm driver. All the nearest neighbors of this vertex in the interconnection graph are receivers of the synchro-wave front[12]. Such a partitioning brings us to a four-color graph. Partitioning can be performed in various ways depending on which rhythm driver point has been chosen. In homogeneous arrays, it can be done rather easily, whereas an arbitrary interconnection graph requires collision detection and the partitioning may be rather sophisticated. Figure 18 presents examples of organizing synchro-wave propagation, one is a two-dimensional array (fig. 18,a) and the other is a heterogeneous interconnection graph (fig. 18,b). In any case, the synchro-stratum should provide the following order of the events:

$$+T_{1i}(k) \rightarrow +a_i(k) \rightarrow -T_{1i}(k) \rightarrow -a_i(k) \rightarrow \{+T_{2j}[Ar_i](k)\},$$
$$+T_{2j}(k) \rightarrow +b_j(k) \rightarrow -T_{2j}(k) \rightarrow -b_j(k) \rightarrow \{+T_{1i}[Br_j](k+1)\}. \tag{13}$$

---

[12] Any cycle in the graph can be used as a source of synchro-waves.

a)

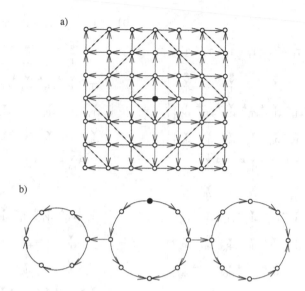

b)

Fig. 18. Examples of organizing the propagation of synchro-waves: a) in a two-dimensional array, b) in a heterogeneous graph

and for the rhythm driver:

$$+ T_{1i}(k) \rightarrow +a_i(k) \rightarrow -T_{1i}(k) \rightarrow -a_i(k) \rightarrow +T_{1i}(k+1).$$

The choice between wave and parallel synchronization strongly depends on the problem being solved, although parallel synchronization is generally preferred.

3.5 Synchro-Stratum Specifications and Implementations

For the case of 2-track 2-phase synchronization of a one-dimensional array (fig. 8,a), we managed to find a sufficiently simple synchro-stratum implementation. Its behavior is specified in fig. 19,a. The line above the graph indicates the correspondence of local synchro-stratum signals to prototype synchronization signals T_1 and T_2. In the graph itself, signals $\pm T_j$ stand for the changes of the output synchro-stratum signal which initiates the functioning of j-th automaton. Signals $\pm P_j$ stand for the changes of j-th automaton acknowledgment signal; signals $\pm h_j$ correspond to the changes of local intermediate variable h_j of the synchro-stratum. Deriving a synchro-stratum module from this signal graph gives the following gate equations:

$$T_j = \overline{T_{j-1} + h_j + T_{j+1}}, \quad h_j = \overline{h_{j-1} + P_j(T_j + T_{j-1}T_{j+1}) + h_{j+1}}. \quad (14)$$

One can trace from the graph of fig. 19,a that the synchro-stratum adds a delay of $D_{ss} = 6\tau_{gate}$ (τ_{gate} is the delay of one gate) to the automata delay.

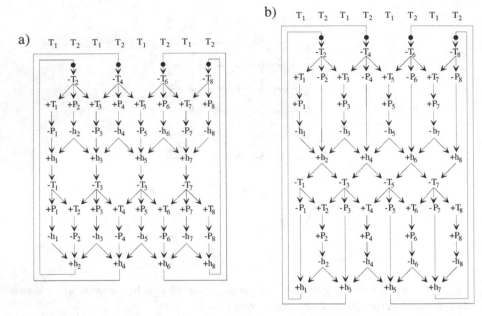

Fig. 19. Signal graphs for 2-track 2-phase synchronization of the array from 8 automata: first version (a), second version (b)

The CMOS implementation has 18 transistors; each module is connected by four wires with adjacent modules.

The size and quality of a synchro-stratum strongly depends on the way of introducing internal variables. In fig. 19,b, the second version of the signal graph is shown with the same number of internal variables. From this graph it is easy to derive the equations for synchro-stratum module gates:

$$T_j = \overline{T_{j-1} + h_{j-1}h_{j+1} + T_{j+1}}, \quad h_j = \overline{h_{j-1} + P_j + h_{j+1}}. \tag{15}$$

In CMOS implementation, these gates require 4 transistors less than the gates (14). Both graphs of fig. 19 is allow concurrency between even and odd automata in their opposite phases of operation that considerably increases the performance of the processor stratum.

Figure 20 shows a fragment of the signal graph unfolding that describes the synchro-stratum built for the case of 4-track 2-phase synchronization in a one-dimensional array. This signal graph specifies the behavior of a well-known circuit which is a one-dimensional pipeline [8]. The line above the graph points to a correspondence between synchro-stratum output signals T_j that activate the automata and the prototype synchro-signals T_1–T_4. Signals $\pm T_j(k)$ mean the changes of T_j at the moments k of logical time. The $\oplus$ symbol marks the connections into which the automata A_j are inserted with their handshake signals. The bold arrows coming to vertices $+T_j(k)$ determine the state change condition for the j-th automaton (the state of register R_1); the dotted arrows to vertices

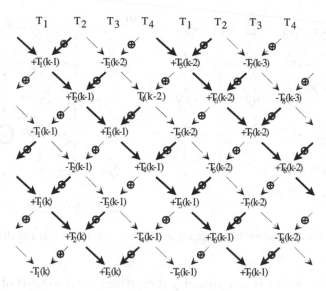

Fig. 20. Signal graphs unfolding for 4-track synchronization

$-T_j(k)$ determine the condition for this state to be held in the j-th automaton (by changing the state of register R_2). It is easy to see that the synchro-stratum is implemented by simple C-elements: $T_j = T_{j-1}\overline{P}_{j+1} + T_j(T_{j-1} + \overline{P}_{j+1})$ where $\overline{P}_{j+1}$ is the acknowledgment signal of the $(j+1)$-th automaton.

The structure of a one-dimensional array with such a synchro-stratum is shown in fig. 21. In this circuit, the total extra delay added by the synchro-stratum is $D_{ss} = 4\tau_c = 8\tau_{gate}$ where τ_c is a C-element delay. The complexity of a synchro-stratum module is determined by the size of the C-element implementation (8–12 transistor for CMOS); the number of wires connecting it with other modules is 2.

The last synchro-stratum circuit differs from the others described here and in [1–4] by its interaction asymmetry and the way how automata are inserted

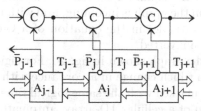

Fig. 21. One-dimensional asynchronous array for the synchronous prototype with 4-track 2-phase synchronization

a)   b)

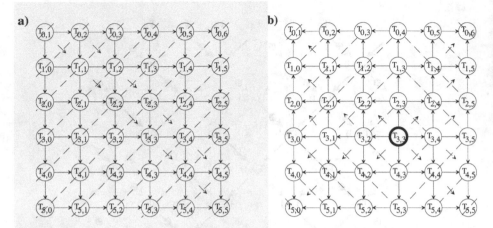

Fig. 22. 2D-arrays: with line-front synchro-wave (a); with rhythm driver (b)

into it.[13] The interaction asymmetry determines the directions of the propagation of synchronization signals and the synchro-stratum is a pipeline, whereas the synchro-strata discussed earlier are oscillating structures. This difference becomes noticeable if the inter-automata connection graph degree is more than 2.

Figure 22 demonstrates two possible structures of synchro-wave propagation in a 2D-array: for synchro-waves with a line-front (fig. 22,a) and for those propagating from a single-point rhythm driver (fig. 22,b).

From the graph of fig. 22,a, directly follows the automaton equation for the array element forming the signal T_{ij}:

$$T_{i,j} = T_{i-1,j}T_{i,j-1}\overline{T}_{i+1,j}\overline{T}_{i,j+1} + T_{i,j}(T_{i-1,j} + T_{i,j-1} + \overline{T}_{i+1,j} + \overline{T}_{i,j+1}).$$

This is an equation of a four-input C-element. If we replace $\overline{T}_{i+1,j}$ and $\overline{T}_{i,j+1}$ respectively by $\overline{P}_{i+1,j}$ and $\overline{P}_{i,j+1}$, which is equivalent to inserting $A_{i+1,j}$ and $A_{i,j+1}$ into the synchro-stratum circuit by their handshake signals, we will obtain the equation of a synchro-stratum module.

For the single-point rhythm driver wave-propagation structure (fig. 22,b), it is also easy to build a synchro-stratum using 4-input C-elements. When deriving C-element equations which determine the inter-element connections, one should use the following rule: the equation contains a variable without inversion if the corresponding arrow in the graph is incoming, and with inversion if it is outgoing. For example, all the variables in the equation of a C-element which acts as a rhythm driver must be inverted.

Let us return to the graph shown in fig. 20. For signals $\pm T_j(k)$, logical time moments k are shown which change in accordance with the synchro-wave order. Each synchro-wave is marked with the same logical time moment. In a usual synchronous specification of a cellular 1D-array, automaton equations for cells are in the form $S_j(k+1) = F_j[S_{j-1}(k), S_j(k), S_{j+1}(k)]$ independent of the way how

---

[13] A_j is inserted into wire gap T_j after the fork; nevertheless, the circuit stays delay-insensitive to wire delays.

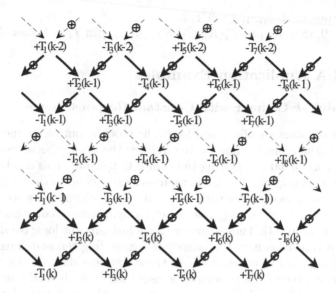

Fig. 23. Signal graph unfolding for 4-track parallel synchronization

synchronization is done. The introduction of a synchro-signal system requires concretizing the procedures of state change and inter-automata data exchange. In the signal graph we are discussing, signal $+T_j(k)$ initiates forming a new state $S_j(k)$ in the master register while the slave register keeps the state of the previous time moment $S_j(k-1)$. At event $-T_j(k)$ the new state is written to the slave register and the state $S_j(k)$ is allowed to be read from the master register. Hence, the initial synchronous specification can be correctly reproduced in asynchronous logical time.

In section 3.3 we demonstrated how to transform wave synchronization into parallel synchronization by a simple change of the initial marking of logical time moments in their signal graphs. However, this requires changing the form of cellular automata equations. A fragment of the synchro-stratum signal graph unfolding for a synchronous prototype defined as a 1D-array with 4-track 2-phase parallel synchronization is given in fig. 23.

The nodes of this graph in which logical time moments change cause state transitions in the automata (state change of the registers R_1). Thus the graph defines the following rules of cellular automata state transition and data exchange:

- for automata $A_{j=4i+1}$, $i = 0, 1, 2, 3, \ldots$
  if $T_j = 0$, then $R_{1,j} := F_j(R_{2,j-1}, R_{2,j}, R_{2,j+1})$; if $T_j = 1$, then $R_{2,j} := R_{1,j}$;
- for automata $A_{j=4i+2}$, $i = 0, 1, 2, 3, \ldots$
  if $T_j = 1$, then $R_{1,j} := F_j(R_{2,j-1}, R_{2,j}, R_{2,j+1})$; if $T_j = 0$, then $R_{2,j} := R_{1,j}$;
- for automata $A_{j=4i+3}$, $i = 0, 1, 2, 3, \ldots$
  if $T_j = 1$, then $R_{1,j} := F_j(R_{2,j-1}, R_{2,j}, R_{2,j+1})$; if $T_j = 0$, then $R_{2,j} := R_{1,j}$;

– for automata $A_{j=4i+4}$, $i = 0, 1, 2, 3, ...$
   if $T_j = 0$, then $R_{1,j} := F_j(R_{2,j-1}, R_{2,j}, R_{2,j+1})$; if $T_j = 1$, then $R_{2,j} := R_{1,j}$;

4   GALA Application Examples

4.1   Modulo-k Counter with Constant Response Time

Modular-k counters are often used for cyclic process control. To increase control efficiency, in such counters one has to minimize the latency between changing the input counting signal and getting the completion signal. This can be done using carry-look-ahead circuits which add their own extra delay to the counting cycle or using asynchronous counters with constant response time [5], whose complexity is pretty high. Several years ago, we suggested synchronous counters with delayed carry propagation [11]. These counters have insignificant logic overhead and for every input transition have the latency not exceeding the switching time of one simple flip-flop. Let us consider one of these counters shown in fig. 24.

The zeroth bit of the counter is a usual toggle with dual-polarity control. The remaining bits are built as master-slave toggles with unipolar control: the odd digits fire when $T = 1$; even digits have dual implementation and fire when $T = 0$. The sequence of master flip-flops states differs from the sequence of binary numbers.

Every counter digit can be in one of the four states for which we will introduce the following designations: 0,1 – the states of master and slave latches are different, $0^*, 1^*$ – the states of master and slave latches are the same. For example, the sequence of a 5-bit counter states is shown in fig. 25.

When the clock signal T changes its value from 0 to 1, the zeroth bit turns into state $\{0,1\}$; when T switches from 1 to 0, it turns into states $\{0^*, 1^*\}$. Every next bit, with the corresponding value of T, turns into states $\{0^*, 1^*\}$ if the preceding bit is in state 0^* or 1 and into states $\{0,1\}$ if the preceding bit is in state 1^* or 0. In time moments $T = 0$, the counter produces the following sequence of numbers: 10, 15, 12, 13, 6, 3, 0, 1, 2, 7, 4, 5, 14, 11, 8, 9, 26, 31, 28, 29, ... However, note that the counting cycle in an n-bit counter is equal to 2^n.

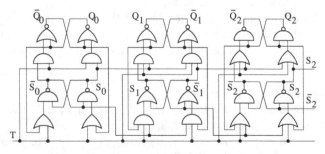

Fig. 24. Three-stage counter circuit

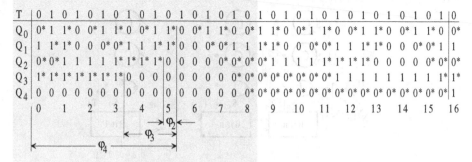

Fig. 25. State sequence of 5-bit counter

It is easy to see that, as compared to a usual binary counter, the value sequences of the suggested counter bits have constant phase shifts starting from Q_2. If we measure the phase shifts by the number of T changes, the phase shift of the j-th bit depends on the phase shift of the preceding bit, as $\varphi_j = \varphi_{j-1} + 2^{j-1} - 1$ for $j \geq 2$. For the initial condition $\varphi_1 = 0$, the solution of this equation is $\varphi_j = 2^j - j - 1$. According to this solution, the sequence of phase shifts, starting from the zero digit, is: 0, 0, 1, 4, 11, 26, 57, ... A simple expression for a phase shift allows one to transform binary numbers into the states of counter bits. This can be done, for example, using the following procedure.

In the state sequence given above, the odd combinations are marked with ordinal numbers which are decimal equivalents of binary numbers. For every j-th bit, number R_j is calculated using the formula:

$$R_j = \left(\left\lceil \frac{(2N+1) - \varphi_{n-1} + \varphi_j}{2^j} \right\rceil - 1 \right)_{\mathrm{mod}\ 4}, \quad j = 0, 1, 2, ..., n-1, \quad (16)$$

where n is the number of bits in the counter,
N is the decimal equivalent of the binary number, $0 \leq N \leq 2^n - 1$,
$\lceil a \rceil$ means that a is rounded off to the nearest larger integer,
$(a)_{\mathrm{mod}\ 4}$ is the remainder of dividing a by 4.
R_j can take the values from the set $\{0,1,2,3,-1,-2,-3\}$. The state Q_j of the j-th digit is defined in accordance with the following rules: if $R_j = 0$, then $Q_j = 0$; if $R_j = 1, -3$, then $Q_j = 0^*$; if $R_j = 2, -2$, then $Q_j = 1$; if $R_j = 3, -1$, then $Q_j = 1^*$.

Note that the counter state that corresponds to the zero binary combination changes in accordance with the counter length and can be easily calculated using the procedure described above. This state is the overflow signal for modulo-2^n counting. For example, in a 5-bit counter the zero value of the binary code corresponds to the state $0\ 1^*\ 0^*\ 1\ 0^*$.

To organize counting with modulo $K \leq 2^n$, one can use the following technique: every time the overflow signal arrives, at the first counting signal of the next cycle, we can assign the initial state of the counter equal to $2^n - K + 1$.

Sometimes, it is more convenient to form the overflow signal not by the counter internal state but using an extra $(n+1)$-th bit. Doing so, the zero state

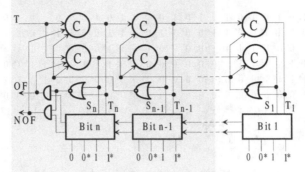

Fig. 26. Asynchronous structure of modulo-K counter with constant response time

would certainly change. The overflow signal would be produced when the most significant bit becomes equal to 1. After this, the first counting signal should reset this bit back to 0.

A serious shortcoming of such a counter is its high capacitive load on the counting signal, as the counter is built using 1-track synchronization. It is easy to build a similar counter with 4-track 2-phase synchronization if to assume that every counting signal is in phase with synchro-signal T_1. Since such a counter is a 1D-array, we can obtain its asynchronous implementation with a synchro-stratum built on two-input C-elements (see fig. 20), using the way described above.

The structure of an asynchronous modulo-K counter with constant response time for the case of an odd number of bits is given in fig. 26. If the number of bits is even, the two AND gates with outputs NOF and OF should be replaced by OR gates. The synchro-stratum in this structure consists of two C-element rows that form a pipeline register. The output signals T_j of the first row control the counter bits functioning in the counting mode while the output signals S_j of the second row control setting the initial state.

Every counter bit has four set inputs that correspond to states 0, 0*, 1 and 1*. One of these inputs should be in the active state, others — in passive. The set input can only assume its active value when S_j is in the active state.

The acknowledgment signals P_j are produced with NOR-gates. This is admissible due to the following reason. When the synchro-stratum is functioning, the duration of the cycle of signal T_j (S_j) is not less than $10t_{gate}$, i.e. T_j (S_j) keeps its value for, at least, $5t_{gate}$. This time must be enough for one simple flip-flop in the j-th bit of the counter to fire since its switching time is not more than $2t_{gate}$. Thus, 2.5-fold time margin is provided. When necessary, the delays of the NOR-gates can be increased. For example, this is necessary when producing signals NOF (no overflow) and OF (overflow).

When the counting modulo is K, to $2K$ changes of signal T the counter replies by $2(K-1)$ changes of NOF and 2 changes of OF.

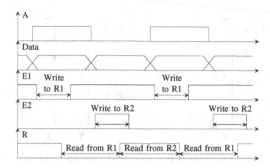

Fig. 27. The time diagram

The number of synchro-stratum C-elements in the asynchronous counter implementation can be reduced almost twice using the following approach. Let the synchro-stratum consist of $\lceil n/2 \rceil$ elements and let the output signals T_j and S_j synchronize the array automata. Every automaton A_j, except for the last one, contains two (j-th and $(n - j - 1)$-th) bits of the counter. The last automaton $A_{\lceil n/2 \rceil}$ contains two bits if n is even and one bit if it is odd. We could prove that such a "curved" counter also functions correctly but the proof is beyond this discussion.

4.2 One-Two-One Track Asynchronous FIFO

Here we apply our GALA approach to constructing the logical circuit of a very fast asynchronous FIFO buffer. This FIFO is a register pipeline with control logic providing maximum throughput. It can be used, for example, in the Line Interface Module (LIMO) that implements the direct ATM-over-fiber transport mechanism [12]. The initial specification for the FIFO design is taken from this work.

Data Rate and Input/Output Protocol. The input data arrive in 8-byte (64 bit) words with a frequency of 300MHz, accompanied by signal A. This signal acts as an external synchro-signal, so data change at its every edge (fig. 27). The mode of data change is NRTZ (non-return to zero); the frequency of A change is 150 MHz (the period is 6.6 ns).

When the receiving device is a usual FIFO, we should form two changes of Enable signal at every edge of A[14] within 3.3 ns, accept the coming word into the input register and rewrite it into the next FIFO register[15], making the input register ready for the next word. Below, we will discuss the possibility of attaining the maximum performance. When the word is 64 bits wide, the main delay in writing is associated with charging the capacitances and propagating

---

[14] This is usually done by the inverse of an asynchronous toggle element.
[15] Two more changes of Enable signal.

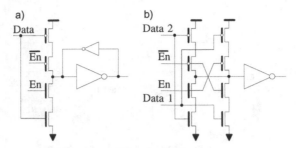

Fig. 28. The latch (a) and the multiplexor (b)

the signal via the Enable wire. The number of changes of Enable in the receiving cycle can be reduced using a different FIFO architecture.

Let us introduce two receiving registers $R1$ and $R2$. On the positive edge of A, the data is written into $R1$, on its negative edge - into $R2$. Writing into $R1$ (by Enable signal $E1$) occurs at the same time with reading from $R2$; the same is true for writing into $R2$ (by Enable signal $E2$) and reading from $R1$ (fig. 27). Thereby we introduce the structure of a One-Two-One Track FIFO. The output head should provide for alternate reading of data from the tracks, forming the Request signal R.

Basic Circuits. FIFO behavior largely depends on the type of register latches being used and on the way of forming the Enable signal. In recent years, latches with weak transistors became popular (e.g. Svensson's latch [12,13]. This is concerned with the possibility of reducing the capacity load on Enable signal (two transistors) and single wire data inputs. On several grounds that will be clear below, we will use the latch given in fig. 28,a. For gathering data from two tracks into one we also need a multiplexer, which can be built as shown in fig. 28,b.

Although these circuits require both Enable signal and its inversion, this can be efficiently used when organizing a driver for the Enable signal. The switching time of Enable signal is determined by two factors. First, by the behavior of the Enable wire as a line with distributed RC-parameters. The delay of signal propagation through the line is $\tau_{line} = RCl^2/2$ where R and C are distributed parameters per a unit of length and l is the length of the line. The delay is reduced by line segmentation and incorporating intermediate inverters. Second, the delay reduction is restricted by the permissible density of current in the wire[16].

To charge the total capacity C up to voltage V by permissible wire I a certain time $\tau_{line} = CV/I$ is necessary. In this case, the delay can be reduced by increasing the wire width[17] and/or by wire segmentation. Since in any case a powerful

---

[16] The density in aluminum is $10^5 A/cm = 1mA/\mu^2$ for direct current and $2 \div 3mA/\mu^2$ for alternating current.

[17] The wire capacity will increase at the same time.

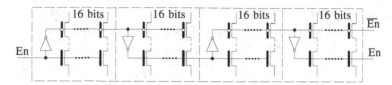

Fig. 29. Enable wire driving

driver (chain of inverters) is necessary for Enable wire switching, a segmentation like the one in fig. 29 obviously makes sense.

Furthermore, there is one more reason for segmentation. Actually, an asynchronous FIFO requires that the moments of register writing completion are indicated; this inserts a significant extra delay. However, the time required to switch Enable is considerably longer than the time of switching the latches. Segmenting the Enable wire provides that Enable signals always arrive in the latches in an orderly fashion and strengthens the possibility of using the switching delay of Enable as a parallel embedded delay for the registers.

Strategy of Synchronization and Synchro-Stratum Design. The synchronous prototype for FIFO is a synchronous shift register, with A signal used as a synchro-signal. However, the capacitive load on it becomes too big. Asynchronous shift is more preferable, and not only for this reason. As follows from section 3, the synchro-stratum structure depends on the chosen way of synchronization. Here we will discuss the two-track shift register with 6-phase synchronization (fig. 30). Each track is a register with 3-phase synchronization. The even synchro-signals control the shift of data in one register, and the odd synchro-signals in the other register. In fig. 30, arrows show the conditions of forming signal edges in asynchronous implementation. Dotted arrows point out the direction of data movement in both tracks.

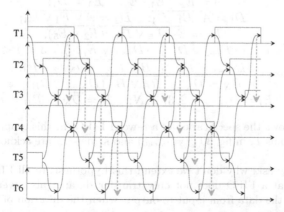

Fig. 30. Six-phase synchronization of a two-track shift register

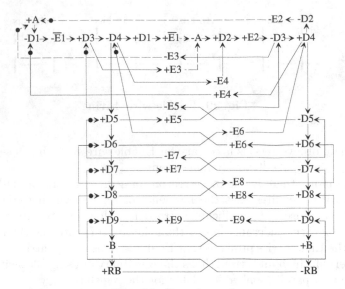

Fig. 31. Signal graph

From the timing diagrams in fig. 27 and fig. 30, taking into account the output sequencing, we can construct a signal graph model for the entire device (fig. 31).[18] It is important that we have no handshakes here, neither at the input nor at the output channel. As for the input, we should start from the hypothesis that between two adjacent changes of A the transient processes in the input circuits must be completed.[19] The arcs shown in the signal graph as dotted lines are given just to provide the correctness of the diagram in the procedure of formal synthesis of control circuits.

Using the specification in fig. 31, logical equations are derived for the elements of the device:

$$A = \overline{E_2 \vee \overline{E}_1 \cdot E_3}; \quad \overline{E}_1 = D_1;$$
$$D_1 = \overline{A \cdot E_4 \cdot D_4}; \quad D_2 = \overline{A \vee E_4 \vee D_4};$$
$$D_3 = \overline{E_2 \cdot E_5 \vee D_4 \cdot (E_2 \vee E_5)};$$
$$D_j = \overline{D_{j-1} \cdot E_{j+2} \vee D_{j+1} \cdot (D_{j-1} \vee E_{j+2})}, \quad 3 < j < N-1;$$
$$D_{N-1} = \overline{D_{N-2} \cdot B \vee D_N \cdot (D_{N-2} \vee B)};$$
$$D_N = \overline{D_{N-1} \cdot R_B \vee B \cdot (D_{N-1} \vee R_B)};$$
$$E_j = D_j, \quad j = 2, 3, ..., N; \quad B = \overline{D}_N; \quad R_B = \overline{B}.$$

---

[18] Figure 31 shows the specification of a 8-word FIFO. In this graph signals D_i correspond to signals T_j in fig. 30 ($j = i_{mod6}$) and signals E_i are acknowledgment signals to D_i.

[19] A reader may ask: why don't we extend this hypothesis to all FIFO registers? The answer is that a FIFO does not only transfer data; it also averages the delay of propagating the data from input to output when the duration of data processing is data-dependent.

The corresponding circuit is given in fig. 32. In this circuit the output signal R_A (next word request) of the input head can be used for checking the correctness of data reception. "Delay" is incorporated in the output head in order to restrict the speed of the output data. Alternatively, the environment can be used instead of the explicit delay if the interface between the FIFO and the environment is supported by handshake signals. The circuit which controls data moves in the FIFO is similar to the circuit of an asynchronous distributor patented in [14].

Discussing the Results. The circuit in fig. 32 is a principal solution that, generally speaking, can be improved by physical design. However, it is enough for the aim pursued here, i.e. for the demonstration of an example of building synchro-stratum by means of global synchronization of the FIFO registers.

As one can see from fig. 31, the delay of the full cycle of signal A is equal to $8\tau_{gate} + 4\tau_{line}$ were τ_{line} is the delay of the enable signal Ej of the register Rj. The cyclic delay of the FIFO is $6\tau_{gate} + 2\tau_{line}$. Hence, the bottleneck of the FIFO throughput is the input head. Note that the suggested FIFO has a latency close to the absolute minimum for register FIFOs: in an empty FIFO, switching of B signal starts $(N + 1)\tau_{gate} + \tau_{line}$ after A has changed where N is a number of FIFO registers.

Generally speaking, data can move independently through parallel tracks of the FIFO. However, it doubles the number of control gates. The possibility of using independent tracks depends on the way the adjacent words in the packet interact with each other while the data is being processed.

4.3   Arbiter-Free Control Logic for Counterflow Pipeline Processor

Regardless of its possible practical application, the counterflow pipeline processor architecture of [15–18] is a very interesting object for studying the behavior of asynchronous devices and their design. In all publications about the counterflow architecture we know of, the behavior specification contains arbitration situations and the respective implementations include arbiters (mutual exclusion elements). However, for today, fully asynchronous computing systems are largely unknown. The only way to apply asynchrony is via its evolutionary penetration into a synchronous environment. However, in this case, the arbiters of asynchronous devices would start to work as synchronizers whose operation is unreliable. A simple calculation of the failure probability shows that asynchronous devices with arbiters are often not applicable in synchronous environment.

One of the main sources of arbitration conditions in the counterflow architecture is the need to provide for the meeting of every instruction with every data set. Here we will try to demonstrate that using the GALA methodology based on decomposing the device into a synchro-stratum and a processor stratum allows us to build arbitration-free implementations for the counterflow architecture. Our claim is based on the fact that for the processor stratum we can use a synchronous prototype in which we can naturally avoid arbitration.

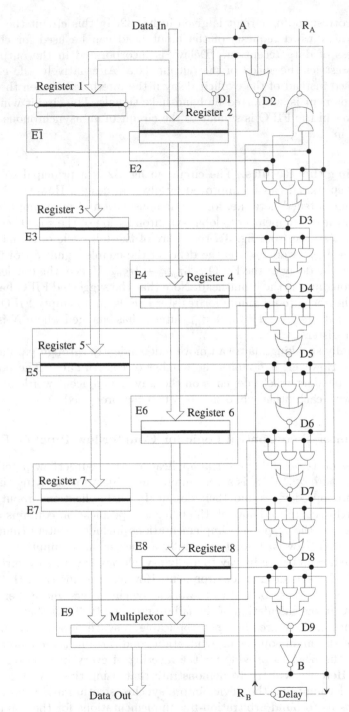

Fig. 32. One-two-one track FIFO

The synchronous prototype should be supplemented by logic that provides the handshake interaction with the synchro-stratum.

Synchronous Prototype of the Counterflow Pipeline Processor. As an initial specification in the GALA methodology we will use the synchronous prototype description shown in fig. 33. The structure consists of two register arrays (pipelines) to ensure the instruction flow and data flow move in two opposite directions (from top to bottom and from bottom to top, respectively). Every instruction from the instruction flow must be executed when meeting the respective data set. For this purpose, every pair of registers I_j and D_j (instructions and data) is provided with a local processor P_j that processes the data according to the current instruction.

Let us consider the simplest type of synchronization that is double-track. It uses two synchro-sequences T_1 and T_2 which change as ... $\to +T_1 \to -T_1 \to +T_2 \to\to -T_2 \to +T_1 \to$ ... . When $T_1 = 1$, the instructions are passed from registers I_{2i} to registers I_{2i+1}, the data sets are passed from registers D_{2i} to registers D_{2i-1}, and processors P_{2i+1} execute the respective instructions over the respective data. When $T_2 = 1$, the instructions are passed from registers I_{2i-1} to registers I_{2i}, the data sets are passed from registers D_{2i+1} to registers D_{2i}, and processors P_{2i} execute the respective instructions over the respective data. Actually, more sophisticated interconnection schemes and synchronization modes could be suggested, for example those that support concurrency between processor operation and data/instruction movement. However, this would just complicate the statement, without changing the principles of the solution we suggest here.

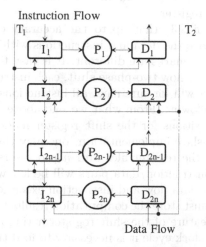

Fig. 33. Synchronous prototype of a counterflow pipeline processor

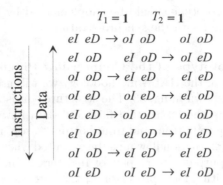

Fig. 34. Example of shifting instructions and data in counterflow registers

Using a Shift Register as the Prototype of an Asynchronous Pipeline.
The next question we have to discuss is organizing the interaction in the register files. The simplest synchronous prototype of an asynchronous pipeline when using a synchro-stratum is a shift register. The structure using shift registers is shown in fig. 33. To store and shift n bits of information (n k-bit words) we should have at least $2n$ memory cells ($2n$ k-bit registers). So, a shift register is a prototype of a non-dense pipeline [8]. Let us mark the instructions and data in the respective flows as even and odd. The marked instructions and data will be referred to as eI, oI, eD, oD. Now let us consider an example of two counterflow registers changing their states. Let the registers be in the state determined by the left column of instructions/data pairs in fig. 34. When $T_1 = 1$, the registers pass to the state that corresponds to the middle column. When $T_2 = 1$, their state corresponds to the right column. The arrows show the actively clocked positions in the shift registers.

We can see from fig. 34 that up to the accuracy of enumeration the odd numbered registers have the data and instructions with equal marks and in the even numbered one the marks are different. It is easy to check that in the case of a synchronous counterflow two-phase shift, each instruction will meet all data sets and each data set will for sure meet all instructions.

Let us note the following. From what we said above about the doubled number of register file positions for the shift register model and from the general knowledge of master-slave implementation, one may think that it is enough to have $2n$ positions in the register files and n processors. However, this way as many as half of the instruction/data pairs will be left without processing. Also note that making the data flow and instruction execution concurrent in time is difficult because we must store the computation results together with the current data set. A special feature of the shift register acting as a synchronous prototype is that in every clock cycle it is necessary to feed the register file with new instructions and data. Actually, this is inconsistent with our concept of asynchronous behavior. This problem will be discussed later, when we talk about incorporating synchro-stratum to make control asynchronous.

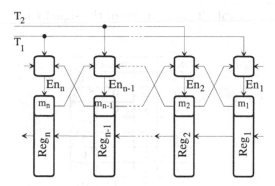

Fig. 35. Synchronous dense pipeline circuit

Building a Synchronous Dense Pipeline and Using It as a Prototype.
One can remove the necessity of renewing input instructions and data at every
clock cycle and increase the informational capacity of the register files by using
a dense synchronous pipeline as a prototype (a pipeline that can be filled with
data without gaps). The structure of a synchronous pipeline is shown in fig. 35.
Every register has a control circuit that produces a signal (En) that enables
writing the register with data.

The main problem of building a dense pipeline is how to separate the adjacent
data words. For this purpose, an even/odd marker can be provided, which is an
extra bit m_j accepting alternating values for successive data (instructions or
data sets). For example, $m_j = 1$ will correspond to odd data and $m_j = 0$ to
even data. Here is the truth table (table 2) for the function of En_j signal that
enables the data transfer from Reg_{j-1} to Reg_j.

The best definition of the function on the "don't care" positions is shown in
brackets. With this definition, the logic function of the enable signal (taking into
account clocking) looks like $En_j = (m_{j-1} \oplus m_{j+1})T_j$. Thus, it becomes possible
to implement a dense synchronous pipeline.

Synchronizing two dense synchronous counterflow pipelines by the same
synchro-sequences guarantees that all instructions will meet all data sets, just
like in a shift register used as a synchronous prototype. However, a new problem
arises here associated with the fact that the same instruction can repeatedly
meet the same data set and the same data set can repeatedly meat the same
instruction.

If we are going to use synchronous dense pipelines we imply that information
may be written in the pipeline and read out not every clock period. Otherwise
a dense pipeline doesn't have a sense. In this situation the distribution of instructions and data in the pipelines may vary in a wide range. One of possible
distributions is used in the example shown in fig. 36.

When the pipelines are initially filled (the left column of instructions/data
pairs) and $T_2 = 1$, data $2D$ meets instruction $4I$ (middle column) for the first
time. When $T_1 = 1$ (right column), the edge of instruction $4I$ continues to

Table 2. Truth table of the signal En_j

m_{j+1}	m_j	m_{j-1}	En_j
0	0	0	*(0)
1	0	0	*(1)
0	1	0	0
1	1	0	1
0	0	1	1
1	0	1	0
0	1	1	*(1)
1	1	1	*(0)

interact with data $2D$ and the edge of data $2D$ continues to interact with instruction $4I$. The simplest way of avoiding repeated execution of instructions
over the same data is to add two extra markers (bits), εd_j to the data and εi_j
to the instructions. Marker $\varepsilon d_j = 1$ if data jD were used by an instruction with
even/odd index equal to 1, and $\varepsilon d_j = 0$ if data jD were used by an instruction
with even/odd index equal to 0. Marker $\varepsilon i_j = 1$ if instruction jI has processed
data with even/odd index equal to 1, and $\varepsilon i_j = 0$ if instruction jI has processed
data with even/odd index equal to 0. Then, if instruction kI with even/odd bit
mi_k and data lD with even/odd bit md_l arrived to processor P_j, the instruction
will process the data only if $(md_l \oplus \varepsilon i_k)(mi_k \oplus \varepsilon d_l) = 1$ (this condition takes
value 1 if instruction kI meets the corresponding data lD for the first time only).

Synchro-Stratum Implementation. In spite of the type of the chosen
pipeline, we used the same type of synchronization, namely two-track two-phase
synchronization. While synchro-pulse $T_1 = 1$ or $T_2 = 1$ is active, the following
sequence of actions must be executed:

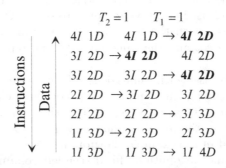

Fig. 36. Example of state transitions in two counterflow pipelines

- Writing (or not) the new data and instructions to the respective positions of the pipelines;
- Checking the conditions of instruction execution;
- Executing the instruction or canceling the execution, depending on the conditions;
- If the instruction was executed, writing the result to the data pipeline and modifying the instruction in the instruction pipeline (if necessary).

We will not discuss here in detail the control over all this sequence of actions. What is important for us is the following:

- Shifting the data and instructions to positions d_j and i_j occurs with the front edge of synchro-signal $+T_j$ (T_j is the signal that synchronizes the j-th position in the pipelines).
- The signal of shift completion (it can be formed in a number of ways; we do not discuss them here) initiates the processor functioning.
- The completion of the processor operation initiates saving the results.
- The completion of saving the results initiates the falling edge of the synchro-signal $-T_j$.

If we provide that the synchro-stratum receives the signal of operation completion at the j-th position ($\pm P_j$), then relying on the above rules, we can build a signal graph shown in fig. 37 that specifies the behavior of the Synchro-Stratum.

In fig. 37, the signals $\pm ReqL$, $\pm AckL$, $\pm ReqR$, $\pm AckR$ determine the left and right interfaces. Variables a_j are the internal variables of the synchro-stratum. From this graph we can derive the Boolean functions for the synchro-stratum gates:

$$T_j = \overline{T_{j-1} + a_{j-1}a_{j+1} + T_{j+1}},\ (2 < j < n-1);$$
$$a_j = \overline{a_{j-1} + P_j + a_{j+1}},\ (1 < j < n);$$
$$T_1 = \overline{AckL + a_0a_2 + T_2};\ T_n = \overline{T_{n-1} + a_{n-1}a_{n+1} + AckR};$$
$$a_0 = \overline{AckL + a_1};\ a_{n+1} = \overline{a_n + AckR};$$
$$ReqL = \overline{a_1 + P_1};\ ReqR = \overline{P_n + a_n}.$$

The synchro-stratum circuit constructed in accordance with these functions is shown in fig. 38.

Discussing the Results. From our standpoint, the major shortcoming of the previously known asynchronous circuit [18] for control of a stage of a counterflow pipeline processor was the necessity to incorporate the arbiters. The reason for having arbitration was that, in order to make the instructions meet the respective data sets the simultaneous shift of instructions and data was prohibited.

We have demonstrated that a synchronous implementation of a counterflow pipeline processor exists which contains no arbitration. Using it, we have built an asynchronous circuit of a synchro-stratum that controls the operation of the pipelines. This circuit contains two gates for every stage of the pipelines. The

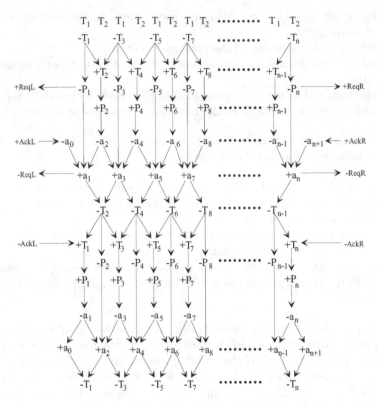

Fig. 37. Fragment of the unfolded signal graph describing the synchro-stratum behavior

pipeline stages themselves can be built in various ways. The only requirement to them is the necessity to produce a completion signal. Such signals are used to organize the handshake interaction with the synchro-stratum.

The pipeline throughput is determined by the worst case delay of one stage which, as we can see from fig. 37, is equal to

$$4\tau_g + max(2\tau_g + \tau_{P_{2j-2}}^+, \tau_{P_{2j-1}}^-, 2\tau_g + \tau_{P_{2j}}^+) + max(\tau_{P_{2j-2}}^-, 2\tau_g + \tau_{P_{2j-1}}^+, \tau_{P_{2j}}^-)$$

where τ_g is the delay of a synchro-stratum gate, $\tau_{P_j}^+$ and $\tau_{P_j}^-$ are delays of the active phase and the preparatory phase of the instruction execution respectively. If say all instructions have the same duration of the active phase and $\tau_{P_j}^+ > \tau_{P_j}^-$, then the pipeline stage delay will be $8\tau_g + \tau_{P_j}^+ + \tau_{P_{j-1}}^+$. Note that this expression does not include the delay of the preparatory phase, because for the even (odd) positions of the pipeline this phase is partially overlapped with the active phase of instruction execution for the odd (even) positions. It is easy to see that as in the case of ordinary pipeline, the maximum throughput of counterflow pipelines is reached when they are half-filled. In this case the delay of the pipeline stage will be $8\tau_g + \tau_{P_j}^+ + \tau_{P_j}^-$.

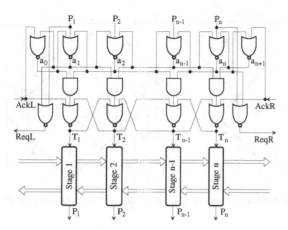

Fig. 38. Structure of the counterflow pipelines in the GALA representation

4.4   Wave Propagation Cellular Array

Let us consider a two-dimensional automata array designed for wave algorithms. In such an array, computing is synchronized by the edges of the signal waves that propagate in it. Ignoring the essence of this computing, we will try to answer the only question: can signal waves propagate asynchronously? According to the above, the answer is "yes" if a corresponding synchronous prototype is available. Let us show the possibility of building a cellular automaton for a synchronous prototype.

Every automaton in a two-dimensional array is connected with its four direct neighbors by two-directional links. The sources (centers) of wave initiation are arbitrary automata of the array in arbitrary time moments (cycles). Every source can initiate one or several waves. We will not discuss here the mechanisms of reactivating the same center. We will also make no distinction between the edge of waves propagating from different active centers. The problem of wave recognition can be solved at the level of data exchange between cellular processors.

If the array contains one source, for example A_{ij}, the wave propagates as shown in fig. 22,b. The shape of the wave is a square rotated 45°. Note that the corners of the square and its sides use different ways of propagation. The corners move towards West (W), South (S), East (E) and North (N); their movement is made possible by the automaton when it receives a corresponding signal from the direction of E, N, W or S. The sides move towards SW, SE, NE and NW. The condition for their movement is that every automaton on the square side accepts the appropriate signals from both directions.

It is reasonable to separate the signals that control the movement of corners with the signals that control the movement of sides. In order to do this, let the cellular automaton have two inputs and two outputs for each direction. Let the binary signals arriving at inputs x_{1W}, x_{1S}, x_{1E}, x_{1N} and taken from outputs y_{1W}, y_{1S}, y_{1E}, y_{1N} control the movement of the sides, and let the signals arriving

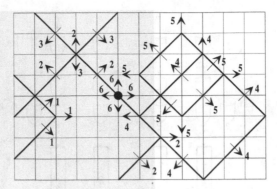

Fig. 39. Edge propagation of waves from several sources in a 2D cellular array

at inputs x_{2W}, x_{2S}, x_{2E}, x_{2N} and taken from outputs y_{2W}, y_{2S}, y_{2E}, y_{2N} control the movement of the corners. Then the conditions of producing the output signals of the cellular automaton can be written as simple logical functions [20]:

$$y_{2N} = x_{2S}, \ y_{2S} = x_{2N}, \ y_{2W} = x_{2E}, \ y_{2E} = x_{2W},$$
$$y_{1N} = x_{1S}(x_{1E} + x_{1W}) + x_{2W} + x_{2E},$$
$$y_{1S} = x_{1N}(x_{1E} + x_{1W}) + x_{2W} + x_{2E},$$
$$y_{1W} = x_{1E}(x_{1S} + x_{1N}) + x_{2S} + x_{2N},$$
$$y_{1E} = x_{1W}(x_{1S} + x_{1N}) + x_{2S} + x_{2N}.$$

It is easy to check that in an array of such automata edges of different waves can move apart propagating in opposite directions, cross or merge partially or fully. The part where two or more waves merge begins to propagate as an edge of one wave. As an example, fig. 39 shows a pattern of five wave fronts in a two-dimensional array, halted at a certain moment. The waves are propagating from five initiation centers and at the moment the sixth center has just appeared as designated by a bold dot. The directions are indicated by arrows each marked with the number of the wave.

In a synchronous implementation of a cellular array that uses 2-track 2-phase synchronization system, the cellular automata are split into two subsets: in one of them the automata have an even sum of indexes and in the other one — an odd sum. These subsets are synchronized by signals of different tracks. Using the approach described above, from such a synchronous prototype an asynchronous implementation can be designed. To do this, a synchro-stratum that corresponds to the prototype synchronization system should be incorporated into the array. Producing completion signals can be ensured using any workable approach.

---

[20] These functions pay respect to that wave propagation through side automata which are the diagonal neighbors of a vertex automaton differs from wave propagation through other side automata.

5   Conclusion

Strange as it might sound but when we had finished this work, we felt deep disappointment rather than satisfaction. Why should we have been racking our brains over the puzzle of organizing the global synchronization of asynchronous arrays for several years, inventing sophisticated examples and trying to find solutions to them, reading adverse reviews and planning work on these problems for some years into the future? A trivial solution was on the surface!

Of course, the issue is not closed. The approach suggested here, as well as any general solution, is good for all cases and bad in every particular one. For example, using this approach, one can implement a bit pipeline, but that will not be as good as the traditional implementation. Therefore, it is very important to understand what question we have just obtained the answer to.

Following this work, we can claim that *for a processor array of any dimension, for any multiprocessor system with a König interconnection graph and for any distributed synchronous (in the sense of using a clock, common for the whole system) algorithm or a system of algorithms, one can uniformly design a system of "asynchronous synchronization." To this end, it is sufficient to use compatible processors and a synchro-stratum of cells as shown in fig. 17.*

The main result on the global synchronization of asynchronous processor arrays and multiprocessor systems stated here corresponds to the case of a synchronous prototype with *two-track two-phase master-slave synchronization*. As it was shown above, other possible synchronization disciplines may be of interest, too.

In the above discussion about GALA (Globally Asynchronous – Locally Arbitrary) methodology, we focused on its first aspect which is Global Asynchrony. Local Arbitrariness assumes a wide range of ways to provide the handshake signals between Synchro-Stratum and Processor (Automaton) Stratum. It is possible to use self-timing, current sensors, start-stop local clocks, parallel incorporated delays (including data-dependent delays) etc. The reader interested in our results in this area can familiarize themselves with [6,8,23-27].

References

[1] V. I. Varshavsky, T.-A. Chu, "Self-Timing - Tools for Hardware Support of Parallel, Concurrent and Event-Driven Process Control," *Proceedings of the Conference on Massively Parallel Computing Systems (MPCS)*, May 1994, pp. 510-515.

[2] V. I. Varshavsky, V. B. Marakhovsky, T.-A. Chu, "Logical Timing (Global Synchronization of Asynchronous Arrays)", *Parallel Algorithm/Architecture Synthesis*, International Symposium, Aizu-Wakamatsu, Japan, IEEE CS Press, March 1995, pp. 130-138.

[3] V. Varshavsky, V. B. Marakhovsky, T.-A. Chu, "Asynchronous Timing of Arrays with Synchronous Prototype", *Proceedings of the Second International Conference on Massively Parallel Computing Systems (MPCS'96)*, Ischia, Italy, May 1996, pp. 47-54.

[4] V.I.Varshavsky, V.B.Marakhovsky, "Global Synchronization of Asynchronous Arrays in Logical Time", *Parallel Algorithm/Architecture Synthesis*, The Second International Symposium, Aizu-Wakamatsu, Japan, IEEE CS Press, March 1997, pp. 207-215.

[5] C.D.Nielsen, *Delay-Insensitive Design with Constant Response Time*, Technical Report ID-TR: 1994-134, Technical University of Denmark, DK-2800 Lyngby, Denmark, Jan. 1994.

[6] M.Kishinevsky, A.Kondratyev, A.Taubin, and V.Varshavsky, *Concurrent Hardware. The Theory and Practice of Self-Timed Design*, J.Wiley & Sons, 1993.

[7] V.Varshavsky, *Hardware Support of Parallel Asynchronous Processes*, Helsinki University of Technology, Digital Systems Laboratory. Series A: Research Reports: No 2; Sept. 1987.

[8] V.Varshavsky, M.Kishinevsky, V.Marakhovsky et al., *Self-timed Control of Concurrent Processes*, Ed. by V.Varshavsky, Kluver Academic Publishers, 1990.

[9] V.Varshavsky, M.Kishinevsky, V.Marakhovsky et al., "Asynchronous Distributer," USSR Inventory Certificate No. 1064461, *The Inventions Bulletin*, No. 48, 1983.

[10] D.König, *Theorie der Endichen und Unendlichen Graphen*, Leipzig, Akad. Verlag M.B.H., 1936, 258SS; N.Y., Chelsea, 1950. Zbl, 15, 375.

[11] V.Varshavsky, A.Kondratyev, V.Marakhovsky, "Counting Device", USSR Patent Certificate No. 1594684, *The Inventions Bulletin*, 1990, No.35.

[12] T.-A. Chu, "10 Gbps ATM LIMO", *ACORN Networks Inc.*, http://www.acorn-networks.com/index.html, 1997.

[13] S.B.Furber, and J.Liu, "Dynamic Logic in Four-Phase Micro-pipelines", *Advanced Research in Asynchronous Circuits and Systems*, Second International Symposium, Aizu-Wakamatsu, Japan, March 18-21, 1996, IEEE, pp.11-16.

[14] V.Varshavsky, A.Kondratyev, N.Kravchenko, and B.Tsyrlin, "Asynchronous Distributor", USSR Patent Certificate No.1598142, *The Inventions Bulletin*, No.37, 1990.

[15] R.F.Sproull, I.E.Sutherland, C.E.Molnar, *Counterflow Pipeline Processor Architecture*, Technical Report SMLI TR-94-25, Sun Micro-systems Laboratories, Inc., CA 94043, April 1994.

[16] R.F.Sproull, I.E.Sutherland, and C.E.Molnar, "The Counterflow Pipeline Processor Architecture", *IEEE Design and Test of Computers*, 11(3), Fall 1994, pp.48-59.

[17] W.H.F.J.Kurver and I.M.Nedelchev, "Synchronous Implementation of the SCPP-A Counterflow Pipeline Processor", *IEE Proceedings, Computers and Digital Techniques*, 143(5), Sept. 1996, pp.287-294.

[18] B.Coates, J.Ebergen, J.Lexau, S.Fairbanks,I.Jones, A.Ridgway, D.Harris, and I.Sutherland, "A Counterflow Pipeline Experiment", *In proc. of International Symposium on Advanced Research in Asynchronous Circuits and Systems*, April 1999, pp.161-172.

[19] V.Varshavsky, "Asynchronous Interaction in Massively Parallel Computing Systems", *Proceedings of the IEEE First International Conference on Algorithms and Architectures for Parallel Processing*, Australia, Brisbane, April 1995, Vol.2, pp.951-953.

[20] V.Varshavsky, V. Marakhovsky and V. Peschansky, "Synchronization of Interacting Automata", *Mathematical System Theory*, 1970, Vol. 4, No. 3, pp. 212-230.

[21] V.I.Varshavsky, V.B.Marakhovsky, "One-Two-One Track Asynchronous FIFO", *Proceedings of the 1998 IEEE Asia-Pacific Conference on Circuits and Systems, (APCCAS-98)*, Chiagmai, Thailand, 1998, pp.743-746.

[22] V. I.Varshavsky, V. B.Marakhovsky, "Asynchronous Control Logic Design for Counterflow Pipeline Processor", *Proceedings of the 9th International Symposium on Integrated Circuits and Systems (ISIC-2001)*, Singapore, 2001, pp.177-181. 1998, pp.743-746.

[23] V. I.Varshavsky, V. B.Marakhovsky, and R. A.Lashevsky, "Asynchronous Interaction in Massively Parallel Computing Systems", *Proceedings of the IEEE First International Conference on Algorithms and Architectures for Parallel Processing*, Australia, Brisbane, 1995, Vol.2, pp. 481–492.

[24] V. I.Varshavsky, V. B.Marakhovsky, M.Tsukisaka, "Data-Controlled Delays in the Asynchronous Design", *IEEE International Symposium on Circuits and Systems, ISCAS'96*, Atlanta, USA, 1996, Vol. 4, pp. 153–155.

[25] V. I.Varshavsky, "Does Current Sensor Make Sense?" *Proceedings of the 7th International Symposium on IC Technology, Systems & Applications (ISIC-97)*, Singapore, 1997, pp. 471-473.

[26] V. I.Varshavsky, M.Tsukisaka, "Current Sensor on the Base of Permanent Prechargable Amplifier", *The 9th Great Lake Symposium on VLSI*, Ann Arbor, USA, 1999, pp. 210-213.

[27] V. I.Varshavsky, V. B.Marakhovsky, M.Tsukisaka, A.Kato, "Current Sensor — Transient Process Problems", *Proceedings of the 8th International Symposium on Integrated Circuits, Devices & Systems (ISIC-99)*, Singapore, 1999, pp. 163-166.

Synthesis of Reactive Systems: Application to Asynchronous Circuit Design

Josep Carmona[1], Jordi Cortadella[2], and Enric Pastor[1]

[1] Universitat Politècnica de Catalunya
Computer Architecture Department, Barcelona, Spain
[2] Universitat Politècnica de Catalunya
Software Department, Barcelona, Spain

Abstract. Synthesis bridges the gap between specification and implementation by systematically transforming one model into another and approaching the primitives of the specification to those realizable by the implementation. This work faces the problem of the synthesis of reactive systems, in which there is an explicit distinction between input and output actions. The transformations used during synthesis must preserve the properties that characterize the correct interaction between the system and the environment. The concept of *I/O compatibilty* is proposed to define this correctness, and is used to provide a set of transformations for the synthesis of reactive systems.

The theoretical contributions of the work are applied to the synthesis of asynchronous circuits. Petri nets are used as specification model, and a set of structural methods are proposed for the transformations of the model and the synthesis of digital circuits.

1 Introduction

A reactive system is a concurrent system in which the behavior explicitly manifests an interaction with the environment. Unlike other models to express concurrency, reactive systems have a clear distinction between the actions performed by the environment (input events) and those performed by the system (output events). Additionally, a reactive system may also have internal actions not observable by the environment.

I/O automata [16] were proposed as a model for discrete event systems in which different components interact asynchronously. The distinction between input, output and internal events is fundamental to characterize the behavior of real-life systems. While a system can impose constraints on when to perform output or internal actions, it cannot impose any constraint on when an input action can occur. For this reason, input actions are always enabled in any state of an I/O automata.

In this work, we deal with the synthesis problem of reactive systems. Given a system and its environment, a synchronization protocol is committed in such a way that, at any state, the environment is guaranteed to produce only those input actions acceptable by the system. For the specification of this type of

J. Cortadella et al. (Eds.): Concurrency and Hardware Design, LNCS 2549, pp. 108–151, 2002.

systems, one might use I/O automata with a dummy state that is the sink of any input action not acceptable by the system.

We want to solve the following problem: given the specification of a reactive system, generate an implementation realizable with design primitives that commits the protocol established with the environment. In this particular work, we focus on the synthesis of asynchronous circuits, where the events of the system are rising and falling signal transitions and the design primitives are logic gates.

The specification formalism used for the synthesis of asynchronous circuits is Petri nets [18], an event based model that can express concurrency explicitly. For this reason, the state explosion problem may arise when state-level information is required for synthesis. This paper will tackle this problem by using structural techniques for synthesis.

1.1   Overview

A reactive system is assumed to interact with an environment (see Fig. 1(a)). Both, the system and the environment have behaviors that can be described with some model for concurrent systems.

A reactive system has an alphabet of input, output and internal events $\Sigma = \Sigma_I \cup \Sigma_O \cup \Sigma_{INT}$. The environment also has another alphabet $\Sigma' = \Sigma'_I \cup \Sigma'_O \cup \Sigma'_{INT}$. A necessary condition for a system and an environment to talk to each other is that their alphabets can be "connected", i.e. $\Sigma_I = \Sigma'_O$ and $\Sigma_O = \Sigma'_I$, as shown in Fig. 1(a). This paper is an attempt to formalize and answer questions such as

Which is the class of systems that can correctly dialogue with a given environment?
How can a system be transformed so that the dialogue with its environment is not affected?
What does "correct dialogue" mean?

To understand the rest of this section, we will give an informal and intuitive idea of what "correct dialogue" means. We will say that two systems have a correct dialogue when

- every output event produced by one of them is expected by the other as an input event (safeness), and
- if one of them is only waiting for input events, the other one will eventually produce one of them (liveness).

Figures 1(b-d) depict an example to illustrate the main issues discussed in this paper. The models used to describe behavior are marked graphs, a subclass of Petri nets with no choice places, in which events represent rising (+) or falling (-) transitions of digital signals. The goal is to synthesize a circuit that can have a correct dialogue with the environment. We will assume that the components of the circuit have arbitrary delays. Likewise, the environment may take any arbitrary delay to produce any enabled output event.

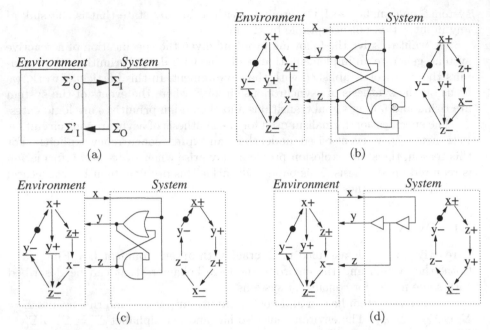

Fig. 1. (a) Connection between system and environment, (b) mirrored implementation of a concurrent system, (c) valid implementation with concurrency reduction, (d) invalid implementation

Let us first have a look at Fig. 1(b). The marked graph in the environment can be considered as a specification of a concurrent system. The underlined transitions denote input events. Thus, an input event of the environment must have a correspondence with an output event of the system, and vice versa. The behavior denoted by this specification can be informally described as follows:

> In the initial state, the environment will produce the event $x+$. After that, the environment will be able to accept the events $y+$ and $z+$ concurrently from the system. After the arrival of $z+$, the environment will produce $x-$, that can occur concurrently with $y+$. Next, it will wait for the system to sequentially produce $z-$ and $y-$, thus leading the environment back to the initial state.

The circuit shown in Fig. 1(b) behaves as specified by the adjacent marked graph. In this case, the behavior of the system is merely a mirror of the behavior of the environment. For this reason, the dialogue between both is correct.

Let us analyze now the system in Fig. 1(c). In this case, the circuit implements a behavior in which $y+$ and $z+$ are produced sequentially. Still, the system can maintain a correct dialogue, since the environment is able to accept more behaviors than the ones produced by the system. We can observe that, even though the behavior is less concurrent, the implementation is simpler.

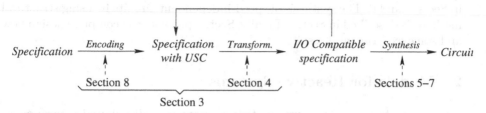

Fig. 2. Synthesis framework for asynchronous circuits

Let us finally look at Fig. 1(d), in which the events $z+$, $y+$ and $x-$ are produced sequentially in this order. Due to this reduction in concurrency, two buffers are sufficient to implement such behavior. Even though the set of traces produced by the system is included in the set of traces produced by the environment, the dialogue between both is not correct. To illustrate that, let us assume the events $x+$ and $z+$ have been produced from the initial state. We are now in a state in which $x-$ is enabled in the environment (output event) but not enabled in the system. This violates one of the conditions for a correct dialogue: if an output event is enabled in one component, the corresponding event must also be enabled in the other component. In practice, if the environment would produce $x-$, the circuit could react with the event $z-$ before $y+$ is produced.

The previous examples suggest that a theory to characterize the fact that two systems can talk to each other is required. We will call *Input/Output-compatibility* this characterization. We will show that the well-known concepts of bisimulation and observational equivalence [17] are not appropriate to analyze properties related to the dialogue between systems, since there is no explicit distinction between input and output events.

Finally, the theory presented in this paper will be applied to a specific area of hardware design: asynchronous circuits. We will provide a kit of transformations that will assist in improving the quality of gate implementations by either reducing the complexity of the circuit or its performance.

Figure 2 depicts the synthesis framework for asynchronous circuits proposed in this work. It is also used to introduce the sections of this paper. Initially, a concurrent specification is given to express the protocol established between system and environment. The specification must be transformed to properly encode the states of the system and guarantee a logic implementation. After the transformations required for encoding (Sect. 8), the specification is said to have the *Unique State Coding* property. Synthesis is performed by transforming the specification in such a way that the behavior is realizable by logic gates. In order to circumvent the state explosion problem, the transformations are performed on the structure of the specification, and not on its state-level representation (Sect. 4). In either case, the transformations performed for encoding and synthesis must preserve the correctness of the interaction with the environment. This correctness is called *I/O compatibility* and it is presented and discussed in Sect. 3. Some basic theory on the synthesis of asynchronous circuits is presented in Sects. 5 and 6. The synthesis of speed-independent circuits by using structural methods is described in Sect. 7. Finally, Sect. 9 presents the complete design flow and some experimental results.

2   Models for Reactive Systems

Reactive systems [11] are systems that operate in a distributed environment. The events in a reactive system can be either input events, output events or internal events. An input event represents a change in the environment for which the system must react. In contrast, an output event can force other systems in the environment to react to. Finally, an internal event represents system's local progress, not observable in the environment. Typical examples of reactive system are a computer, a television set and a vending machine. The events executed in a reactive system are assumed to take arbitrary but finite time.

Two models for the specification of reactive systems are presented in this section: Transition systems and Petri nets.

2.1   Transition Systems

Definition 1 (Transition System). *A Transition System (TS) [1] is a* 4-tuple $A = (S, \Sigma, T, s_{in})$ *where*

- *S is the set of states*
- *Σ is the alphabet of events*
- *$T \subseteq S \times \Sigma \times S$ is the set of transitions*
- *$s_{in} \in S$ is the initial state*

Figure 3(a) depicts an example of TS. The initial state is denoted by an incident arc without source state.

Reachability in a TS The transitions are denoted by (s, e, s') or $s \xrightarrow{e} s'$. An event is said to be *enabled* in the state s, denoted by the predicate $\mathsf{En}(s, e)$, if $(s, e, s') \in T$, for some s'. The *reachability relation* between states is the transitive closure of the transition relation T. The predicate $s \xrightarrow{\sigma} s'$ denotes a *trace* of events σ that leads from s to s' by firing transitions in T. A state s is *terminal* if no event is enabled in s. A TS is *finite* if S and T are finite sets.

Language of a TS A TS can be viewed as an automaton with alphabet Σ, where every state is an accepting state. For a TS A, let $L(A)$ be the corresponding language, i.e. its set of traces starting from the initial state.

The synchronous product of two transition systems is a new transition system which models the interaction between both systems [1].

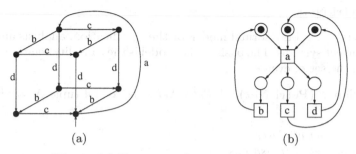

(a)   (b)

Fig. 3. (a) Transition System. (b) Petri net

Definition 2 (Synchronous Product). *Let* $A = (S^A, \Sigma^A, T^A, s_{in}^A)$, $B = (S^B, \Sigma^B, T^B, s_{in}^B)$ *be two TSs. The synchronous product of A and B, denoted by $A \times B$ is another TS (S, Σ, T, s_{in}) defined by*

- $s_{in} = \langle s_{in}^A, s_{in}^B \rangle \in S$
- $\Sigma = \Sigma^A \cup \Sigma^B$
- $S \subseteq S^A \times S^B$ *is the set of states reachable from s_{in} according to the following definition of T.*
- *Let* $\langle s1, s1' \rangle \in S$.
  - *If* $e \in \Sigma^A \cap \Sigma^B$, $s_1 \xrightarrow{e} s_2 \in T^A$ *and* $s_1' \xrightarrow{e} s_2' \in T^B$, *then* $\langle s_1, s_1' \rangle \xrightarrow{e} \langle s_2, s_2' \rangle \in T$
  - *If* $e \in \Sigma^A \setminus \Sigma^B$ *and* $s_1 \xrightarrow{e} s_2 \in T^A$, *then* $\langle s_1, s_1' \rangle \xrightarrow{e} \langle s_2, s_1' \rangle \in T$
  - *If* $e \in \Sigma^B \setminus \Sigma^A$ *and* $s_1' \xrightarrow{e} s_2' \in T^B$, *then* $\langle s_1, s_1' \rangle \xrightarrow{e} \langle s_1, s_2' \rangle \in T$
  - *No other transitions belong to T*

When the events of a TS are interpreted as events of a reactive system, the notion of *reactive transition system* arise:

Definition 3 (Reactive Transition System). *A Reactive Transition System (RTS) is a TS (S, Σ, T, s_{in}) where Σ is partitioned into three pairwise disjoint subsets of input (Σ_I), output (Σ_O) and internal (Σ_{INT}) events. $\Sigma_{OBS} = \Sigma_I \cup \Sigma_O$ is called the set of observable events.*

Properties of Reactive Systems Some definitions depending on the interpretation of the events arise in a reactive transition system.

Definition 4 (Livelock). *A livelock is an infinite trace of only internal events. A RTS is* livelock-free *if it has no livelocks.*

Definition 5 (Input-Proper). *An RTS is* input-proper *when for every internal transition $s \xrightarrow{e} s'$, with $e \in \Sigma_{INT}$ and for every input event $i \in \Sigma_I$, $\mathsf{En}(s', i) \implies \mathsf{En}(s, i)$. In other words, whether or not an input event is enabled in a given state depends only on the observable trace leading to that state.*

Definition 6 (Mirror Operator). *The* mirror *of A, denoted by $\overline{A}$, is another RTS identical to A, but in which the input and output alphabets of A have been interchanged.*

2.2   Petri Nets

Petri Nets [21, 18] is a formal model for the specification, analysis and synthesis of concurrent systems. The basis of the model is the causality relation established between the set of events.

Definition 7 (Petri Net). *A Petri Net (PN) is a 4-tuple $N = (P, T, F, M_0)$ where*

- *P is the set of places*
- *T is the set of transitions*
- *$F : (P \times T) \cup (T \times P) \to \mathbb{N}$ is the flow relation*
- *$M_0 : P \to \mathbb{N}$ is the initial marking*

An example of PN is shown in Fig. 3(b).

Paths A *path* in a PN is a sequence $u_1 \ldots u_r$ of nodes such that $\forall i, 1 \le i < r :$ $(u_i, u_{i+1}) \in F$. A path is called *simple* if no node appears more than once on it.

Reachability in a PN Given a node x of N, the set $^\bullet x = \{y \mid (y, x) \in F\}$ is the pre-set of x and the set $x^\bullet = \{y \mid (x, y) \in F\}$ is the post-set of x. A transition t is *enabled* in marking M if each place $p \in {}^\bullet t$ is marked with at least $F(p, t)$ tokens. When a transition t is enabled, it can *fire* by removing $F(p, t)$ tokens from place $p \in {}^\bullet t$ and adding $F(t, q)$ tokens to each place $q \in t^\bullet$. A marking M' is *reachable* from M if there is a sequence of firings $t_1 t_2 \ldots t_n$ that transforms M into M', denoted by $M[t_1 t_2 \ldots t_n\rangle M'$. A sequence of transitions $t_1 t_2 \ldots t_n$ is a *feasible sequence* if it is firable from M_0. The set of reachable markings from M_0 is denoted by $[M_0\rangle$. A marking is a *home marking* if it is reachable from every marking of $[M_0\rangle$. Let $R \subseteq [M_0\rangle$ be the set of markings where transition t_i is enabled. Transition t_j *triggers* transition t_i if there exists a reachable marking M such that $M[t_j\rangle M'$, $M \notin R$ and $M' \in R$. Transition t_j *disables* transition t_i if there exists a reachable marking M enabling both t_i and t_j, but in the marking M' such that $M[t_j\rangle M'$, t_i is not enabled.

Petri Net Subclasses A place in a PN is *redundant* if its elimination does not change the behavior of the net. A PN is *place-irredundant* if it does not have redundant places. A Petri net is called *ordinary* when for every pair of nodes (x, y), $F(x, y) \le 1$. All the Petri nets appearing in this chapter are ordinary[1]. If restrictions are imposed on the structure of the net, several subclasses can be defined [18]. Three subclasses are of interest in this paper:
- A *State Machine* (SM) is a PN such that each transition has exactly one input place and one output place.
- A *Marked Graph* (MG) is a PN such that each place has exactly one input transition and one output transition.

---

[1] Given that we deal with ordinary nets, we will abuse language and say $e \in F$ instead of $F(e) = 1$.

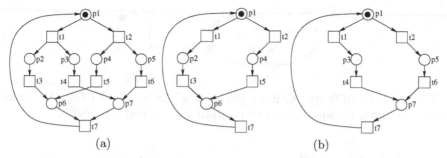

Fig. 4. (a) Free-choice petri net. (b) SM-cover of PN from (a)

- A *Free-choice Petri net* (FC) is a PN such that if $(p, t) \in F$ then ${}^\bullet t \times p^\bullet \subseteq F$, for every place p.

Liveness and Safeness A PN is *live* iff every transition can be infinitely enabled through some feasible sequence of firings from any marking in $[M_0\rangle$. A PN is *safe* if no marking in $[M_0\rangle$ assigns more than one token to any place. In the rest of the chapter, live and safe Petri nets will be assumed.

Free-Choice Decomposition A free-choice live and safe Petri net (FCLSPN) can be decomposed into a set of strongly-connected state-machines (marked graphs). An *SM-cover* (*MG-cover*) of a FCLSPN is a subset of state machines (marked graphs) such that every place (transition) is included at least in one state machine (marked graph). Moreover, a FCLSPN can be also decomposed into a set of strongly-connected *one-token* state-machines, i.e. state-machines that at most contain one token at any reachable marking [10].

A FCLSPN is shown in Fig. 4(a). A one-token SM-cover of PN of Fig. 4(a) is shown in Fig. 4(b).

Concurrency Relations The Concurrency Relation [6] between pairs of nodes $(P \cup T)$ of a PN is defined as a binary relation $\mathcal{CR}$, such that given places p_i, p_j and transitions t_i, t_j:

$$(t_i, t_j) \in \mathcal{CR} \Leftrightarrow [\exists M \in [M_0\rangle : M[t_i t_j\rangle \wedge M[t_j t_i\rangle];$$
$$(p, t_i) \in \mathcal{CR} \Leftrightarrow [\exists M \in [M_0\rangle : M[t_i\rangle M' \wedge M(p) > 0 \wedge M'(p) > 0];$$
$$(p_i, p_j) \in \mathcal{CR} \Leftrightarrow [\exists M \in [M_0\rangle : M(p_i) > 0 \wedge M(p_j) > 0].$$

Polynomial algorithms for the computation of the concurrency relations of a FCLSPN have been presented in [14].

As in the case of the TS model, a transition in a PN can represent an event occurring in a reactive system.

Definition 8 (Reactive Petri Net). *A Reactive Petri Net (RPN) is a* 3-tuple $((P, T, F, M_0), \Sigma, \Lambda)$ *where*

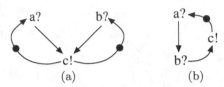

(a)   (b)

Fig. 5. (a) IO-RPN specification. (b) RPN which is not IO-RPN (the suffices ? and ! are used to denote input and output events, respectively)

- (P, T, F, M_0) *is a PN*
- Σ *is a set of events defined as in the case of RTS*
- $\Lambda : T \to \Sigma$

A RPN A has an associated reactive transition system $\text{RTS}(A)$, in which each reachable marking corresponds to a state and each transition t between a pair of markings to an arc labeled with $\Lambda(t)$. A RPN A is *deterministic* if $\text{RTS}(A)$ is deterministic. Along this paper, only deterministic RPNs are considered.

When restrictions are imposed on the structure of a RPN, several subclasses can be defined. The IO-RPN class contains those free-choice deterministic RPNs fulfilling both that there is not an input event triggering another input event, and the transitions in the post-set of a *choice* place are all input events:

Definition 9 (I/O Reactive Petri Net). *An IO-RPN is a deterministic free-choice RPN where the following conditions hold:*

1. $\forall t_1, t_2 \in T : (t_2 \in (t_1^\bullet)^\bullet \wedge \Lambda(t_1) \in \Sigma_I \Rightarrow \Lambda(t_2) \notin \Sigma_I)$.
2. $\forall p \in P : (|p^\bullet| \geq 2 \Rightarrow \forall t \in p^\bullet : \Lambda(t) \in \Sigma_I)$.

Figure 5(a) presents an example of IO-RPN. The RPN of Fig. 5(b) does not belongs to the IO-RPN class because input transition a triggers input transition b. The IO-RPN class possesses some nice properties, which will be discussed in Sects. 8 and 9.

3   Relations of Reactive Systems

In the first part of this section, the *observational equivalence* relation [17] is introduced. Afterwards, a set of conditions that ensure a correct dialogue between two reactive systems is presented: the *I/O compatibility*. Both notions are compared and the relations among them are outlined. Finally, the I/O compatibility is used for defining the set of conditions establishing when an object can be considered as a correct realization of a reactive system (*I/O preserving realization*). Formal proofs of the theorems appearing in this section can be found in [4].

3.1   Observational Equivalence

The *observational equivalence* relation between two reactive systems was introduced by Milner in [17]. The relation identifies those systems whose observable behavior is identical.

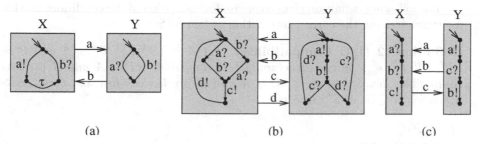

Fig. 6. Connection between different reactive systems (the suffixes ? and ! are used to denote input and output events, respectively)

Definition 10. *Let $A = (S^A, \Sigma^A, T^A, s_{in}^A)$ and $B = (S^B, \Sigma^B, T^B, s_{in}^B)$ be two RTSs. A and B are observational equivalent $(A \approx B)$ if $\Sigma_{OBS}^A = \Sigma_{OBS}^B$ and there exists a relation $R \subseteq S^A \times S^B$ satisfying*

1. *$s_{in}^A R s_{in}^B$.*
2. *(a) $\forall s \in S^A, \exists s' \in S^B$ s.t. sRs'.*
   (b) $\forall s' \in S^B, \exists s \in S^A$ s.t. sRs'.
3. *(a) $\forall s_1 \in S^A, s_1' \in S^B$: if $s_1 R s_1'$, $e \in (\Sigma_{OBS}^A)$ and $s_1 \xrightarrow{e} s_2$ then $\exists \sigma_1, \sigma_2 \in (\Sigma_{INT}^B)*$ such that $s_1' \xrightarrow{\sigma_1 e \sigma_2} s_2'$, and $s_2 R s_2'$.*
   (b) $\forall s_1 \in S^A, s_1' \in S^B$: if $s_1 R s_1'$, $e \in (\Sigma_{OBS}^A)$ and $s_1' \xrightarrow{e} s_2'$ then $\exists \sigma_1, \sigma_2 \in (\Sigma_{INT}^A)*$ such that $s_1 \xrightarrow{\sigma_1 e \sigma_2} s_2$, and $s_2 R s_2'$.

The two RTSs of Fig. 6(a) are observational equivalent, because every observable sequence of one of them can be executed in the other. Figures 6(b)-(c) depict examples of non-observationally equivalent systems.

3.2   I/O Compatibility of Reactive Systems

A formal description of the conditions needed for having a correct dialogue between two RTSs is given in this section. We call this set of conditions *I/O compatibility*. The properties of the I/O compatibility can be stated in natural language:

(a) *Safeness: if system A can produce an output event, then B must be prepared to accept the event.*
(b) *Liveness: if system A is blocked waiting for a synchronization with B, then B must produce an output event in a finite period of time.*

Two RTSs are *structurally I/O-compatible* if they share the observational set of events, in a way that they can be connected.

Definition 11 (Structural I/O Compatibility). *Let $A = (S^A, \Sigma^A, T^A, s_{in}^A)$ and $B = (S^B, \Sigma^B, T^B, s_{in}^B)$ be two RTSs. A and B are structurally I/O compatible if $\Sigma_I^A = \Sigma_O^B$, $\Sigma_O^A = \Sigma_I^B$, $\Sigma^A \cap \Sigma_{INT}^B = \emptyset$ and $\Sigma^B \cap \Sigma_{INT}^A = \emptyset$.*

The following definition gives a concise formalization of the conditions needed for characterizing the correct interaction of two RTSs:

Definition 12 (I/O Compatibility). *Let $A = (S^A, \Sigma^A, T^A, s_{in}^A)$ and $B = (S^B, \Sigma^B, T^B, s_{in}^B)$ be two structurally I/O compatible RTSs. A and B are I/O compatible, denoted by $A \rightleftharpoons B$, if A and B are livelock-free and there exists a relation $R \subseteq S^A \times S^B$ such that:*

1. $s_{in}^A R s_{in}^B$.
2. Receptiveness:
    (a) If $s_1 R s_1'$, $e \in \Sigma_O^A$ and $s_1 \xrightarrow{e} s_2$ then $\mathsf{En}(s_1', e)$ and $\forall s_1' \xrightarrow{e} s_2' : s_2 R s_2'$.
    (b) If $s_1 R s_1'$, $e \in \Sigma_O^B$ and $s_1' \xrightarrow{e} s_2'$ then $\mathsf{En}(s_1, e)$ and $\forall s_1 \xrightarrow{e} s_2 : s_2 R s_2'$.
3. Internal Progress:
    (a) If $s_1 R s_1'$, $e \in \Sigma_{INT}^A$ and $s_1 \xrightarrow{e} s_2$ then $s_2 R s_1'$.
    (b) If $s_1 R s_1'$, $e \in \Sigma_{INT}^B$ and $s_1' \xrightarrow{e} s_2'$ then $s_1 R s_2'$.
4. Deadlock-freeness:
    (a) If $s_1 R s_1'$ and $\{e \mid \mathsf{En}(s_1, e)\} \subseteq \Sigma_I^A$ then $\{e \mid \mathsf{En}(s_1', e)\} \not\subseteq \Sigma_I^B$.
    (b) If $s_1 R s_1'$ and $\{e \mid \mathsf{En}(s_1', e)\} \subseteq \Sigma_I^B$ then $\{e \mid \mathsf{En}(s_1, e)\} \not\subseteq \Sigma_I^A$.

Let us consider the examples of Fig. 6. In Fig. 6(a), the receptiveness condition fails and therefore X and Y are not I/O compatible. However, the RTSs of Fig. 6(b) are I/O compatible. Finally, Fig. 6(c) presents an example of violation of the deadlock-freeness condition.

Condition 4 has a strong impact on the behavior of the system. It guarantees that the communication between A and B has no deadlocks (see theorem 3).

Lemma 1. *Let A, B be two RTSs such that $A \rightleftharpoons B$, let R be an I/O compatible relation between A and B and let $A \times B = (S, \Sigma, T, s_{in})$ be the synchronous product of A and B. Then, $\langle s, s' \rangle \in S \Rightarrow sRs'$*

Theorem 1 (Safeness). *Let A, B be two RTSs such that $A \rightleftharpoons B$, and a trace $\sigma \in L(A \times B)$ of their synchronous product such that $s_{in} \xrightarrow{\sigma} \langle s, s' \rangle$. If A can fire an output event in s, then the same event is enabled in state s' of B.*

Theorem 2 (Absence of Livelocks). *Let A, B be two RTSs such that $A \rightleftharpoons B$, and let $A \times B$ be the synchronous product of A and B. Then, $A \times B$ is livelock-free.*

The I/O compatibility relation represents implicitly a *liveness property*, stated in the following theorem:

Theorem 3 (Liveness). *Let A, B be two RTSs such that $A \rightleftharpoons B$, and a trace $\sigma \in L(A \times B)$ of their synchronous product such that $s_{in} \xrightarrow{\sigma} \langle s, s' \rangle$. If only input events of A are enabled in s, then there exists some trace $\langle s, s' \rangle \xrightarrow{\sigma'} \langle s, s'' \rangle$ such that some of the input events of A enabled in s are also enabled in s'' as output events of B.*

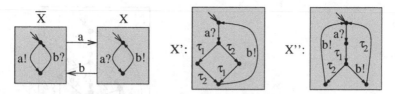

Fig. 7. Relation between I/O compatibility and observational equivalence

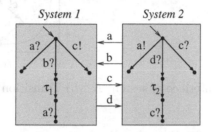

Fig. 8. Two I/O compatible systems that are not input-proper

3.3   A Sufficient Condition for I/O Compatibility

A sufficient condition for having I/O compatibility between two reactive systems can be obtained when combining the notions of observational equivalence and input-properness:

Theorem 4. *Let* $A = (S^A, \Sigma^A, T^A, s_{in}^A)$, $B = (S^B, \Sigma^B, T^B, s_{in}^B)$ *be two livelock-free RTSs with* $\Sigma_I^A = \Sigma_O^B$ *and* $\Sigma_O^A = \Sigma_I^B$. *If* A *and* B *are input proper and* $A \approx B$, *then* $A \rightleftharpoons B$.

When considering a system A and some I/O compatible system B, any transformation of B preserving both input-properness and observational equivalence will lead to another I/O compatible system:

Theorem 5. *Let* $A = (S^A, \Sigma^A, T^A, s_{in}^A)$, $B = (S^B, \Sigma^B, T^B, s_{in}^B)$ *and* $C = (S^C, \Sigma^C, T^C, s_{in}^C)$ *be three RTSs. If* $A \rightleftharpoons B$, $B \approx C$, $\Sigma_I^B = \Sigma_I^C$, $\Sigma_O^B = \Sigma_O^C$ *and* C *is input-proper then* $A \rightleftharpoons C$.

Figure 7 shows an example of application of Theorem 5. The transformation of X which leads to X' is the insertion of the internal events τ_1 and τ_2. It preserves both observational equivalence and input-properness, and then, $\overline{X}$ and X' can safely interact.

Finally, it must be noted that I/O compatibility does not require input-properness, as shown in Fig. 8. This occurs when the non-input-proper situations are not reachable by the interaction of the two systems. For the sake of simplicity, only input-proper systems will be considered along this paper.

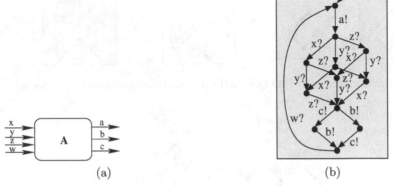

(a)   (b)

Fig. 9. (a) Interface of system A, (b) Transition System model

3.4   Realizations of a Reactive System

In this section, it is of interest to characterize when the specification of a reactive system is correctly realized by a given implementation. For this purpose, two RTSs representing specification's and implementation's behavior are compared. The I/O compatibility can be used to determine when a pair ⟨specification, implementation⟩ represents a correct realization: for specification A, the system $\overline{A}$ represents a model of the environment where a possible implementation B must correctly interact.

Definition 13 (I/O Preserving Realization). *Let A and B be two RTSs, A representing the specification of a reactive system. B realizes A ($A \models B$) iff $\overline{A} \rightleftharpoons B$.*

Let us illustrate the concept with the example of system A, specified in Fig. 9. It observes events x, y, z and w, and generates events a, b and c (Fig. 9(a)). The behavior of such system is specified with the RTS of Fig. 9(b). Figure 10 depicts the RTSs of four possible realizations of system A.

The reactive transition system 10(a) violates the input-proper property and can cause a malfunction in the entire system: if the realization of the internal event λ takes a long delay, 10(a) is imposing that after event a has been generated, the environment must wait before generating the events x, y and z. Therefore, if implementation 10(a) was used, the system(s) in the environment responsible of generating events x, y and z must be re-synthesized. However, the insertion of λ in 10(b) leads to an input-proper RTS. Sometimes it is necessary to insert internal events in the specification, in order to fulfill some implementability conditions (see Sect. 8).

The reactive transition system 10(c) is a correct realization of system A, because it represents a modification of the specification 9(b), where the concurrency of the output events b and c is reduced: the environment will observe 10(c)'s

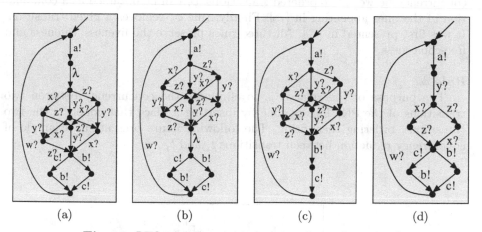

(a)   (b)   (c)   (d)

Fig. 10. RTS of different implementations of system A

events in a more restricted (but still expected) order. The transition system 10(d) represents an erroneous realization of system A: it is restricting the way input events must be received from the environment.

4   Synthesis of Reactive Systems

The action of synthesis can be defined as the process of combining transformations that preserve certain properties. In this section we are interested in transformations applied to a reactive system that preserve the I/O compatibility.

Highly concurrent systems suffer from the well-known *state explosion problem*: the set of states of a system can be exponentially large with respect to its set of events. Therefore, when dealing with large concurrent systems, statebased models like transition systems are not suitable for its representation. On the contrary, event-based models like Petri nets circumvent this problem by representing the system as a set of causality relations between the events. In this section we use the Petri net model as the formal model for specifying a system.

A kit of synthesis rules is presented in this section. It is based on the application of Petri net transformations over a RPN. The kit of transformations is defined in Sect. 4.1. Section 4.2 presents those transformations that preserve the I/O compatibility.

4.1   Kit of PN Transformations

Three rules are presented for modifying the structure of a FCLSPN. The rule ϕ_r is used for sequencing two concurrent transitions. It was first defined in [2]. Here a reduced version is presented. Rule ϕ_i does the opposite: it increases the concurrency between two ordered transitions. ϕ_i can be obtained as a combination of the ones appearing in [18]. Finally, rule ϕ_e removes a given transition. It was first presented in [15]. All three rules preserve the liveness, safeness and free-choiceness.

Rule ϕ_r

The purpose of the rule ϕ_r is to eliminate the concurrency between two transitions of the PN. This is done by inserting a place that connects the two transitions, ordering their firing. The following figure presents an example of concurrency reduction between transitions t_i and t_j.

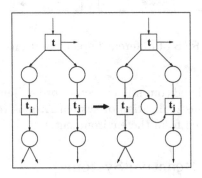

The formal definition of the rule is:

Let $N = (P, T, F, M_0)$, $N' = (P', T, F', M_0')$ be two FCLSPNs, and transitions $t_i, t_j \in T$. Then, $\phi_r(N, t_i, t_j) = N'$ if:

Conditions on N:

1. $\{t\} = {}^\bullet({}^\bullet t_i) = {}^\bullet({}^\bullet t_j)$
2. ${}^\bullet t_i = \{p_i\} \wedge |p_i^\bullet| = 1$
3. ${}^\bullet t_j = \{p_j\} \wedge |p_j^\bullet| = 1$
4. $M_0(p_i) = M_0(p_j)$

Conditions on N':

1. $P' = P \cup \{p\}$
2. $F' = F \cup \{(t_i, p), (p, t_j)\}$
3. $M_0' = M_0 \cup \{p \leftarrow 0\}$

Rule ϕ_i

Inversely to rule ϕ_r, rule ϕ_i removes the causality relation between two ordered transitions, making them concurrent. The following figure presents an example of increase of concurrency between transitions t_i and t_j.

The formal definition of the rule is:

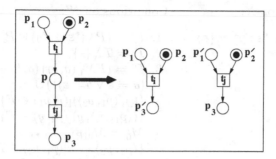

Let $N = (P, T, F, M_0)$, $N' = (P', T', F', M'_0)$ be two FCLSPNs, and transitions $t_i, t_j \in T$. In the following definition, places p'_k represent new places originated from places either in ${}^\bullet t_i$ $(k = i)$ or in $t^\bullet_j$ $(k = j)$. Then, $\phi_i(N, t_i, t_j) = N'$ if:

Conditions on N:

1. $\{(t_i, p), (p, t_j)\} \subseteq F$
2. $|{}^\bullet p| = |p^\bullet| = 1$
3. $\forall q \in {}^\bullet t_i : |q^\bullet| = 1$
4. $t_i \notin (t^\bullet_j)^\bullet$

Conditions on N':

1. $P' = (P \setminus \{p\}) \cup \{p'_i | p_i \in {}^\bullet t_i\} \cup \{p'_j | p_j \in t^\bullet_j\}$
2. $F' = (F \setminus \{(t_i, p), (p, t_j)\}) \cup$
   $\{(y, p'_i) | (y, p_i) \in F\} \cup \{(p'_i, t_j) | (p_i, t_i) \in F\} \cup$
   $\{(p'_j, y) | (p_j, y) \in F\} \cup \{(t_i, p'_j) | (t_j, p_j) \in F\} \cup$
   $\{(y, p'_j) | (y, p_j) \in F \land y \neq t_j\}$
3. $M'_0 = M_0 \cup \{p'_k \leftarrow M_0(p_k) + M_0(p)\}$

Rule ϕ_e

The rule ϕ_e eliminates a transition from the PN. The following figure presents an example of elimination of transition ε.

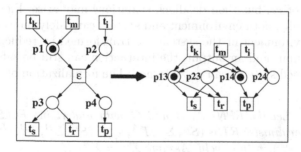

The formal definition of the rule is:

Let $N = (P, T, F, M_0)$, $N' = (P', T', F', M'_0)$ be two FCLSPNs, transition $\varepsilon \in T$ and let $P_\varepsilon = ({}^\bullet \varepsilon) \times (\varepsilon^\bullet)$. Then, $\phi_e(N, \varepsilon) = N'$ if:

Conditions on N:

1. $\forall p : p \in {}^{\bullet}\varepsilon : p^{\bullet} = \{\varepsilon\}$

Conditions on N':

1. $P' = (P \setminus ({}^{\bullet}\varepsilon \cup \varepsilon^{\bullet})) \cup P_{\varepsilon}$
2. $T' = T \setminus \{\varepsilon\}$
3. $F' = (F \setminus \{(a,b) \,|\, (a,b) \in F \wedge$
   $(a = \varepsilon \vee b = \varepsilon)\}) \cup$
   $\{(y, \langle p_1, p_2 \rangle) | (y, p_1) \in F\} \cup$
   $\{(\langle p_1, p_2 \rangle, y) | (p_2, y) \in F\}$
4. $M_0' = M_0|_{P \setminus ({}^{\bullet}\varepsilon \cup \varepsilon^{\bullet})} \cup$
   $\{\langle p_1, p_2 \rangle \leftarrow k | \langle p_1, p_2 \rangle \in P_{\varepsilon} \wedge$
   $k = M_0(p_1) + M_0(p_2)\}$

where $f|_C$ represents the restriction of function f to set C.

4.2   I/O Compatible Transformations over RPN

The I/O compatible relation operator ($\rightleftharpoons$) can be lifted to RPNs:

Definition 14 (I/O Compatible Relation over RPN). *Let A and B be two RPNs with corresponding RTSs RTS(A) and RTS(B). $A \rightleftharpoons B$ if RTS$(A) \rightleftharpoons$ RTS(B).*

For each transformation of the kit presented in Sect. 4.1, the following sections enumerate those situations where the transformation can be applied to the underlying FCLSPN of a deterministic RPN while preserving the I/O compatible relation.

I/O Compatible Application of ϕ_r

The application of $\phi_r(A, e_1, e_2)$ preserves $\rightleftharpoons$ when neither e_1 nor e_2 is an input transition. In fact, it is sufficient to require only e_2 to be non-input for the preservation of $\rightleftharpoons$, but then deadlock situations may arise. Figure 11 exemplifies this: initially, both environment and system can safely interact. Moreover, if either the environment or the system are transformed by reducing concurrency between an input and an output, the interaction can still be safe. However, the two transformed systems can not interact. The formalization of the transformation is:

Theorem 6. *Let the RPNs A, B and C with underlying FCLSPN and corresponding deterministic RTSs $(S^A, \Sigma^A, T^A, s_{in}^A)$, $(S^B, \Sigma^B, T^B, s_{in}^B)$ and $(S^C, \Sigma^C, T^C, s_{in}^C)$, respectively. Assume $\Sigma^C = \Sigma^B$. If*

1. $A \rightleftharpoons B$
2. $\phi_r(B, e_1, e_2) = C$, with $e_1, e_2 \notin \Sigma_I^B$

then $A \rightleftharpoons C$.

Proof. See appendix.

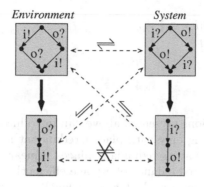

Fig. 11. Different possibilities for reducing concurrency

I/O Compatible Application of ϕ_i

The application of ϕ_i preserves $\rightleftharpoons$ when:

1. at least one of the transitions involved is internal, and
2. no internal transition is inserted as trigger of an input transition

The purpose is to avoid the increase of concurrency between two observable transitions, in order to forbid the generation of unexpected traces either on the environment's or on the system's part. More formally:

Theorem 7. *Let the RPNs A, B and C with underlying FCLSPN and corresponding deterministic RTSs $(S^A, \Sigma^A, T^A, s_{in}^A)$, $(S^B, \Sigma^B, T^B, s_{in}^B)$ and $(S^C, \Sigma^C, T^C, s_{in}^C)$. Assume $\Sigma^C = \Sigma^B$. If*

1. *$A \rightleftharpoons B$*
2. *$\phi_i(B, e_1, e_2) = C$, with either $e_1 \in \Sigma_{INT}^B$ or $e_2 \in \Sigma_{INT}^B$*
3. *B is input-proper*
4. *$\forall e \in (e_2^\bullet)^\bullet : e \notin \Sigma_I^B$*

then $A \rightleftharpoons C$.

Proof. See appendix.

I/O Compatible Application of ϕ_e

Rule ϕ_e only preserves $\rightleftharpoons$ when applied to internal transitions.

Theorem 8. *Let the RPNs A, B and C with underlying FCLSPN and corresponding deterministic RTSs $(S^A, \Sigma^A, T^A, s_{in}^A)$, $(S^B, \Sigma^B, T^B, s_{in}^B)$ and $(S^C, \Sigma^C, T^C, s_{in}^C)$. Assume $\Sigma_{OBS}^C = \Sigma_{OBS}^B$. If*

1. $A \rightleftharpoons B$
2. $\phi_i(B, e) = C$, with $e \in \Sigma_{INT}^B$
3. B is input-proper

then $A \rightleftharpoons C$.

Proof. See appendix.

The transformations presented above can introduce redundant places in the target net. For dealing only with place-irredundant nets, the kit is augmented with a rule for eliminating redundant places. Linear programming techniques exist that decide the redundancy of a place efficiently [23]. Moreover, each time a transformation is performed, it can be locally determined the potential redundant places, and therefore the redundancy checking is only applied to a few places.

Section 9 depicts an example of application of the rules presented in this section. The kit of rules is there used for synthesizing an asynchronous circuit.

5   Asynchronous Circuits

Asynchronous circuits are digital circuits that react to the changes of their input signals according to the functionality of the gates of the circuit [3]. Synchronous circuits can be considered as a particular case of asynchronous circuits in which some specific design rules and operation mode are imposed.

In general, any arbitrary interconnection of gates is considered an asynchronous circuit. The synthesis problem consists in generating a proper interconnection of gates that commits a correct interaction with the environment according to some specified protocol.

This section presents the models used in this work for the specification and synthesis of asynchronous circuits.

5.1   State Graphs

Asynchronous circuits can be modeled with a RTS, where the events represent changes in the value of the system signals. The VME Bus Controller example in Fig. 12 will be used for illustrating the concepts. The interface is depicted in Fig. 12(a), where the circuit controls data transfers between the bus and the device. Figure 12(b) shows the timing diagram corresponding to the read cycle.

Binary Interpretation A transition labeled as x_i+ (x_i-) denotes a rising (falling) of signal x_i: it switches from 0 to 1 (1 to 0). Figure 13 shows the RTS specifying the behavior of the bus controller for the read cycle. Each state of an asynchronous circuit can be encoded with a *binary vector*, representing the signal values on that state. The set of encoded states are *consistently encoded* if no state can have an enabled rising (falling) transition $a+$ ($a-$) when the value of the signal in that state is 1 (0) (see Sect. 6 for a formal

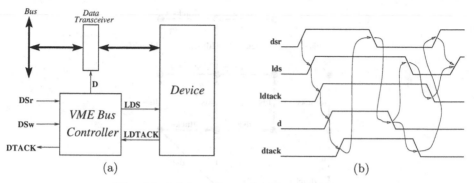

Fig. 12. (a) Interface, (b) Timing diagram

definition of consistency). Correspondingly, for each signal of a RTS representing an asynchronous circuit, a partition of the states of the RTS can be done by separating the states where the signal has value one, from those where the signal has value zero. This partition can only be done when the underlying asynchronous circuit is consistently encoded. Figure 14(a) shows the partition induced by considering signal lds in the RTS of Fig. 13. Each transition from LDS=0 to LDS=1 is labeled with lds+ and each transition from LDS=1 to LDS=0 is labeled with lds−. A binary vector can be assigned to each state if such partition is done for each signal of the system. The encoded transition system is called *State Graph.*

Definition 15 (State Graph). *A State Graph (SG) is a* 3-tuple $A = (A', \mathcal{X}, \lambda)$ *where*

- *$A' = (S, \Sigma, T, s_{in})$ is a RTS*
- *$\mathcal{X}$ is the set of signals partitioned into inputs ($\mathcal{I}$), observable outputs ($\mathcal{O}bs$) and internal outputs ($\mathcal{I}nt$), and $\Sigma = \mathcal{X} \times \{+, -\} \cup \{\varepsilon\}$, where all transitions not labeled with the silent event (ε) are interpreted as signal changes*
- *$\lambda : S \to \mathbb{B}^{|\mathcal{X}|}$ is the state encoding function*

Figure 14(b) shows the SG of the bus controller.

We will denote by $\lambda_x(s)$ the value of signal x is state s. The following definitions relate signal transitions with states. They will be used later to derive Boolean equations from an SG.

Definition 16 (Excitation and Quiescent Regions). *The positive and negative excitation regions (ER) of signal $x \in X$, denoted by* ER$(x+)$ *and* ER$(x-)$, *are the sets of states in which $x+$ and $x-$ are enabled, respectively, i.e.*

$$\mathsf{ER}(x+) = \{s \in S \mid \exists s \xrightarrow{x+} s' \in T\}$$
$$\mathsf{ER}(x-) = \{s \in S \mid \exists s \xrightarrow{x-} s' \in T\}$$

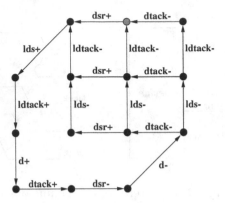

Fig. 13. Transition System specifying the bus controller

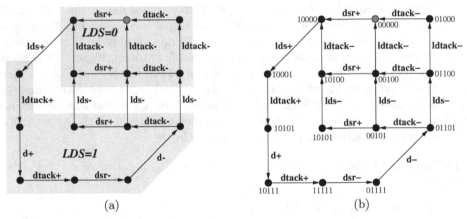

(a)   (b)

Fig. 14. (a) Partition induced by signal lds, (b) State graph of the read cycle. States are encoded with the vector (dsr,dtack,ldtack,d,lds)

The *positive* and *negative* quiescent regions (QR) *of signal* $x \in X$, *denoted by* QR($x+$) *and* QR($x-$) *are the sets of states in which* x *has the same value, 1 or 0, and is stable, i.e.*

$$\text{QR}(x+) = \{s \in S \mid \lambda_x(s) = 1 \ \wedge \ s \notin \text{ER}(x-)\}$$
$$\text{QR}(x-) = \{s \in S \mid \lambda_x(s) = 0 \ \wedge \ s \notin \text{ER}(x+)\}$$

5.2 Signal Transition Graphs

As in the case of the RTS model, events of a RPN can represent signal changes of an asynchronous circuit. The model is called *Signal Transition Graph* [22].

Definition 17. *A Signal Transition Graph (STG) is a 3-tuple* $(N, \mathcal{X}, \Lambda)$, *where*

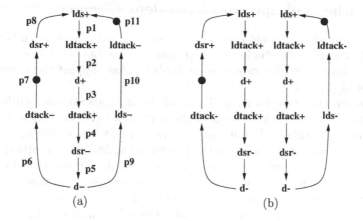

Fig. 15. (a) Signal Transition Graph specifying the bus controller, (b) State machine cover

- $N = (P, T, F, M_0)$ *is a Petri net*
- $\mathcal{X}$ *and* Σ *are defined as in the case of the SG.*
- $\Lambda : T \to \Sigma$

Adjacency Transition x_{i*} is said to be a *predecessor* of x_{j*} if there exists a feasible sequence $x_{i*}\sigma x_{j*}$ that does not include other transitions of signal x. Conversely, x_{j*} is a *successor* of x_{i*}. We will also say that the pair (x_{i*}, x_{j*}) is *adjacent*. The set of predecessors (successors) of x_{i*} is denoted by $prev(x_{i*})$ ($next(x_{i*})$).

An example of STG specifying the bus controller is shown in Fig. 15. Places of the STG with only one predecessor and one successor transition, are not shown graphically as convention. The RTS associated to an STG is an SG. The SG associated to the STG of Fig. 15 is shown in 14(b).

Concurrency Relations Concurrency relations can be naturally extended to nodes and signals in a STG. The *Signal concurrency relation* between a node $u_j \in P \cup T$ and a signal $x \in \Lambda$ is defined as a binary relation $\mathcal{SCR}$, such that $(u_j, x) \in \mathcal{SCR} \Leftrightarrow \exists x_{i*} : (u_j, x_{i*}) \in \mathcal{CR}$.

The class of STGs with underlying IO-RPN are defined. This class will be used in Sects. 8 and 9.

Definition 18. *An IO-STG is an STG with underlying IO-RPN.*

Figure 15(a) shows an example of IO-STG.

6   Synthesis of Speed-Independent Circuits

Speed-independent (SI) circuits is the class of asynchronous circuits that work correctly regardless the delay of their components (gates). Currently, there is a robust theory, design flow and some tools [8] that support the automatic synthesis of SI circuits.

However, one of the major problems of the methods used for synthesis is that they require an explicit knowledge of the state graph. Highly concurrent systems often suffer the state explosion problem and, for this reason, the size of the state graph can be a limiting factor for the practical application of synthesis methods.

In this section, some basic concepts on the logic synthesis of SI circuits are presented. We refer the reader to [8] for a deeper theory on how to implement SI circuits. In this paper, we will focus on the main step in synthesis: the derivation of the Boolean equations that model the behavior of the digital circuit.

In Sects. 7, 8 and 9, a synthesis framework that only uses structural methods on STGs to derive the Boolean equations will be provided. By only using structural methods, the computational complexity associated to the state explosion problem is avoided.

6.1   Implementability as a Logic Circuit

This section defines a set of properties that guarantee the existence of a SI circuit. They are defined at the level of SG, but can be easily extended to STGs. Instead of giving new definitions for STGs, we will simply consider that a property holds in an STG if it holds in its underlying SG.

The properties are the following: boundedness, consistency, complete state coding and output persistency.

Boundedness. A necessary condition for the implementability of a logic circuit is that the set of states is finite. Although this seems to be an obvious assumptions at the level of SG, it is not so obvious at the level of STG, since an STG with a finite structure may have a infinite number of reachable markings.

Consistency. As shown in Fig. 14, each signal x_i defines a partition of the set of states. The consistency of an SG refers to the fact that the events x_i+ and x_i- are the only ones that cross these two parts according to their meaning: switching from 0 to 1 and from 1 to 0, respectively. This is captured by the definition of consistent SG.

Definition 19 (Consistent SG). *An SG is consistent if for each transition* $s \xrightarrow{e} s'$ *the following conditions hold:*

- *if* $e = x_i+$*, then* $\lambda_i(s) = 0$ *and* $\lambda_i(s') = 1$*;*
- *if* $e = x_i-$*, then* $\lambda_i(s) = 1$ *and* $\lambda_i(s') = 0$*;*
- *in all other cases,* $\lambda_i(s) = \lambda_i(s')$*.*

where λ_i *denotes the component of the encoding vector corresponding to signal* x_i*.*

Complete State Coding This property can be illustrated with the example of Fig. 14(b), in which there are two states with the same binary encoding: 10101. Moreover, the states with the same binary code are behaviorally different. This fact implies that the system does not have enough information to determine how to react by only looking at the value of its signals.

The distinguishability of behavior by state encoding is captured by the following two definitions.

Definition 20 (Unique State Coding). *[6] An SG satisfies the* Unique State Coding (*USC*) *condition if every state in S is assigned a unique binary code. Formally, USC means that the state encoding function, λ, is injective.*

Definition 21 (Complete State Coding). *[6] An SG satisfies the* Complete State Coding (*CSC*) *condition if for every pair of states $s, s' \in S$ having the same binary code the sets of enabled non-input signals are the same.*

Both properties are sufficient to derive the Boolean equations for the synthesized circuit. However, given that only the behavior of the non-input signals must be implemented, encoding ambiguities for input signals are acceptable.

Output Persistency This property is required to ensure that the discrete behavior modeled with SG has a robust correspondence with the real analog behavior of electronic circuits.

Definition 22 (Disabling). *An event x is said to* disable *another event y if there is a transition $s \xrightarrow{x} s'$ such that y is enabled s but not in s'.*

Definition 23 (Output Persistency). *An SG is said to be output persistent if for any pair of events x and y such that x disables y, both x and y are input signals.*

In logic circuits, disabling an event may result in non-deterministic behavior. Imagine, for example, that an AND gate has both inputs at 1 and the output at 0. In this situation, the gate starts the process to switch the signal towards 1 in a continuous way. If one of the inputs would fall to 0 during this process, the output would interrupt this process and start moving the signal to 0, thus producing an observable glitch. To avoid these situations, that may produce unexpected events, the property of output persistency is required.

6.2   Boolean Equations

This sections describes the procedure to derive Boolean next-state functions for output signals from an SG. The procedure defines an incompletely specified function from which a gate implementation can be obtained after Boolean minimization.

An incompletely specified n-variable *logic function* is a mapping $F : \{0, 1\}^n \rightarrow \{0, 1, -\}$. Each element $\{0, 1\}^n$ is called a *vertex* or binary code.

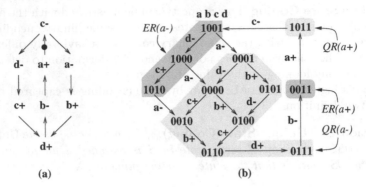

Fig. 16. Example *abcd*: (a) Signal Transition Graph, (b) State Graph

A *literal* is either a variable x_i or its complement $\overline{x_i}$. A *cube* c is a set of literals, such that if $x_i \in c$ then $\overline{x_i} \notin c$ and vice versa. Cubes are also represented as an element $\{0, 1, -\}^n$, in which value 0 denotes a complemented variable $\overline{x_i}$, value 1 denotes a variable x_i, and $-$ indicates the fact that the variable is not in the cube. A *cover* is a set of implicants which contains the on-set and does not intersect with the off-set (on-set and off-set are defined below).

Given a specification with n signals, the derivation of an incompletely specified function F^x for each output signal x and for each $v \in \mathbb{B}^n$ can be formalized as follows:

$$F^x(v) = \begin{cases} 1 & \text{if } \exists\, s \in \mathsf{ER}(x+) \cup \mathsf{QR}(x+) : \lambda(s) = v \\ 0 & \text{if } \exists\, s \in \mathsf{ER}(x-) \cup \mathsf{QR}(x-) : \lambda(s) = v \\ - & \text{if } \not\exists\, s \in S : \lambda(s) = v \end{cases}$$

The set of vertices in which $F^x(v) = 1$ is called the *on-set* of signal x ($\mathsf{ON}(x)$), whereas the codes in which $F^x(v) = 0$ is called the *off-set* of x (($\mathsf{OFF}(x)$).

The previous definition is ambiguous when there are two states, s_1 and s_2, for which $\lambda(s_1) = \lambda(s_2) = v$, $s_1 \in \mathsf{ER}(x+) \cup \mathsf{QR}(x+)$ and $s_2 \in \mathsf{ER}(x-) \cup \mathsf{QR}(x-)$. This ambiguity is precisely what the CSC property avoids, and this is why CSC is a necessary condition for implementability.

Figure 16 depicts an STG and the corresponding SG. Figure 17 shows the Karnaugh maps of the incompletely specified functions for signals a and d.

For the incompletely specified functions, other circuit architectures can also be derived [8].

7   Structural Approximations for Logic Synthesis

Most of the existing frameworks for the synthesis of SI circuits from STG specifications rely on the explicit computation of the underlying SG to check implementability conditions and generate Boolean equations [7] (see Sect. 6). Unfortunately, the underlying SG of a highly concurrent system can be exponential in

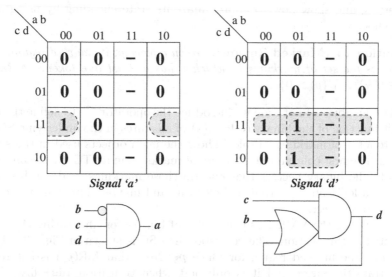

Fig. 17. Complex gate implementation for the *abcd* example

the size of the STG specification, which leads to the well-known state explosion problem.

This section describes how to link structure and behavior with polynomial complexity if the STG specification has an underlying FCLSPN, thus avoiding exponentiality. The method is based on the analysis of the concurrency relations and state machine decompositions of the STG. States are never generated, instead their encoding vectors are approximated by logic functions with various degrees of accuracy. State explosion is avoided by using a conservative approximation of the state graph, but providing computationally efficient algorithms that generate minimized implementations comparable to those generated by state-based tools. This section presents a general overview of results developed elsewhere. We refer to [19, 20] for further details and proofs.

7.1 Structural Approximations of the State Graph

Initially we introduce a technique to approximate the underlying SG of an STG. This approximation will be used to check the USC conditions in Sect. 7.2, and to provide approximate logic functions for the logic synthesis process in Sect. 7.4. The structural approximation of the SG is based on a simple concept: characterize the states in which a given place is marked, this is the so called *marked region*. The goal is to derive a simple logic function to approximate each marked region.

Marked Regions and Cover Cubes A set of markings, named *marked region*, define the correspondence between the basic structural elements of an STG and its underlying SG. We will introduce this basic region, derive its fundamental properties, and show how to approximate its state encoding by using a single cover cube.

Definition 24 (Marked Region). *Given a place p, its marked region, denoted $MR(p)$, is the set of markings in which p has at least one token, i.e. $MR(p) = \{M \in [M_0\rangle : M(p) > 0\}$.*

With an abuse of notation we introduce the operator $\frown$ to define the characteristic function of the binary codes $\lambda(s)$ of all states in the underlying SG equivalent to a set of markings. Table 1 show the main objects used in the synthesis process. The first column refers to sets of markings in a STG, the second column refers to the binary vectors that encode those markings, and the last column refers to a logic function that includes all (and maybe more) binary vectors in the previous object.

We will use the VME Bus Controller of Fig. 15 for illustrating the concepts presented in this section. The corresponding SG is shown in Fig. 19. Figure 19 highlights the marked region for place p_8. Note that $MR(p_8)$ is entered after firing transition dsr+ and it is only left when transition lds+ fires. The binary codes corresponding to those markings are characterized by $\widehat{MR}(p_8) = \{10101, 10100, 10000\}$.

A cover cube for a MR must cover the binary encoding of all markings in the region. To make the approximation more accurate this cube should be the smallest among possible (with the largest number of literals) [13]. Any signal that does not change in the MR of a place (is not concurrent to the place) is represented by a corresponding literal in a cover cube. The value of this signal can be determined by an interleave relation. *Interleaving* characterizes the position of a node with respect to a pair of adjacent signal transitions.

Definition 25 (Interleave Relation). *The* Interleave Relation *is a binary relation $\mathcal{IR}$ between nodes in $P \cup T$ and pairs of adjacent transitions x_{i*} and x_{j*} of a signal x such that, a node u_j is interleaved with (x_{i*}, x_{j*}) $(u_j \in \mathcal{IR}(x_{i*}, x_{j*}))$, if there exists a simple path from x_{i*} to x_{j*} containing u_j.*

Proposition 1 (Consistent Place Interleaving). *In a consistent STG if a place p is interleaved with a pair of adjacent transitions (x_i+, x_i-) then p cannot be interleaved with any other adjacent pair (x_j-, x_j+) and vice versa.*

Proposition 1 guarantees that if a place p is non-concurrent to signal x and interleaved between two adjacent transitions (x_i+, x_i-) $((x_i-, x_i+))$, then all binary codes in $\widehat{MR}(p)$ have value 1 (0) for signal x. This property is the basis to approximating markings by computing a single *cover cube* for each marked region. We can see in Fig. 15(a) that place p_8 is interleaved between dtack- and dtack+ because the path dtack- $\rightarrow$ dsr+ $\rightarrow$ lds+ $\rightarrow$ ldtack+ $\rightarrow$ d+ $\rightarrow$ dtack+ exists. Furthermore, all markings in $MR(p_8)$ are encoded with dtack $= 0$.

Proposition 2 (Boolean Approximation for a MR [13]). *The cover cube C_p for $MR(p)$ is the smallest cube that covers $\widehat{MR}(p)$ such that for every signal x:*

Table 1. Main objects used during structural synthesis

Marking	Binary code	Cover
$MR(p_i)$	$\widehat{MR}(p_i)$	$cv(p_i)$
$ER(x_{i*})$	$\widehat{ER}(x_{i*})$	$cv_{ER}(x_{i*})$
$QR(x_{i*})$	$\widehat{QR}(x_{i*})$	$cv_{QR}(x_{i*})$

1. *if x non-concurrent to p $((p,x) \notin \mathcal{SCR})$ then*

$$C_p^x = \begin{cases} 0 \ if \ b = 0 \ in \ \widehat{MR}(p), \\ 1 \ if \ b = 1 \ in \ \widehat{MR}(p). \end{cases}$$

2. *if x concurrent to p then $C_p^x = -$;*

where C^x indicates the x-th component bit of C.

Given a place p, a literal must appear in the cube for any non-concurrent signal x to p $((x,p) \notin \mathcal{SCR})$. For any arbitrary place p the value of the signal x in a corresponding cover cube is determined by checking if p is interleaved between pairs of adjacent rise-fall or fall-rise transitions. Property 1 guarantees that the value of signal x is the same for all the adjacent pairs for which p is in $\mathcal{IR}$. Therefore, the *Interleave Relation* gives a polynomial-time algorithm (for free-choice STG) to determine the value of literal C_p^x:

$$C_p^x = \begin{cases} 1 \ if \ \exists \ adjacent \ (x_i+, x_i-) : p \in \mathcal{IR}(x_i+, x_i-) \ , \\ 0 \ if \ \exists \ adjacent \ (x_i-, x_i+) : p \in \mathcal{IR}(x_i-, x_i+) \ , \\ - \ otherwise \ . \end{cases}$$

Figure 18 shows the state machines for the STG depicted in Fig. 15. All places in this STG are implicit, thus only place names are shown. Every place in each state machine is annotated with its corresponding cover cube. Going back to Fig. 19 we can analyze cube $C_{p_8} = $ 10-0-. $MR(p_8)$ is entered after firing dsr+ thus the positive value for this signal. Neither dtack nor d fire inside $MR(p_8)$ thus their value remains constant. The correct value to assign is 0 since p_8 is interleaved between a negative and a positive transition for both signals. Finally, both ldtack and lds fire inside $MR(p_8)$ thus their value is undefined.

7.2   State Coding Verification

The USC property [6] requires that no pair of different markings share the same binary encoding. Checking this definition requires the generation of the under-lying SG of the STG and all pairwise intersection of states checked to be empty.

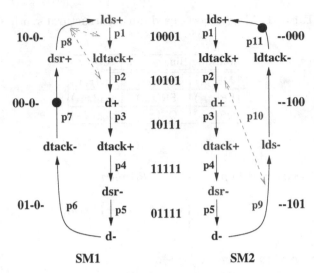

Fig. 18. SM-cover and cover cubes for the STGin Fig. 15. Cubes encoded with the vector (dsr,dtack,ldtack,d,lds)

Detection of Coding Conflicts The objective of this section is to provide an efficient algorithm to check USC. The methodology is based on the approximate analysis of the underlying SG. Further details and proofs can be found in [20].

In addition to marked regions, the structure of the STG is applied by using a set of SM that completely covers the places in the STG. Such set is called an SM-cover, and any place in the STG should be included in at least one component of the cover. Given the MR for all places and a SM-cover SMC, the following theorem provides *sufficient conditions* to detect USC conflicts.

Theorem 9 (Sufficient Conditions for USC). *Given a SM-cover SMC, a STG with underlying FCLSPN satisfies the USC property if*

$$\forall\, SM \,\in\, SMC, \forall p_i, p_j \text{ covered by } SM, \; i \neq j \Rightarrow \widehat{MR}(p_i) \cdot \widehat{MR}(p_j) = \emptyset$$

Theorem 9 cannot be considered a *necessary* conditions due to the existence of state machines that contain more than one token. Assume the existence of one SM with two places p_1 and p_2 that contain a token in the same marking M. Then $M \in MR(p_1)$, $M \in MR(p_2)$, and therefore $\widehat{MR}(p_1) \cdot \widehat{MR}(p_2) \neq \emptyset$. If it can be guaranteed that all SM in the SM-cover satisfy the *one-token-per-SM* restriction, then Theorem 9 is also a necessary condition.

Theorem 9 can be relaxed to obtain a conservative rule to check USC violations by using cover cubes. Intersections between marked regions $\widehat{MR}(p_i) \cdot \widehat{MR}(p_j) \neq \emptyset$ can be detected as intersections between cover cubes, i.e. $\mathcal{C}_{p_i} \cdot \mathcal{C}_{p_j} \neq \emptyset$. However, due to the conservative nature of the approximation, all non-empty intersections between cover cubes ($\mathcal{C}_{p_i} \cdot \mathcal{C}_{p_j} \neq \emptyset$) must be considered as a potential USC violation.

Figure 18 shows the state machines for the STG depicted in Fig. 15 annotated with its coding conflicts detected following Theorem 9. SM1 contains two coding conflicts, one between p_8 and p_1 and a second between p_8 and p_2. SM2 contains one coding conflict between p_2 and p_9. Conservatively we have to assume that the STG does not satisfy the USC property.

7.3   Refinement of the State Graph Approximations

Many cube intersections detected by Theorem 9 could be *fake* due to the lossy approximation provided by cover cubes. Fake coding conflicts degrade the quality of the results obtained by the methodology. An STG satisfying the USC property may have to be encoded due to the existence of fake conflicts, and the number of state signals inserted in a STG not satisfying the USC property may be increased due to the additional conflicts to be solved.

Figure 19 shows a case of fake coding conflict. The states included in the marked regions $MR(p_1)$, $MR(p_2)$, and $MR(p_8)$ are shadowed. The states covered by the cover cube $\mathcal{C}_{p_8}$ are grouped in the dotted region. $\mathcal{C}_{p_8}$ clearly overestimates $MR(p_8)$ because it also includes $MR(p_1)$, even though $\widehat{MR}(p_1) \cdot \widehat{MR}(p_8) = \emptyset$. On the other side, $\mathcal{C}_{p_8}$ also includes $MR(p_2)$, but this is a real conflict because $\widehat{MR}(p_2) \cdot \widehat{MR}(p_8) \neq \emptyset$.

Fake conflicts can be detected and eliminated if the information provided by the SM-cover is correlated. Even though the process will remain conservative, experimental results demonstrate that most fake coding conflicts can be eliminated with little effort.

Fake conflict elimination relies on the observation that the information in a SM is complemented by the rest of elements in the SM-cover. A place may be covered by several SMs, containing coding conflicts in all or in none of them. In that case the information provided by the SM-cover is congruent. However, if a place has no coding conflicts in one state machine SM_i but has conflicts in a second state machine SM_j, we can infer from SM_i that the cover cubes in SM_j are overestimated.

Theorem 10 (Relaxed Sufficient Conditions for USC). *Given a SM-cover SMC, a STG with underlying FCLSPN satisfies the USC property if*

$$\forall p_i \in P :$$
$$\exists SM \in SMC \wedge p_i \in SM : [\forall p_j \in SM, \ i \neq j \ \Rightarrow \ \widehat{MR}(p_i) \cdot \widehat{MR}(p_j) = \emptyset]$$

This result can be exported to the particular case in which the binary codes in the marked regions are approximated by cover cubes. Note that the empty intersection between pairs of places $\mathcal{C}_{p_i} \cdot \mathcal{C}_{p_j} = \emptyset$ is only a sufficient condition to determine that no coding conflict exists.

From the previous theorem we can deduce that places without coding conflicts in one SM can be used to eliminate fake conflicts in some other SM. The fake conflict elimination can be applied in a single step by applying Theorem 10, thus eliminating the coding conflicts for a place p_i in all state machines that

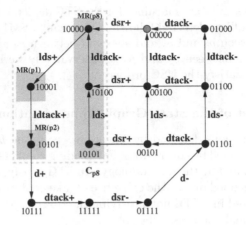

Fig. 19. Real and fake USC coding conflicts

cover that place if a SM covering p_i exists such that the cover cube of no other place in SM interests with $\mathcal{C}_{p_i}$.

This technique can be extended by considering that for a given pair of places $\widehat{\mathrm{MR}}(p_i) \cdot \widehat{\mathrm{MR}}(p_j) = \emptyset$ (even though $\mathcal{C}_{p_i} \cdot \mathcal{C}_{p_j} \neq \emptyset$) if we have previously eliminated all the coding conflicts for place p_i or p_j.

The analysis of the coding conflicts in Fig. 18 shows that the coding conflict between places p_1 and p_8 at SM_1 is a *fake conflict*. Note that p_1 has a conflict at SM_1 but has no conflicts at SM_2, therefore the cover cube for p_8 is overestimating $\mathrm{MR}(p_8)$.

Given that a single cube approach is clearly insufficient we introduce a new approximation function for places, named *cover function* $\mathrm{cv}(p)$. Initially, cover functions will take the same value than cover cubes, i.e. $\mathrm{cv}(p) = \mathcal{C}_p$. However, the value of the cover function can be iteratively refined every time a fake conflict is eliminated.

Formally, the *refinement* of the cover function $\mathrm{cv}(p)$ by a SM is an algorithm that builds a new cover as a result of restricting $\mathrm{cv}(p)$ to the sum of the cover functions of any place $p_i \in$ SM that is concurrent to p; that is:

$$\mathrm{cv}(p) \leftarrow \sum_{p_i \in \mathrm{SM}\,:\,(p,p_i)\in\mathcal{CR}} \mathrm{cv}(p_i) \cdot \mathrm{cv}(p)$$

Place p_8 can be refined by using the information provided by SM_2. Places p_9, p_{10} and p_{11} are concurrent to p_8, so $\mathrm{cv}(p_8)$ should be refined as

$$\mathrm{cv}(p_8) \leftarrow \mathrm{cv}(p_8) \cdot [\mathrm{cv}(p_9) + \mathrm{cv}(p_{10}) + \mathrm{cv}(p_{11})] = 10\text{--}00 + 1010\text{--}$$

Therefore $\mathrm{cv}(p_8)$ no longer includes $\mathrm{MR}(p_1)$ and the fake conflict is no longer present.

7.4   Structural Approximations for Signal Regions

The structural generation of Boolean equations for SI circuits that satisfy the synthesis conditions described in Sect. 6 requires conservative approximations of the signal regions $\mathrm{ER}(x_{i*})$ and $\mathrm{QR}(x_{i*})$.

We define $\mathrm{cv_{ER}}(x_{i*})$ to be a cover function for the binary codes in $\widehat{\mathrm{ER}}(x_{i*})$; and $\mathrm{cv_{QR}}(x_{i*})$ a cover function for the binary codes in $\widehat{\mathrm{QR}}(x_{i*})$. This section will show how to build both $\mathrm{cv_{ER}}(x_{i*})$ and $\mathrm{cv_{QR}}(x_{i*})$ by using the cover functions of individual places previously introduced in Sect. 7.1.

An *excitation region* $\mathrm{ER}(x_{i*})$ corresponds to the set of markings in which transition x_{i*} is enabled. Let $\mathrm{EPS}(x_{i*})$ be the set of places in the pre-set of x_{i*}. $\mathrm{ER}(x_{i*})$ is easily expressed as the intersection of marked regions for places in $\mathrm{EPS}(x_{i*})$:

$$\mathrm{ER}(x_{i*}) = \bigcap_{p \in \mathrm{EPS}(x_{i*})} \mathrm{MR}(p)$$

Hence the binary codes in $\widehat{\mathrm{ER}}(x_{i*})$ are covered by a function $\mathrm{cv_{ER}}(x_{i*})$ created as the intersection of the cover functions of places in $\mathrm{EPS}(x_{i*})$:

$$\mathrm{cv_{ER}}(x_{i*}) = \bigcap_{p \in \mathrm{EPS}(x_{i*})} \mathrm{cv}(p)$$

A marking is in the *quiescent region* $\mathrm{QR}(x_{i*})$ if it can be reached by firing a feasible sequence $\sigma_1 x_{i*} \sigma_2$ such that no successor transition $x_{j*} \in next(x_{i*})$ is enabled in any prefix of σ_2. In the previous sections we have shown that feasible sequences can be associated to simple paths in the PN. Hence we can informally state that the cover functions of all places interleaved between adjacent transitions x_{i*} and $x_{j*} \in next(x_{i*})$ can be used to build $\mathrm{cv_{QR}}(x_{i*})$.

Hence, the domain of places required to approximate $\mathrm{QR}(x_{i*})$ should include all places interleaved between x_{i*} and some transition $x_{j*} \in next(x_{i*})$. This domain is denoted $\mathrm{QPS}(x_{i*})$, i.e.

$$\mathrm{QPS}(x_{i*}) = \{p \mid \exists x_{j*} \in next(x_{i*}) : p \in \mathcal{IR}(x_{i*}, x_{j*}) \wedge p \notin {}^\bullet x_{j*}\}$$

The binary codes in $\widehat{\mathrm{QR}}(x_{i*})$ are covered by a function $\mathrm{cv_{QR}}(x_{i*})$ created as the union of the cover functions of places in $\mathrm{QPS}(x_{i*})$:

$$\mathrm{cv_{QR}}(x_{i*}) = \bigcup_{p \in \mathrm{QPS}(x_{i*})} \mathrm{cv}(p)$$

As an example we will build the $\mathrm{cv_{ER}}$ and $\mathrm{cv_{QR}}$ (see Fig. 20) approximations for signal dtack in Fig. 15. $\mathrm{ER}(\text{dtack+})$ and $\mathrm{cv_{ER}}(\text{dtack-})$ is build as $\mathrm{cv_{ER}}(\text{dtack+}) = \mathrm{cv}(p_3) = 10111$, and $\mathrm{cv_{ER}}(\text{dtack-}) = \mathrm{cv}(p_6) = 01\text{-}0\text{-}$ The covers $\mathrm{cv_{QR}}(\text{dtack+})$ and $\mathrm{cv_{QR}}(\text{dtack-})$ are approximated by the sets of places $\mathrm{QPS}(\text{dtack+}) = \{p_4, p_5\}$, and $\mathrm{QPS}(\text{dtack-}) = \{p_7, p_8, p_1, p_2\}$

The resulting covers are: $\mathrm{cv_{QR}}(\text{dtack+}) = \mathrm{cv}(p_4) + \mathrm{cv}(p_5) = \text{-}1111$, and $\mathrm{cv_{QR}}(\text{dtack-}) = \mathrm{cv}(p_7) + \mathrm{cv}(p_8) + \mathrm{cv}(p_1) + \mathrm{cv}(p_2) = 00\text{-}0\text{-} + 10\text{-}00 + 1010\text{-} + 10\text{-}01$.

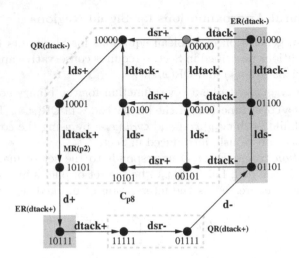

Fig. 20. Regions for output signal `dtack`

Starting from this region approximations logic minimization can be applied in order to derive the final logic equations that implement signal `dtack` (see Sect. 6). The on-set of the signal is build as:

$$\mathsf{ON}(\texttt{dtack}) = \mathsf{cv}_{\mathsf{ER}}(\texttt{dtack+}) \cup \mathsf{cv}_{\mathsf{QR}}(\texttt{dtack+}) = 1\text{-}111 + \text{-}1111$$

and the off-set as:

$$\mathsf{OFF}(\texttt{dtack}) = \mathsf{cv}_{\mathsf{ER}}(\texttt{dtack-}) \cup \mathsf{cv}_{\mathsf{QR}}(\texttt{dtack-}) =$$
$$= 0\text{-}\text{-}0\text{-} + 10\text{-}00 + 1010\text{-} + 10\text{-}01$$

In case we choose to implement the on-set of the function we will obtain a circuit equivalent to the following logic equation:

$$\texttt{dtack} = (\texttt{dsr} + \texttt{dtack}) \cdot \overline{\texttt{ldtack}} \cdot \overline{\texttt{d}} \cdot \overline{\texttt{lds}}$$

8   State Encoding

One of the conditions for the SI implementation of an specification is to have a correct encoding (see Sect. 6). This section presents a technique for transforming an specification in order to force a correct encoding. The method presented guarantees a solution for the encoding problem and tackles the problem in linear complexity for the class of FCLSPNs. The technique is based on the insertion of a signal for each place of the STG, mimicking the token flow on that place.

8.1   A Structural Encoding Transformation

The method presented has been inspired on previous work for the direct synthesis of circuits from Petri nets. One of the relevant techniques was proposed in [24], where a set of cells that mimic the token flow of the Petri net was abutted for producing a circuit structure isomorphic to the original net. This type of cells, called David cells, were initially proposed in [9].

Figure 21 depicts a very simple example on how these cells can be abutted to build a distributor that controls the propagation of activities along a ring. The behavior of one of the cells in the distributor can be summarized by the following sequence of events:

$$\cdots \;\rightarrow\; \underbrace{c_{i-1}-}_{\substack{i\text{-th cell} \\ \text{excitation}}} \;\rightarrow\; \underbrace{a_i+ \;\rightarrow\; \hat{a}_i-}_{i\text{-th cell setting}} \;\rightarrow\;$$

$$\rightarrow \; \underbrace{\hat{a}_{i-1}+ \;\rightarrow\; a_{i-1}- \;\rightarrow\; c_{i-1}+}_{(i-1)\text{-th cell resetting}} \;\rightarrow\; \underbrace{c_i-}_{\substack{(i+1)\text{-th cell} \\ \text{excitation}}} \;\rightarrow\; \cdots$$

In [24], each cell was used to represent the behavior of one of the transitions of the Petri net. The approach presented in this paper is based on encoding the system by inserting a new signal for each place with a behavior similar to a David cell.

Let $S = \langle\langle P, T, F, M_0\rangle, \mathcal{X}, \Lambda\rangle$ be an STG with underlying FCLSPN. The Structural Encoding of S derives the STG $Enc(S)$ in which a new internal signal sp has been created for each place $p \in P$, and the transformation rule described in Fig. 22 has been applied to each transition $t \in T$. The new transitions appearing in $Enc(S)$, labelled with $sp*$, will be called *E-transitions* along the paper.

Proposition 3 ([5]). *$Enc(S)$ is FCLSPN. It is consistent and observational equivalent to S, and has the USC property.*

Proposition 3 guarantees the fulfillment of the main properties needed in the synthesis framework presented in Sect. 7.

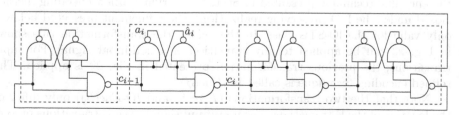

Fig. 21. Distributor built from David cells [12]

1. Create the *silent* transitions ε_1 and ε_2.

2. For each place $p \in {}^\bullet t$, create a new transition with label $sp-$ and insert new arcs and places for creating a simple path from ε_1 to ε_2, passing through $sp-$.

3. For each place $p \in t^\bullet$, substitute the arc (t, p) by the arc (ε_2, p), create a new transition labeled as $sp+$ and insert new arcs and places for creating a simple path from t to ε_1, passing through $sp+$.

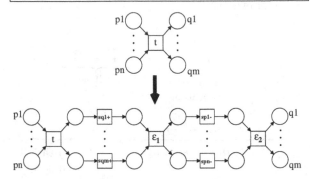

Fig. 22. Transformation rule for each transition $t \in T$

8.2 I/O-Preserving Structural Encoding Transformation

The previous section presents a method for transforming a specification by the insertion of internal signals. In order to reason about the correctness of the method, i.e. whether the transformed specification can safely interact in its assumed environment, we can check if the transformed specification and the environment (the mirror of the initial specification) are I/O compatible. This is analog to checking whether the transformed specification realizes the initial specification (see Definition 13).

However, the encoding technique presented in the previous section does not guarantee to preserve the I/O preserving realization with respect to the initial STG, because condition 2(a) of the I/O preserving realization can be violated in the interaction between S and $Enc(S)$. In this section we present a refinement of the encoding technique presented in Sect. 8.1, deriving a new encoding method closed under the I/O preserving realization. The refinement presented below is only valid for the IO-STG class. In that class, the transformation rule shown in Fig. 23 can be applied to any transition of a non-input signal. For input transitions, the previous transformation presented in Fig. 22 is applied. This refined encoding technique is called $IO\text{-}Enc(S)$.

Note that the two transformations ($Enc(S)$ and $IO\text{-}Enc(S)$) only differ on the location of the E-transitions. For non-input signals, the E-transitions precede the transformed transition.

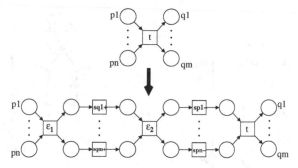

Fig. 23. Transformation rule for non-input signals to preserve the I/O interface

The proofs for preserving free-choiceness, liveness, safeness, consistency, observational equivalence and ensuring USC are similar to those presented in the previous section when applied to the class of IO-STGs [5]. It is important to note that this new technique is closed under the I/O preserving realization:

Proposition 4. *Let S be an IO-STG with underlying FCLSPN and SG(S) input-proper. Then $S \models$ IO-Enc(S).*

Proof. The encoding preserves both the input-properness and the observational equivalence. Theorem 5 guarantees the I/O preserving realization between S and IO-Enc(S)

Moreover, the *IO-Enc* technique ensures to fulfill the speed-independent conditions for implementability.

Proposition 5 ([5]). *Let S be a consistent and output-persistent IO-STG with underlying FCLSPN. Then IO-Enc(S) fulfills the speed-independent conditions.*

Figure 24 depicts an example of the I/O preserving structural encoding.

9   Automatic Synthesis of Asynchronous Circuits

Some of the structural techniques presented in previous sections can be combined to derive a structural framework for the synthesis of asynchronous circuits. The main properties of the framework presented below are:

1. It always guarantees to find a solution.
2. Only polynomial algorithms are involved.
3. The quality of the solutions obtained is comparable to the methods that require an explicit enumeration of the state space.

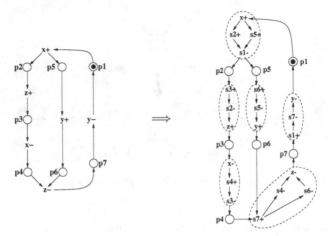

Fig. 24. Structural encoding (x is input and y and z are outputs)

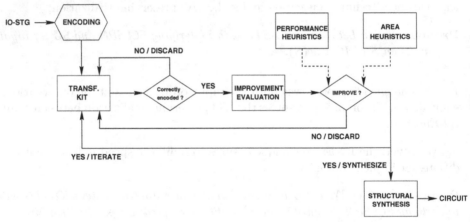

Fig. 25. Framework for the structural synthesis of asynchronous circuits

9.1 Design Flow

This section presents an automatic methodology that starts from an IO-STG specifying the control part of a circuit and ends up with a set of Boolean equations both implementing the specification and fulfilling the SI conditions. The core of the framework is the idea of Petri net transformation: in the initial step, we apply the encoding transformation of Sect. 8.2 which ensures to have a correct encoding and preserves the I/O preserving realization with respect to the specification. Then, Petri net transformations (those from the kit presented in Sect. 4.1) are applied iteratively in order to improve the quality of the solution. Figure 25 presents the framework.

A natural strategy that can be mapped in the framework of Fig. 25 is to try to eliminate the maximum number of signals inserted in the encoding step

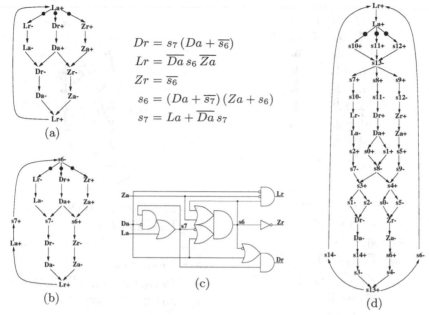

$$Dr = s_7 \left(Da + \overline{s_6}\right)$$
$$Lr = \overline{Da}\, s_6\, \overline{Za}$$
$$Zr = \overline{s_6}$$
$$s_6 = \left(Da + \overline{s_7}\right)\left(Za + s_6\right)$$
$$s_7 = La + \overline{Da}\, s_7$$

Fig. 26. Case study: adfast

while preserving a correct encoding. Once no more signals can be deleted, start to apply iteratively any transformation from the kit until an admissible solution is obtained. In this way, an exploration of the solution space is performed iteratively, by modifying locally causal dependencies and concurrency relations between the events of the system.

9.2 An Example

Let us present an example of application of the framework presented in the previous section. The example corresponds to a specification of an *analog-to-digital fast converter* with three input signals (Da, La and Za) and three output signals (Dr, Lr and Zr). The specification is shown in Fig. 26(a). This IO-STG does not have a correct encoding. Figure 26(d) shows the IO-STG obtained after applying the structural encoding rules. The new internal signals $s_0...s_{14}$ correspond to the 15 places in the initial specification.

From the IO-STG in Fig. 26(d), a sequence of eliminations of internal signals have been applied, always preserving a correct encoding. The resulting IO-STG and the corresponding circuit are shown in Fig. 27(a), where only five extra signals remain. A typical way of measuring the quality of the circuit is to estimate the area needed for its implementation; a good heuristic is the number of literals in the Boolean equations. In the case of the IO-STG in Fig. 27(a), this number is 35.

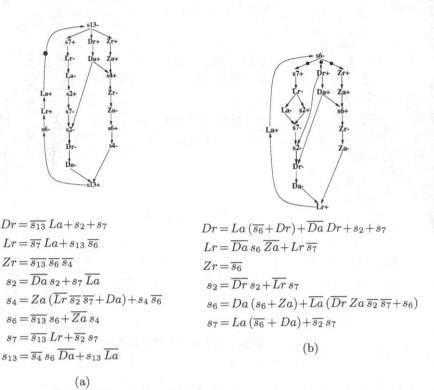

$$Dr = \overline{s_{13}}\, La + s_2 + s_7$$
$$Lr = \overline{s_7}\, La + s_{13}\, \overline{s_6}$$
$$Zr = \overline{s_{13}}\, \overline{s_6}\, \overline{s_4}$$
$$s_2 = \overline{Da}\, s_2 + s_7\, \overline{La}$$
$$s_4 = Za\,(\overline{Lr}\, \overline{s_2}\, \overline{s_7} + Da) + s_4\, \overline{s_6}$$
$$s_6 = \overline{s_{13}}\, s_6 + \overline{Za}\, s_4$$
$$s_7 = \overline{s_{13}}\, Lr + \overline{s_2}\, s_7$$
$$s_{13} = \overline{s_4}\, s_6\, \overline{Da} + s_{13}\, \overline{La}$$

(a)

$$Dr = La\,(\overline{s_6} + Dr) + \overline{Da}\, Dr + s_2 + s_7$$
$$Lr = \overline{Da}\, s_6\, \overline{Za} + Lr\, \overline{s_7}$$
$$Zr = \overline{s_6}$$
$$s_2 = \overline{Dr}\, s_2 + \overline{Lr}\, s_7$$
$$s_6 = Da\,(s_6 + Za) + \overline{La}\,(\overline{Dr}\, Za\, \overline{s_2}\, \overline{s_7} + s_6)$$
$$s_7 = La\,(\overline{s_6} + Da) + \overline{s_2}\, s_7$$

(b)

Fig. 27. Intermediate solutions in the design space

Figure 27(b) reports one of the intermediate solutions (31 literals) explored after obtaining the solution in Fig. 27(a). The transformations of increase and reduction of concurrency have also been applied in the exploration: note in Figs. 27(a)-(b) the position of transition s_6- with respect to transitions $Lr+$ and $La+$. Figures 26(b) and 26(c) depict the final IO-STG, the Boolean equations and the circuit after applying the transformations and doing logic synthesis. This solution, which has been obtained mechanically, is identical to the one generated by the CAD tool petrify [7].

9.3   Experimental Results

The synthesis strategy described above has been applied to a set of benchmarks. Initially, none of the specifications had the CSC property. The results are reported in Table 2.

The columns labeled with *"petrify"* indicate the characteristics of the circuit obtained by the tool petrify. The number of inserted signals to solve CSC conflicts and the number of literals of the Boolean equations are reported.

The columns labeled with *"struct. encoding"* report the characteristics of the circuit after having applied first the encoding technique and then the elimination

Table 2. Experimental results

benchmark	states	petrify		struct. encoding		str. enc. + optim.	
		#CSC	lit.	#CSC	lit.	#CSC	lit.
adfast	44	2	14	5	35	2	14
vme-fc-read	14	1	8	2	14	1	8
nak-pa	56	1	18	3	35	1	18
m-read1	1882	1	38	2	43	1	40
m-read2	8932	8	68	13	95	10	70
duplicator	20	2	18	5	36	3	18
mmu	174	3	29	7	53	3	34
seq8	36	4	47	22	147	4	47

of internal signals. It is interesting to observe that the number of signals required to solve encoding conflicts when using the "local" encoding provided by the places is significantly larger than the number of signals required when "global" encoding methods are used.

The results of the final circuit, after having explored the design space with the set of transformations, are reported in the columns labeled *"str. enc. + optim."*. It can be observed that the quality of the solution can be highly improved by playing with the concurrency of the internal signals. In many cases, the obtained result is the same as the one generated by petrify. In other cases, the results are similar but with more internal signals than the ones inserted by petrify(e.g. master-read2, duplicator). This corroborates a known fact that states that the reduction of internal signals does not always implies an improvement on the quality of the circuit.

10 Conclusions

Asynchronous circuits are just a subclass of reactive systems in which the state is represented by a vector of Boolean variables. However, the underlying theory to synthesize asynchronous circuits can be extended to other classes of systems.

This work has defined I/O compatibility as a key concept to characterize the correct interaction between system and environment. The rationale behind this concept is the following: one can always decide when an output or internal action must be performed as long as this does not break the correct interaction with the environment. This freedom to choose *"when"*, opens a design space that can be explored to obtain the most appropriate realization for a behavior.

Typically, synthesis must consider a trade-off between complexity and performance. By sequentializing concurrent behaviors, one can derive systems with less complexity, at the expense of reducing the performance. By allowing more concurrent behaviors, the system's cost may increase, but possibly providing

more performance. It is mainly the degree of concurrency what opens the space
of solutions and drives the strategies to explore it.

Acknowledgments

This work has been partially funded by the Ministry of Science and Technology
of Spain under contract TIC 2001-2476, ACiD-WG (IST-1999-29119) and a grant
by Intel Corporation.

References

[1] A. Arnold. *Finite Transition Systems*. Prentice Hall, 1994. 112
[2] G. Berthelot. Checking Properties of Nets Using Transformations. In G. Rozen-
     berg, editor, *Advances in Petri Nets 1985*, volume 222 of *Lecture Notes in Com-
     puter Science*, pages 19–40. Springer-Verlag, 1986. 121
[3] Janusz A. Brzozowski and Carl-Johan H. Seger. *Asynchronous Circuits*. Springer-
     Verlag, 1995. 126
[4] J. Carmona and J. Cortadella. Input/Output Compatibility of Reactive Systems.
     In *Fourth International Conference on Formal Methods in Computer-Aided Design
     (FMCAD)*, Portland, Oregon, USA, November 2002. Springer-Verlag. 116
[5] J. Carmona, J. Cortadella, and E. Pastor. A structural encoding technique for the
     synthesis of asynchronous circuits. In *Int. Conf. on Application of Concurrency
     to System Design*, June 2001. 141, 143
[6] Tam-Anh Chu. *Synthesis of Self-Timed VLSI Circuits from Graph-Theoretic Spec-
     ifications*. PhD thesis, MIT Laboratory for Computer Science, June 1987. 115,
     131, 135
[7] J. Cortadella, M. Kishinevsky, A. Kondratyev, L. Lavagno, and A. Yakovlev.
     Petrify: a tool for manipulating concurrent specifications and synthesis of asyn-
     chronous controllers. *IEICE Transactions on Information and Systems*, E80-
     D(3):315–325, March 1997. 132, 146
[8] J. Cortadella, M. Kishinevsky, A. Kondratyev, L. Lavagno, and A. Yakovlev. *Logic
     synthesis of asynchronous controllers and interfaces*. Springer-Verlag, 2002. to
     appear. 130, 132
[9] René David. Modular design of asynchronous circuits defined by graphs. *IEEE
     Transactions on Computers*, 26(8):727–737, August 1977. 141
[10] M. Hack. *Analysis of production schemata by Petri nets*. M.s. thesis, MIT, Febru-
     ary 1972. 115
[11] D. Harel and A. Pnueli. On the development of reactive systems. In Krzystof R.
     Apt, editor, *Logic and Model of Concurrent Systems*, volume 13 of *NATO ASI*,
     pages 477–498. Springer-Verlag, October 1984. 112
[12] Michael Kishinevsky, Alex Kondratyev, Alexander Taubin, and Victor Var-
     shavsky. *Concurrent Hardware: The Theory and Practice of Self-Timed Design*.
     Series in Parallel Computing. John Wiley & Sons, 1994. 141
[13] Alex Kondratyev and Alexander Taubin. Verification of speed-independent cir-
     cuits by stg unfoldings. In *Proc. International Symposium on Advanced Research
     in Asynchronous Circuits and Systems*, pages 64–75, November 1994. 134
[14] A. Kovalyov and J. Esparza. A polynomial algorithm to compute the concurrency
     relation of free-choice signal transition graphs. In *Proceedings of the International
     Workshop on Discrete Event Systems, WODES'96*, pages 1–6, August 1996. 115

[15] A. V. Kovalyov. On complete reducibility of some classes of Petri nets. In *Proceedings of the 11th International Conference on Applications and Theory of Petri Nets*, pages 352–366, Paris, June 1990. 122

[16] Nancy A. Lynch and Mark R. Tuttle. An introduction to input/output automata. In *CWI-Quarterly*, volume 2, pages 219–246, Centrum voor Wiskunde en Informatica, Amsterdam, The Netherlands, September 1989. 108

[17] R. Milner. *A Calculus for Communicating Processes*, volume 92 of *Lecture Notes in Computer Science*. Springer Verlag, 1980. 111, 116, 151

[18] Tadao Murata. Petri nets: Properties, analysis and applications. *Proceedings of the IEEE*, 77(4):541–574, April 1989. 109, 114, 122

[19] Enric Pastor. *Structural Methods for the Synthesis of Asynchronous Circuits from Signal Transition Graphs*. PhD thesis, Universitat Politècnia de Catalunya, February 1996. 133

[20] Enric Pastor, Jordi Cortadella, Alex Kondratyev, and Oriol Roig. Structural methods for the synthesis of speed-independent circuits. *IEEE Transactions on Computer-Aided Design*, 17(11):1108–1129, November 1998. 133, 136

[21] C. A. Petri. *Kommunikation mit Automaten*. PhD thesis, Bonn, Institut für Instrumentelle Mathematik, 1962. (technical report Schriften des IIM Nr. 3). 114

[22] L. Y. Rosenblum and A. V. Yakovlev. Signal graphs: from self-timed to timed ones. In *Proceedings of International Workshop on Timed Petri Nets*, pages 199–207, Torino, Italy, July 1985. IEEE Computer Society Press. 128

[23] Manuel Silva, Enrique Teruel, and José Manuel Colom. Linear algebraic and linear programming techniques for the analysis of place/transition net systems. *Lecture Notes in Computer Science: Lectures on Petri Nets I: Basic Models*, 1491:309–373, 1998. 126

[24] Victor I. Varshavsky, editor. *Self-Timed Control of Concurrent Processes: The Design of Aperiodic Logical Circuits in Computers and Discrete Systems*. Kluwer Academic Publishers, Dordrecht, The Netherlands, 1990. 141

A   Proofs of Section 4

Proof. (of Theorem 6) (*Case* $\{e_1, e_2\} = \{o_1, o_2\} \subseteq \Sigma_O^B$. *The other cases are similar*).

Let R' be the relation between A and B. Define R as:

$$\forall s \in S^A, s'' \in S^B, s' \in S^C : sR's'' \wedge s_{in}^B \xrightarrow{\sigma} s'' \wedge s_{in}^C \xrightarrow{\sigma} s' \Leftrightarrow sRs'$$

- **Condition 1:** taking $\sigma = \lambda$ implies $s_{in}^A R s_{in}^C$.
- **Condition 2(a):** let $s_1 R s_1'$, and suppose $s_1 \xrightarrow{e} s_2$ with $e \in \Sigma_O^A$. Figure 28 depicts the situation. Condition 2(a) of R' ensures that there exists $s_2'' \in S^B$ s.t. $s_1'' \xrightarrow{e} s_2''$ and $s_2 R' s_2''$. By definition of R, σ is enabled both in s_{in}^B and s_{in}^C. Then, each place marked by the sequence σ in B is also marked in C, because the flow relation of B is included in the flow relation of C. Given that the initial marking of B is preserved in C and the set of predecessor places for each input event is also preserved, implies that e is also enabled in s_1'. The definition of R makes each s_2' s.t. $s_1' \xrightarrow{e} s_2'$ to be related with s_2.

- **Condition 2(b):** let $s_1 R s'_1$, and suppose $s'_1 \xrightarrow{e} s'_2$ with $e \in \Sigma_O^C$. The set of predecessor places of e in B is a subset or is equal to the one in C. Moreover, given that both the initial marking of B is identical to the one in C, and each place marked by the sequence σ in B is also marked in C, implies that e is also enabled in s''_1, i.e. $s''_1 \xrightarrow{e} s''_2$. Condition 2(b) of R' ensures that $\mathsf{En}(s_1, e)$, and each s_2 such that $s_1 \xrightarrow{e} s_2$ is related by R' with s''_2. The definition of R induces that each such s_2 is related with s'_2.
- **Condition 3(a):** let $s_1 R s'_1$, and suppose $s_1 \xrightarrow{e} s_2$ with $e \in \Sigma_{INT}^A$, then a similar reasoning of Condition 2(a) can be applied.
- **Condition 3(b):** let $s_1 R s'_1$, and suppose $s'_1 \xrightarrow{e} s'_2$ with $e \in \Sigma_{INT}^C$, then a similar reasoning of Condition 2(b) can be applied.
- **Condition 4(a):** let $s_1 R s'_1$, and suppose $\{e|\mathsf{En}(s_1, e)\} \subseteq \Sigma_I^A$. Condition 4(b) of R' ensures that $\{e|\mathsf{En}(s''_1, e)\} \not\subseteq \Sigma_I^B$. If the non-input event enabled in s''_1 is different from o_2, then similar reasoning of previous cases guarantees that the event is also enabled in s'_1. If the event enabled in s''_1 is o_2 and no non-input event is enabled in s'_1, we will proof that o_2 is also enabled in s'_1. Assume the contrary: o_2 is enabled in s''_1 but no non-input event is enabled in s'_1. Applying the same reasoning of case 2(a) we can conclude that the place p such that $\{p\} = {}^\bullet o_2$ in B has a token in the marking M corresponding to state s'_1. Moreover, the liveness of C ensures that from M there is a feasible sequence δ (let δ be minimal) reaching a marking M' where o_1 is enabled. The minimality of δ, together with the fact that the new place p' added by ϕ_r between o_1 and o_2 is unmarked in M (otherwise o_2 is enabled in s'_1, because $\{p, p'\} = {}^\bullet o_2$ in C) imply that $o_2 \notin \delta$, and therefore $M'(p) = 2$, which contradicts the safeness of C.
- **Condition 4(b):** let $s_1 R s'_1$, and suppose $\{e|\mathsf{En}(s'_1, e)\} \subseteq \Sigma_I^C$, then similar reasons of the previous cases ensure that $\{e|\mathsf{En}(s''_1, e)\} \subseteq \Sigma_I^B$ and Condition 4(b) of R' ensures that $\{e|\mathsf{En}(s_1, e)\} \not\subseteq \Sigma_O^A$.

Finally, it can be proven that the language of $\mathsf{RTS}(C)$ is a subset of the language of $\mathsf{RTS}(B)$. Therefore, no infinite trace of internal events can exist in C implying that C is livelock-free. $\square$

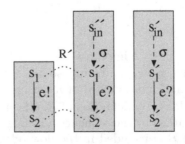

Fig. 28. Conditions 2(a) from the proof of Theorem 6

Proof. (of Theorem 7) Conditions 1-4 of transformation ϕ_i ensure to preserve both the observational equivalence and the input-properness of B. Theorem 5 induces $A \rightleftharpoons C$.   □

Proof. (of Theorem 8) If the observational languages of two deterministic systems coincide, then they are observational equivalent [17]. It can be proven that the observational language of C is the same to the one of B. Moreover, C is also input proper and therefore, applying the determinism of B and Theorem 5 implies $A \rightleftharpoons C$.   □

Decomposition in Asynchronous Circuit Design[*]

Walter Vogler[1] and Ralf Wollowski[2]

[1] Institut für Informatik, Universität Augsburg
vogler@informatik.uni-augsburg.de
[2] FB Elektro- und Informationstechnik, Universität Kaiserlautern
wollo@rhrk.uni-kl.de

Abstract. Signal Transition Graphs (STGs) are a version of Petri nets for the specification of asynchronous circuit behaviour. It has been suggested to decompose such a specification as a first step; this leads to a modular implementation, which can support circuit synthesis by possibly avoiding state explosion or allowing the use of library elements.
We present a decomposition algorithm and formally prove it correct, where an interesting aspect is the use of a bisimulation with angelic nondeterminism. In contrast to similar approaches in the literature, our algorithm is very generally applicable. We show that transition contraction – the main operation in the algorithm – can be applied with fewer restrictions than known so far. We also prove that deletion of redundant places can be used in the algorithm, which turns out to be very useful in examples.

1 Introduction

Signal Transition Graphs (STGs), see e.g. [Wen77, RY85, Chu86], are a version of Petri nets for the specification of asynchronous circuit behaviour; they are supported by the tools petrify (e.g. [CKK+97]) and CASCADE [BEW00], which in many cases can synthesize a circuit from an STG. The transitions are labelled with input or output signals;[1] the latter are thought to be controlled by the circuit, the former by its environment. In such a setting, I,O-automata [Lyn96] require that in each state each input can occur, and the same holds for the language theoretic framework of [Dil88]; in STGs though, the occurrence of an input signal in some state might not be specified, which formulates the assumption on the environment not to produce this signal.

Being Petri nets, STGs allow a causality-based specification style, and they give a compact representation of the desired behaviour since they represent concurrency explicitly. As a first step in the synthesis of a circuit corresponding

---

[*] This work was partially supported by the DFG-project 'STG-Dekomposition' Vo615/7-1 / Wo814/1-1.

[1] Usually, the labels in STGs are not signals, but rising and falling edges of signals, which for each signal are required to alternate; this is of minor importance for our theoretical development, so we abstract from this distinction for the larger part of this paper.

J. Cortadella et al. (Eds.): Concurrency and Hardware Design, LNCS 2549, pp. 152–190, 2002.
© Springer-Verlag Berlin Heidelberg 2002

to a given STG N, one usually constructs the reachability graph, where one might encounter the state explosion problem; i.e. the number r of reachable states (markings) might be too large to be handled. To avoid this, one could try to decompose the STG into components C_i; their reachability graphs taken together can be much smaller than r since r might be the product of their sizes. Even if this is not achieved, several smaller components might be easier to handle: depending on the circuit synthesis method, further steps might easily take quadratic time in the number of states, or the reachability graph of N might even be too large for the available memory space. Decomposition can also be useful independently of size considerations: there are examples where N cannot be handled by a specific synthesis method, while the C_i can; also, one may be able to split off a library element, and this is valuable in particular for arbiters, which are complicated to synthesize.

Thus, instead of synthesizing one large circuit from N, we decompose N into components C_i, synthesize a circuit from each C_i (e.g. using tools or library look-ups) and compose these circuits into one system of communicating circuits. In this paper, we only deal with the decomposition.

[Chu87a, Chu87b, KKT93] suggest decomposition methods for STGs, but these approaches can only deal with very restricted net classes. [Chu87a] only decomposes live and safe free choice nets, which cannot model controlled choices or arbitration, and makes further restrictions; e.g. each transition label is allowed only once (which makes the STG deterministic in the sense of language theory), and conflicts can only occur between input signals. The conference version [Chu87b] restricts attention even further to marked graphs, which have no conflicts at all.

The method in [Chu87a] constructs for each output signal s a component C_i that generates this signal; C_i has as inputs all signals that – according to the net structure – may directly cause s. The component is obtained from the STG N by contracting all transitions belonging to the signals that are neither input nor output signals for this component. This contraction is required to be tr-preserving (as defined in [Chu87a]), and it might be necessary to add further signals to the inputs to ensure this.

In [Chu87a], it is stated that the parallel composition of the C_i – i.e. the (modular) *implementation* – has the same language as N; in the restricted setting of [Chu87a], this is the same as having isomorphic reachability graphs. Clearly, this isomorphism is very strict and not a necessary requirement for an implementation to be correct. On the other hand, language equivalence is too weak in general, since it ignores which choices are possible during a run, and in particular it ignores deadlocks; it seems that in general some form of bisimilarity would be more suitable. The formal proofs for the correctness statement in [Chu87a] are very involved.

A similar decomposition method is described in [KKT93]; only marked graphs with only output signals are considered and the treatment is quite informal. In contrast to [Chu87a], a component can generate several output signals and different components can generate the same signal; this gives more flexibility, but additional components are needed to collect occurrences of the same signal generated by different components.

Further, rather informal, considerations of this decomposition method can be found in [BW93, Wol97]. We finally mention [KGJ96] where fork/join machines are decomposed, which are a restricted form of free choice STGs. In contrast to our setting, the decomposition is already uniquely traced out by the given fork/join structure; correctness only holds under fundamental mode conditions and is not formally proved.

In this paper, we have a fresh look at the decomposition problem. In particular, we will suggest a method where there are no restrictions on the graph-theoretic structure of the given STG N; to some degree we will even deal with arc weights greater 1 and unsafe nets, which is a bit unusual for STGs, but can be useful e.g. for modelling bounded counters. Also in one of our examples, unsafe nets turn up as intermediate steps, although all resulting components are safe; thus, it is a clear advantage that we can deal with unsafe nets. There are restrictions on the labelling, e.g. conflicts between input and output signals are not allowed; an STG violating this restriction cannot be turned into a reliable (i.e. hazard-free) digital circuit. STGs are required to be deterministic; but very importantly, we allow several transitions to have the same label.

Our method is based on [Chu87a, Chu87b], but components may generate several output signals. We start from a partition of the output signals and construct for each class of the partition a component C_i; the component has as inputs all signals that – according to the net structure – may directly cause one of its outputs. C_i is obtained from N by contracting stepwise all transitions belonging to the signals that are neither input nor output signals for this component.

As [Chu87a, BW93, Wol97], we suggest to apply mainly *secure* t-contractions, already studied in [And83], but we also allow the deletion of redundant places (see e.g. [Ber87] for an early reference). Secureness is a part of being tr-preserving in the sense of [Chu87a], but in contrast to tr-preservation in general, it is easy to check from the *local* net structure. Thus, only in our version the steps of the decomposition algorithm become efficient. Also in our approach, it might be necessary to add further input signals to a component during the stepwise contraction process; we give local graph-theoretic, i.e. easy, conditions when this is the case.

If we regard transition t as internal, i.e. as labelled with the empty word λ, then [Chu87a] shows that the tr-preserving contraction of t preserves the language. This is actually true for all secure contractions, as e.g. already indicated in [And83]. After presenting basic definitions of STGs in Section 2, we have a closer look at contractions in Section 3, also considering bisimilarity and non-secure contractions and introducing redundant places.

In Section 4, we describe our method in detail. We give a flexible description based on the notion of admissible operation which allows not only secure contractions to be used but *any* admissible operation; this notion gives structure to our correctness proof and makes it partially reusable. It is thus easier to see that also the deletion of redundant places can be used, and also non-secure contractions under certain conditions, e.g. if each transition label occurs only once as in [Chu87a]. This of course depends on our correctness criterion, which has the following important features.

- We ensure that the composition of the C_i is free of what e.g. Ebergen calls computation interference [Ebe92], where one component produces an output that is an unspecified input for another; it seems that this problem is ignored in [Chu87a, Chu87b].
- We only consider behaviour where the environment behaves as specified by the original STG N, i.e. the composition of the components might specify additional inputs, but we ignore these and any subsequent behaviour since they cannot occur if the implementation runs in an appropriate environment. The same is done e.g. in [Dil88, Ebe92], so both these features are not new – but new in the context of STG decomposition.
- We achieve both these features with a bisimulation-like correctness definition. Since we restrict ourselves in this paper to the case that N and the C_i are deterministic, bisimilarity actually coincides with language equivalence; but there are several reasons for choosing a bisimulation style: First, for future extensions to nondeterministic STGs, the additional distinctive power of bisimulation will be important. Second, although one could argue that the explicit treatment of markings in the definition of a bisimulation is not as elegant as the definition of the language, markings have to be treated anyway in order to deal with computation interference. In fact, the treatment of markings and the explicit requirements how input and output signals of one system are matched by the other system, should better clarify the notion of correctness – and this is the third reason. Fourth, the chosen style will be technically useful in our correctness proof.
  Interestingly, our proof technique is based on a kind of angelic bisimulation, where internal transition occurrences only serve to find a matching behaviour, but are not required to be matched on their own.

The main contribution of this paper is that – transferring the first and second of these features to the area of STG decomposition – we obtain a more generally applicable decomposition method with a much easier correctness proof compared to [Chu87a]. We show that also deletion of redundant places and – under certain circumstances – non-secure contractions are admissible in our approach. We present some examples for our method in Section 5; further examples as well as a supporting tool are in preparation. Additional research topics are discussed in the conclusion in Section 6. This paper is the full version of an extended abstract that can be found in the proceedings of the 22nd Conference Foundations of Software Technology and Theoretical Computer Science FSTTCS 2002.

2   Basic Notions of Signal Transition Graphs

In this section, we introduce the kind of Petri nets we study in this paper, some standard behaviour notions, and the operation of parallel composition. For general information on ordinary Petri nets, the reader is referred to e.g. [Pet81, Rei85]. A *Signal Transition Graph* or *STG* is a net that models the desired behaviour of an asynchronous circuit. Its transitions are labelled with signals from some alphabet Σ or with the empty word λ, and we distinguish between input and output signals. A transition labelled with λ represents an internal, unobservable signal, which can be an internal signal between components of a circuit. In this paper, we use λ-labelled transitions only in intermediate phases of our algorithm.

Thus, an *STG* $N = (P, T, W, l, M_N, In, Out)$ is a labelled net consisting of finite disjoint sets P of *places* and T of *transitions*, the *arc weight* $W : P \times T \cup T \times P \to \mathbb{N}_0$, the *labelling* $l : T \to In \cup Out \cup \{\lambda\}$, the *initial marking* $M_N : P \to \mathbb{N}_0$ and the disjoint sets $In \subseteq \Sigma$ and $Out \subseteq \Sigma$ of *input* and *output* signals; $\mathbb{N}_0$ denotes the natural numbers including 0. We usually use a, b, c for input and x, y, z for output signals; if $l(t) \in In$ ($l(t) \in Out$ resp.) then t is an input (an output resp.) transition, drawn as a black (a white resp.) box; if $l(t) = \lambda$, then t is an *internal* transition, drawn as a line or a box with two lines in it. When we introduce an STG N or N_1 etc., then we assume that implicitly this introduces its components P, T, W, ... or P_1, T_1, ... etc.

We say that there is an *arc* from $x \in P \cup T$ to $y \in P \cup T$ if $W(x, y) > 0$. For each $x \in P \cup T$, the *preset* of x is $^\bullet x = \{y \mid W(y, x) > 0\}$ and the *postset* of x is $x^\bullet = \{y \mid W(x, y) > 0\}$. If $x \in {}^\bullet y \cap y^\bullet$, then x and y form a *loop*. A *marking* is a function $P \to \mathbb{N}_0$ giving for each place a number of *tokens*. We now define the basic firing rule.

- A transition t is *enabled* under a marking M, denoted by $M[t\rangle$, if $W(., t) \leq M$.

  If $M[t\rangle$ and $M' = M + W(t, .) - W(., t)$, then we denote this by $M[t\rangle M'$ and say that t can *occur* or *fire* under M yielding the follower marking M'.
- This definition of enabling and occurrence can be extended to sequences as usual: a finite sequence $w \in T^*$ of transitions is *enabled* under a marking M, denoted by $M[w\rangle$, and yields the follower marking M' when *occurring*, denoted by $M[w\rangle M'$, if $w = \lambda$ and $M = M'$ or $w = w't$, $M[w'\rangle M''$ and $M''[t\rangle M'$ for some marking M'' and transition t. If w is enabled under the initial marking, then it is called a *firing sequence*.
- We extend the labelling to sequences of transitions as usual, i.e. $l(t_1 \ldots t_n) = l(t_1) \ldots l(t_n)$; note that internal signals are automatically deleted in this *image* of a sequence. With this, we lift the enabledness and firing definitions to the level of signals: a sequence v of signals from Σ is *enabled* under a marking M, denoted by $M[v\rangle\rangle$, if there is some transition sequence w with $M[w\rangle$ and $l(w) = v$; $M[v\rangle\rangle M'$ is defined analogously. If $M = M_N$, then v is called a *trace*. The *language* $L(N)$ is the set of all traces. We call two STGs *language equivalent* if they have the same traces.
- A marking M is called *reachable* if $M_N[w\rangle M$ for some $w \in T^*$. The STG is *k-bounded* if $M(p) \leq k$ for all places p and reachable markings M; it is *safe* if it is 1-bounded and *bounded* if it is k-bounded for some k.

Often, STGs are assumed to be safe and to have only arcs with weight 1. In the first place, we are interested in such STGs; but we also deal with bounded STGs with larger arc weights, in particular since they can turn up in our decomposition algorithm. Note that there is no additional problem to synthesise a circuit from such an STG if the reachability graph is used as an intermediate construction [VYC$^+$94, Wol97].

The idea of input and output signals is that only the latter are under the control of the circuit modelled by an STG. The STG requires that certain outputs are produced provided certain inputs have occurred, namely those outputs that are enabled under the marking reached by the signal occurrences so far. At the same time, the STG describes assumptions about the environment that controls the input signals: if some input signal is not enabled, the environment is supposed not to produce this input at this stage; if it does, the specified system may show arbitrary behaviour, and it might even malfunction. Inputs and outputs will become really important in Section 4.

In this paper, we deal with specifications that completely specify the desired behaviour in the sense of determinism (except for intermediate stages in our decomposition algorithm): an STG is *deterministic* if it does not have internal transitions and if for each of its reachable markings and each signal s, there is at most one s-labelled transition enabled under the marking. It is useful to distinguish two forms how determinism can be violated.

- Two different transitions t_1 and t_2 are *enabled concurrently* under a marking M if $W(., t_1) + W(., t_2) \leq M$, i.e. if there are enough tokens for both transitions together. If both transitions are labelled with the same signal $s \in \Sigma$, then s is *enabled auto-concurrently* under M. An STG is *without auto-concurrency*, if no signal is enabled auto-concurrently under any reachable marking.
- Two different transitions t_1 and t_2 are *in conflict* under a marking M if they are not enabled concurrently under M, but $M[t_1\rangle$ and $M[t_2\rangle$. If both transitions are labelled with the same signal $s \in \Sigma$, then s is *in auto-conflict* under M and the STG has a *dynamic auto-conflict*.
- Two different transitions t_1 and t_2 – and also the signals labelling them – are *in structural conflict* if $^\bullet t_1 \cap {}^\bullet t_2 \neq \emptyset$. If both transitions are labelled with the same signal $s \in \Sigma$, then s is *in structural auto-conflict* and the STG *has* such a conflict. If t_1 is an input (or a λ-labelled) and t_2 an output transition, then they form a *structural input/output conflict* (or a *structural λ/output conflict*) and the STG *has* such a conflict.

Figure 1 shows on the left an STG with a structural but without a dynamic auto-conflict. The STG on the right has a dynamic (and thus also a structural) auto-conflict; without the marked place in the middle, it would have auto-concurrency instead of an auto-conflict.

Clearly, an STG without internal transitions is deterministic if and only if it is without auto-concurrency and without dynamic auto-conflict; the latter is ensured if there are no structural auto-conflicts. Note that internal transitions

Fig. 1.

enabled concurrently or being in conflict do not introduce auto-concurrency or -conflict.

Simulations are a well-known important device for proving language inclusion or equivalence. A *simulation from* N_1 *to* N_2 is a relation S between markings of N_1 and N_2 such that $(M_{N_1}, M_{N_2}) \in S$ and for all $(M_1, M_2) \in S$ and $M_1[t\rangle M_1'$ there is some M_2' with $M_2[l_1(t)\rangle\rangle M_2'$ and $(M_1', M_2') \in S$. If such a simulation exists, then N_2 can go on simulating all signals of N_1 forever.

Theorem 1. *If there exists a simulation from* N_1 *to* N_2*, then* $L(N_1) \subseteq L(N_2)$.

Proof. easy induction. □

Often, nets are considered to have the same behaviour if they are language equivalent. But just as often this is not enough: consider the STGs in Figure 2, which all have the language $\{\lambda, send, send\ receive\}$; they model different channels for the communication of one message: the STG on the right can deadlock without the occurrence of any visible signal by firing the λ-transition, i.e. the channel can refuse to accept a message; the middle one can deadlock after *send*, i.e. it just forgets the message it has accepted in the *send*-action; the STG on the left will stop working only after the message was sent and received. This – clearly important – difference is taken into account by the more detailed behaviour equivalence bisimilarity.

A relation B is a *bisimulation* between N_1 and N_2 if it is a simulation from N_1 to N_2 and B^{-1} is a simulation from N_2 to N_1. If such a bisimulation exists, we call the STGs *bisimilar*; intuitively, the STGs can work side by side such that

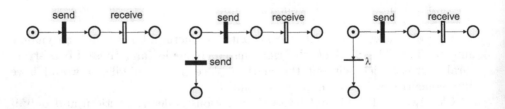

Fig. 2.

in each stage each STG can simulate the signals of the other. This is more than just requiring that there is a simulation from N_1 to N_2 and one from N_2 to N_1: the latter is true for the STGs in Figure 2 although they are not bisimilar. For deterministic STGs, language equivalence and bisimulation coincide; the second and the third STG in Figure 2 are not deterministic (due to a dynamic auto-conflict, an internal transition resp.).

In the following definition of *parallel composition* ||, we will have to consider the distinction between input and output signals. The idea of parallel composition is that the composed systems run in parallel synchronizing on common signals. Since a system controls its outputs, we cannot allow a signal to be an output of more than one component; input signals, on the other hand, can be shared. An output signal of one component can be an input of one or several others, and in any case it is an output of the composition. A composition can also be ill-defined due to what e.g. Ebergen [Ebe92] calls computation interference; this is a semantic problem, and we will not consider it here, but later in the definition of correctness.

The parallel composition of STGs N_1 and N_2 is defined if $Out_1 \cap Out_2 = \emptyset$. Then, let $A = (In_1 \cup Out_1) \cap (In_2 \cup Out_2)$ be the set of common signals. If e.g. s is an output of N_1 and an input of N_2, then an occurrence of s in N_1 is 'seen' by N_2, i.e. it must be accompanied by an occurrence of s in N_2. Since we do not know a priori which s-labelled transition of N_2 will occur together with some s-labelled transition of N_1, we have to allow for each possible pairing. Thus, the *parallel composition* $N = N_1 \parallel N_2$ is obtained from the disjoint union of N_1 and N_2 by combining each s-labelled transition t_1 of N_1 with each s-labelled transition t_2 from N_2 if $s \in A$. In the formal definition of parallel composition, $*$ is used as a dummy element, which is formally combined e.g. with those transitions that do not have their label in the synchronization set A. (We assume that $*$ is not a transition or a place of any net.) Thus, N is defined by

$$P = P_1 \times \{*\} \cup \{*\} \times P_2$$

$$T = \{(t_1, t_2) \mid t_1 \in T_1, t_2 \in T_2, l_1(t_1) = l_2(t_2) \in A \}$$
$$\cup \{(t_1, *) \mid t_1 \in T_1, l_1(t_1) \notin A \}$$
$$\cup \{(*, t_2) \mid t_2 \in T_2, l_2(t_2) \notin A \}$$

$$W((p_1, p_2), (t_1, t_2)) = \begin{cases} W_1(p_1, t_1) & \text{if } p_1 \in P_1, \ t_1 \in T_1 \\ \text{or} \\ W_2(p_2, t_2) & \text{if } p_2 \in P_2, \ t_2 \in T_2 \end{cases}$$

$$W((t_1, t_2), (p_1, p_2)) = \begin{cases} W_1(t_1, p_1) & \text{if } p_1 \in P_1, \ t_1 \in T_1 \\ \text{or} \\ W_2(t_2, p_2) & \text{if } p_2 \in P_2, \ t_2 \in T_2 \end{cases}$$

$$l((t_1, t_2)) = \begin{cases} l_1(t_1) & \text{if } t_1 \in T_1 \\ l_2(t_2) & \text{if } t_2 \in T_2 \end{cases}$$

$$M_N = M_{N_1} \dot{\cup} M_{N_2}, \text{ i.e. } M_N((p_1, p_2)) = \begin{cases} M_{N_1}(p_1) & \text{if } p_1 \in P_1 \\ M_{N_2}(p_2) & \text{if } p_2 \in P_2 \end{cases}$$

$$In = (In_1 \cup In_2) - (Out_1 \cup Out_2)$$
$$Out = Out_1 \cup Out_2$$

Clearly, one can consider the place set of the composition as the disjoint union of the place sets of the components; therefore, we can consider markings of the composition (regarded as multisets) as the disjoint union of markings of the components; the latter makes clear what we mean by the restriction $M|_{P_i}$ of a marking M of the composition.

We will denote a marking $M_1 \dot{\cup} M_2$ of the composition also by (M_1, M_2). By definition of $\|$, the firing $(M_1, M_2)[(t_1, t_2)\rangle(M_1', M_2')$ of N corresponds to the firings $M_i[t_i\rangle M_i'$ in N_i, $i = 1, 2$; here, the firing of $*$ means that the empty transition sequence fires. Therefore, all reachable markings of N have the form (M_1, M_2), where M_i is a reachable marking of N_i, $i = 1, 2$.

If the components do not have internal transitions, then also their composition has none. To see that N is deterministic if N_1 and N_2 are, consider different transitions (t_1, t_2) and (t_1', t_2') with the same label that are enabled under the reachable marking (M_1, M_2). The transitions differ in at least one component, say the first, and since it cannot be the case that t_1 is a transition while $t_1' = *$ (then we would have $l((t_1, t_2)) \in In_1 \cup Out_1$ but $l((t_1', t_2')) \notin In_1 \cup Out_1$), t_1 and t_1' are different transitions with the same label enabled under the reachable marking M_1, which contradicts that N_1 is deterministic. But note that N might have structural auto-conflicts even if none of the N_i has.

It should be clear that, up to isomorphism, composition is associative and commutative. Therefore, we can define the parallel composition of a family (or collection) $(C_i)_{i \in I}$ of STGs as $\|_{i \in I} C_i$, provided that no signal is an output signal of more than one of the C_i. We will also denote the markings of such a composition by $(M_1, \ldots, M_n)$ if M_i is a marking of C_i for $i \in I = \{1, \ldots, n\}$. It is not hard to see that $N_1 \| N_2$ is deterministic if N_1 and N_2 are.

3   Transition Contraction and Redundant Places

We now introduce and study transition contraction (see e.g. [And83] for an early reference), which will be most important in our decomposition procedure. For the reader who is only interested in the method but not the proofs, it suffices to understand the following definition and the definitions of secure contraction and redundant place at the end of the section after Theorem 7.

Definition 2. Let N be an STG and $t \in T$ with $W(., t), W(t, .) \in \{0, 1\}$, $^{\bullet}t \cap t^{\bullet} = \emptyset$ and $l(t) = \lambda$. We define the t-contraction $\overline{N}$ of N by

$$\overline{P} = \{(p, *) \mid p \in P - (^{\bullet}t \cup t^{\bullet})\}$$
$$\cup \{(p, p') \mid p \in {}^{\bullet}t, p' \in t^{\bullet}\}$$
$$\overline{T} = T - \{t\}$$

$$\overline{W}((p, p'), t_1) = W(p, t_1) + W(p', t_1)$$
$$\overline{W}(t_1, (p, p')) = W(t_1, p) + W(t_1, p')$$
$$\overline{l} = l|_{\overline{T}}$$
$$M_{\overline{N}}((p, p')) = M_N(p) + M_N(p')$$
$$\overline{In} = In \quad \overline{Out} = Out$$

In this definition, $* \notin P \cup T$ is a dummy element; we assume $W(*, t_1) = W(t_1, *) = M_N(*) = 0$. We say that the markings M of N and $\overline{M}$ of $\overline{N}$ satisfy the *marking equality* if for all $(p, p') \in \overline{P}$

$$\overline{M}((p, p')) = M(p) + M(p').$$

The first requirement about the arc weights of t is presumably more a convenience and not so essential for our results, compare [And83]. It is motivated by the usual, though not necessary, assumption that STGs are safe and have no arc weights greater 1. Note that a contraction might destroy these properties: if N has arc weight 1, this might not be true anymore after contracting some t.; if t' has an arc with weight > 1 after the contraction, we cannot contract t' anymore, although this might have been possible in N; see also the discussion of the following example. For the moment, we only remark that comparable approaches would not even allow such 'destructive' contractions; we will consider generalizations in the future. The second requirement about the absence of loops seems difficult to avoid.

Figure 3 (a) shows a part of a net and the result when the internal transition is contracted. (Observe: if we merge the a- and the c-labelled transition and label it with λ, then this λ-labelled transition cannot be contracted anymore in $\overline{N}$, since it has an arc of weight 2 to the place $(1, 3)$.) In many cases, the preset or the postset of the contracted transition has only one element, and then the result of the contraction looks much easier as e.g. in Figure 3 (b).

We make the following easy observation:

Lemma 3. *If $t \in T_1$ satisfies the requirements of Definition 2 and $N_1 \parallel N_2$ is defined, then $(t, *)$ satisfies the requirements of 2 in $N_1 \parallel N_2$ and $\overline{N_1 \parallel N_2} = \overline{N_1} \parallel N_2$ (up to isomorphism), i.e. contraction and parallel composition commute.*

For the rest of this section, we fix an STG N with a transition t satisfying the requirements of Definition 2 and denote its t-contraction by $\overline{N}$. Furthermore, we define the relation $\mathcal{B}$ as $\{(M, \overline{M}) \mid M \text{ and } \overline{M} \text{ satisfy the marking equality}\}$.

The first theorem will show that contraction preserves behaviour in a weak sense, i.e. that all the traces of N will still be possible in $\overline{N}$. We begin with an important lemma which relates the transition firing of a net before and after contraction in two markings related by the marking equality.

Lemma 4. *Let M and $\overline{M}$ be markings of N and $\overline{N}$ satisfying the marking equality.*

1. *$M[t\rangle M'$ implies $\overline{M}((p, p')) = M'(p) + M'(p')$.*

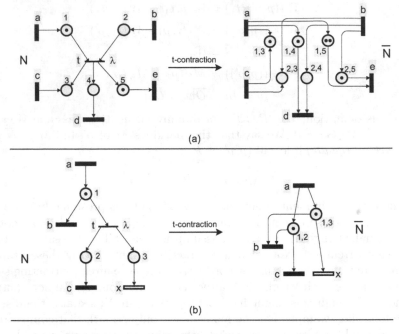

Fig. 3.

2. If $M[t_1\rangle M'$ for $t_1 \neq t$, then $\overline{M}[t_1\rangle\overline{M'}$, and M' and $\overline{M'}$ satisfy the marking equality.

3. $M[v\rangle\rangle M_1$ implies $\overline{M}[v\rangle\rangle\overline{M}_1$ such that also M_1 and $\overline{M}_1$ satisfy the marking equality.

Proof. 1. t removes a token from p and adds a token to p', hence $M(p) + M(p') = M'(p) + M'(p')$. This argument fails in general if ${}^\bullet t \cap t^\bullet \neq \emptyset$.

2. $W((p,p'),t_1) = W(p,t_1) + W(p',t_1) \leq M(p) + M(p') = \overline{M}((p,p'))$; hence, $\overline{M}[t_1\rangle\overline{M'}$ for some $\overline{M'}$.
   $\overline{M'}((p,p')) = \overline{M}((p,p')) - \overline{W}((p,p'),t_1) + \overline{W}(t_1,(p,p'))$; according to the marking equality and the definition of $\overline{W}$, the latter is $M(p) - W(p,t_1) + W(t_1,p) + M(p') - W(p',t_1) + W(t_1,p') = M'(p) + M'(p')$.

3. Apply the first two parts inductively to show that $M[w\rangle M_1$ implies $\overline{M}[w'\rangle\overline{M}_1$ such that also M_1 and $\overline{M}_1$ satisfy the marking equality, where w' is w after deleting all occurrences of t; then we are done, since $l(t) = \lambda$.   □

Theorem 5. $\mathcal{B}$ *is a simulation from N to $\overline{N}$; in particular, $L(N) \subseteq L(\overline{N})$.*

Proof. This follows from the last part of Lemma 4, since the initial markings satisfy the marking equality.   □

The next two results show that under additional assumptions contraction preserves behaviour in a stronger sense, i.e. the t-contraction is bisimilar or at least language-equivalent in these cases. In both theorems, the third part is what is really needed for the remainder of the paper. A further comment on the assumptions can be found after Theorem 7.

Theorem 6. *Assume that* $(^\bullet t)^\bullet \subseteq \{t\}$. *Then:*

1. $\mathcal{B}$ *is a bisimulation from* N *to* $\overline{N}$.
2. *If* t_1 *and* t_2 *with* $t_1 \neq t_2$ *are concurrently enabled under a reachable marking* $\overline{M}$ *of* $\overline{N}$, *then there is a reachable marking* M' *of* N *that satisfies the marking equality with* $\overline{M}$ *and also enables* t_1 *and* t_2 *concurrently.*
3. *The contraction preserves boundedness and freedom from auto-concurrency.*

Proof. First observe that the third part follows from the other two, hence we concentrate on these. In particular, each reachable marking of $\overline{N}$ satisfies the marking equality with some reachable marking of N; hence, if N is k-bounded, then $\overline{N}$ is $2k$-bounded.

If $^\bullet t = \emptyset$, then $\overline{P} = P - t^\bullet$ and the marking $\overline{M}$ satisfying the marking equality with some marking M of N is given by $\overline{M} = M|_{\overline{P}}$. Since t can put arbitrarily many tokens onto $t^\bullet$, both claims are quite easy to see; hence, let $^\bullet t \neq \emptyset$.

$\mathcal{B}$ is a simulation by Lemma 4, hence we only have to show that $\mathcal{B}^{-1}$ is a simulation, too. Let $(M, \overline{M}) \in \mathcal{B}$ and $\overline{M}[t_1\rangle M_1$. Firing t under M as often as possible gives a marking M' that still satisfies the marking equality with $\overline{M}$ by Lemma 4 and $M'(p_0) = 0$ for some $p_0 \in {}^\bullet t$. (For the latter, we use $W(p_0, t) = 1$ according to the precondition on t according to Definition 2.) We check the places $p \in P$ to see that M' enables t_1:

$p \notin {}^\bullet t \cup t^\bullet$: $\quad W(p, t_1) = \overline{W}((p, *), t_1) \leq \overline{M}((p, *)) = M'(p)$
$p \in {}^\bullet t$: $\qquad W(p, t_1) = 0$ by assumption
$p \in t^\bullet$: $\qquad W(p, t_1) = W(p_0, t_1) + W(p, t_1) = \overline{W}((p_0, p), t_1) \leq \overline{M}((p_0, p))$
$\qquad\qquad = M'(p_0) + M'(p) = M'(p)$

Now we have $M'[t_1\rangle M_1'$ for some M_1' and $(M_1', M_1) \in \mathcal{B}$ by Lemma 4. Since a sequence of t's followed by t_1 has the same label as just t_1, we have shown the first part.

For the second part, one finds M' as above, and also the check that M' enables t_1 and t_2 concurrently is very similar; e.g. for $p \notin {}^\bullet t \cup t^\bullet$, we have:
$$W(p, t_1) + W(p, t_2) = \overline{W}((p, *), t_1) + \overline{W}((p, *), t_2) \leq \overline{M}((p, *)) = M'(p) \qquad \square$$

Theorem 7. *Assume that* $^\bullet(t^\bullet) = \{t\}$; *in particular,* $t^\bullet \neq \emptyset$. *Further, assume that* $\exists p_0 \in t^\bullet : M_N(p_0) = 0$; *then:*

1. $\{(\overline{M}, M) \in \mathcal{B}^{-1} \mid \exists q_0 \in t^\bullet : M(q_0) = 0\}$ *is a simulation from* $\overline{N}$ *to* N; N *and* $\overline{N}$ *are language equivalent.*
2. *If* t_1 *and* t_2 *with* $t_1 \neq t_2$ *are concurrently enabled under a reachable marking* $\overline{M}$ *of* $\overline{N}$, *then there is a reachable marking* M' *of* N *that satisfies the marking equality with* $\overline{M}$ *and also enables* t_1 *and* t_2 *concurrently.*
3. *The contraction preserves boundedness and freedom from auto-concurrency.*

Proof. First observe that the third part follows from the other two, hence we concentrate on these. In particular, each reachable marking of $\overline{N}$ satisfies the marking equality with some reachable marking of N; hence, if N is k-bounded, then $\overline{N}$ is $2k$-bounded.

To show the first part, observe that the initial markings are related by hypothesis. Now assume $(\overline{M}, M)$ is in the given relation, $q_0 \in t^\bullet$ with $M(q_0) = 0$, and $\overline{M}[t_1\rangle M_1$.

We choose $p_1 \in t^\bullet$ such that $m = W(p_1, t_1) - M(p_1)$ is maximal; since $W(q_0, t_1) - M(q_0) = W(q_0, t_1) \geq 0$, m is not negative. We check that t can fire m times under M: for all $p \in {}^\bullet t$, we have $M(p) + M(p_1) = \overline{M}((p, p_1)) \geq \overline{W}((p, p_1), t_1) = W(p, t_1) + W(p_1, t_1)$, and thus $M(p) \geq W(p_1, t_1) - M(p_1) + W(p, t_1) \geq m$. Firing t under M m times gives a marking M', which satisfies the marking equality with $\overline{M}$ by Lemma 4. By choice of p_1, we have: (∗) $M'(p_1) = W(p_1, t_1)$ and $M'(p) \geq W(p, t_1)$ for all $p \in t^\bullet$.

We check that t_1 is enabled under M' by considering all places p:

$p \notin {}^\bullet t \cup t^\bullet$: $W(p, t_1) = \overline{W}((p, *), t_1) \leq \overline{M}((p, *)) = M'(p)$

$p \in t^\bullet$:   see (∗)

$p \in {}^\bullet t$: $W(p, t_1) + W(p_1, t_1) = \overline{W}((p, p_1), t_1) \leq \overline{M}((p, p_1)) = M'(p) + M'(p_1)$
        $= M'(p) + W(p_1, t_1)$ by (∗), hence $W(p, t_1) \leq M'(p)$

Now we have $M'[t_1\rangle M_1'$ for some M_1'. Since $W(t_1, p_1) = 0$ by hypothesis, we have $M_1'(p_1) = 0$ by (∗). Therefore (M_1, M_1') is in the given relation by Lemma 4. As above, since a sequence of t's followed by t_1 has the same label as just t_1, we have shown the first claim.

Language equivalence follows since, together with Theorem 5, we have simulations in both directions.

The second part can be shown in a similar way. If $\overline{M}$ is reachable, it is related to some reachable M by the simulation of the first part; let $q_0 \in t^\bullet$ with $M(q_0) = 0$.

We construct M' as above and check that M' enables t_1 and t_2 concurrently as above by adding in the above argument to every atomic term containing t_1 an analogous term containing t_2. E.g. we choose $p_1 \in t^\bullet$ such that $m = W(p_1, t_1) + W(p_1, t_2) - M(p_1)$ is maximal; due to q_0, m is not negative.   □

If the preconditions of Definition 2 and Theorem 6 or 7 are satisfied, then we call the contraction of t *secure*.

The last two theorems show that, for a secure contraction of t, each reachable marking of $\overline{N}$ can be determined from a reachable marking of N via the marking equality. Furthermore, a marking M of N enabling t will be related to the same marking of $\overline{N}$ as the marking M' with $M[t\rangle\rangle M'$. This implies that the contracted net has at most as many reachable markings as N, and it justifies a respective stricter claim about marked graphs, which we will make in Section 5.

To explain the definition of a secure contraction, assume that there are transitions t_1 and t_2 with $t_1 \neq t \neq t_2$, $p_1 \in {}^\bullet t_1 \cap {}^\bullet t$ and $p_2 \in t_2^\bullet \cap t^\bullet$. After contracting t,

t_2 can put a token onto (p_1, p_2) and t_1 can take it, such that, intuitively speaking, the token flows from the postset of t back to the preset; clearly, this can lead to completely new behaviour in $\overline{N}$, such that on the one hand we cannot expect language equivalence, while on the other hand auto-concurrency could be introduced.

We conclude this section by defining redundant places; the deletion of such a place (including the incident arcs) is another operation that can be used in our decomposition algorithm. A place p of an STG N is (structurally) *redundant* (see e.g. [Ber87]) if there is a set of places Q with $p \notin Q$, a valuation $V : Q \cup \{p\} \to \mathbb{N}$ and some $c \in \mathbb{N}_0$ which satisfy the following properties for all transitions t:

- $V(p)M_N(p) - \sum_{q \in Q} V(q)M_N(q) = c$
- $V(p)(W(t,p) - W(p,t)) - \sum_{q \in Q} V(q)(W(t,q) - W(q,t)) \geq 0$
- $V(p)W(p,t) - \sum_{q \in Q} V(q)W(q,t) \leq c$

If the third item holds (at least) for all output transitions t, we call p *output-redundant*; this is, to the best of our knowledge, a new concept.

The first two items ensure that p is something like a linear combination of the places in Q with factors $V(q)/V(p)$. Indeed, for the case $c = 0$, the first item says that p is such a combination initially; the second item, in the case of equality, says that this relationship is preserved when firing any transition. The proof that p is indeed redundant argues that the valuated token number of p is at least c larger than the valuated token sum on Q for all reachable markings, while the third item says that each transition or at least each output transition needs at most c 'valuated tokens' more from p than from the places in Q; this shows that for the enabling of a transition the presence or absence of p does not matter. Therefore, the deletion of a redundant place in N turns each reachable marking of N into one of the transformed STG that enables the same transitions, hence the deletion gives a bisimilar STG.

A special case of a redundant place is a *loop-only place*, i.e. a marked place p such that p and t form a a loop with arcs of weight 1 for all $t \in {}^\bullet p \cup p^\bullet$. Another simple case is that of a duplicate: place p is an (extended) *duplicate* of place q, if for all transitions t $W(t,p) = W(t,q)$, $W(p,t) = W(q,t)$ and $M_N(p) \geq M_N(q)$.

4   Decomposing a Signal Transition Graph

For this section, we assume that we are given a fixed STG N as a specification of some desired behaviour. Our aim is to decompose it into a collection of components $(C_i)_{i \in I}$ that together implement the specified behaviour; in particular, this should help to avoid the state explosion problem, and therefore we have to avoid the complete state exploration for N. For the casual reader, it suffices to read the first two subsections.

In particular in the area of circuit design, it seems most often to be the case that, if an input or output is specified, then its effects are specified without any choices; therefore, we assume that N is *deterministic*. To see the absence of dynamic auto-conflicts easily, we also require N to be *free of structural auto-conflicts*. The specifier is in particular responsible for avoiding auto-concurrency; in many cases, its absence can be proven by place invariants. In this paper, we will concentrate on the construction of components that are also deterministic.

We further assume that N is *free of structural input/output conflicts*; this ensures that there are no dynamic input/output conflicts, which are very hard to implement, since the input, which is under the control of the environment, might occur at roughly the same time as the output, which is under the control of the system, and can therefore not prevent the output as specified; technically, this may even lead to malfunction. In applications, N will be bounded and most often even safe; but our results also hold in the general case.

In the first subsection, we define when a collection of components is a correct implementation of N, which – to repeat – we assume to be deterministic and free of structural auto-conflicts and structural input/output conflicts; in the second, we describe our decomposition algorithm, which uses what we call admissible operations. In the third subsection, we prove that it indeed produces correct components, and in the fourth, we show that certain contractions and place deletions are admissible.

4.1   Correctness Definition

Components $(C_i)_{i \in I}$ are correct if their parallel composition 'somehow' matches the behaviour prescribed by the STG N; for this, their composition must of course be defined according to the definition in Section 2, but it must also be well-defined in the sense of being free of computation interference, see [Ebe92]. To compare the behaviour of N and $\|_{i \in I} C_i$, one could require language equivalence, as Chu does in [Chu87a, Chu87b], but this is actually too restrictive; one could also take a more liberal refinement notion that is still language based, like Dill does in [Dil88]. Our idea of correctness is very close to the notion of [Dil88, Ebe92], but we will define correctness in a bisimulation style.

We have discussed this choice in the introduction; recall that, in particular, the chosen style will be technically useful in our correctness proof. We now give the formal definition and comment on it afterwards.

Definition 8. A collection of deterministic components $(C_i)_{i \in I}$ is a *correct decomposition* or a *correct implementation* of a deterministic STG N, if the parallel composition C of the C_i is defined, $In_C \subseteq In_N$, $Out_C \subseteq Out_N$ and there is a relation $\mathcal{B}$ between the markings of N and those of C with the following properties.

1. $(M_N, M_C) \in \mathcal{B}$
2. For all $(M, M') \in \mathcal{B}$, we have:
   (a) If $a \in In_N$ and $M[a\rangle\rangle M_1$, then either $a \in In_C$ and $M'[a\rangle\rangle M'_1$ and $(M_1, M'_1) \in \mathcal{B}$ for some M'_1 or $a \notin In_C$ and $(M_1, M') \in \mathcal{B}$.
   (b) If $x \in Out_N$ and $M[x\rangle\rangle M_1$, then $M'[x\rangle\rangle M'_1$ and $(M_1, M'_1) \in \mathcal{B}$ for some M'_1.
   (c) If $x \in Out_C$ and $M'[x\rangle\rangle M'_1$, then $M[x\rangle\rangle M_1$ and $(M_1, M'_1) \in \mathcal{B}$ for some M_1.

(d) If $x \in Out_i$ for some $i \in I$ and $M' |_{P_i} [x\rangle\rangle$, then $M'[x\rangle\rangle$. (no *computation interference*)

Here, and whenever we have a collection $(C_i)_{i \in I}$ in the following, P_i stands for P_{C_i}, Out_i for Out_{C_i} etc.

In this definition, we allow C to have fewer input and output signals than N; the reasons are as follows: There might be some input signals that are not relevant for producing the right outputs; we allow that such an input signal of N is not a signal of C. Practically, this means that the environment might still produce this signal, but C completely ignores it such that no connection must be built for this signal. Whereas N makes some assumptions on the environment regarding these inputs, C does not – hence, the environment of C might produce these signals any time, but we are sure that C will never malfunction due to an unexpected input of such a signal.

Analogously, there might be outputs that actually never have to be produced; if N has such outputs, this presumably indicates an error in the specification since most likely these outputs were intended to occur. In fact, our algorithm only produces C with $Out_C = Out_N$.

In contrast, N might very well contain irrelevant inputs, in particular in the following case: N specifies a system that is itself a component of a larger system, and these inputs are important in other parts; when the designer has not realized this, it is useful that our algorithm might detect such so-called *globally irrelevant* inputs.

Figure 4 shows a simple example of an STG N and a decomposition into two components C_1 and C_2 that can be constructed by our algorithm; a is only an input of N but not of any component, but still the latter is a correct implementation as demonstrated by $\mathcal{B} = \{(1, (12, 123)), (2, (12, 123)), (3, (3, 123)), (4, (45, 4)), (5, (45, 5))\}$. (Here we have identified a marking of N or a component with its single marked place.)

The first three clauses of Part 2 are as usual; the first says that an input allowed by the specification is also allowed by C (or ignored), the second that specified outputs can be made by C, and the third that it does not make others. It should be remarked that in b) the then-part could simply require $M'[x\rangle\rangle$:

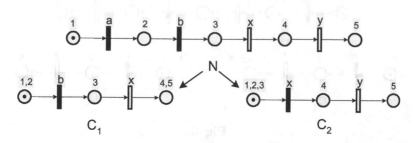

Fig. 4.

due to determinism there is only one follower marking in C, which due to c) matches M_1, the unique follower marking in N. More interestingly, it would also be possible to require only $M'[y\rangle\rangle$ for some $y \in Out_C$: again, c) would ensure that this output is specified and the ensuing behaviour matches the specification; but this clause would only say that, in case of *several* specified outputs, at least *one* will be performed. Whether the others are possible or not cannot be observed, since once an output is performed, it cannot be checked whether others had been possible as well; this view is e.g. taken in [Seg93]. Note that the situation is different in a setting with symmetric handshake communication: there, a communication is under the control of both partners, and the environment can test for the possibility of a specific communication by offering just this one; this is not possible in our setting, since outputs are under the control of the system only. Our decomposition algorithm guarantees the stronger form of correctness given in clause b) above.

Remarkably, there is no clause requiring a match for inputs of C. If $M'[a\rangle\rangle\ M_1'$ for some input a, then either $M[a\rangle\rangle\ M_1$, in which case the uniquely defined M_1' and M_1 match by a), or the input is not specified; in the latter case, the environment is not supposed to supply it, such that we can ignore this potential behaviour of C which will never occur in an appropriate environment, i.e. one that satisfies the assumption of the specification.

The usefulness of this feature is demonstrated by the simple example in Figure 5: C_1 and C_2 are an intuitively correct decomposition of N (again obtainable by our algorithm), since together they answer an input a by x and a following b by y, just as specified. But in $C_1 \parallel C_2$, which is just the disjoint union of C_1 and C_2, b is enabled initially in contrast to N. Note that this implies that N and $C_1 \parallel C_2$ are not language equivalent, as e.g. required in [Chu87a, Chu87b].

The fourth clause is a requirement that could easily be overlooked: if, in state M', C_i on its own could make an output x that is an input of some C_j, but not allowed there, then there simply exists no x-labelled transition enabled under M' due to the definition of parallel composition; but x is under the control of C_i, so it might certainly produce this output, and we must make sure that it is present in C, i.e. does not lead to a failure of C_j for instance.

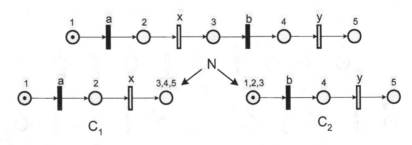

Fig. 5.

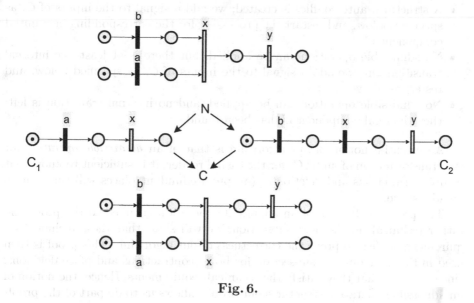

Fig. 6.

An example is shown in Figure 6. The parallel composition C of C_1 and C_2 looks very much the same as N, and they certainly have the same language - they are even bisimilar. But putting circuits for C_1 and C_2 together, C_1 will possibly produce output x after receiving input a, although x cannot occur in C after a alone; this occurrence is not specified in N, and therefore C_1 and C_2 should not be a correct decomposition of N – and they are indeed not one due the fourth clause.

Remark 1. Since N and C are deterministic, there is a smallest $\mathcal{B}$ as above if there is one at all, and its elements correspond one-to-one to the reachable markings of the composition of the *mirror* of N with C; the mirror of N is N with input and output signals exchanged, it is the maximal environment compatible with the system specification N. Such a composition is sometimes considered in the definition of a correct implementation, see e.g. [Ebe92].

4.2   The Decomposition Algorithm

We start with an outline of our algorithm, where the unknown notions will be described in this and the next subsection:

Given are a deterministic STG N free of structural auto- and input/output-conflicts as a specification, and a feasible partition of its signals. These define an initial decomposition $(C_i)_{i \in I}$. We process one C_i after the other as follows:

We repeatedly apply admissible operations to C_i until one of the following occurs:

- A structural auto-conflict is created; we add a signal to the inputs of C_i as specified below, and restart the processing for the corresponding new initial component C_i.
- No admissible operation can be applied, but there is at least one internal transition left; we add a signal to the inputs of C_i as specified below, and restart as above.
- No admissible operation can be applied, and no internal transition is left; then the final component C_i has been found.

An essential notion of our algorithm is that of an *admissible operation* for the transformation of an STG; for the casual reader, it is sufficient to know that secure contractions and deletion of (output-)redundant places will turn out to be admissible.

The precise definition of an admissible operation is tuned to the proof and rather technical; in the next subsection, we will show that these technical requirements suffice to prove the correctness of our algorithm. This proof is then used in the next but one subsection for both, contractions and place deletions, since we show that they satisfy the technical requirements. Hence, the notion of an admissible operation structures our proofs, allows us to do part of the proofs only once instead of twice, and it supports a possible future reuse of this proof part. Additionally, it becomes clear that also non-secure contractions might be used under appropriate conditions.

We will define an admissible operation in three steps; for understanding this subsection, it is enough to know that each admissible operation is a *tc/pd-operation*, i.e. a transition contraction or the deletion of a place (and its incident arcs). We will introduce the further properties as they are needed in the correctness proof; we hope this makes the definition easier to understand.

To initialize the algorithm, one has to choose a *feasible partition* of the signals of N, i.e. a family $(In_i, Out_i)_{i \in I}$ for some set I such that the sets Out_i, $i \in I$, are a partition of Out_N and for each $i \in I$ we have $In_i \subseteq In_N \cup Out_N$, and furthermore:

(C1) If output signals x and y of N are in structural conflict, then $x \in Out_i$ implies $y \in Out_i$ for each $i \in I$. The rationale for this is similar to the one for disallowing input/output conflicts in N: the requirement ensures that output signals that could be in a dynamic conflict in N are produced by the same component; otherwise, the component responsible for x might be ready to produce this output signal; when y occurs at this time in another component, it must immediately prevent x as specified – and this is very hard to implement and may easily lead to malfunction.

(C2) If there are $t, t' \in T_N$ with $t^\bullet \cap {}^\bullet t' \neq \emptyset$ and $l_N(t') \in Out_i$ for some $i \in I$, then $l_N(t) \in In_i \cup Out_i$. ($l_N(t)$ *gives concession to* $l_N(t')$.)

For a feasible partition, the *initial decomposition* is $(C_i)_{i \in I}$, where each *initial component* $C_i = (P, T, W, l_i, M_N, In_i, Out_i)$ is a copy of N except for the labelling and the signals; $l_i(t) = l(t)$ if $l(t) \in In_i \cup Out_i$ and $l_i(t) = \lambda$ otherwise.

Now to each C_i repeatedly an admissible operation is applied until either no λ-labelled transitions are left, in which case a a component of the decomposition has been found, or one of the following failures occurs:

- The C_i transformed last has a structural auto-conflict. Then the last operation was a contraction of some t, and one adds $l(t)$ to In_i and starts the algorithm for this i again from the new initial C_i; alternatively, it suffices to undo the last contractions on C_i up to and including the first contraction of a transition labelled $l(t)$, if this saves time.
- There are internal transitions in C_i, but no known admissible operation is applicable. In this case, one adds $l(t)$ to In_i for some internal transition t and restarts as above.

The reason for the backtracking and addition of an input in the first case is as follows. We take the structural auto-conflict as an indication of a dynamic auto-conflict. Such a dynamic auto-conflict shows that t was labelled in N with a signal C_i should better know about in order to decide which of the two equally labelled transitions to fire.

As an example which also shows that we might get different components if contractions are applied in different orders, consider N in Figure 7 and the construction of a component generating x. Taking c as only input is feasible, and contracting the transitions that were y-, b- and a-labelled in this order gives the component shown in the middle; here it is not clear whether x should be generated upon input of c or not. Now we undo the last contraction and add a as input signal; this gives the component on the left, which does what is required. Alternatively, we could have contracted the last two transitions the other way round, i.e. the a-labelled before the b-labelled transition; then we would undo the contraction of the b-labelled transition and obtain the component on the right, which is alright as well.

Note that this treatment of structural auto-conflicts might be over-cautious, because it could be that despite the structural auto-conflict there actually is no dynamic auto-conflict. To check this, one would – in general – perform a state exploration, which here we try to avoid. In a computer-aided procedure this is presumably the place for human intervention which could possibly supply a proof that there actually is no dynamic auto-conflict requiring a restart.

There might even be some more room for improvement: even if C_i has a dynamic auto-conflict, this might occur under a marking that is in fact not reachable if C_i runs in the environment formed by the other components and an 'outer' environment as specified by N.

As indicated, if a failure occurs, the algorithm is restarted; therefore, in each step, for some C_i either the number of internal transitions goes down or it stays the same and the number of places decreases – since each admissible operation is a tc/pd-operation – or the number of signals (which is bounded by $|In_N \cup Out_N|$) increases in case of a restart. Thus, eventually a decomposition will be found in any case.

Of course, this decomposition might not be useful since the C_i might be too large – in an extreme case, some C_i could be equal to N except for the labelling.

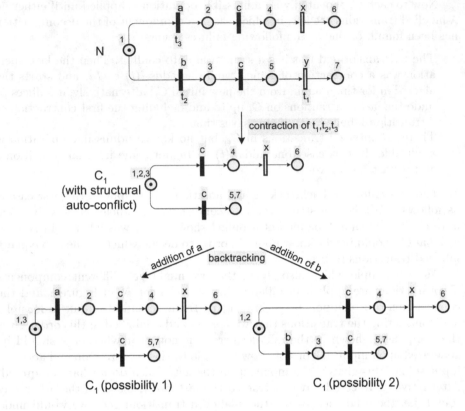

Fig. 7.

But even in this case, the result might be useful if e.g. an arbiter has been split off; see Section 5. Also, one cannot expect to fight state explosion successfully in all cases; and in any case, our algorithm works more often than the approaches presented in the literature so far. In the examples we have checked, which will be discussed in Section 5, the algorithm performed quite well.

Finally, it should be pointed out that finding a feasible partition from a partition of the output signals and checking whether a secure contraction can be applied and whether a structural auto-conflict was generated can be easily done by local graph-theoretic considerations. The same can be said about checking for loop-only places and duplicates; checking for output-redundant places in general is non-local, but it can also be done without generating the reachability graph.

4.3 The Correctness Proof

Each admissible operation will be pre-admissible in the following sense:

Definition 9. An operation is *pre-admissible* if it is a tc/pd-operation that when applied to an STG without dynamic auto-conflicts and satisfying (a) and

(b) below preserves freeness from auto-concurrency and gives an STG satisfying (a) and (b) again:

(a) There is neither a structural input/output nor a structural λ/output conflict.
(b) If t_2 is an output transition and $t_1{}^\bullet \cap {}^\bullet t_2 \neq \emptyset$, then t_1 is not an internal transition.

Two easy consequences of this definition are formulated in the following lemma, which will be needed when proving correctness formulated in Theorem 13.

Lemma 10.   *1. At each stage of the algorithm, each C_i satisfies (a) and (b) of Definition 9 and is free of dynamic auto-conflicts.*
   2. When the algorithm terminates, the resulting C_i and hence also C are deterministic.

Proof. The initial C_i satisfy (a), since by assumption on N an output transition of C_i can in N only be in structural conflict with another output transition, which will also be an output transition of C_i due to condition (C1) in the definition of a feasible partition. They satisfy (b) by condition (C2) of this definition. Furthermore, they are free of dynamic auto-conflicts since N is.

Hence, the first claim follows from Definition 9 and the fact that we restart the algorithm in case a structural auto-conflict turns up.

For the second claim observe that, by assumption and Part 1, there are no internal transitions and no dynamic auto-conflict. Since there is no auto-concurrency initially, there is also none in the end due to Definition 9 and Part 1. The result follows, as already observed in Section 2.   □

We now come to the central notion in our correctness proof; it is a variant of a bisimulation with an angelic treatment of internal transitions, and it is (like a loop invariant) needed to describe in what sense the intermediate stages of our algorithm are correct. If there is an internal transition in an initial C_i, then this corresponds to a signal of the system that this component does not 'see'; if we assume that by some angelic intervention such a transition, which is internal to C_i and not connected in any way to the outside, fires if the signal occurs, then the C_i together work as intended, and this sort of behaviour is captured with an angelic bisimulation. For the final C_i, an angelic bisimulation guarantees correctness, since there are no internal transitions.

Clearly, if we synthesized a circuit for an intermediate C_i with internal transitions, we could not assume that the internal signals of the circuit would behave well, i.e. in accordance with the angelic bisimulation. Hence, this is not a 'real-life' correctness notion; angelic correctness is just a mathematical tool for our proof.

We regard it as highly interesting that this kind of bisimulation is useful even though we do not assume any angelic nondeterminism in our correctness definition (8). In the future, we will study decompositions where components communicate with each other by signals that are internal to the implementation;

these internal signals will certainly have to be of a different kind compared to the λ-transitions we study here.

Definition 11. A collection of components $(C_i)_{i \in I}$ is an *angelically correct decomposition* or *implementation* of a deterministic STG N, if the parallel composition C of the C_i is defined, $In_C \subseteq In_N$, $Out_C \subseteq Out_N$ and there is an angelic bisimulation relation $\mathcal{B}$ between the markings of N and those of C, i.e. $\mathcal{B}$ satisfies the following properties.

1. $(M_N, M_C) \in \mathcal{B}$
2. For all $(M, M') \in \mathcal{B}$, we have:
   (a) If $a \in In_N$ and $M[a\rangle\rangle M_1$, then either $a \in In_C$ and $M'[a\rangle\rangle M_1'$ and $(M_1, M_1') \in \mathcal{B}$ for some M_1' or $a \notin In_C$ and $M'[\lambda\rangle\rangle M_1'$ and $(M_1, M_1') \in \mathcal{B}$ for some M_1'.
   (b) If $x \in Out_N$ and $M[x\rangle\rangle M_1$, then $M'[x\rangle\rangle M_1'$ and $(M_1, M_1') \in \mathcal{B}$ for some M_1'.
   (c) If $x \in Out_i$ for some $i \in I$ and $M'|_{P_i}[x\rangle\rangle$, then some M_1' and M_1 satisfy $M'[x\rangle\rangle M_1'$, $M[x\rangle\rangle M_1$ and $(M_1, M_1') \in \mathcal{B}$.

This definition looks very much like Definition 8; the differences are that here $[x\rangle\rangle$ in C might involve additional λ-transitions besides an x-labelled transition, that in 2(a) internal transitions are allowed to match an input of N that is not one of C, and that 2(c) is a combination of 8.2(c) and (d) and guarantees a matching only for some M_1' – this is an angelic part of the definition. It is also angelic that we do not require a match for the firing of only internal transitions in C.

We come to the final definition of an admissible operation, which leads to the correctness result.

Definition 12. We call a pre-admissible operation applied to some member of a family $(C_i)_{i \in I}$ that satisfies (a) and (b) of Definition 9 *admissible* if it preserves angelic correctness w.r.t. N.

Theorem 13. *When the algorithm terminates, the resulting C_i are a correct decomposition of N.*

Proof. Due to $\mathcal{B} = \{(M, (M, \ldots, M) \mid M \text{ is reachable in } N\}$, the initial decomposition is angelically correct. The defining clauses for an angelic bisimulation are satisfied, since the firing of a transition t in N or in some C_i can be matched by firing all copies of this transition in N and all the C_i.

Admissible operations preserve angelic correctness by definition, since the C_i always satisfy conditions (a) and (b) of Definition 9 by Lemma 10. Hence, the resulting C_i are an angelically correct decomposition of N.

Furthermore, the C_i and C are deterministic by Lemma 10. Therefore, (a), (b) and (c) of Definition 11 immediately give (a), (b) and (d) of Definition 8. Further, M_1' in (c) of 8 is uniquely determined by M' and x by determinism of C, thus it is the M_1' in (c) of 11 and therefore also (c) of 8 follows. $\quad\square$

4.4   Admissible Operations

It remains to present some admissible operations, and to show in particular that secure contractions are admissible. For this, we give two lemmata corresponding to pre- and full admissibility.

Lemma 14.   *1. A contraction applied to an STG satisfying conditions (a) and (b) of Definition 9 preserves these properties.*
2. Secure contractions are pre-admissible.

Proof. The second claim follows from the first and Theorems 6 and 7. Hence, we concentrate on the first claim.

So assume contraction of t is applied to some STG S satisfying conditions (a) and (b). Assume the result violates (a) due to some input or internal transition t_1 and some output transition t_2. Then there are places $pi \in {}^{\bullet}t_i$ such that $p1 \in {}^{\bullet}t$ and $p2 \in t^{\bullet}$ or vice versa; compare Figure 8(a). In the first case, t and t_2 violate (b) in S; in the second case, t and t_2 violate (a) in S.

Finally, assume the result violates (b) due to some internal transition t_1 and some output transition t_2. Then there are places $p1 \in t_1{}^{\bullet}$ and $p2 \in {}^{\bullet}t_2$ such that $p1 \in {}^{\bullet}t$ and $p2 \in t^{\bullet}$ or vice versa; compare Figure 8(b). In the first case, t and t_2 violate (b) in S; in the second case, t and t_2 violate (a) in S. (Note that in this

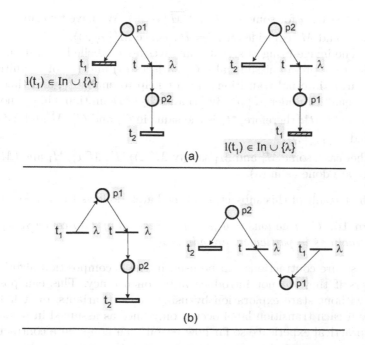

(a)

(b)

Fig. 8.

case the contraction is not secure, but such contractions are considered in the first part, too.)   □

The following is the essential lemma for the treatment of contractions; it shows what we need (a) and (b) of Definition 9 for in our approach.

Lemma 15. *Contraction applied to some member of a family $(C_i)_{i \in I}$ that satisfies (a) and (b) of Definition 9 preserves angelic correctness w.r.t. N.*

Proof. Assume contraction of t is applied to C_j and results in $\overline{C_j}$, $\overline{C}$ resp.; assume further that $\mathcal{B}$ is an angelic bisimulation for N and $(C_i)_{i \in I}$. We define $\overline{\mathcal{B}}$ as $\{(M, \overline{M}) \mid$ there is $(M, M') \in \mathcal{B}$ such that M' and $\overline{M}$ satisfy the marking equality $\}$. Similarly, we will denote by $\overline{M_1}$ the marking of $\overline{C}$ that satisfies the marking equality with the marking M_1 of C.

We check that $\overline{\mathcal{B}}$ is an angelic bisimulation for N and $(C_i')_{i \in I}$, where C_j' is $\overline{C_j}$ and $C_i' = C_i$ otherwise. Clearly, the initial markings of N and $\overline{C}$ are related since the initial markings of N and C are.

So let $(M, \overline{M}) \in \overline{\mathcal{B}}$ due to $(M, M') \in \mathcal{B}$.

(a) Let $a \in In_N$ and $M[a\rangle\rangle M_1$. Either $a \in In_C$ and for some M_1' $M'[a\rangle\rangle M_1'$ and $(M_1, M_1') \in \mathcal{B}$; then we get $\overline{M}[a\rangle\rangle \overline{M_1}$ by Lemma 4.3 and $(M_1, \overline{M_1}) \in \overline{\mathcal{B}}$. Or $a \notin In_C$ and for some M_1' $M'[\rangle\rangle M_1'$ and $(M_1, M_1') \in \mathcal{B}$; again we get $\overline{M}[\rangle\rangle \overline{M_1}$ by Lemma 4.3 and $(M_1, \overline{M_1}) \in \overline{\mathcal{B}}$.

(b) analogously.

(c) Let $x \in Out_i$ for some $i \in I$ and $\overline{M}|_{P_i'}[x\rangle\rangle$. We have two subcases:

$i \neq j$: $\overline{M}$ and M' coincide on $P_i' = P_i$, hence $M'|_{P_i}[x\rangle\rangle$.

$i = j$: The image-firing of signal x involves an x-labelled transition t_1. Since contractions are pre-admissible, also C_j' satisfies (a) and (b) of Definition 9; by (b), only firing internal transitions cannot help to enable t_1, and thus t_1 must already be enabled under $\overline{M}|_{P_j'}$. By (a) and (b) of Definition 9 in C_j, no place in ${}^\bullet t_1$ can be in ${}^\bullet t \cup t^\bullet$; therefore, ${}^\bullet t_1$ is the same in C_j and C_j', $\overline{M}$ and M' coincide on ${}^\bullet t_1$, and $M'|_{P_i}[x\rangle\rangle$.

In either case, some M_1' and M_1 satisfy $M'[x\rangle\rangle M_1'$, $M[x\rangle\rangle M_1$ and $(M_1, M_1') \in \mathcal{B}$, and we are done as in (a).   □

The first result of this subsection immediately follows from these lemmata.

Theorem 16. *Contractions that preserve freeness of auto-concurrency, i.e. secure contractions in particular, are admissible.*

Thus, secure contractions can be used in the decomposition algorithm, but also others if they do not introduce auto-concurrency. This can possibly be checked without state exploration by using place invariants, or it holds automatically if each transition label occurs only once as assumed in [Chu87a]. We have no practical experience so far how useful such non-secure contractions can be; whenever we wanted to apply such a contraction, we were able to make it secure by first applying a place deletion as described in the following.

We have already argued in Section 3, that the deletion of an redundant place gives a very similar STG; the deletion turns each reachable marking of the original STG into one of the transformed STG that enables the same transitions, hence the deletion gives a bisimilar STG. Still, it is not completely obvious that such deletions are admissible operations, since the latter are defined w.r.t. the structure of STGs, which certainly changes, and since such a deletion can increase the concurrency.

Theorem 17. *The deletion of an (output-)redundant place is an admissible operation.*

Proof. To check pre-admissibility, take an STG S that is without dynamic auto-conflicts and satisfies properties (a) and (b) of Definition 9.

First assume that the deletion introduces auto-concurrency, say the equally labelled transitions t and t' are concurrent under the reachable marking M'. Then, $M' = M|_{P_i - \{p\}}$ for some reachable marking of S, and t and t' are also enabled under M – this holds for any place deletion. Since they cannot be concurrent by assumption, they must be in conflict; this is a contradiction since S does not have dynamic auto-conflicts.

Since the deletion of a place does not add structural conflicts or arcs, it is clear that (a) and (b) of Definition 9 are preserved.

To conclude the proof, it follows from the above observation, that an angelic bisimulation for N and C before a deletion can be turned into one for N and C after the deletion by omitting p from each marking of C. This can clearly not disturb 1 and 2(a) and (b) of Definition 11, and output-redundancy ensures (c). $\qquad\square$

5   Examples

We will now demonstrate our algorithm for some realistic examples. In these examples, we will use labels like $a+$ and $a-$, which really denote rising and falling edges of the signal a. To fit them into the approach presented here, one can either regard the $+$ and $-$ as comments and the a-labelled transitions as toggle-transitions that let rising and falling edges of a alternate. Alternatively, we can regard $a+$ and $a-$ as signals in the sense of this paper; the only adaptations needed are the following: we only consider feasible partitions, where $a+ \in In_i$ iff $a- \in In_i$ and the same for Out_i; when the algorithm has to be restarted and some $a+$ is added to In_i, we also add $a-$ and vice versa. This ensures that each STG has either both edges of a signal as outputs or none, and the same for inputs. (The latter view involves a little change of the algorithm, but the correctness proof still works without any changes.)

We will discuss two examples in some detail; for more details see http://www.eit.uni-kl.de/beister/eng/projects/deco_examples/main_examples.html

With the benchmark examples in the table below[2] (circulation in the STG-community), we demonstrate the possible savings w.r.t. the number of reachable

---

[2] Where 6-8 have been adapted slightly for our approach

markings – by listing the name, the number for this STG, and the numbers for the components of the best decomposition we have found so far. Examples 1-4 are so-called marked graphs (see below); even such a simple case as FIFO *cannot* be decomposed with the decomposition methods given in the literature so far, since the deletion of loop-only places is necessary (just as in mread-8932) and since during the construction places with 2 or more tokens arise; the latter is no problem for us since we do not restrict ourselves to the treatment of safe nets.

no	name	reach. markings	for the components					
1	FIFO	832	26	12	12	8	4	4
2	nak-pa	58	21	7	6	6		
3	adfast	44	21	12				
4	mread-8932	8932	36	36	18	18	12	10
5	pe-rcv-ifc	65	53	25				
6	tsend_csm	35	25	16				
7	mux2	99	63	33				
8	locked2	166	34	20	20			

Examples 5-8 are free-choice nets, each of them having some labels occurring more than once; hence, the methods of [Chu87a, KKT93] are not applicable. Restarts were needed in 5,6 and 8. Globally irrelevant inputs were found in 7 and 8.

We will have a closer look at the first example now; FIFO is the specification of a FIFO-queue controller, see Figure 9. It has already been studied and decomposed somewhat informally in [BW93]. This STG is particularly simple, since it is a marked graph, where the arc weights are 1 and each place has exactly one transition in its preset and one in its postset; thus, there are no conflicts.

Admissible operations preserve these properties; thus, every well-defined contraction is secure. The only possible obstacle for contracting an internal transition is a loop. If we assume that no transition is dead in N, i.e. each can be fired under some reachable marking, then each cycle must contain a token; since a loop generated by the algorithm arises from a cycle in the marked graph N, the loop place is marked and deleting it is an admissible operation. Therefore, in examples like this there will never be the need for a restart. Furthermore, if we can find an initial decomposition where each component has at least one λ-transition, then each component will have fewer reachable markings than N in the end; compare the last paragraph of Section 3 and observe that the deletion of a redundant place never increases the number of reachable markings.

In our example, the deletion of loop-only places turns out to be necessary indeed; note that so far place deletions have not been discussed in the literature about STG decomposition. In fact, it is also very convenient to delete redundant places early; in this example, several duplicates can be found. We repeat that – although N and all the constructed components are safe – one does come across places with more than one token on them. Hence, it is important that we do not restrict ourselves to the treatment of safe nets.

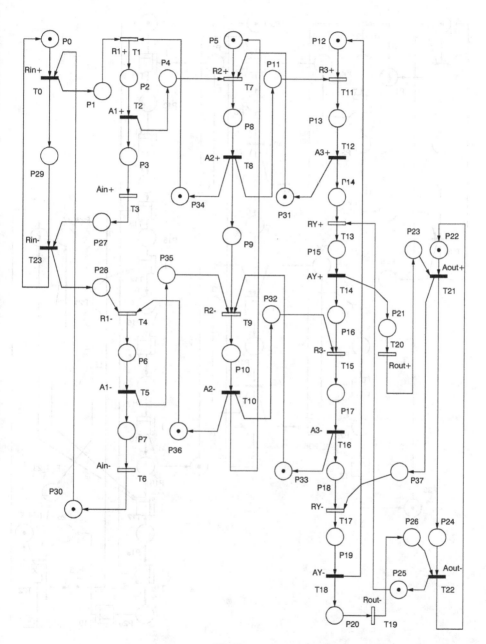

Fig. 9.

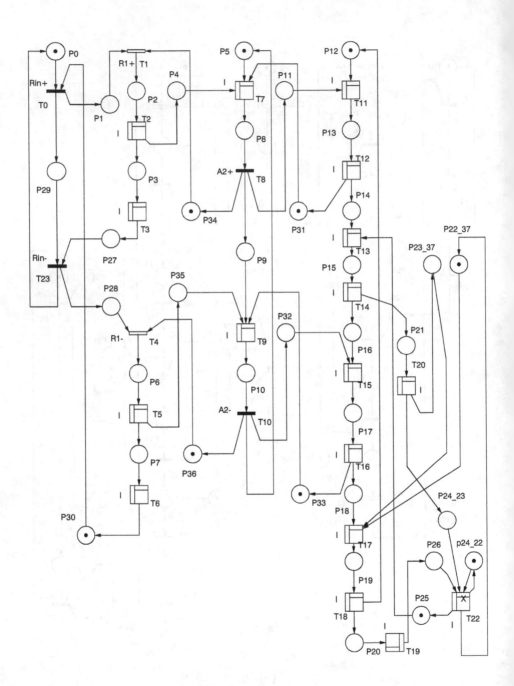

Fig. 10.

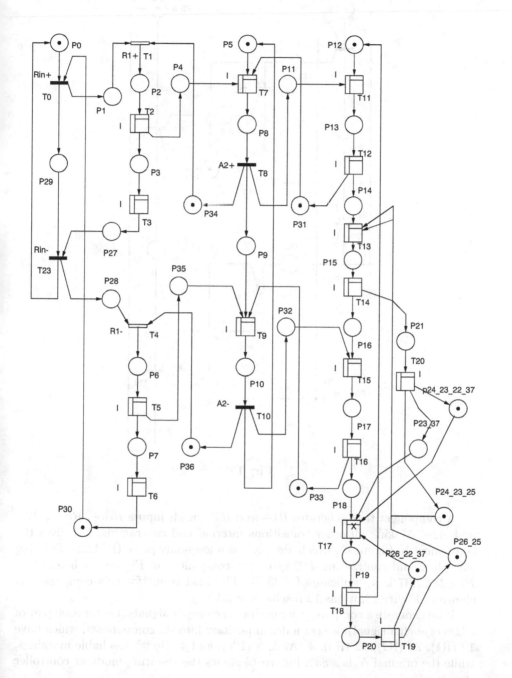

Fig. 11.

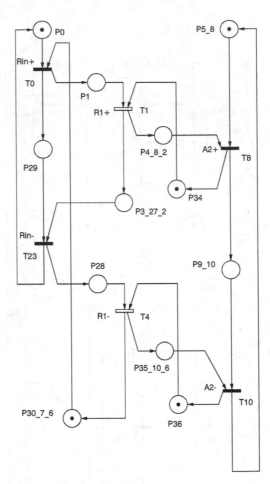

Fig. 12.

A component that generates $R1+$ and $R1-$ needs inputs $Rin+$, $Rin-$, $A2+$ and $A2-$. Making all other transitions internal and contracting $T21$ gives the component in Figure 10, which already has a loop-only place (P24_22). Deleting this place and contracting $T22$ gives the component in Figure 11; here, place $P24\_23\_22\_37$ is a duplicate of $P23\_37$. The final result for this component is shown in Figure 12; it has 12 reachable markings.

If we generate a component for each of the output signals (i.e. for each pair of edges of such a signal), we get a decomposition into six components, which have 12 (R1), 26 (R2), 12 (R3), 4 (Ain), 8 (RY), and 4 (Rout) reachable markings, while the original N has 832. Figure 13 shows the resulting modular controller structure.

Our final example demonstrates that our algorithm can deal with arbitration, and it gives a case where one finds a well known circuit specification as

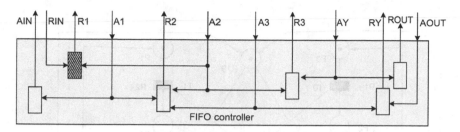

AIN RIN R1   A1   R2   A2   A3   R3   AY   RY ROUT AOUT

FIFO controller

Fig. 13.

component in a correct decomposition. Figure 14 shows the STG specification of a low latency arbiter known from literature [YKK+96]. Upon a request $R1+$ or $R2+$, the circuit arbitrates with $A1+$ or $A2+$, i.e. there is a critical input race between $R1+$ and $R2+$ [WB00]. In parallel to the arbitration, the circuit requests a resource itself with $R+$. When it gets the resource $(G+)$, it grants it depending on the arbitration with $G1+$ or $G2+$. When the resource is returned with $R1-$ or $R2-$, it returns the resource and all signals are returned to the original level. (Note that the place $P4$ is not safe.)

Critical race behaviour cannot be correctly implemented by a pure logic circuit; additional analogue circuitry is needed to avoid anomalous behaviour like metastability. Present day STG-based tools, therefore, cannot handle such behaviour. The problem is usually solved by using specific library elements, in particular a so-called two-way mutual exclusion (ME) element (e.g. [YKK+96]). This solution burdens the designer with the task to split off an ME-element; our decomposition method can give support here – with results that we have proven to be correct – and we will demonstrate this now.

A component for the generation of the $Ai*$, $i = 1, 2$ and $* \in \{+, -\}$, must have the $Ri*$ as inputs according to the definition of a feasible partition. The corresponding initial C_1 is shown in Figure 15.

The secure contractions of $T12$, $T13$, $T6$ and $T7$ give the STG in Figure 16, and the further secure contractions of $T4$ and $T5$ give the STG in Figure 17.

The remaining internal transitions do not allow a secure contraction; but place $P18\_14$ is redundant due to $Q = \{P11, P12, P23\_15, P24\_16\}$ with $V \equiv 1$. After deletion of this place, we can perform the secure contractions of $T14$ and $T15$, which gives the STG in Figure 18. The places in 'the middle column' except for $P19$ can be shown to be redundant, and deleting them gives the standard STG representation of the ME-element (e.g. [YKK+96]). (Note that one of the deleted places is a loop-only place.)

This example is concerned with splitting off a library element and not with savings in the state space. In fact, the second component that generates the other output signals $R*$ and $Gi*$, $i = 1, 2$ and $* \in \{+, -\}$, is not smaller than N. But it does not specify critical races (because the $Ai*$ are inputs for this component), and can therefore be implemented with the known STG-based methods.

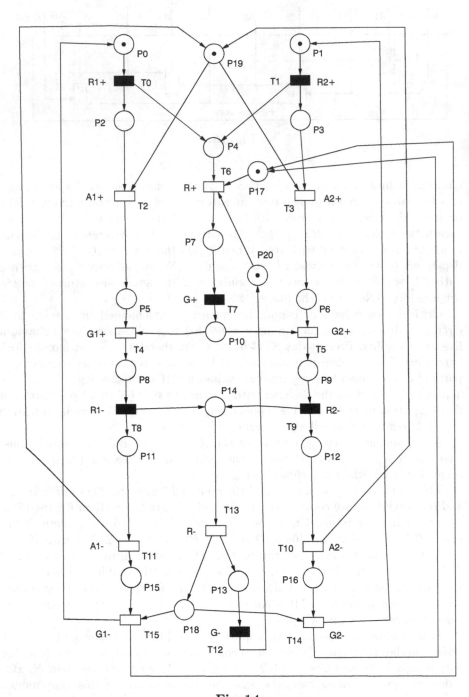

Fig. 14.

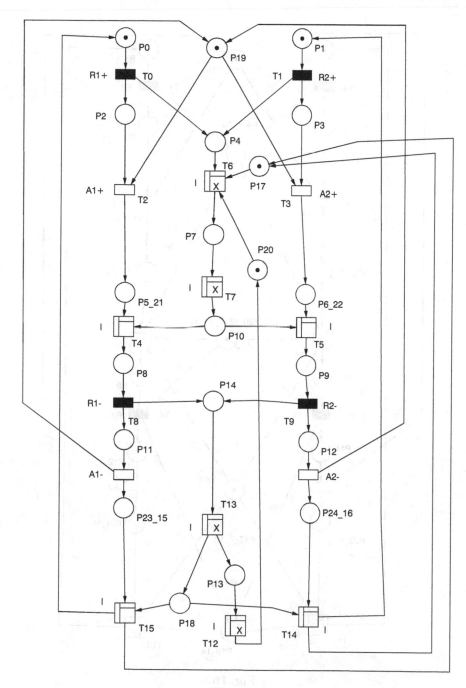

Fig. 15.

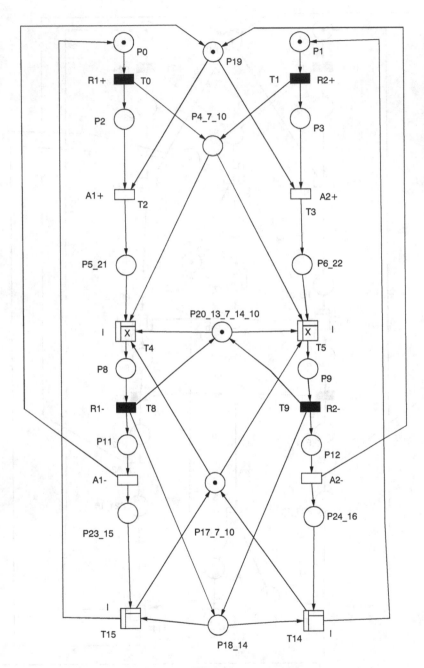

Fig. 16.

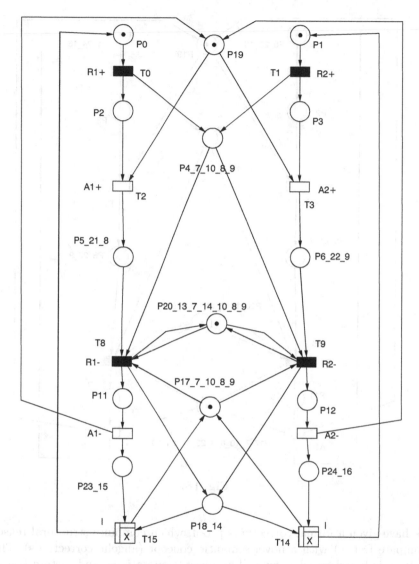

Fig. 17.

6   Conclusion and Future Work

STG decomposition can help in the synthesis of circuits: it may avoid state explosion, it supports the use of library elements, and it leads to a modular implementation that can be more efficient. We have presented a decomposition algorithm that is much more generally applicable than those known from literature; in particular, we do not restrict ourselves to live and safe free-choice nets or to marked graphs, and we do not require that each label occurs only once.

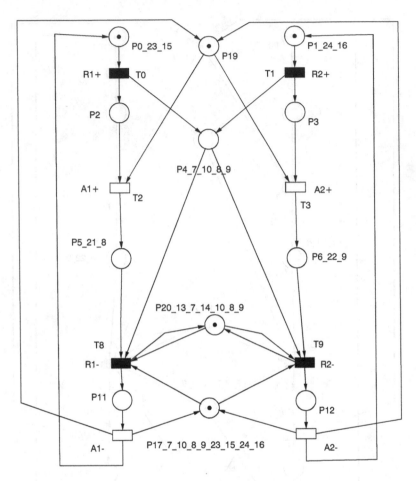

Fig. 18.

We have given a formal correctness proof, which combines structural reasoning (compare Def. 9) with a novel semantic concept (angelic correctness). The algorithm is based on what we call admissible operations, and certain transition contractions and place deletions have been shown to be admissible. We have demonstrated the usefulness of our algorithm with some practical examples.

There are a number of open problems we will tackle in the near future. The first one concerns determinism: we have assumed that the given STG-specification N, its components C_i we have constructed, and their parallel composition C are deterministic. One would get much more freedom in finding components, if one allowed internal signals for the communication between components; then the composition C would not be deterministic anymore, and to treat such STGs it becomes essential to use some form of bisimulation that is not angelic. Also for N, it can be useful to allow nondeterminism: e.g. to treat arbitration in general, it can be necessary to have several enabled and conflicting transitions with the same label, and in [YKK$^+$96], it is argued that auto-conflicts are very useful when modelling so-called OR-causality; internal transitions can also be useful purely for syntactic convenience.

Of course, we have to study more examples; for this, integration of the decomposition algorithm into a tool is needed, and this is already under way. One question then is how useful non-secure contractions and output-redundant, but not redundant place deletions are. Another aspect is that we would like to see examples where it is useful to continue in the algorithm in cases where there is a structural auto-conflict but no dynamic auto-conflict; see the discussion in Section 4.2.

Depending on the choice of a feasible start partition and on the choices of signals for restarts (which for the first kind of failure in Section 4.2 depend on the order of the transition contractions), we can arrive at different decompositions – compare Figure 7. We want to study quality criteria (like the overall or the maximal number of reachable markings) for decompositions and methods to find good decompositions.

Finally, as argued in [WB00], STGs are not always sufficient to specify the desired behaviour; as an improvement, gSTGs are suggested. Therefore, we want to generalize our approach to gSTGs, and we also want to generalize our correctness criterion to take concurrency into consideration, where it seems to be natural to require the modular implementation to exhibit at least the concurrency prescribed in the specification.

Acknowledgment

The authors thank Ben Kangsah for helping with the figures and working out part of the examples, and they thank the referees for valuable comments, which helped to improve the presentation of this paper.

References

[And83]   C. André. Structural transformations giving B-equivalent PT-nets. In Pagnoni and Rozenberg, editors, *Applications and Theory of Petri Nets*, Informatik-Fachber. 66, 14–28. Springer, 1983. 154, 160, 161

[Ber87]   G. Berthelot.   Transformations and decompositions of nets.   In W. Brauer et al., editors, *Petri Nets: Central Models and Their Properties*, Lect. Notes Comp. Sci. 254, 359–376. Springer, 1987. 154, 165

[BEW00]   J. Beister, G. Eckstein, and R. Wollowski. Cascade: a tool kernel supporting a comprehensive design method for asynchronous controllers. In M. Nielsen, editor, *Applications and Theory of Petri Nets 2000*, Lect. Notes Comp. Sci. 1825, 445–454. Springer, 2000. 152

[BW93]   J. Beister and R. Wollowski. Controller implementation by communicating asynchronous sequential circuits generated from a Petri net specification of required behaviour. In G. Caucier and J. Trilhe, editors, *Synthesis for Control Dominated Circuits*, 103–115. Elsevier Sci. Pub. 1993. 154, 178

[Chu86]   T.-A. Chu. On the models for designing VLSI asynchronous digital systems. *Integration: the VLSI Journal*, 4:99–113, 1986. 152

[Chu87a]   T.-A. Chu. *Synthesis of Self-Timed VLSI Circuits from Graph-Theoretic Specifications*. PhD thesis, MIT, 1987. 153, 154, 155, 166, 168, 176, 178

[Chu87b]   T.-A. Chu. Synthesis of self-timed VLSI circuits from graph-theoretic specifications. In *IEEE Int. Conf. Computer Design ICCD '87*, pages 220–223, 1987. 153, 154, 155, 166, 168

[CKK+97]   J. Cortadella, M. Kishinevsky, A. Kondratyev, L. Lavagno, and A. Yakovlev. Petrify: a tool for manipulating concurrent specifications and synthesis of asynchronous controllers. *IEICE Trans. Information and Systems*, E80-D, 3:315–325, 1997. 152

[Dil88]   D. Dill. *Trace Theory for Automatic Hierarchical Verification of Speed-Independent circuits*. MIT Press, Cambridge, 1988. 152, 155, 166

[Ebe92]   J. Ebergen. Arbiters: an exercise in specifying and decomposing asynchronously communicating components. *Sci. of Computer Programming*, 18:223–245, 1992. 155, 159, 166, 169

[KGJ96]   P. Kudva, G. Gopalakrishnan, and H. Jacobson. A technique for synthesizing distributed burst-mode circuits. In *33rd ACM/IEEE Design Automation Conf.*, pages 67–70, 1996. 154

[KKT93]   A. Kondratyev, M. Kishinevsky, and A. Taubin. Synthesis method in self-timed design. Decompositional approach. In *IEEE Int. Conf. VLSI and CAD*, pages 324–327, 1993. 153, 178

[Lyn96]   N. Lynch. *Distributed Algorithms*. Morgan Kaufmann Publishers, San Francisco, 1996. 152

[Pet81]   J. L. Peterson. *Petri Net Theory*. Prentice-Hall, 1981. 156

[Rei85]   W. Reisig. *Petri Nets*. EATCS Monographs on Theoretical Computer Science 4. Springer, 1985. 156

[RY85]   L. Rosenblum and A. Yakovlev. Signal graphs: from self-timed to timed ones. In *Proc. Int. Work. Timed Petri Nets*, Torino, Italy, 1985. 152

[Seg93]   R. Segala. Quiescence, fairness, testing, and the notion of implementation. In E. Best, editor, *CONCUR 93*, Lect. Notes Comp. Sci. 715, 324–338. Springer, 1993. 168

[VYC+94]   C. Vanbekbergen, C. Ykman-Couvreur, B. Lin, and H. de Man. A generalized signal transition graph model for specification of complex interfaces. In *European Design and Test Conf.*, pages 378–384. IEEE, 1994. 157

[WB00]   R. Wollowski and J. Beister. Comprehensive causal specification of asynchronous controller and arbiter behaviour. In A. Yakovlev, L. Gomes, and L. Lavagno, editors, *Hardware Design and Petri Nets*, pages 3–32. Kluwer Academic Publishers, 2000. 183, 189

[Wen77]   S. Wendt. Using Petri nets in the design process for interacting asynchronous sequential circuits. In *Proc. IFAC-Symp. on Discrete Systems, Vol.2*, Dresden, 130–138. 1977. 152

[Wol97]   R. Wollowski. *Entwurfsorientierte Petrinetz-Modellierung des Schnittstellen-Sollverhaltens asynchroner Schaltwerksverbünde*. PhD thesis, Uni. Kaiserslautern, FB Elektrotechnik, 1997. 154, 157

[YKK+96]   A. Yakovlev, M. Kishinevsky, A. Kondratyev, L. Lavagno, and M. Pietkiewicz-Koutny. On the models for asynchronous circuit behaviour with or causality. *Formal Methods in System Design*, 9:189–233, 1996. 183, 189

Functional and Performance Modeling of Concurrency in VCC

William LaRue, Sherry Solden, and Bishnupriya Bhattacharya

Cadence Design Systems
2655 River Oaks Parkway, San Jose, CA 95134

Abstract. VCC®(Virtual Component Co-Design) is a system level software tool that supports the design of concurrent systems by specifying the functional model as a set of interconnected functional blocks, the system architecture, and the mapping between functional blocks and architectural elements. VCC provides functional simulation, performance estimation, and refinement of the model to implementation. This chapter provides a brief tutorial on the VCC tool. It describes the model of concurrency in VCC's default discrete event model of computation. While modeling a system, the importance of separating the behavioral model from the implementation architecture is emphasized. The techniques used to model performance and implementation of the architecture components, as a set of collaborating services, are explained in some detail. Customization of the model of computation, and communication between functional blocks is also discussed. An example is provided that demonstrates the dataflow model of computation implemented on top of the VCC infrastructure. Finally the automatic generation of an implementation from VCC (in terms of HDL and/or C, and the communication code) is described.

1 Introduction

Modern systems under design are increasingly composed of highly complicated functionality encompassing both software and hardware, linked together by a complex communication network, usually all residing on the same chip, giving rise to today's system-on-chip (SoC) [1]. Clearly, the design of such systems from conception through incremental refinement, and validation, to final implementation, requires a robust system-level tool that enables, assists, and accelerates such complete design flows. VCC is such a system-level tool.

VCC supports the specification of both the behavior (algorithms) and the architecture of an embedded system. The mapping of behavior to the system architecture is an essential part of the specification. Apart from functionality, performance models of a building block can also be specified. These specifications can be used to confirm the correctness of the algorithms, and estimate the performance of the system by software simulation of the design, and finally to create implementations of the system.

J. Cortadella et al. (Eds.): Concurrency and Hardware Design, LNCS 2549, pp. 191–227, 2002.

Traditionally system-level design has been performed using high-level modeling languages, such as C, Java and C++. They offer the advantage, with respect to Hardware Description Languages (HDLs), of higher level data types, and sometimes object oriented design methodologies. The purpose of executable modeling is to gain insight into the overall system functionality, as well as to gather performance requirements for both communication and computation, by means of appropriate instrumentation of the model. These models are generally thrown away after this information has been gathered, and HDL designing has begun.

Recently, a trend has emerged to actually use these high-level models, written in languages such as C++ (e.g., SystemC [2], OCAPI [3]) and extensions of C (e.g., SpecC [4]), also for the analysis of communication and architectural refinement. This provides a continuum of abstraction levels from purely functional sequential, to purely functional concurrent, to time-annotated concurrent, all the way down to "RTL in C++" (e.g., OCAPI [3], CoWare® [5]). The obvious advantage is the reduction of the "semantics gap" between the levels (there is no syntactic gap), and the possibility to re-use high-level models as testbenches for lower-level models. Sophisticated design environments for DSP algorithms like SPW® [6], CoCentric®System Studio [7], and Simulink® [8] have always used C and/or C++ as a modeling language for the internals of a block. The problem in all these cases has always been to use the right mechanism to introduce communication, concurrency, and synchronization into originally sequential languages such as C and C++, or languages with virtual-machine-dependent, software-oriented concurrency such as Java. SystemC, OCAPI, VCC, SpecC are all attempts to introduce "standard" mechanisms for this purpose which are suitable for system-level design. They mostly focus on providing several communication models ("channels") which can be refined down to the bus transaction level. Such refinement can be done, in an object-oriented flavor, by providing different implementations of the same interface, where the fixed interface is all that the communicating processes care about.

VCC uses a mechanism similar to the above approaches for both functional modeling, i.e. concurrent blocks written in C or C++, and communication refinement, i.e. channels whose models can be changed and refined without altering the connected blocks. However, it is radically different from them, since it provides a mechanism, based on the Y-chart paradigm (see [9], [10]), to ease the creation of refined models from the mapping of functionality onto architecture. This mechanism is used to simplify the creation of the complex performance model that depicts the effects of architectural choices such as the use of one or more processors, the HW/SW partitioning, the use of different bus hierarchies, and so on, on the functional model. The latter imposes requirements, called in the following "uses of architectural services", on the underlying architecture, called in the following "implementation of architectural services". The result is a performance annotation that can be used to execute simulations in the time domain, collect bus and CPU utilization statistics, schedule Gantt charts, perform power analysis, and so on.

Finally, the same mapping information can also be used to derive a high-level model of the system architecture, in the form of top-level hardware netlist, RTOS customizations (tasks, priorities, etc.) and, more importantly, a testbench that can be used directly to drive the co-verification model after detailed implementation, using the same stimuli that had been used during functional validation and performance analysis, and to compare against the same outputs. This testbench re-use throughout the design flow, is one of the key benefits of the design paradigm advocated in this chapter, based on computation and communication refinement, driven by function-architecture mapping.

The rest of this chapter provides a brief tutorial on the VCC tool, explaining the concepts discussed above in more details.

1.1 Behavioral Specification

In VCC, a behavior is described in terms of a block diagram where blocks communicate with each other through ports and communication arcs. Each block is hierarchical (that is, another block diagram) or a leaf level block. Leaf level blocks are specified with textual programming languages such as C and C++, an FSM editor, or imported from another design tool. Fig. 1 shows a simple VCC behavior diagram.

The leaf level blocks produce data or tokens on their output ports. The leaf level blocks connected to those outputs, consume that data, are activated (their code is run), and produce output data. The services associated with the ports control the transportation of the data. The model of computation associated with each behavior controls the activation of the behavior. The services and models of computation are both user definable and stored in VCC libraries.

In VCC behaviors are executable - they can be simulated. We call this kind of simulation a *behavioral simulation*. Behavioral simulation allows the system designer to verify the system's intended behavior before implementation and answer the question "am I designing the right function?" The behavioral specification also provides the traffic or load for the estimation of the performance of the overall system.

1.2 Architectural Specification

The *architecture* of the system is how that function is implemented in hardware and software. The architectural specification in VCC is a block diagram consisting of interconnected architectural resource. Common architectural resources include software schedulers, CPUs, busses, bus-bridges, caches, timers, DMAs, ASICs, and memories. The architecture is specified at a high-level. For example, the busses are graphically shown as a single, wide line representing a bundle of physical wires, and are not broken down into individual wires, one for each bit of an n-bit data value that is transmitted on the bus. We call this kind of architecture a *relaxed* architecture as opposed to a *refined* architecture. Fig. 2 shows a simple VCC Architecture diagram.

1.3   Mapping

VCC supports Function/Architecture Co-Design at the system level by separating the behavior (*e.g.*,function, application) of an embedded system from its implementation (architecture) [9]. A behavior can be partitioned across a single architecture in a variety of ways

The relationship between behavior and architecture is described by a *mapping*. A mapping is a correspondence between entities in the behavior (these go by a variety of names; tasks, processes, behavioral blocks, behaviors) and entities in the architecture on which those tasks are implemented. For example, an MPEG decoder in the behavior may be implemented on an ASIC in the architecture and a portion of a protocol stack in the behavior might be implemented as software running on a CPU. The designer can compare the performance of different mapping configurations using VCC. Fig. 3 shows a VCC mapping diagram.

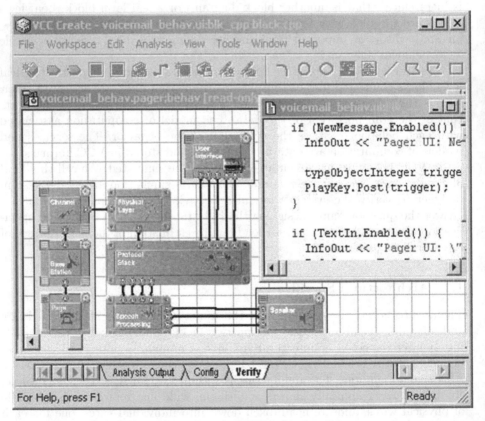

Fig. 1. An example VCC behavior diagram

Scheduling: Multiple tasks mapped to a processor in the architecture imply some kind of arbitration between these tasks. The arbitration is handled by the scheduling policy on the processor model. For example, if two tasks are mapped to the same CPU and are ready to execute then the choice of a non-preemptive scheduler would run one task to completion and then the other. Other possible schedulers include round robin and parallel scheduling of tasks.

Communication: In any hardware/software system, tasks in the behavior need to communicate with each other. If two behaviors are connected (in the behavior diagram), but mapped to different architectural resources, then a communication path through the architectural resources must be found so that the communication specified in the behavior can be implemented. VCC can find such a path if it is unique or the communication path between the behaviors can be explicitly mapped. A detailed performance simulation or implementation of the design requires additional information to be specified about the communication between behaviors. Associating a *pattern* (from a VCC library) with the communication

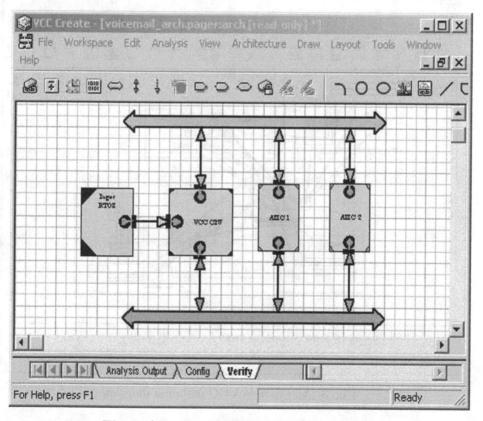

Fig. 2. An example VCC architecture diagram

specifies this information. A pattern specifies the mechanism for the communication between the behaviors. For example, a common pattern for software-to-software communication might specify that the communication is implemented by a shared variable protected by a semaphore. Without the semaphore protection, the sender might overwrite the shared variable before the receiver is able to read the variable.

2   Models of Computation

The model of computation [11] controls the interaction between behaviors, their requirements for activation, and their order of execution. The default model of computation for VCC is discrete event, but other models of computation can be written in C++ and added to the VCC library by defining them using the VCC simulator API.

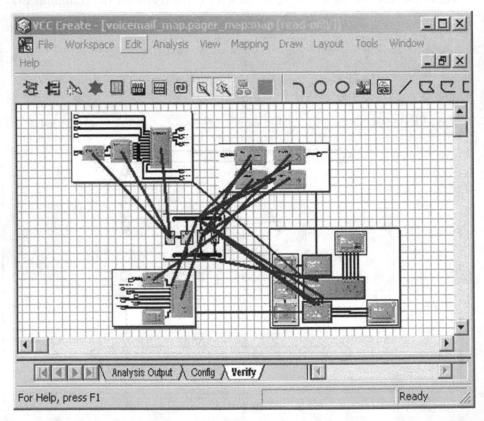

Fig. 3. An example VCC mapping diagram

2.1   Basic Simulator API

The simulator provides a C++ API for authoring models of computation. The same API is used to author services and blackbox C++ models. The term black-box is used because VCC has no visibility into behaviors written in C++. The information in this subsection on the basic simulator API applies to all models of computation and isn't specific to the discrete event MOC.

Port to Port Communications with Services: The communication between behaviors is done through *services*. The simulator provides a reference to the service declaration associated with each port in the design. The service declaration, which is stored in a VCC library and is not a part of the simulator, determines the API available for that particular port.

Event Scheduling: An event object, which is derived from the VCC Event class, is created on the heap, and then scheduled on the simulation master calendar with the VCC event scheduling API. Every event has a time, priority, sequence number, and handler function. Events are ordered by time, priority is used to order equal time events, and sequence number is used to order equal time and priority events. This algorithm ensures a deterministic ordering of events. An event's handler function is called when it reaches the head of the ordered list.

New threads of control are created in the simulator by the event scheduling mechanism. If an event is scheduled for the current time, the effect is the same as creating a new thread.

Semaphores: Semaphores are provided as the fundamental mechanism for event synchronization within VCC. The simulator implements a semaphore class with three primary member functions wait(), post(), and getValue(). The wait() function blocks the calling thread until the semaphore count is greater than zero, then it decrements the count. The post() function increments the semaphore count, and if there are any threads blocked (waiting) on the semaphore, one will be unblocked. If multiple threads are waiting on the same semaphore, there is no defined order for their unblocking by posts to that semaphore. The getValue() function returns the semaphore count.

The semaphore mechanism is commonly used to implement functions that block until some operation is complete. A frequently used mechanism is to schedule an event to process a request, and then wait on a semaphore. The handler for the event then posts to that semaphore when the processing is complete. This unblocks the calling thread.

Delay Models: Each behavior has a delay model associated with it to support performance estimation. The delay model specifies the time required to execute the behavior, and accounts for interruptions in processing such as being preempted by a higher priority behavior.

The model of computation runs a behavior by calling the activate() function on its associated delay model. Once the behavior processing time has been modeled, the delay model calls the model of computation to start the reaction. The model of computation then calls a function in the behavior to do the reaction. The behavior will not be activated again until the reaction is complete.

The simulator supplies a dummy delay model during functional simulation so that the same model of computation can be shared between functional and performance simulation.

2.2 Discrete Event MOC

Discrete event (DE) is the default model of computation (MOC) in VCC. The key attributes of the discrete event model of computation are:

- Each behavior is treated as an independent process.
- These processes communicate via message passing from output ports to input ports.
- Blocks are awakened by receiving messages from other blocks or from timers.
- Data can be lost if the sending behavior sends additional data before the receiver checks its inputs.

Message Passing through Post(), Value(), Enabled(): A behavior produces an output by calling the Post() function with a data token. This causes any behaviors connected to that output to be activated. When a behavior is run, it may test for the presence of inputs by calling the Enabled() function on its inputs or internal timers. The Enabled() function returns true, if an input is present. If an input is enabled, then its value can be extracted with the Value() function.

Block Activation through Run(), Await(): The model of computation calls the Run() function of the behavior to start the first reaction. The reaction continues until either the Run() function returns or the function Await() is called. Await() saves the state of the behavior, ends the reaction, and returns control to the simulator. If the last reaction ended with a call to Await(), then the next reaction causes the behavior to be resumed at the next statement. If the last reaction ended with the return of the Run() function, then the start of the next reaction causes the Run() function to be called again.

Await() has optional arguments to support waiting for the presence of particular combinations of inputs or timers. In some cases, several inputs are needed to perform a computation. This can be handled by supplying a port expression to Await(). If the behavior has two inputs: I1 and I2, then, Await(I1 & I2), waits until inputs are available on both I1 and I2. Alternatively, you can wait on either I1 or I2 as Await(I1 | I2). After waiting on a set of inputs, the Enabled() function can be used to check which ports are active. These capabilities support both static and dynamic conditional block activation of arbitrary complexity.

2.3   User Defined Models of Computation

In VCC, the default model of computation used in the interactions between behavioral blocks is assumed to be discrete event. However, VCC provides a flexible framework to customize the MOC assumed by the behavioral blocks. The framework consists of a specification for the activation semantics of the block as well as *service declarations* and *service definitions* that specify the communication between blocks.

The communication between blocks is described through a customizable port interface that lets each MOC specify the function names through which the block belonging to that MOC can access its input/output ports (e.g., read/write vs. Value/Post); the semantics of each function (e.g., blocking vs. non-blocking); and port parameters (e.g., the data rate at a dataflow port). The customizable block interface allows the specification of the activation semantics (e.g. OR semantics, where a block maybe fired when any input receives data vs. AND semantics, where a block maybe fired only when all inputs receive data) of a block belonging to that MOC.

Customizable Port Interface: The port interface is specified as a C++ class, called the *service declaration*, which specifies the structure of the communication between blocks, usually as pure virtual functions. This class is templated with the data type of the port. The service declaration class inherits from a class in the simulator (VCC_InputPortDeclaration or VCC_OutputPortDeclaration) that provides some common functionality like finding connectivity on the wire, interacting with probes, interactive simulation, etc. The port interface is implemented as another C++ class, called the *service definition* that inherits from the service declaration class and provides implementations for the interface functions. Examples of service declarations and service definitions for the dataflow MOC can be found further down this section. By default, each port assumes that it is communicating with another port belonging to the same MOC. To interface with other MOCs, *converter services* have to be provided. At the very minimum, every MOC is required to provide converter services to/from the discrete event MOC.

In a behavior diagram, every behavioral block declares its MOC and the simulator automatically inserts the communication services as specified by that MOC. If the block communicates with another block that has a different MOC, then the simulator inserts the appropriate converter services that translate between the MOC pair. If no direct converter is available between two MOCs, moc1 and moc2, the conversion is performed by first converting from moc1 to discrete event and then from discrete event to moc2.

Customizable Block Interface: A MOC is implemented with a C++ class, and blackbox behaviors inherit from this MOC class. The class hierarchy is shown in Fig. 4. FxBlackboxCPPInterface is a simulator class that provides

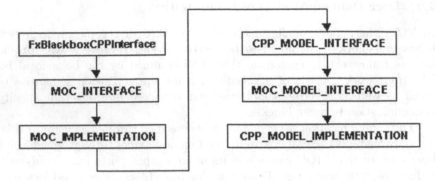

Fig. 4. The class hierarchy for specifying a behavioral block belonging to a particular MOC

some common functionality to all MOCs like parameters, error reporting, interactive simulation control, interface to the delay model for performance simulation, etc. A MOC must call the API provided in this class for block activation. The MOC_INTERFACE class derives from the FxBlackboxCPPInterface class and is also a part of the simulator. This class is templated by the input and output port service declarations of this MOC. The functionality it provides is type-specific iterators for input and output ports.

The next class in the inheritance chain (MOC_IMPLEMENTATION) is particular to each MOC, and is authored by the MOC developer. This class implements the activation semantics (firing rule) of a block using the simulator internal API from FxBlackboxCPPInterface and the port service declaration APIs accessible through the parent MOC_INTERFACE class. In particular, a MOC has to interface with the delay model to implement the activation semantics of a block. This happens through two pre-defined delay model API routines: activate() – called by the MOC specific code to inform the simulator that the behavior associated with the delay model is ready to run – and registerRunCallback(Callback *) – causes the supplied callback to be invoked when the simulator is able to run the behavior. For example, the MOC author can register a callback which when invoked calls a particular member method in the behavior class (e.g., Run()).

The next three classes shown in the hierarchy chain are particular to the behavioral block being described and are jointly filled in by the tool and the behavior author. The CPP_MODEL_INTERFACE class is automatically generated by a common fabricator module in the simulator and stored in the file black_interface.h. It provides a type-specific service declaration reference for each port, such that port functions can be called in the block as portName.fn(a1, a2, ...). The MOC_MODEL_INTERFACE class comes next. This is an optional class generated by a MOC-specific fabricator in the simulator. This class is stored in the file custom_interface.h, and provides MOC-specific functionality. An example custom MOC class for the dataflow MOC is shown later in this section. CPP_MODEL_IMPLEMENTATION is the final class in the inheritance chain authored by the behavior author. The simulator fabricator generates templates for this class in files black.h and black.cpp. The behavior author fills in this template using port interface service declaration APIs, parameters of the behavior and its ports, and simulator internals accessible through its parent classes.

The default discrete event MOC in VCC is implemented using this general MOC scheme described above and is not hard-coded into the tool.

The Dataflow MOC in VCC: As discussed earlier in this section, VCC provides the general infrastructure of customizing the model of computation assumed in the interactions between the behavioral blocks. We now validate that general concept by a concrete example demonstrating the *dataflow* (DF) MOC implemented in VCC.

In the dataflow MOC, behavioral blocks (*actors*) communicate with each other via edges that represent first-in-first-out FIFO channels. This communication is lossless is the sense that tokens are never lost between blocks – the FIFOs are responsible for queuing up tokens sent from the output of one actor to the input of another. Each dataflow block, when it is executed (*fired*), consumes a certain number of tokens on each input port (called the *data rate* at that port), and produces a certain number of tokens on each output port. The block is fired only when all input ports have the requisite numbers of tokens. Another property of a dataflow edge is its *delay* ($>=0$) , which represents the number of initial tokens on that edge. To avoid confusion with the concept of timed delay in VCC, we will refer to these delay tokens as *initial tokens* present at simulation time zero. Thus, dataflow primarily differs from VCC's default discrete event MOC in:

- **lossless communication** between blocks via queues, as opposed to the discrete event MOC where tokens can be lost if they are not processed by the receiver before the buffer is overwritten by the sender.

- **AND firing rule** of a block, as opposed to the OR rule where a block is fired whenever any input receives a token

In *static dataflow* (SDF) [12], the number of tokens consumed and produced by a block on each firing is a constant number known at compile time. In *dynamic dataflow* (DDF – a DDF domain is implemented in Ptolemy [13]), the token consumption/production pattern can vary during a simulation run, as long as the block informs the simulator about the firing rule in effect for its next activation. SDF limits expressive power to static applications only but provides the benefit of strong compile-time analysis (e.g. static scheduling [14]). On the other hand, DDF provides increased expressive power at the cost of limited compile-time analysis, where all scheduling has to be done at run-time. Here, we demonstrate DDF (which is necessarily a superset of SDF) implemented in VCC.

It is relatively straightforward to extend the dataflow modeling techniques described in this section to other conceptually similar MOCs like Kahn Process Networks [15] and a slightly modified version of KPNs as implemented in the YAPI [10] system.

The Behavioral Block Class Hierarchy: The code segment below shows the common base class in the class hierarchy of all behavioral blocks in the dataflow MOC. The MOC_IMPLEMENTATION class of Fig. 4 is represented by the VCC_MOC_Dataflow_moc class. This class inherits from the simulator's MOC_INTERFACE class templated by the input and output port service declarations of the dataflow MOC. It overloads the simulator's internal Init__() routine to call registerRunCallback() in the delay model, and schedules the Run_() routine to be invoked when the behavior block is activated.

```
// code segment
// VCC_MOC_Dataflow_moc is the MOC_IMPLEMENTATION class for the
// dataflow MOC.
// This class is common to all dataflow behavioral blocks
class VCC_MOC_Dataflow_moc : public MOC_INTERFACE
<VCC_DataflowServices_InputPort_serviceDecl<class typeObject> ,
VCC_DataflowServices_OutputPort_serviceDecl<class typeObject>>
{
public:
    virtual void Run_();
private:
    class runCallback : public Callback
    {
    public:
        runCallback(VCC_MOC_Dataflow_moc &model) : model_(model) { }
        void invoke() { model_.Run_(); }
    private:
        VCC_MOC_Dataflow_moc &model_;
    };
    void Init__()
    {
        Callback *cb = new runCallback(*this);
        asFxDelayModel()->registerRunCallback(cb);
    }
};
```

For each specific behavioral block, VCC custom fabricates the next three classes after MOC_IMPLEMENTATION in the class hierarchy of Fig. 4. The code segment below shows these three custom fabricated classes for the the *down-sampler* block in the dataflow MOC. The downsampler block is a static dataflow block with one input port "in" and one output port "out". The "factor" parameter determines the decimation ratio of the block – it consumes "factor" number of tokens at its input port and transfers one of these tokens to its output port. The CPP_MODEL_INTERFACE class in black_interface.h declares the input and output port as references to the dataflow input and output port service declarations respectively. The MOC_MODEL_INTERFACE class is automatically generated by a code generator that is customized for the dataflow model of computation. It declares the pure virtual function Run() (to be overloaded and filled in by the behavior author), and itself overloads the Run_() method to call the user-written Run() and other member methods declared in the dataflow input and output port service declaration APIs (described later in this section). The user-written Run() function in the CPP_MODEL_IMPLEMENTATION class assumes that requisite numbers of tokens are present at all the input ports of this block. The Run() function then processes this input data and writes the output data into the output ports, using the dataflow port API routines, like read() and write(). Thus the functionality of a dataflow behavioral block is split between these two classes – one (MOC_MODEL_INTERFACE) automatically fabricated by the tool, and the other (CPP_MODEL_IMPLEMENTATION) filled in by the behavior author. For the downsampler block, the user-written code transfers the last received input token from the input port to the output port. The fabricated code then takes over to deliver the generated token to all the fanouts of the output port, and checks if the block is ready to run again, which is a possibility for dynamic dataflow blocks due to changes in the firing rule that may have happened during the current block activation.

```
// code segment
// Classes below are custom fabricated for each dataflow
// behavioral block
// black_interface.h
class CPP_MODEL_INTERFACE : public VCC_MOC_Dataflow_moc
{
public:
    VCC_DataflowServices_InputPort_serviceDecl
        <typeObjectInteger> &in; // input port
    VCC_DataflowServices_OutputPort_serviceDecl
        <typeObjectInteger> &out; // output port
    VCC_InternalServices_Parameter_serviceDecl
        <typeObjectInteger> &factor; // parameter
};
// custom_interface.h
class MOC_MODEL_INTERFACE : public CPP_MODEL_INTERFACE
{
public:
    void Run_()
    {
        Run();
        out.DeliverTokens();
        in.FireBlockIfReady();
    }
    virtual void Run() = 0;
};
```

```
// black.h, black.cpp
class CPP_MODEL_IMPLEMENTATION : public MOC_MODEL_INTERFACE
{
public:
    void Init() { ratio = factor.Value(); }
    void Run() { out.write( in.read(ratio - 1)); }
private:
    int ratio;
};
```

The Port API: Our implementation of the dataflow MOC defines a different interface for dataflow blocks to communicate with their input/output ports than the Value()/Enabled()/Post() interface provided for discrete event blocks. This interface is specified in the dataflow input and output port service declaration classes shown in the code segment below. The dataflow input port interface defines a read(int i=0) method for accessing the ith input token, while the output port interface defines a write(typeObject &token, int i=0) method for writing the ith output token. In addition, both inputs and outputs support GetDataRate() and SetDataRate(int rate) methods. It is not necessary to provide a dataflow equivalent of the Enabled() method defined for discrete event input ports, since the dataflow MOC ensures that a dataflow block is fired only when all inputs have sufficient tokens. The remaining member methods in the two classes shown below are used either by the MOC_MODEL_INTERFACE class in a dataflow behavioral block, (shown earlier in this section) or by the input port service definition class (VCC_DataflowServices_InputPort_serviceDefn) that appears later in this section.

```
// code segment
// The dataflow input port service declaration class
template<class portType>
class VCC_DataflowServices_InputPort_serviceDecl :
    virtual public VCC_InputPortDeclaration
{
public:
    virtual const int GetDataRate() const = 0;
    virtual void SetDataRate(int rate) = 0;
    virtual typeObject &read(int index=0) const = 0;
    virtual void FireBlockIfReady() = 0;
protected:
    virtual bool CanFire() = 0;
    virtual void DequeueTokensAndPutInBuffer() = 0;
};
// The dataflow output port service declaration class
template<class portType>
```

```
class VCC_DataflowServices_OutputPort_serviceDecl :
    virtual public VCC_OutputPortDeclaration
{
public:
    virtual const int GetDataRate() const = 0;
    virtual void SetDataRate(int rate) = 0;
    virtual void write(typeObject &data, int index=0) = 0;
    void DeliverTokens() = 0;
};
```

Another important class in defining the communication strategy between input and output dataflow ports is the DataflowComm class shown below. This class defines a simple private interface for a dataflow output port to communicate with a dataflow input port through the member method receiveNewDFToken(typeObject *token). The exact mechanism of this communication appears later in this section in the output port service definition class (VCC_DataflowServices_OutputPort_serviceDefn). This interface is private in the sense that only the communicating input and output services are aware of this class and not the behavioral blocks.

```
// code segment
// The dataflow communication class between input and output ports
template<class portType>
class VCC_DataflowServices_DataflowComm_serviceDecl
{
public:
    virtual void receiveNewDFToken(typeObject *token) = 0;
};
```

The Port API Implementation: The input port service definition class and the output port service definition class implement the respective service declarations described above. The input port service definition class is shown first in the code segment below. It multiply inherits from the input port service declaration class and the DataflowComm class. Each input port maintains its own queue and its own internal buffer of size equal to the port data rate. Initial tokens are specified as a parameter on a dataflow input port and are inserted into the port's internal queue at time 0 (in the Init0() routine). Whenever the port receives a new token (sent by its driver output port) in receiveNewDFToken(), it queues up that token and checks if the block is ready to fire in FireBlockIfReady().

```
// code segment
// The dataflow input port service definition class
class VCC_DataflowServices_InputPort_serviceDefn : virtual public
VCC_DataflowServices_DataflowComm_serviceDecl<typeObject>,
```

```
virtual public VCC_DataflowServices_InputPort_serviceDecl<typeObject> {
public:
    void receiveNewDFToken(typeObject *data)
    {
        queue_.enqueueValue_(data);
        numTokens_++;
        FireBlockIfReady();
    }
    const int GetDataRate() const { return dataRate_; }
    void SetDataRate(int rate)
    {
        dataRate_ = rate;
        AllocateBuffer_();
    }
    typeObject &read(int index=0) const
    {
        if (index >= dataRate_)
            ErrorOut("Out of range indexing into input buffer");
        return **(buffer_[index]);
    }
    void Init0(); // overloaded simulator internal method
    void Init(); // overloaded simulator internal method
    void FireBlockIfReady();
protected:
    bool CanFire()
    {
        if (numTokens_ >= dataRate_)
            return TRUE;
        else
            return FALSE;
    }
    void DequeueTokensAndPutInBuffer();
private:
    void AllocateBuffer_();
    FxInputQueue_ queue_;
    typeObject **buffer_;
    int dataRate_;
    int numTokens_;
};
```

The member method FireBlockIfReady() is shown separately in the code segment below. In this method, if every dataflow input port has sufficient tokens then all input ports are asked to de-queue port rate number of tokens and copy these into their internal port buffer (DequeueTokensAndPutInBuffer()), and the simulator is instructed to fire the block through the delay model API. This ultimately results in the behavior block's Run() function being invoked, as explained in Section 2.1. While the block is running, the read(int i) method indexes into the input port internal buffers and accesses the ith token.

```
// code segment
// The FireBlockIfReady() member method of the dataflow
// input port service definition class
void VCC_DataflowServices_InputPort_serviceDefn::FireBlockIfReady()
{
    VCC_MOC_Dataflow_moc *model = (VCC_MOC_Dataflow_moc *)model();
    const VCC_Vector<VCC_DataflowServices_InputPort_serviceDecl
        <typeObject>> &inPorts = model->inputs();
    int i, numInputs = inPorts.entries();
    for (i=0; i<numInputs; i++) {
        VCC_DataflowServices_InputPort_serviceDecl<typeObject>
            *inPort = inPorts[i];
        if (!(inPort->CanFire())) return;
    }
    for (i=0; i<numInputs; i++) {
        VCC_DataflowServices_InputPort_serviceDecl<typeObject>
            *inPort = inPorts[i];
        inPort-> DequeueTokensAndPutInBuffer();
    }
    model->asFxDelayModel()->activate();
}
```

The output port service definition class is shown next in the code segment below. Each output port service definition class maintains its own internal buffer of size port data rate and a list of fanout input ports that it is connected to. During simulation initialization in Init0(), the output port queries the simulator for all destination connections and fills in this list of fanout ports typed as Dataflow-Comm classes. When the block runs, it performs write(typeObject &token, int i) calls which puts the token into the ith output buffer slot. After the user-written code completes execution, DeliverTokens() is called on each output port (see the MOC_MODEL_INTERFACE::Run() routine earlier in this section), which picks up every token written into the output port buffer and delivers it to all the fanout input ports via the receiveNewDFToken() interface API.

```
// code segment
// The dataflow output port service definition class
class VCC_DataflowServices_OutputPort_serviceDefn :
virtual public VCC_DataflowServices_OutputPort_serviceDecl<typeObject> {
public:
    const int GetDataRate() const { return dataRate_; }
    void SetDataRate(int rate)
```

```
    {
        dataRate_ = rate;
        AllocateBuffer_();
    }
    void write(typeObject &data, int index=0)
    {
        if (index >= dataRate_)
            ErrorOut("Out of range indexing into output buffer");
        buffer_[index] = data.deepCopy();
    }
    void Init0() // overloaded simulator internal method
    {
        VCC_Vector<VCC_InputPortDeclaration> dests = inputsOnNet();
        numFanOuts_ = dests.entries();
        for(int i=0; i<numFanOuts_; i++)
        {
            VCC_DataflowServices_DataflowComm_serviceDecl<typeObject>
                *dest = (VCC_DataflowServices_DataflowComm_serviceDecl
                <typeObject>*) dests[i]->queryDeclaration
                ("VCC_DataflowServices.DataflowComm:serviceDecl");
            fanOut_.append(dest);
        }
    }
    void Init(); // overloaded simulator internal method
    void DeliverTokens()
    {
        int i, j;
        for (i=0; i<dataRate_; i++) {
        for (j=0; j<numFanOuts_; j++) {
                VCC_DataflowServices_DataflowComm_serviceDecl
                    <typeObject> *thisFanOut = fanOut_[j];
                thisFanOut->receiveNewDFToken(buffer_[i]);
            }
        }
    }
private:
    void AllocateBuffer_();
    typeObject **buffer_;
    int dataRate_;
    VCC_Vector<VCC_DataflowServices_DataflowComm_serviceDecl
        <typeObject>> fanOut_;
    int numFanouts_;
};
```

If a dataflow block is not connected to another dataflow block, but to a block belonging to a different MOC, then the simulator inserts a converter service definition in between the two blocks. For this purpose, the dataflow MOC provides converter services that translate to/from the discrete event MOC. These converters are simple to write. For example, the converter from a discrete event output to a dataflow input inherits from the DiscreteEventComm class (which has a similar interface structure as the DataflowComm class shown earlier in this section), and overloads the receiveNewDEToken() method to call the Dataflow-Comm::receiveNewDFToken() method of the dataflow input port. The discrete event output port implements Post() to call receiveNewDEToken(). That call is intercepted by the DE-DF converter and translated to a receiveNewDFToken() call implemented by the dataflow input port.

An Example Mixed MOC Simulation: Fig. 5 shows a mixed MOC simulation in VCC consisting of discrete event blocks and dataflow blocks. The "Adder" and the "Dnsmpl" are dataflow blocks, while all the source and sink blocks are discrete event. Each input of the adder is driven by a discrete event "Counter", parameterized by the initial start value and the time period after which the next incremented output is produced. The first adder input starts counting at 0 and gets incremented after every 5.0 time units, while the second adder input starts at 10 and is incremented after every 10.0 time units. The adder output drives a downsampler block that is set up to decimate by a factor of 4. The downsampler output goes to a discrete event "Sink" block that prints the received input.

The simulator binds the appropriate input and output port service definitions according to the MOCs of each pair of communicating behavioral blocks. In this example, simulation probes (represented by the arrows) are inserted at the two adder input ports, the adder output port, and at the downsampler output port to monitor the token values arriving at these ports during the simulation run. The simulation is executed for 50.0 time units and the probe results are charted in the form of a table as shown in Fig. 6.

The probe outputs in Fig. 6 demonstrate the two essential features of the dataflow MOC as explained earlier in this section:

- **Lossless Communication**: Although the first adder input runs twice as fast as the second adder input, additional tokens at the first input are not discarded, but rather queued up and used in the next adder activation. In this case, a discrete event adder would have discarded every other token arriving at its first input. For example, at time unit 10.0 at the first input port, for a discrete event adder, token 2 would have overwritten token 1 from time unit 5.0 and the adder output would have been 13. Instead, the dataflow adder queues up token 1 from time unit 5.0 and uses that to produce output 12 at time unit 10.0.
- **AND Activation**: The adder is not activated at time units 5.0, 15.0, 25.0, ..., when only the first input has data but not the second input. Instead, the adder runs at time units 0.0, 10.0, 20.0,...., when both inputs have data.

As expected, the downsampler block decimates by a factor of 4 and transmits every fourth adder output (at time units 30.0, 70.0, ...) to the sink, discarding the remaining input tokens.

3   Communications Services

As mentioned in Section 2.1, the communication between behaviors in VCC occurs through services. Each model of computation defines communication interfaces called service declarations for input and output ports. The service declarations are in the form of an abstract base class that specifies the interface as a set of pure virtual functions.

Each service declaration has one or more service definitions that implement the functions defined by the abstract base class. VCC selects the service definition based on the architecture and mapping definitions for the design. The appropriate service definition is instantiated by the simulator and bound to the port references in the behavior.

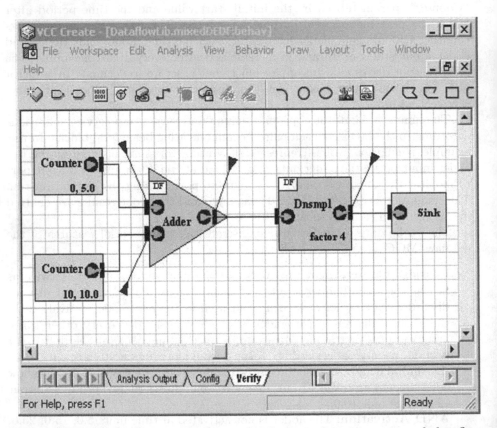

Fig. 5. A mixed MOC simulation in VCC using discrete event and dataflow behavioral blocks

Time	Adder input1	Adder input2	Adder output	Dnsmpl output
0	0	10	10	-
5	1	-	-	-
10	2	11	12	-
15	3	-	-	-
20	4	12	14	-
25	5	-	-	-
30	6	13	16	16
35	7	-	-	-
40	8	14	18	-
45	9	-	-	-
50	10	15	20	-

Fig. 6. Probe outputs charted in the form of a table for the mixed MOC simulation of Fig. 5

The flexibility of using different services for the same port communication interface is necessary in order to support simulation of the same behavior functionally, or mapped to different architectural resources.

3.1 Behavioral Services

Behavioral services implement the communication between the behaviors. Each behavior has a model of computation associated with it. The model of computation defines the behavioral services that are used to implement the communication between the behaviors and control the activation of the behaviors.

3.2 Architectural Services

In VCC, the "behavior" of an architectural resource (e.g., a DMA controller) is modeled through an *architectural service* [16]. An architectural service is a C++ class that is attached or *bound* to the body of an architectural resource or to a port on an architectural resource. Every architectural service implements one or more *service declarations*. A service declaration specifies an interface for the architectural service as an abstract base class in C++. A service declaration can have any number of architectural services that implement it. Additionally, an architectural service can declare that it needs one or more other services to help it do its job. In this case we say that an architectural service *uses* another architectural service. VCC comes with a library of architectural services for common components such as busses, memories, DMAs, and caches. Users are not restricted to using these services but can modify them or create their own.

3.3   Schedulers

In a performance simulation, schedulers arbitrate between the behaviors to model the contention for time-shared resources such as processors. In VCC, schedulers serve the role of the RTOS scheduler by determining when the behaviors run.

The schedulers supplied with VCC support static, FCFS, priority, and round robin scheduling. The VCC scheduling framework supports hierarchical or nested scheduling of behaviors. For example, a set of behaviors can be scheduled statically and then treated as a single task on a round robin scheduler. The VCC scheduler framework is also extendable by implementing a new scheduling service in C++. The scheduler runs the behaviors by calling the functions start(), suspend(), resume(), and abort() of the behaviors of the delay model. The scheduler implements the functions activation() and finish() that are called by the delay models of the behaviors.

3.4   Communication Patterns

In addition to modeling the communication between architecture elements, services are used to model the full communication path between behaviors. The protocol for communication between behaviors is specified as a communication pattern. VCC uses the communication pattern to select a set of cooperating services that implement a realistic communication protocol between the behaviors. Different services are bound to implement the communication depending on the mechanism, and arbitration of the communication. For example, one pattern in the VCC library specifies that the communication takes place between a sender behavior implemented in hardware and a receiver behavior implemented in software, with communication taking place through a register, and activation of the receiver by interrupts.

Fig. 7 shows a behavior running in software sending data to a behavior running on an ASIC. This communication may involve RTOS "memcpy" from the Standard C Library which in turn uses the memory access service which in turn uses the master bus adapter on the CPU to send tokens across the bus to a register on the ASIC. In order to send tokens on a bus, the master bus adapter requests ownership of the bus using the arbitration service on the bus. Finally the token reaches the ASIC register and the ASIC polls the presence register before processing the data. A much more complicated pattern is needed to support HW->SW interrupts. The ASIC completes processing and wants to hand the completed data to another software task. In this communication, the ASIC must send an interrupt across the interrupt bus, which in turn uses the interrupt controller on the processor. The interrupt controller calls the appropriate interrupt vector. The interrupt vector uses services on the data bus to copy the data from the ASIC register into the processor memory space. The interrupt vector then schedules the software task on the RTOS.

The communication patterns can be represented by a sender and receiver service. The sender source implements the "output" port service declaration (Post() function) and the receiver service implements the "input" port service

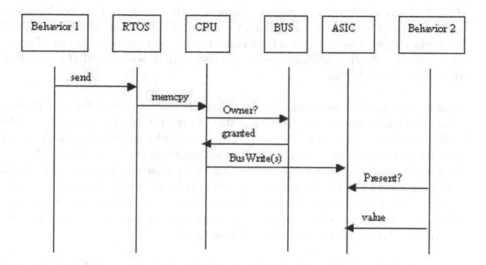

Fig. 7. A message sequence chart describing the Register Mapped communication pattern from the VCC library

declaration (Enabled() and Value() functions). The sender and receiver services can "use" services implemented by the architecture elements to which the behavior is mapped. For example, the register mapped pattern would have a "sender" pattern that "uses" services supported by the RTOS/processor and the "receiver" pattern "uses" services supported by the ASIC. Fig. 8 is an example of the services used in a "Register Mapped" pattern. The Post() function is implemented by the "RegisterMappedSWSender" service. This sender pattern uses the "Standard C Library API" which is implemented on the RTOS by the "Standard C Library" Service. The "Standard C Library" service uses the "CPU Memory API" which is implemented on the processor by the "CPU Memory" service. The "CPU Memory" service uses the "Master Adapter API" that is implemented by the "FCFS Bus Adapter" on the CPU port that writes the data to the "Bus Slave Adapter" on the ASIC port. In addition, the ASIC supports a "ASIC Memory API" which provides the "RegisterMappedReceiver" service a way to read the data when the Value() function is called.

The "sender" and "receiver" services only need to get the communication started and let the binding of services across the architecture topology transfer the data to its appropriate destination. Thus the "sender" and "receiver" patterns are reusable across different architecture platforms. For example, the "Register Mapped" sender and receiver services don't need to know the type of data bus that is used. In Fig. 8, the data bus is modeled as first-come-first-served. The bus adapters can be replaced with different bus models and the pattern will still work.

Some of the commonly used patterns available in the VCC library are enumerated below.

Direct Connect: A direct connect communication pattern is a hardware-to-hardware pattern that assumes the source and destination behaviors are mapped to hardware (ASICs) and a direct pin connection exists between the two. The direct connect pattern is implemented as a direct update and immediate activation of the receiver behavior.

Polling: The polling communication patterns are hardware-to-software patterns. The communication occurs through either a register or shared memory. The polling patterns assume a polling task runs periodically, monitoring the ASIC for new data. If data is present, the polling task activates the destination behavior. The sender and receiver services written for this pattern neglect the polling task and only model the time when the destination is activated determined by the polling period. The sender determines when the polling task runs next based on the current time, the polling start time, and the polling period. It then schedules the destination behavior to activate at this time.

Interrupt Patterns: The interrupt patterns are hardware-to-software patterns that assume the source behavior in a connection is mapped to hardware. The communication takes place either through a register or shared memory. The

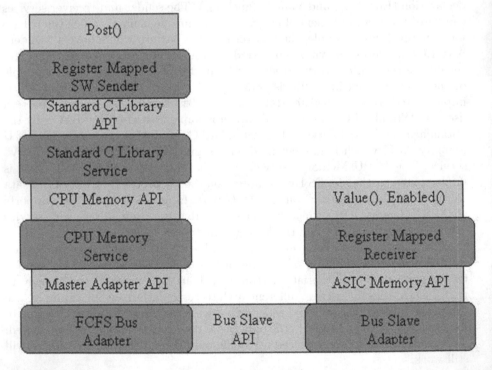

Fig. 8. Service bindings for the Register Mapped communication pattern from the VCC library

receiver behavior is activated by the sender, but no data transfer occurs until the receiver behavior does a read.

Semaphore Protected: The semaphore protected pattern is a software-to-software pattern where the receiver is prevented from reading an incomplete transfer by a software semaphore.

Unprotected: Unprotected patterns are software-to-software patterns where there is no coordination between the communicating processes.

4 Refinement

VCC supports a methodology of continuous refinement of the design from abstract towards concrete. The user begins the design process with a pure behavioral design. This design should first be analyzed for correct behavior using a functional simulator. Once the algorithm is behaving as expected, the design can be incrementally mapped to the architecture diagram. As the user makes more design decisions the accuracy of the performance analysis increases. For example, if the behaviors are implemented in software then the scheduling of the tasks on the RTOS causes the tasks to be run sequentially instead of in parallel as modeled in a pure functional simulation. The functional simulation serves as an executable specification to ensure that the design continues to operate correctly as more details are added to the design through refinement. This section defines the incremental mapping steps from functional simulation to fully mapped design. These steps don't have to be followed in the exact order mentioned and can be combined into larger steps.

Once the design has been sufficiently refined, then probes are added to record scheduler and bus activity, delays through the system, and other metrics of interest. Analysis of this data identifies the critical paths in the design as well as busses and schedulers which are overloaded. The performance of the design can then be improved by changing the mapping of the behaviors to the architectural elements or increasing the speed of architectural elements.

4.1 Functional Simulation

Functional simulation is used to verify the integrity of your behavioral design. You can check the data on the outputs to verify correctness. Functional simulation assumes that the implementation has infinite resources (computational processes, communication processes and memory).

Simulation time is shorter than in performance analysis because the functional blocks are executed with minimal scheduling overhead based on your model of computation (e.g., Discrete Event or Dataflow). It is also simpler to debug your design without the impact of architecture resource like RTOS, processors, caches, DMAs, bus bridges, etc.

4.2   Performance Impact of Behaviors Running in Software vs. Hardware

The first refinement step is the partitioning of the behavioral design into hardware and software. In VCC, the partitioning is accomplished by mapping each behavior instance to the architecture resource (RTOS for software and ASIC for hardware). In addition, the user must specify for each behavior instance, a performance model of running this behavior on a specific architecture resource. The performance analysis of this mapped design will show delays of running the tasks in hardware vs. software. VCC supports two alternatives for specifying a performance model for a behavior, *Delay Script Model* and *Annotated Model*.

The simplest model is a Delay Script Model that supports delay statements interspersed with sampling of inputs and posting of outputs. An example is shown below.

```
delay_model()
{
      /* Wait before reading input */
      delay('20e-6');
      /* Now read the input */
      input(inA);
      run();
      /* Wait before posting the outputs */
      delay('10e-6');
      /* Post the output */
      output(outX);
      /* Wait between outputs, if needed. */
      delay('10e-6');
      output(outY);
      /* Wait for internal state to finish */
      delay('10e-6');
}
```

VCC wraps the Delay Script Model around the behavior model causing the input events, the block itself and the posting of outputs to be appropriately delayed. This model is useful for data-dominated blocks, but more difficult to write for control-dominated blocks because of the many branching constructs that must be duplicated in the Delay Script Model.

The Annotated Performance Model is much better for defining a performance model for control-dominated behaviors. The performance delays are associated with statements in the original behavioral model. During performance analysis, the annotated behavior is executed causing delays along the way. Therefore when a particular branch is executed, the delays annotated in that branch are also executed while skipping delays associated with branches not executed. Similarly, if a delay is annotated inside a looping construct, the delay will be accumulated for each iteration of the loop.

The performance models associated with behaviors cause the appropriate delay during performance analysis. The user can place probes on ports and then display the data on a timeline chart. If the throughput through the system is too slow, the user may choose to move some of the behaviors to hardware. Another choice is to increase the clock speed on the processor (delays in performance model may be expressed as clock cycles instead of absolute time).

4.3   Performance Impact of RTOS Scheduling Software Tasks

Multiple behaviors running on an RTOS contend for execution time on the processor. Thus the RTOS must arbitrate between the behaviors by implementing a scheduling policy (such as round robin scheduling, priority-based scheduling and so forth). In VCC, the scheduling policy is defined as an architectural service on the RTOS. If the scheduling policy supports priority or task ordering, the user specifies this information as a parameter on the mapping link.

The performance impact of scheduling involves two fundamental concepts: activation and reaction. A task is activated when it has enough inputs to run. The task requests service from the RTOS and remains in the activated state until the RTOS runs the task. Once the RTOS determines the task should run next, the RTOS sends a message to the task to start the reaction. The task runs (using the performance model of the behavior instance as described in Section 4.2). When the task is finished it sends a message to the RTOS that the reaction has ended. Finally the task is deactivated because it has run to completion and now waits for its next set of inputs.

In some RTOS models preemption is supported. This is modeled by extending the above description to support two new messages (suspend() and resume()). The scheduler may receive a request of activation by a second behavior that has higher priority than the currently running task. In this scenario, the RTOS sends a suspend() message to the running task, runs the higher priority task and then sends a resume() message to the original task. During the suspension, the state of the task must be saved so that it can be resumed at a later time. If the preemption occurs after the input sampling phase, it delays the outputs by the duration of the preemption. If preemption occurs during input sampling, computation might be affected. Input values might be overwritten before they are sampled, or new events might arrive that were not available originally. It is precisely these effects that need to be understood through performance analysis.

VCC performance analysis supports Gantt-style probes that collect data regarding task activations, starts, suspends, resumes and finishes. Fig. 9 is an example of a Gantt-style chart that displays when tasks were activated (asterisks), how long it waited to be started by the RTOS, and how long it took for the reaction (triangles). The Gantt-style chart also shows whether a behavior has been preempted and when it was resumed. In Fig. 9, three behavior tasks are run on the RTOS. The BURST_BASIC_FIFO asks for activation (asterisks) and then reacts (triangles). The MAC and the CONTROLLER are run sequentially. If the CONTROLLER requested activation before the MAC was completed, the

Gantt chart would show that the RTOS arbitrated the multiple requests causing the CONTROLLER to be delayed until after the MAC was done.

4.4   Performance Impact of Bus Loading

The loading of a bus is another factor in the overall system performance. By mapping behaviors onto different architectural resources, certain communications must be over a bus. The impact of communication over a bus can be specified as arbitration and transfer delay.

Bus arbitration is needed when multiple transfers are requested simultaneously. If the bus is a time-sliced bus then arbitration is not necessary. If the bus is arbitrated by priority, then a request and acknowledge ownership protocol must be defined between the bus and the bus masters.

The transfer delay accounts for the delay associated with transferring data across the bus. The bus model must calculate how many bus transactions are required for a data token of specific size. Finally the bus model must specify how long it takes for each bus transaction.

Some busses support preemption and can be handled by extending the bus model with additional suspend() and resume() messages (similar to the RTOS model).

VCC can automatically determine which communications are over a bus. If there is a single bus between the architecture resources, VCC can also automatically determine which bus should be loaded by this communication. In more complicated architectures, the user should explicitly map a behavioral net to the bus to be loaded. The bus must specify the arbitration model and the transfer delay model. Probes can be placed on the bus during performance analysis to collect data regarding the load of the bus. This data can be analyzed to see the traffic on the bus (average load as well as peak load). For example, in Fig. 10, the bus has traffic from behaviors mapped to ASIC1. The Filter sends data on the bus, followed by the Equalizer and the Slicer. The bus arbiter serializes these three transactions.

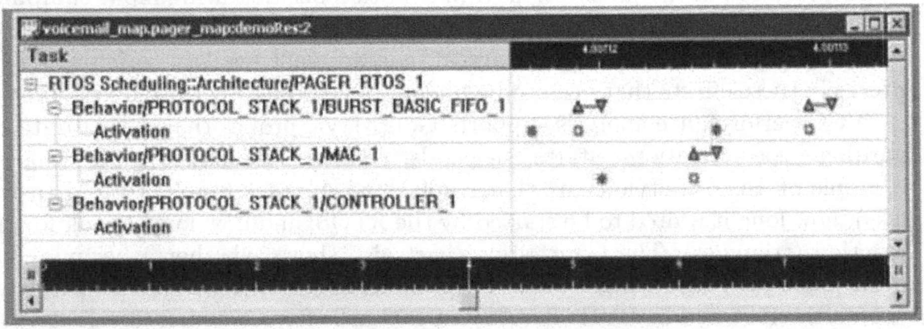

Fig. 9. A Gantt chart in VCC Visualize that demonstrates the impact of RTOS scheduling on system performance

4.5   Channel Refinement from Abstract Tokens

In the behavior diagram, the data communicated between behaviors may be abstract tokens (video frames) instead of bit-vectors. If the behaviors are implemented in hardware then the tokens must be converted to bit-vectors. The disassembly of token into bit-vectors must be done on one side and then the reassembly of the token must be done on the other side. The up and down converters for this data token must be compatible with each other.

Since this refinement is only needed if the communication occurs in hardware, VCC supports channel refinement in the mapping diagram. Refinement in the mapping has the advantage of not modifying the original behavioral design, thus making the behavioral design reusable in other mappings.

The mapping refinement requires instantiating the up-down converters into the mapping diagram. Instead of mapping the behavioral net to a bus in the architecture, it is mapped to the refinement instance. The refinement instance itself is then mapped to the architecture. Thus the up and down converter may be mapped to hardware or software and the communication between the two must also be mapped to a bus. The performance analysis will now show the impact of running the up and down converters. The bus load of transferring bit-vectors across the bus instead of the high level tokens should not be significantly different assuming the original bus model could calculate the size of the abstract token and can preempt in the middle of a transaction.

4.6   Performance Impact of Specific Communication Patterns

Communication patterns are a simple mechanism to represent and reuse complex models of detailed communications behavior or protocols. An earlier step in the refinement process maps communications to busses in the architecture

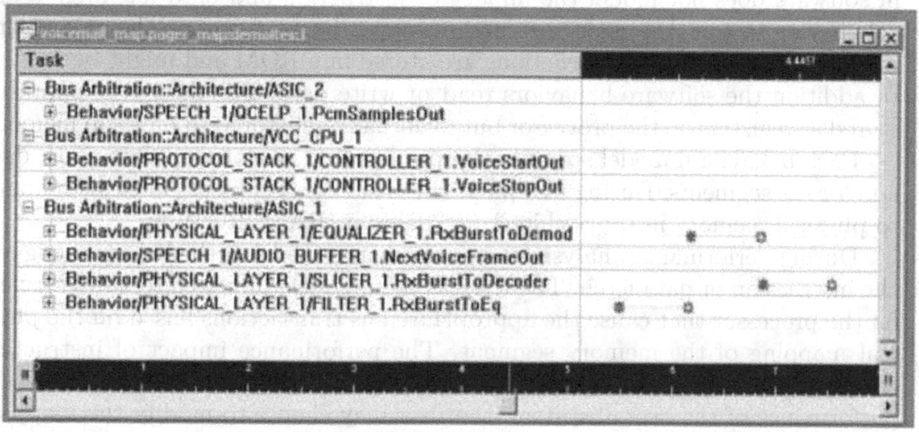

Fig. 10. A Gantt chart in VCC Visualize that demonstrates the impact of bus loading on system performance

diagram. This bus load represents only the delay of sending the data from the source to a register on destination architecture resource. In modern architectures, additional communication protocols are used. For example, architectures support shared memories on the bus. Instead of writing data to the register on the ASIC, the data may be written to the shared memory. A trigger might be sent to the ASIC to indicate that the data is in the shared memory and when the ASIC is ready it accesses the data from the shared memory. The performance impact is that the sender of the data doesn't have to wait until the ASIC has read the data. In more complicated architectures there are caches, DMAs, Bus Bridges, interrupt busses, and so forth which support more efficient communication patterns. To build correct system models, each pattern must be modeled for delay and resource sharing, leading to the methods described.

VCC supports patterns and architectural services to support performance modeling of communication patterns. The user can choose an existing pattern from a library or may create new communication patterns. In the mapping diagram, the user instantiates an instance of the pattern, sets the parameters, maps the behavioral net to the pattern and sets additional parameters on the mapping link. An example of a parameter on the pattern might be the shared memory to which the data should be written.

In performance analysis, the impact of choosing different communication patterns can be seen by delays of the data through the design. Performance impact might also be seen on the bus traffic. For example, the choice of interrupt or polling pattern will impact the load on data bus as well as the scheduling of the polling task. To improve the performance of the overall system, the user may choose different communication patterns or alter pattern parameters.

4.7   Performance Impact of Instruction and Data Fetching

Earlier in the refinement process, the performance delays of running a behavior in software does not model the impact of instruction and data fetching. When a behavior is run, the code instructions must be loaded into the processor's memory. In general, the instructions are stored in a ROM and might be cached. In addition the software behaviors read or write data. The data is temporarily stored as registers on the processor but eventually get stored to physical memory.

Each behavioral model specifies the number and size of each data code, data and/or bss segments. During mapping, these memory segments must be mapped to physical memory in the architecture diagram (RAM, ROM, etc).

During performance analysis, the performance model of the behavior triggers the instruction or data fetch. The fetch is then modeled by architectural services on the processor that cause the appropriate bus transactions based on the physical mapping of the memory segment. The performance impact of instruction and data fetching is task delay as well as additional bus traffic. To improve the performance of the overall system, the user may choose to modify the mapping of the memory segments to faster memories or analyze the locality of data to improve caching.

4.8 Impact of Refinement on Simulation Run Times

The refinements described in this section often have a very large impact on the run time of the simulation models. In functional simulation, the output of a block is moved to the input of another block, and the downstream block is activated with a single event on the global queue. In a performance simulation where the behaviors and communication are mapped, the same operation would require many events and context switches. In simulations with detailed modeling of the bus effects we have seen simulation run times hundreds of times slower than functional simulation.

The performance of VCC simulations is platform dependent. When run on architectures that have a low context switch overhead, the simulation performance is much better. RISC architectures where many registers must be saved when switching between threads have a higher context switching overhead than processors with fewer registers. In some cases where simulation performance is dominated by context switching overheads, very fast and expensive workstations have been relatively slow when running VCC simulations.

5 Links to Implementation

Once the system performance meets the needs of the designer, the next step is to implement the specified design. The implementation of the design should match the design previously simulated. This requires implementing the model of concurrency as well as the individual behaviors and services. VCC supports assembly of both the hardware and software implementation of the mapped design. A complete design consists of the following: an RTL-level netlist representing the top-level architecture diagram, hardware for each of the architecture instances in the diagram, ANSI-C software for each of the tasks mapped to software and configuration/startup files for assembling the target software and finally the communication between the software and hardware. If the design is to be simulated in a downstream tool (HDL simulator) then VCC also supports reusable testbenches and probe support for correlating results between the functional simulation, performance simulation, and implementable designs.

5.1 RTL Level Netlist

The RTL-level netlist for the top-level architecture diagram converts the relaxed architecture diagram into a pin-accurate netlist. The designer defines a refined interface file for each architecture instance that lists all the pins (name and direction). In addition, the user defines a refined interface file for the busses in the diagram. In order to connect the instances to the bus, the user provides a rule-based connectivity model. The simplest rule is to connect by name. For example, if the bus has a signal called "data" then it should be connected to the signal called "data" on the architecture instance. If the signal names don't match then more complicated rules can be specified for connecting them. The rules can be parameterized by model parameters, instance-level parameters or even mapping parameters. This is very useful for defining communication patterns that issue interrupt signals.

Since architecture models can and will be implemented by different vendors, the connectivity model specifies a refined interface to which it can be connected. Thus, if an architecture instance defines rules for connecting to the same interface that the bus supports, VCC can assemble them together. A project, company or a third party standards body might define this interface. The VCI Bus standard is a good example of such an interface, because busses, masters and slaves can be independently implemented to this standard. VCC supports multiple team design by modeling the interface as a refined interface model in a library. The designer specifies for each relaxed port of the architecture element the refined interface model to which it can connect by setting the *connType* parameter.

5.2   Hardware Model Implementation

For each architecture instance in the diagram, an implementation view should be provided. The architecture symbol declares the implementation services supported and the implementation view bound in the configuration selects a service definition for each of the declared services on the symbol. This separation of declaration and definition supports multiple implementations of the same interface. For example, the hardware may be implemented in FPGA or as Custom Layout. The hardware may have alternative implementations representing variations for low power, high speed or minimal area.

An architecture element may be defined by one or more services. For example, an MPEG may be implemented in dedicated hardware. Instead of defining a large block of HDL code, the designer is encouraged to separate the HDL behavior from the communication. In addition, the communication should be layered providing separating HDL blocks for the transaction-based communication down to the signal-based communication. Another service on the dedicated hardware may represent the internal arbitration required to serialize requests to the bus. By providing such separation of interests, the services may be reused in different architecture element and there is a higher chance of mixing and matching these different pieces. For example, if the bus on the architecture changes, then only the service for translating the transaction-based communication down to the signal-based communication needs to be modified. Another example is evaluating the impact of changing communication from register-mapped to shared memory by just changing the transaction-based communication layer.

If the dedicated hardware does not exist, VCC will assemble the hardware block based on the behaviors mapped to this architecture instance. Each behavior mapped to this architecture instance should provide an RTL view of just the behavior. In addition, the RTL view should match the MOC of the behavior. An example of an RTL model that models the Discrete Event MOC has two signals for each behavioral input port. One signal, portA_e, represents the enable pin and the second signal, portA represents the data. The model should only reference the data signal when the enable signal is true. In order to model the OR firing semantics, the RTL model should be written with sensitivity list containing all the enable signals. The lossy semantics of the DE MOC is supported by the combination of the sensitivity list and not accessing the data signal unless the enabled signal is true.

The behavioral nets connecting these behaviors are mapped to patterns. Each pattern has an implementation view that model the communication layer in terms of transactions.

The pattern is also responsible for setting the enabled pin when the data is available and reset it after the reaction is complete. The translation of transaction to signals is modeled by a service (bus adapter) on the architecture instance. In addition, the bus adapter models the arbitration of the different patterns within the instance to the bus. Fig. 11 shows how the hardware is assembled from the implementation models of each behavior, and from the patterns and hardware services in the architecture diagram.

5.3   Testbench Implementation

Testbench behaviors may be modeled by mapping these behaviors to a Test Hardware block. This Test Hardware block may be directly connected to a Dedicated Hardware block or it may be connected to the bus. The testbench behaviors don't have to be implemented at the RTL level as long as it can be wrapped in an RTL-level interface and the target simulator provides an adequate API to schedule events, wait on time, etc. This methodology supports reuse of the same testbench behavior in VCC simulation as well as the target simulation (i.e. HDL simulator).

5.4   Hardware Service Definitions

The service definitions may be RTL models written in standard languages like Verilog or VHDL. VCC supports macro substitution within the provided RTL models. For example, the Verilog may require a destination address to send the data. This address might be dependent on the mapping of the behavior receiving this data. VCC evaluates the macros based on parameter values in the behavior, architecture or mapping design. If the RTL model is even more complicated, the service can be written in Java and can generate the model based on all the design data. An example of a Java service is a RAM generator that can implement RAMs of different sizes.

5.5   Software Configuration

For the software, VCC supports configuration and setup of the target executable. This includes configuration of the RTOS as well as registering processor interrupts.

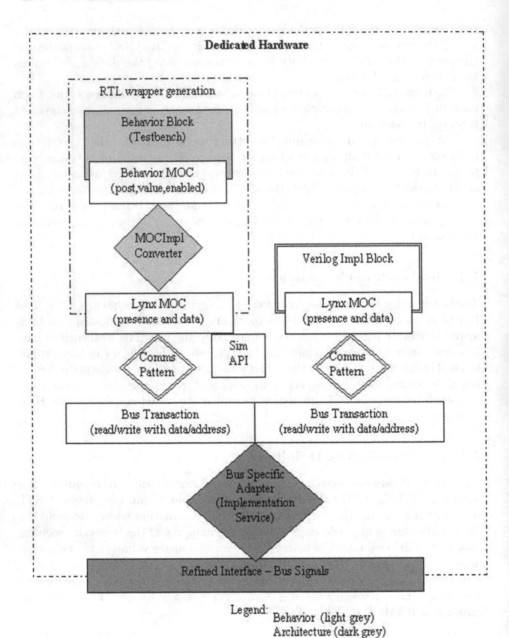

Fig. 11. Assembly of custom behaviors on dedicated hardware

5.6   Software Tasks

Behaviors mapped to an RTOS or static scheduler in the architecture diagram need to provide a software implementation of that behavior. For example, if a behavioral model is defined in whitebox C (a subset of ANSI-C), VCC supports automatic generation of an ANSI-C model. But if a behavioral model is defined in blackbox C++ (a subset of C++), the designer must explicitly provide a software implementation. The software implementation should match the MOC of the original behavior. For discrete event MOC, the ANSI-C model should model the OR firing semantics. The VCC methodology encourages this software to be implemented as macro calls for accessing ports, parameters and behavioral memory interface. These macro calls can then be defined based on the communication pattern chosen in the mapping diagram. For example, two behaviors mapped to the same RTOS might communicate via a semaphore. The port communication that posts data from the source behavior should be a macro that locks the semaphore and sends the data. By specifying this as a macro, the communication can be easily changed to an unprotected software communication or may even be changed to a hardware communication (across a bus) in the scenario where the destination behavior is re-mapped to a dedicated hardware block.

5.7   Software Communication

The implementation view of software patterns can use services provided by the RTOS or processor to which its behavior is mapped. The semaphore service For example, needs to register the semaphore during RTOS configuration. This registration can be supported by a semaphore registration service of the RTOS. This methodology will also prevent semaphore patterns from being used on a simple RTOS that doesn't support this style of communication, because the stripped down RTOS does not provide such a service.

5.8   Software Service Definitions

Software services can be software implementation (ANSI-C, assembly, etc.) or it might be a Java generator which provides more expressiveness in defining the implementation as well as making sure the configuration/setup of the target executable is supported.

5.9   Static Schedulers

The VCC architecture diagram supports static schedulers as well as full service RTOS. A static scheduler represents a single task where the behaviors are run serially based on the designer-specified task order. VCC supports automatic generation of this static scheduler based on the behaviors and the task order parameter values.

6 Summary

VCC supports a flexible model for specifying, simulating, and generating implementations of concurrent systems. The definition of behavior interaction is supported by an extensible set of models-of-computation defining the semantics of behavior invocation and interaction. Design exploration is supported by separate specification of the behavior and architecture. Design exploration is also supported by communication refinement, which is made possible by the separate specification of the interface and implementation of services. After the communication has been specified in detail, an implementation of the model can be generated.

Acknowledgement

We sincerely thank Luciano Lavagno and Grant Martin for their careful review, and invaluable feedback in the writing of this chapter. Many thanks to the entire VCC team for brainstorming, developing, and testing the methodology described here.

References

[1] H. Chang, L. Cooke, M. Hunt, A. McNelly, G. Martin, and L. Todd, *"Surviving the SOC Revolution: A Guide to Platform-Based Design,"* Kluwer Academic Publishers, 1999. 191

[2] T. Grotker, S. Liao, G. Martin, and S. Swan, *"System Design with SystemC,"* Kluwer Academic Publishers, 2002. 192

[3] P. Schaumont, S. Vernalde, L. Rijnders, M. Engels, and I. Bolsens, "Synthesis of multi-rate and variable rate circuits for high speed telecommunications applications," *Proceedings of the European Design and Test Conference,* 1997. 192

[4] D. D. Gajski, J. Zhu, R. Domer, A. Gerstlauer, and S. Zhao, *"SpecC: Specification Language and Methodology,"* Kluwer Academic Publishers, 2000. 192

[5] K. Van Rompaey, D. Verkest, I. Bolsens, and H. D. Man, "CoWare – a design environment for heterogeneous hardware/software systems," *Proceedings of the European Design Automation Conference,* 1996. 192

[6] http://www.cadence.com/products/spw.html 192

[7] J. T. Buck,, R. Vaidyanathan, "Heterogeneous Modeling and Simulation of Embedded Systems in El Greco," *Proceedings of the International Workshop on Hardware-Software Codesign,* 2000. 192

[8] Bob Schutz, "Integrated System Design Environment Lowers Development Risk," *Integrated System Design,* A Miller Freeman Publication, March 1999. 192

[9] F. Balarin, M. Chiodo, P. Giusto, H. Hsieh, A. Jurecska, L. Lavagno, C. Passerone, A. Sangiovanni-Vincentelli, E. Sentovitch, K. Suzuki, and B. Tabbara, *"Hard-Software Co-Design of Embedded Systems: The POLIS Approach,"* Kluwer Academic Publishers, 1997. 192, 194

[10] E. A. de Kock, G. Essink, W. J. M. Smits, P. van der Wolf, J.–Y. Brunel, W. M. Kruijtzer, P. Lieverse, and K. A. Vissers, "YAPI: Application modeling for signal processing systems," *Proceedings of the Design Automation Conference,* 2000. 192, 201

[11] S. Edwards, L. Lavagno, E. A. Lee, and A. Sangiovanni-Vincentelli, "Design of embedded systems: Formal models, validation and synthesis," *Proceedings of the IEEE*, **Vol. 85, No. 3**, March 1997. 196

[12] E. A. Lee, and D. G. Messerschmitt, "Static scheduling of Synchronous dataflow programs for digital signal processing," *IEEE Transactions on Computers*, **Vol. C-36, No. 2**, February, 1987. 201

[13] J. T. Buck, S. Ha, E. A. Lee, and D. G. Messerschmitt, "Ptolemy: A Framework for Simulating and Prototyping Heterogeneous Systems," *International Journal of Computer Simulation*, **Vol. 4**, April, 1994. 201

[14] S. S. Bhattacharyya, P. K. Murthy, and E. A. Lee, "*Software Synthesis from Dataflow Graphs*," Kluwer Academic Publishers, 1996. 201

[15] G. Kahn, "The semantics of a simple language for parallel programming," J. L. Rosenfeld, editor, *Information Processing*, North-Holland Publishing Company, 1974. 201

[16] S. Solden, "Architectural Services Modeling for Performance in HW-SW Co-Design," *Proceedings of the Workshop on Synthesis and System Integration of Mixed Technologies (SASIMI)*, Japan, October, 2001. 211

Modeling and Designing Heterogeneous Systems

Felice Balarin[1], Luciano Lavagno[1], Claudio Passerone[2],
Alberto Sangiovanni-Vincentelli[3], Marco Sgroi[3], and Yosinori Watanabe[1]

[1] Cadence Berkeley Labs, 2001 Addison St. 3rd Floor, Berkeley CA 94704, USA
[2] Politecnico di Torino, C. Duca degli Abruzzi 24, 10129 Torino, Italy
[3] University of California, Berkeley CA 94720, USA

Abstract. We present the modeling mechanism employed in Metropolis, a design environment for heterogeneous embedded systems, and a design methodology based on the mechanism experimented for wireless
communication systems. It is developed to favor the reusability of components in the systems, by decoupling the specification of orthogonal
aspects explicitly over a set of abstraction levels. It uses a single model
to represent designs specified this way, to which not only simulation but
also analysis and synthesis algorithms can be applied relatively easily.
The model uses executable code as well as denotational formulas, classes
of temporal and predicate logic, so that the right level of details of the
design can be defined at each abstraction.

1 Introduction

The ability to integrate an exponentially increasing number of transistors within
a chip, the ever-expanding use of electronic embedded systems to control more
and more aspects of the "real world", and the trend to interconnect more and
more such systems (often from different manufacturers) into a global network,
are creating a nightmarish scenario for embedded system designers. Complexity and scope are exploding into three inter-related but independently growing
directions, while teams are even shrinking in size to further reduce costs. This
problem can only be tackled by a revolutionary approach to system design, which
dramatically raises the level of abstraction, while keeping close control on cost,
performance and power issues.

This paper focuses on embedded systems, which are defined as electronic
systems that use computers and electronics to perform some task, usually to
control some physical system or to communicate information, without being
explicitly perceived as a computer. Thanks to the phenomenal growth exhibited
by the scale of integration, they are preferred means to offer ever-improving
services to a multitude of drivers, callers, photographers, watchers, and so on.

A key characteristic of such systems is the *heterogeneity* both of specification
models, because of the habits and needs of designers from very different application fields, and of implementation mechanisms, because of the variety of tasks
and environmental conditions. For example, block-based design environments,
multi-CPU implementation platforms, critical safety needs and hard deadlines

J. Cortadella et al. (Eds.): Concurrency and Hardware Design, LNCS 2549, pp. 228–273, 2002.
© Springer-Verlag Berlin Heidelberg 2002

are typical of the automotive world. On the other hand, a cellular telephone user interface is designed using software-oriented tools, such as compilers and debuggers, for implementation over a single micro-controller shared with protocol stack management tasks.

This heterogeneity has so far caused a huge fragmentation of the field, resulting in very diverse design methodologies with often scarce tool support. De facto standards in terms of specification models and tools have emerged only in a few areas, namely telecommunications and automotive, essentially because of standardization and integration needs. This is of course problematic for a number of reasons, and a more unified approach to embedded system design, with possible ramifications to general electronic system design, would obviously be a benefit. We are not advocating a single, over-arching super-tool that could solve all design problems, since this is obviously not feasible. This paper proposes an approach with the following key characteristics.

First of all, it leaves the designer relatively free to use the specification mechanism (graphical or textual language) of choice, as long as it has a sound semantical foundation (Model Of Computation).

Secondly, it uses a single meta-model to represent both the embedded system and some abstract relevant characteristics of its environment.

Finally, it separates orthogonal aspects, such as:

1. Computation and communication. This separation is important because:
   - refinement of computation is generally done by hand, or by compilation, or by scheduling, and other complex techniques,
   - refinement of communication is generally done by use of patterns (such as circular buffers for FIFOs, polling or interrupt for hardware to software data transfers, and so on).
2. Functionality and architecture, or "functional specification" and "implementation platform", because they are often defined independently, by different groups (e.g., video encoding and decoding experts versus hardware/software designers in multi-media applications). Functionality (both computation and communication) is "mapped" to architecture in order to specify a given refinement for automated or manual implementation.
3. Behavior and performance indices, such as latency, throughput, power, energy, and so on. These are kept separate because:
   - when performance indices represent constraints they are often specified independent of the functionality, by different groups (e.g., control engineers versus system architects for automotive engine control applications),
   - when performance indices represent the result of implementation choices, they derive from a specific architectural mapping of the behavior.

All these separations result in better *re-use*, because they decouple independent aspects, that would otherwise tie, e.g., a given functional specification to low-level implementation details, or to a specific communication paradigm, or to a scheduling algorithm. It is very important to define only as many aspects

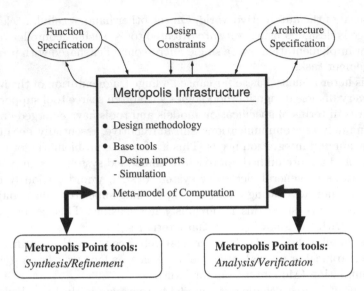

Fig. 1. The Metropolis framework

as needed at every level of abstraction, in the interest of flexibility and rapid design space exploration.

We are developing a design environment called Metropolis, with the characteristics above. A schematic representation of the Metropolis framework is shown in Figure 1: the main infrastructure consists of the internal representation mechanism called the Metropolis meta-model, described in detail in Sections 2 and 3, the design methodology, used in Section 6 to model a communication network, and some base tools for simulation and design imports. It is designed so that point tools such as synthesis or verification algorithms can be easily interfaced to the infrastructure to perform specialized tasks on particular applications, and thus various tools can be interoperated across different abstraction levels over different applications.

We defined the meta-model to be powerful enough, so that the most commonly used abstract Models Of Computation (MOCs) and concrete formal languages could be translated into it, so as not to constrain the application designer to a specific language choice[1].

Another fundamental aspect that we considered throughout this work is the ability to *specify* rather than implement, *execute* reasonably detailed but still fairly abstract specifications, and finally *use the best synthesis algorithms* for a given application domain and implementation architecture. For these reasons we represented explicitly the concurrency available at the specification level, in the form of multiple communicating processes. We used an executable representation for the computation processes and the communication media, in order

---

[1] At least in principle. Of course, time may limit in practice the number of available translators.

to allow both simulation and formal and semi-formal verification techniques to be used. Finally, we restricted that representation, with respect to a full-fledged programming language such as C, C++ or Java, in order to improve both *analyzability* and *synthesizability*.

Unfortunately we were not able to fully remain within the decidable domain (nor, maybe even worse, within the efficiently analyzable domain), because this goal is achievable only with extreme abstraction (i.e. only at the very beginning of a design), or for very simple applications, or in very specialized domains. However, we defined at least a meta-model for which the task of identifying *sufficient conditions* that allow analysis or synthesis algorithms to be applied or speeded up, could be simple enough. Hence our meta-model can be translated relatively easily, under checkable conditions or using formally defined abstractions, into a variety of abstract synthesis- or analysis-oriented models, such as Petri nets, or static dataflow networks, or synchronous extended finite state machines.

The result is a meta-model that uses different classes of objects to represent the basic notions discussed above.

1. Processes, communication media and netlists describe the functional requirements, in terms of input-output relations first, and of more detailed algorithms later.
2. A mechanism of refinement allows one to replace processes and media with sub-netlists representing more detailed behavior.
3. Temporal and propositional logics can be used to describe constraints over quantities such as time or energy. They:
   - initially describe constraints over yet undefined quantities (e.g. latency constraints when describing processes at the untimed functional level using Kahn process networks),
   - then specify properties that must be satisfied by more detailed implementations (e.g. while a Kahn process network is being scheduled on a processor), and
   - finally define assumptions that must be checked for validity (e.g. using a cycle-accurate Instruction Set Simulator to run the scheduled processes in software).

In the rest of the paper we discuss all these notions in detail, and we apply them to a complex, realistic embedded system specification from the communications domain.

2   Metropolis Meta-model

In providing a specification, one needs a capability of describing the following three aspects: *actions*, *constraints*, and their *refinement*. This is true whether it is a specification of a system (behavior or architecture) or of the environment. The Metropolis meta-model has this capability, as presented in this and the next two sections.

A behavior can be defined as concurrent occurrences of sequences of actions [2]. Some action may follow another action, which may take place concurrently with other actions. The occurrences of these actions constitute the behavior of a system that the actions belong to. An architecture can be defined as capacity of actions it can provide. Some actions may realize arithmetic operations, while others may transfer data. Using these actions, one can implement the behavior of the system.

A description of actions can be made in terms of *computation, communication*, and *coordination*. The computation defines the input and output sets, a mapping from the former to the latter, the condition under which inputs are acquired, and the condition under which outputs are made observable. The communication defines a state and methods. The state represents a snapshot of the communication. For example, the state of communication carried out by a stack may represent the number of elements in the stack and the contents of the elements. The communication methods are defined so that they can be used to transfer information. The methods may evaluate and possibly alter the communication state. For the example of the stack, methods called pop and push may be defined. In addition, one may define a method for evaluating the current number of elements available in the stack. Actions for computation and communication often need to be coordinated. For example, one may want to prohibit the use of the pop method, while an element is added to the stack by the push method. Coordination may be specified either by formulas such that desired coordination is realized when actions take place in order to satisfy the formulas, or by algorithms whose execution guarantees the coordination.

In the meta-model, special types of objects called *process* and *medium* are used to describe computation and communication, respectively. For coordination, a special type called *scheduler* can be used to specify algorithms. Alternatively, one can write formulas in the linear temporal logic [6] if one prefers to specify the coordination without committing to particular algorithms. The formulas can be specified in any of the special objects or in hierarchical netlists that define connections of the objects.

When an action takes place, it incurs cost. Cost for a set of actions is often subject to certain constraints. For example, the time interval between two actions may have to be smaller than some bound, or the total power required by a sequence of actions may need to be lower than some amount. The meta-model provides a mechanism that a quantity such as time or power can be defined and associated with actions, and constraints on the quantity can be specified in a form of predicate logic. In the rest of this section, we present more in detail these key points of the meta-model and illustrate them with examples.

---

[2] Here, *behavior* is used as a general term to refer to what a given system does. In the succeeding sections, we define the term more restrictively as a single sequence of observable actions.

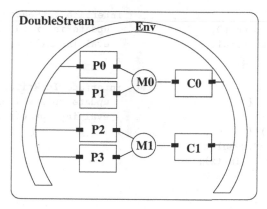

Fig. 2. A netlist of processes and media. The object around the processes is the environment, which is modeled by a medium in this example

2.1 Processes, Media, and Netlists

Figure 2 shows a network of meta-model objects, where rectangles represent processes and circles represent media. It consists of two independent data streams. In each stream, the two processes on the left send integers, and the process on the right receive them. The medium in the middle defines the semantics of this communication.

Processes are active objects in the sense that they take their own actions concurrently with those of other processes. The specifications of the processes in Figure 2 are given in Figure 3-(a). The syntax is similar to that of Java, although the meta-model does not support many of the Java grammar or keywords. As with a class definition in an object-oriented language, a process may declare fields and functions, and may be extended to define other processes under the class hierarchy. The fields and functions may not be accessed by objects other than itself. This restriction enforces communication to be specified explicitly. A process always defines at least one constructor and exactly one function called `thread`, the top-level function to specify the behavior of the process. We call it *thread* because it is given as a sequential program to define a sequence of actions that the process takes. A formal definition of a thread is provided in Section 3, with respect to the execution semantics of the meta-model. A process interacts with other objects through *ports*. A port is a special kind of field with the type being an interface. An interface declares a set of functions with the types of their inputs and outputs, without implementing them (as in Java). A process may access its ports and call functions declared in the corresponding interfaces. The interfaces used in Figure 2 is shown in Figure 3-(b). The keyword `update` indicates that the corresponding function may change the state of a medium that implements the interface. Similarly, `eval` indicates that the function may only evaluate the state but not change it. The meta-model has a use policy that

```
process IntX {                          interface IntReader extends Port {
  port IntReader port0;                   update int readInt();
  port IntWriter port1;                   eval int n();
                                        }
  IntX(){ }
                                        interface IntWriter extends Port {
  void thread() {                         update void writeInt(int data);
    int x;                                eval int space();
    while(true) {                       }
  Rd:   x = port0.readInt();
  Wr:   port1.writeInt(x);
} } }
```

(a)   (b)

Fig. 3. (a) Process used in Figure 2 (b) Interfaces used for the ports of the process (a)

these functions must be implemented so that the implementation is compatible with the semantics of these keywords.

Figure 4 shows the specification of the media used in Figure 2. A medium implements interfaces by providing code for the functions of the interfaces. As with processes, a medium may define fields and functions, where some of the fields may be ports. They may not be accessed by objects other than itself. The only exception is that a function of an interface implemented by the medium object may be called by an object that has a port connected to the medium object. Such connections are specified in netlists, where a port may be connected to a single object of a medium type which implements the port's interface. With such a connection, a call of a function of the interface through the port will execute the code of the function provided in the medium.

Statements called `await` often appear in functions of both processes and media. This is one of the most important constructs, since it is the only one in the meta-model to specify synchronization among processes in the execution code [3]. It is used in a situation where a process needs to wait until a certain condition holds, and once the condition becomes true, the process takes a sequence of actions. We call such a sequence *critical section*. Further, it is possible to specify actions that should not be taken by other processes while the process is in the critical section. We will illustrate the semantics of this construct in this section, while the formal semantics is given in Section 3.

Consider the code of the process shown in Figure 5. Inside the keyword `await`, the parentheses specify a condition to be checked and actions to be excluded. This is followed by a specification of the critical section, inside the braces in

---

[3] Constraint formulas can be used in addition to the execution code to specify synchronization, as described in Section 2.3.

```
medium IntM implements IntWriter,IntReader,IW,IR,IC,IS,IN {
  int storage, space, n;

  IntM(){space = 1; n = 0;}

  update void writeInt(int data) {
    await (space>0; this.IW, this.IS; this.IW)
      await (true; this.IC, this.IS, this.IN; this.IC){
        space = 0; n = 1;
        storage = data;
      }
  }

  update int readInt() {
    await (n>0; this.IR, this.IN; this.IR)
      await (true; this.IC, this.IS, this.IN; this.IC){
        space = 1; n = 0;
        return storage;
      }
  }

  eval int space() {await(true; this.IW, this.IC; this.IS) return space;}

  eval int n() {await(true; this.IR, this.IC; this.IN) return n;}
}

/*
Interfaces used inside IntM
*/
interface IW extends Port {}
interface IR extends Port {}
interface IC extends Port {}
interface IS extends Port {}
interface IN extends Port {}
```

Fig. 4. Medium used in Figure 2

the example. The parentheses consist of three sections separated by semicolons, which are called the *guard*, *test list*, and *set list* respectively.

The guard, a Boolean expression, specifies the condition that must hold when the execution of the critical section begins. In Figure 5, an interface function n() is called in the guard. Suppose that this function returns the number of data elements available in the storage of the corresponding medium object. Then the guard becomes true when both of the media connected to the ports of the process have at least one data element respectively. This is the semantics used in dataflow networks. In general, await is capable of modeling different semantics by using different guards. For example, if the conjunction used in the guard in

```
process Y {
  port IntReader port0;
  port IntReader port1;
  port IntWriter port2;
  ...
  void thread() {
    int z;
    while(true) {
      await {
        (port0.n()>0 && port1.n()>0;
         port0.IntReader, port1.IntReader;
         port0.IntReader, port1.IntReader)
         { z = foo(port0.readInt(),port1.readInt()); }
      }
      port2.writeInt(z);
  } }
  int foo(int x, int y) { ... }
}
```

Fig. 5. Process using an await statement

Figure 5 is replaced by disjunction, then the guard becomes true if at least one of the media has data, which is the semantics employed in discrete event systems.

The test list specifies actions that must not be executing when the critical section starts. The set list specifies actions that should not start while the critical section is executed. In Figure 5 these two lists happen to be the same, but they may differ in general. Each list consists of an arbitrary number of comma-separated elements, and each element specifies an interface of a medium object. The list defines pairs of medium objects and interfaces, where each pair means that no other process can execute a function of the interface implemented in the medium object. For example, in Figure 5, both test list and set list contain an element specifying IntReader interface of the medium connected to port0. This indicates that the critical section is mutually exclusive to the actions for all function calls made by other processes to that medium through IntReader interface (e.g. calls readInt() of that medium). Ports are used to specify medium objects, since specifications of processes and media are often given independently, and exact names of connected objects may not be known when code of an individual object is written.

The specification of the medium shown in Figure 4 also uses await statements in defining its functions. writeInt() writes data only if there is a space to write. The guard of the first await ensures this condition. Its test list specifies that the critical section can be entered only if no other process is executing the critical sections of the functions of IntWriter, i.e. the first await of writeInt() and that of space(). This is so because interfaces specified in the set lists of these await statements, i.e. IW and IS, are specified in the test list. The interface IW listed in its set list is included in test lists of awaits in the functions of

`IntWriter`, and this in turn ensures that the critical sections of those functions cannot be entered when one process is in the critical section of the first `await` of `writeInt()`. This critical section consists of another `await`. Its test list says that the process can further proceed only if no other process is executing the critical sections of the inner `await`s of `writeInt()` and `readInt()`, as well as those in `space()` and `n()`. The critical section then updates the state of the medium to write `data`. Its set list specifies an interface `IC`. This ensures that while this update is made no other process updates or evaluates the state variables, since such actions are always taken inside critical sections of `await` statements whose test lists include `IC`.

The formal syntax of the `await` statement is as follows:

`await{ (guard1; test1; set1) c1; ··· (guardk; testk; setk) ck; }`

Here, `testi` and `seti` denote lists of $p.i$ separated by comma, where p denotes a port and i denotes an interface, while ci denotes a statement for the i-th critical section. As shown here, multiple critical sections can be specified. In its semantics, if there are more than one critical sections that can be entered, the process non-deterministically chooses exactly one of them to execute, and exits the entire `await` statement when the execution of the chosen section is completed. This will be detailed in Section 3.

2.2   Refinement

Once objects are instantiated and connected, some of them may be refined further to provide details of the behavior. Such details are often necessary when particular architecture platforms are considered for implementation. For example, the specification of Figure 2 assumes communication with integers, and each medium has a storage of the integer size. However, the chosen architecture may have only a storage of the byte size, and thus the original communication needs to be implemented in terms of byte-size communication. In the refinement, the semantics of the communication must remain the same as the original when observed from the processes, i.e. the processes can issue functions of reading and writing integers under the exclusion specified in the original medium.

Figure 6-(a) illustrates a refinement of the medium of Figure 4. In general, a refinement of an object is specified as a netlist of objects, and a refinement relation between the netlist and the original object is specified using the `refine` statement. A constructor of the netlist takes as input the object being refined. Some objects contained in the refinement netlist may be provided externally, and thus the constructor may take those objects as additional inputs. It then creates the refinement netlist, establishes the refinement relation between that and the original object, creates internal objects necessary to constitute the netlist, and defines connections among the objects, as well as connections between the objects in the netlist and objects that are connected to the object being refined.

Such a netlist is often specified by a designer who defines architecture platform, and is stored in a library together with the original object being refined. Since this designer is in general different from a system designer who instantiates the platform objects to specify his system, it is usually unknown how the original object is used in a particular system, i.e. the number of objects connecting to or the names of such objects. For this reason, the meta-model provides constructs used in the netlist constructors that take as input the name of the original object and possibly interfaces, and return the information about its adjacent objects. The system designer, who first instantiates the original object to constitute his system behavior, then chooses a particular refinement netlist for the object.

In Figure 6-(a), the refinement netlist `RefIntM` contains three types of media. `ByteM` is the medium with a byte storage. It implements interfaces called `ByteWriter` and `ByteReader`, which are identical with `IntWriter` and `IntReader` except that the size of data is byte. One object of this type is used in the refinement, which may be provided externally. `ByteW` implements the `IntWriter` interface so that each of its objects is connected from a port of an object (such as $P0$ in Figure 2) that originally accesses `IntM` with the interface. The function `writeInt()` is implemented so that it divides the integer into bytes and iteratively calls the write function `writeByte()` of `ByteWriter` while ensuring the exclusion specified originally, i.e. no other process can execute the bodies of the functions of `IntWriter` implemented by the media in this refinement netlist during this period. `ByteR` is the third type, which implements the `IntReader` interface and is connected from a port of an object (such as $C0$ in Figure 2) that originally accesses `IntM` with the interface. As with `ByteW`, in the implementation of `readInt()`, the read function `readByte()` of `ByteReader` is called iteratively to compose an integer.

This refinement netlist is instantiated for each of the original medium objects. The resulting netlist is depicted in Figure 6-(b). Note that both refinement netlists (`RefMO` and `RefMO`) are instantiated with the same byte storage BM in place of `ByteM`. In this way, the byte storage is shared between the refinement netlists. This is possible for this particular refinement, because it allows the object of `ByteM` to be provided externally.

2.3   Coordination Constraints

The specification given in Figure 2 has two independent data streams. However, its refinement illustrated in Figure 6-(b) uses a single object denoted by *BM* as the storage of both streams. This requires coordination between the two streams. For example, data written by the process $P0$ must be read by the process $C0$ rather than $C1$. There are two ways in the meta-model to specify such a coordination. One is to specify a function in an object of the scheduler type that implements an algorithm for the coordination. Such an object can be connected to the process objects of Figure 6-(b), so that the order of execution of these processes is determined by the algorithm.

The other way is to specify formulas in the linear temporal logic. This is more general in the sense that one can specify desired coordination without committing to particular scheduling algorithms. For example, in the constructor of the netlist `DoubleStream` shown in Figure 6-(b), it is possible to add the following code:

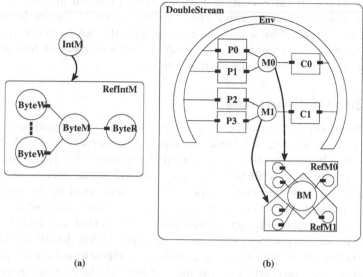

(a)   (b)

Fig. 6. (a) A Refinement of the Medium `IntM` (b) A Refinement of the netlist of Figure 2 using the refinement netlist given in (a). The objects shown with names are instantiated in the netlist `DoubleStream`,while those without names are created inside the refinement netlists of (a)

```
ltl byteMOrder(IntX p, IntX q, IntX r)
  G(end(p, BM.writeByte) -> !beg(q, BM.readByte) U end(r, BM.readByte));

constraint {
  ltl byteMOrder(P0, C1, C0);
  ltl byteMOrder(P1, C1, C0);
  ltl byteMOrder(P2, C0, C1);
  ltl byteMOrder(P3, C0, C1);
}
```

Here, `ltl` is a meta-model keyword to specify an LTL formula, where the formula may be optionally preceded by the name of the formula with arguments as shown in this example. In the formula, keywords `beg` and `end` are used to designate the beginning and the end of an action respectively. Inside these keywords, one specifies the name of a process that takes the action and a piece of code; the latter is made of the name of an object in which the code resides and either a label or the name of a function. For instance, `end(p, BM.writeByte)` denotes the end of the execution by the process `p` of the `writeByte` function defined in the object `BM`. If there are more than one point in the code at which this function is called by the process, then the formula applies at all such points. Section 3 and Section 5 formalize the semantics of these keywords. They are related by the logical and LTL operators to constitute an LTL formula. `->` is a keyword to denote the logical implication. Intuitively, the formula `byteMOrder` means that

if a process p ends the execution of writeByte() defined in the medium object
BM, then the execution of readByte() in BM cannot be begun by a process q
until it is completed by a process r. This formula can be instantiated by using its name, inside a constraint clause as shown above. The four instantiated
formulas specify the desired coordination.

2.4   Quantity Constraints

The value of any design can be divided into three broad categories: functionality,
performance, and cost. All three are equally important, and a design can be
successful only if it meets its goals in all three categories. However, the design
process usually starts only with functional specification, because it is often not
possible to evaluate performance and cost until much later in the design cycle. In
other words, at higher levels of abstraction, performance and cost are constraints
that have to be met, but they depend on quantities that will be defined only at
lower levels of abstractions, when more implementation details are known.

We believe it is important that system specifications include performance
and cost constraints starting at the highest level of abstraction, even if they are
expressed in terms of yet undefined quantities. In this way, global constraints can
be propagated to subsystems, possibly based on rough performance estimates.
Inconsistent, or overly aggressive constraints can be recognized early, and appropriate adjustments can be made (e.g. relaxing some constraints, or adopting
alternative designs).

To specify such constraints in the meta-model, a quantity, such as time,
power, or Quality of Service, must be defined first. This consists of three parts.
The first is the domain of the quantity. For the case of the global time, one may
define real numbers as its domain. Syntactically, quantity is defined as a class
and the domain can be defined by declaring a field in the class with a particular
type, such as double for the global time. The second is a correspondence between
the quantity and actions in the behavior. This is the key in this mechanism, since
constraints become meaningful only if the correspondence between the system's
behavior and the quantity is well defined. To establish the correspondence, the
meta-model considers only the beginning and the end of an action, which are
referred to as *events*. For example, in the DoubleStream netlist, if we consider
as an action the execution of the statement labeled with Wr in Figure 3 by the
process $P0$, the beginning and the end of the execution are the events of this
action. In the meta-model syntax, they are represented by beg(P0, P0.Wr) and
end(P0, P0.Wr) respectively, where P0 is a variable that refers to the process
$P0$. We will present a formal definition of events in Section 3. We then consider
the i-th occurrence of an event e in a given execution of the behavior specified
in a netlist. We denote it by $e[i]$, where i is a natural number. For example,
beg(P0, P0.Wr)$[i]$ denotes the beginning of the i-th execution of the statement
Wr by $P0$ that takes place in executing the behavior of the DoubleStream netlist.
The correspondence between the quantity and actions is established by defining
a function $f(e[i])$ that designates the quantity associated with $e[i]$. In the meta-
model syntax, this is done by declaring a static function in the corresponding

```
final class GTime extends Quantity {
  double gtime;
  static double A(event e, int i){ }  // the annotation of this quantity

  // axioms
  constraint {
    event e1, e2;
    int i, j;
    forall e1,e2,i,j:  GXI.A(e1,i)==GXI.A(e2,j) -> A(e1,i)==A(e2,j);
    forall e1,e2,i,j:  GXI.A(e1,i)<GXI.A(e2,j) -> A(e1,i)<=A(e2,j);
  }
}
```

Fig. 7. A definition of global time quantity in the meta-model

quantity class which takes as input an event variable (of type **event**) and an integer, and returns a value of the type of the domain of the quantity. We call such a function *annotation*, and the meta-model requires that the name of this function must always be **A**. Exactly one annotation function must be declared in each quantity class, where its implementation is not given in the specification.

The third part is a set of axioms of the quantity. For the case of global time, if one event follows another event in a given execution, the global time of the former must be no greater than that of the latter. In the meta-model, first order logic can be used to specify such axioms, which are written in a **constraint** clause using keywords **forall** : and **exists** : for quantifiers. Figure 7 shows an example for the global time quantity. **GXI** used in the axioms is a built-in quantity in the meta-model that designates the global index of a particular occurrence of an event in the current execution of the behavior. The first condition in the axiom says that for given two events e_1 and e_2 and two natural numbers i and j, if $e_1[i]$ and $e_2[j]$ have the same global index in the current execution, their global time must be identical. The second condition says that global time may not decrease as the global index increases. Specifying axioms is important, because some property may be verified to hold only if those axioms are assumed.

Once quantity is defined, one can specify constraints on the quantity annotated with the behavior. The meta-model supports a subset of first order logic called *logic of constraints* for this purpose. Section 5 details this logic, but intuitively it has only one variable, denoted by i in the meta-model, which represents an occurrence of events. This variable is universally quantified implicitly, i.e. the formula must be true for all i. No explicit use of universal or existential quantifiers is allowed. For example, the following code can be added to the constructor of the **DoubleStream** netlist:

```
loc latency(IntX p, IntX r, int C)
  GTime.A(end(r, r.Rd), i) - GTime.A(beg(p, p.Wr), i) < C;
```

```
constraint {
  loc latency(P0, C0, 10);
  loc latency(P1, C0, 10);
  loc latency(P2, C1, 10);
  loc latency(P3, C1, 10);
}
```

Here, `loc` is a meta-model keyword to specify a formula in logic of constraints. The syntax is same with `ltl`. Recall that `end(r, r.Rd)` designates the end of the execution of the statement labeled with `Rd` in Figure 3 by the process `r`. Thus the formula means that the difference in the global time between the i-th occurrence of `beg(p, p.Wr)` and the i-th occurrence of `end(r, r.Rd)` must be less than a given constant C. This formula is then instantiated in a `constraint` clause to specify constraints on the latency between each pair of a writer process and a reader process.

3   Execution Semantics

In this section we sketch the formal execution semantics of the meta-model. The semantics we provide here is not complete. In particular, we will say very little about parts of the meta-model that are similar to standard sequential programming languages, and focus instead on distinctive features such as `await`.

The semantic domain we use to interpret executions of meta-model netlists is a set of sequences of *observable events*. An observable event is a beginning or an ending of an *observable action*, and observable actions are calls of communication media functions. While the behavior is defined by observable actions only, we also use other actions to help us define the semantics. This extended set of actions include all the statements in the program, as well as certain expressions within a statement. A precise definition of an action is given in the next section.

The execution of netlists evolves through a sequence of *states*. A state of the program consists of two parts. The first is the state of the *memory* which consists of assignments to *state variables*. The second part of the state corresponds intuitively to the program counter. We represent this part of the state with states of *action automata*. We associate an action automaton with each action (observable or not). The state of an action automaton indicates whether the corresponding statement or expression is being executed or not. By combining all these states, we can precisely determine the location pointed by the program counter. The transition relation of action automata enforces the proper sequence of the beginning and ending of statement executions.

3.1   Actions, Events and Event Vectors

The set of *actions* of a netlist consists of actions that each process in the netlist can take. The set of actions that a particular process can take includes:

```
process dummy {
  int x,y;
  dummy(){ }

  int minus(int n) { return -n; }

  void thread (){
    x=y=2+2;
    while( x<5 ) {
      x += y+minus(y+1);
} } }
```

Fig. 8. A simple process

- all statements that the process can execute,
- all function calls that the process can make,
- all assignment expressions that the process can execute, i.e. all expressions of the form $x \sim expr$, where x is a variable, $expr$ is an expression, and $\sim$ is one of the assignment operators $=, + =, * =, \ldots$
- all *top-level* expressions that the process can execute: expressions that are statements (i.e. terminated by ;), right-hand sides of assignment expressions, and expressions that appear as arguments in function calls.

For example, the process in Figure 8 has the total of 16 actions which include:

- 7 statements: 3 compound statements (bodies of thread, minus and while), 1 while statement, 1 return, and 2 expression statements (x=y=2+2; and x += y+minus(y+1);),
- 1 function call: minus(y+1),
- 3 assignment expressions: x=y=2+2, y=2+2, and x += y+minus(y+1),
- 5 top-level expressions: -n, 2+2, x<5, y+minus(y+1), and y+1.

None of the actions is observable (hence the process name).

With each action a we associate two *events*, a^+ indicating the start of an execution of a, and a^- indicating the end. For each process P we define the set of events Σ_P that contains a^+ and a^- for each action a of P, and a special symbol $P : nop$, indicating that no events are occuring in P. When no ambiguity can arise, we will abbreviate $P : nop$ to nop. The cross-product of all the sets of events in the system is called the set of *event vectors*. In a system with processes $P_1, \ldots, P_n$, an event vector, say σ is a n-tuple $(\sigma_1, \ldots, \sigma_n)$, where each σ_i is an element of Σ_{P_i}. Occasionally, we will treat an event vector $(\sigma_1, \ldots, \sigma_n)$ as the set $\{\sigma_1, \ldots, \sigma_n\}$, and write expressions such as $\sigma_2 \in \sigma$. Two the representations of σ are equivalent, because Σ_P's are disjoint, and we will make no notational distinction between them.

3.2   State Variables

State variables are defined for objects of communication media and processes. For an object of a communication medium in a given netlist, the instances of the fields of the medium are called the *state variables* of the object. For a process object in the netlist, consider the set of functions that can be called by the object. Specifically, the function `thread` is in the set and if a function f is in the set, all the functions that can be called from f are in the set. The instances of variables declared in the functions in this set, and instances of the fields of the process constitute the *state variables* of the object[4]. In addition, there is a state variable for each action that is also an expression. Intuitively, this state variable is used to temporarily store the value of the expression. Notice that sets of process state variables are disjoint. The set of all state variables is called the *memory*, and an assignment of values to all state variables is called a *memory state*.

For example, the memory of the process in Figure 8 consists of the following state variables: x, y, V_{-n}, $V_{x=y=2+2}$, $V_{y=2+2}$, V_{2+2}, $V_{x+=y+minus(y+1)}$, $V_{x<5}$, $V_{y+minus(y+1)}$, $V_{minus(y+1)}$, and V_{y+1}.

3.3 Action Automata

The execution semantics of a meta-model netlist is defined by the language of *action automata* which are defined over the alphabet containing event vectors. There is at least one action automaton for each action of each process. Before we present action automata for various actions, we first give a general definition of automata. This definition applies to action automata, but could apply to schedulers as well. It is quite a standard definition, except perhaps for the addition of state variables.

We assume that all automata inhabit the same *global state space* which is the cross product of sets of *local states* (one set for each automaton) and the set of *memory states*.

An automaton is given by a set of *local states*, and a set of *local transitions*. The set of local states must contain a state called $INIT$, but otherwise it is an arbitrary finite set. A *local transition* is 5-tuple (p, n, G, E, U) where *present state* p and *next state* n are local states, *guard* G is a subset of global states, *label* E is a set of event vectors, and a set of *memory updates* U is a set of expressions of the form $x := e$, where x is a state variable, and e is either an expression over state variables or keyword **any**.

A *global transition* is a set of local transitions in which every automaton in the system is represented by exactly one of its local transitions.

If s is a global state and $\mathcal{A}$ is an automaton, we use $s(\mathcal{A})$ to denote the component of s that is the local state of $\mathcal{A}$. Similarly, we use $s(x)$ to denote the component of s that is the value of state variable x. Also, if e is some expression over state variables, we use $e|_s$ to denote the value of e at state s.

Given global states s and q and an event vector σ we say that q is a σ-*successor* of s if there exists a global transition t such that:

---

[4] Some functions may be called from different process objects. In this case, distinct instances are created for each variable declared in the functions and they are included in the state variables of the respective process objects.

— s, q and σ satisfy all local transitions in t, i.e. for all automata $\mathcal{A}$, the local transition $(p, n, G, E, U) \in t$ that correspond to $\mathcal{A}$ satisfies the following:

$$s(\mathcal{A}) = p$$
$$q(\mathcal{A}) = n$$
$$s \in G$$
$$\sigma \in E \ ,$$

— q correctly reflects memory updates in t, i.e. for all state variables x:
  - $q(x) = s(x)$ if x is not updated by any of the local transitions in t
  - $q(x) = e|_s$ if $x := e$ appears in the set of memory updates of some local transition in t, e is not **any**, and x is not updated by any other local transition in t.

Notice that $q(x)$ may take any value if x is assigned **any**, or if multiple local transitions in t update x. Also notice that while in this case x may be assigned any value from its domain, **any** is not such a value. In other words, $x :=$ **any** should not be interpreted literally, but rather as an indication of a non-deterministic assignment to x.

We say that a sequence:

$$s_0 \xrightarrow{\sigma_1} s_1 \xrightarrow{\sigma_2} \ldots \xrightarrow{\sigma_i} s_i \xrightarrow{\sigma_{i+1}} \ldots$$

is an *execution* of the meta-model netlist, and also say that $\sigma_1 \sigma_2 \ldots$ is a *behavior* of the netlist if:

— s_0 is the initial state, i.e. $s_0(\mathcal{A}) = INIT$ for every automaton $\mathcal{A}$,
— transition relations are respected, i.e. for all $i > 0$ s_i is a σ_i-successor of s_{i-1}.

Finally, we say that the projection of the behavior to Σ_P is the *thread* of P in a given execution.

This concludes general definitions. Now we are ready to go back to action automata. There are several notational conventions we use to simplify the presentation of action automata. We represent local states with nodes in a graph, and represent local transition (p, n, G, E, U) by an arc from p to n labeled above with G/E and below with elements of U. If the transition is unguarded, i.e. if G contains all global states, then we write just E instead of G/E. If $p = n$, then we label p itself with G/E or E, and omit drawing the self-loop. Some types of label occurs so often that it is useful to introduce special abbreviations for them. For example, if e is an event in Σ_P, then in all automata associated with actions of P, we write e to denote the set:

$$\{\sigma | e \in \sigma\} \ .$$

Similarly, if S is a subset of events in Σ_P, we write S to denote the set:

$$\{\sigma | \exists e \in S : e \in \sigma\} \ .$$

$$Care = \{a^+, a^-, stmt_1^+, stmt_1^-, \ldots, stmt_k^+, stmt_k^-\}$$

$$\xrightarrow{a^+} \boxed{nop} \xrightarrow{stmt_1^+} \boxed{\overline{Care}} \xrightarrow{stmt_1^-} \boxed{nop} \rightarrow \cdots \xrightarrow{stmt_k^+} \boxed{\overline{Care}} \xrightarrow{stmt_k^-} \boxed{nop} \xrightarrow{a^-}$$

Fig. 9. Action automaton $\mathcal{A}[\![a]\!]$ in case a is $\{stmt_1 \ldots stmt_k\}$

With every action automata of process P we associate a subset of Σ_P called the *care set*, denoted with $Care$. Intuitively, an automaton controls the events in its care set, but it is not affected by any other events.

To further reduce the clutter, we do not draw the $INIT$ state, and assume that any transition without present (next) state is coming from (leading to) $INIT$. We also assume that in every action automaton there is a self-loop in the $INIT$ state that is unguarded and labeled with $\overline{Care}$ (we use over-line to denote complementation, i.e. $\overline{Care} = \{\sigma | \forall e \in Care : e \notin \sigma\}$).

3.4 Compound and Conditional Statements

The semantics of compound and conditional statements is a standard one. We show them here mainly to introduce the use of action automata to specify meta-model semantics.

One of the simplest action automaton[5] is the one for a compound statement $\{stmt_1; \ldots stmt_k; \}$ shown in Figure 9. Its care set contains starting and ending events of the compound statement itself, as well as starting and ending events of all the constituent statements. The action automata enforces the usual order of these events.

There are two types of self-loops in Figure 9, some states have self-loops labeled with nop, and some states have self-loops labeled with $\overline{Care}$. Clearly, the process can make no progress while the action automaton is in one of the states labeled with nop. However, while the system is in a state labeled with $\overline{Care}$, actions not in the care set can be executed. Thus, we may say that the action automaton has the control in a state labeled with nop, while it relinquishes control in a $\overline{Care}$-labeled state. But, even in the latter case, the automaton still controls the events in the care set. We will see later that almost all of the states of action automata fall into one of these two categories. The few states that do not fit can be interpreted as the action automaton partially relinquishing control.

Consider, for example, the following piece of code:

```
{f();{g();}}
```

---

[5] This automaton is valid for code that confirms to rules of structured programming, i.e. no **break**, or **continue** statements, and **return** appearing only as the last statement in function's body.

$$Care = \{a^+, a^-, stmt_1^+, stmt_1^-, stmt_2^+, stmt_2^-\}$$

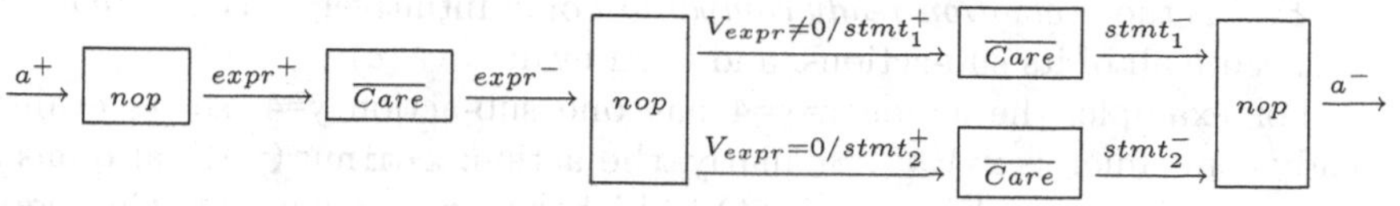

Fig. 10. Action automaton $\mathcal{A}[\![a]\!]$ in case a is if $expr$ then $stmt_1$ else $stmt_2$

that includes two compound statements. One possible execution that is accepted by action automata for both of these compound statements is the following:

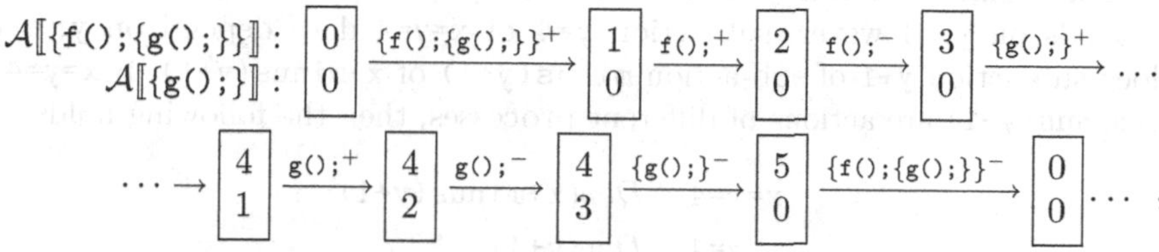

where numbers denote states of automata $\mathcal{A}[\![\{f();\{g();\}\}]\!]$ and $\mathcal{A}[\![\{g();\}]\!]$. We use 0 to denote the $INIT$ state, and number states in Figure 9 with consecutive integers, starting from the left. The execution above is not the only one accepted by the two automata, but all others can be obtained from it by traversing the same cycle a number of times and possibly adding self-loops. On self-loops where both of the automata are in state 0, 2, or 4, any event other than the beginning or ending of $\{f();\{g();\}\}$, $\{g();\}$, $f();$, or $g();$ can occur. These are precisely the states where either both automata are waiting in the $INIT$ state, or $f();$, or $g();$ are being computed, so the control is transfered to other automata. On all other self-loops, only nop can occur.

Another simple action automaton is the one for the conditional statement if $expr$ then $stmt_1$ else $stmt_2$ shown in Figure 10. The conditional expression is evaluated first. The result of evaluation becomes the part of the state stored by the state variable V_{expr}. Based on this result, one of the two statement is executed next.

3.5   Expressions

The semantics of expression varies somewhat from typical sequential programming languages. The difference arises when actions of two processes attempt to read and write the same state variable. In general, our approach is conservative, if there is any possibility of a conflict, the value of an expression is not specified. Otherwise, the value is determined as in standard sequential programming languages. To formalize these notions, we first need several definition.

We say that an action s is a *sub-action* of an action e, if e is an expression, and s is a sub-expression of e. We use $Sub(e)$ to denote the set of sub-actions of e. Given an expression e, we use $\mathcal{E}(e)$ to denote the expression obtained from e by replacing each sub-action s in e with the corresponding state variable V_s. We say $\mathcal{E}(e)$ is the *evaluation-ready companion* of e. Intuitively, to execute e we need to execute all of its sub-actions, and then evaluate $\mathcal{E}(e)$.

For example, the action x=y=4 has one sub-action y=4, so its evaluation-ready companion is x=$V_{y=4}$. Similarly, the action: x+minus(y+1) also has a single sub-action, namely minus(y+1), which has sub-action y+1. Consequently, $\mathcal{E}$(x+minus(y+1)) is x+$V_{minus(y+1)}$, and $\mathcal{E}$(minus(y+1)) is minus(V_{y+1}).

We say that expression e of process P *depends* on a state variable x, if x appears in $\mathcal{E}(e)$. We say that e depends on an action a of some process other than P, if a is an assignment expression of the form $x \sim expr$, and e depends on x. Informally, e depends on a if a is writing a variable that e is reading or writing. We use $Dep(e)$ to denote the set of actions that e depends on.

For example, both x=y=4 and x+minus(y+1) depend on x, but neither one depends on y. However, sub-action y=4 of x=y=4 does depend on y, and so does sub-action y+1 of sub-action minus(y+1) of x+minus(y+1). If x=y=4 and x+minus(y+1) are actions of different processes, then the following holds:

$$x\text{=}y\text{=}4 \in Dep(x\text{+}minus(y\text{+}1))$$
$$y\text{=}4 \in Dep(y\text{+}1) \ .$$

Given a set of actions A we use $Active(A)$ to denote the set of global states in which at least one of the actions in A is being executed, i.e.:

$$Active(A) \ = \ \{s \mid \exists a \in A : \ s(A[\![a]\!]) \neq INIT\} \ .$$

Also, we use $Start(A)$ to denote the set of event vectors that contain the beginning of at least one action in A, i.e.:

$$Start(A) \ = \ \{\sigma \mid \exists a \in A : \ a^+ \in \sigma\} \ .$$

Intuitively, if a state in $Active(A)$ is a σ-successor of a state in $\overline{Active(A)}$, then σ should be an element of $Start(A)$. We invite the reader to check that this is the case for all the action automata presented here.

Now we are ready to examine action automata for expressions. With each expression a we associate $|Sub(a)| + 2$ automata denoted by $A[\![a]\!]$, $A^{sub}[\![a]\!]$, and $A^s[\![a]\!]$, where $s \in Sub(a)$. The purpose of $A[\![a]\!]$ is to monitor whether any of the state variables that a depends on is being modified. If that is the case, then V_a is assigned an arbitrary value. Otherwise, V_a is assigned the standard value. Automaton $A[\![a]\!]$ for expressions that are not assignment expressions is shown in Figure 11. The upper part of the automaton corresponds to the case where no actions in $Dep(a)$ overlap with a, and V_a is assigned the standard value. If at any stage of execution of a an overlap with some action in $Dep(a)$ is detected, the automaton moves to the lower part, and eventually assigns any to V_a.

Automaton $A[\![a]\!]$ for an assignment expression is almost the same as the one in Figure 11, except that memory updates need to be extended to the state variable being assigned. For example, the automaton $A[\![a]\!]$ when a is x+ = $expr$

$Care = \{a^+, a^-\}$

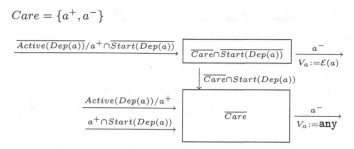

Fig. 11. Action automaton $\mathcal{A}[\![a]\!]$ for an expression a that is not an assignment

can be obtained from the one in Figure 11 by adding $x := x \mid V_{expr}$ to $V_a := \mathcal{E}(a)$, and adding $x := $ **any** to $V_a := $ **any**.

The purpose of automata $\mathcal{A}^{sub}[\![a]\!]$ and $\mathcal{A}^s[\![a]\!]$, $s \in Sub(a)$ (shown in Figure 12) is to ensure that sub-actions of a are properly executed during the execution of a. The automaton $\mathcal{A}^{sub}[\![a]\!]$ ensures that the beginning of a sub-action is followed by its end, i.e. it ensures that only a single sub-action can be executed at a time. The automaton $\mathcal{A}^s[\![a]\!]$ ensures that the end of s must be preceded by the beginning of s, and that s is executed only once for each execution of a. Notice that there is no prescribed order in which sub-actions of a must be executed. Also notice that for leaf expressions (i.e. expressions with no sub-actions) the right state of $\mathcal{A}^{sub}[\![a]\!]$ is unreachable. It follows that while a process is computing a leaf expression, it cannot start or end any other action.

The automaton $\mathcal{A}^{sub}[\![a]\!]$ in Figure 12 is not valid for function calls. For these types of actions $\mathcal{A}^{sub}[\![a]\!]$ needs to ensure that the body of the function is executed after all the arguments, and that results are properly communicated up to the

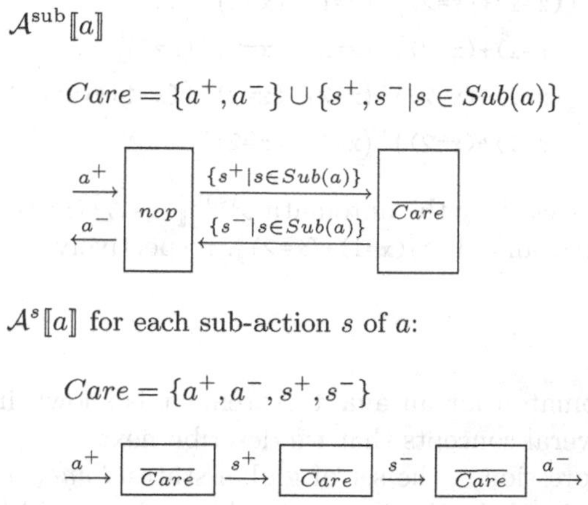

$\mathcal{A}^{sub}[\![a]\!]$

$Care = \{a^+, a^-\} \cup \{s^+, s^- \mid s \in Sub(a)\}$

$\mathcal{A}^s[\![a]\!]$ for each sub-action s of a:

$Care = \{a^+, a^-, s^+, s^-\}$

Fig. 12. Action automata for sub-actions of an expression a that is not a function call

$$Care = \{a^+, a^-, stmt_1^+, stmt_1^-, \ldots, stmt_k^+, stmt_k^-\}$$

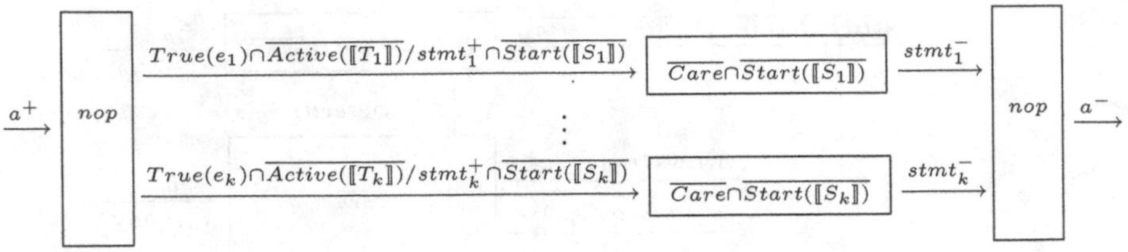

Fig. 13. Automaton $\mathcal{A}[\![a]\!]$ in case a is $\texttt{await}\{(e_1; T_1; S_1)stmt_1; \cdots (e_k; T_k; S_k) stmt_k; \}$

enclosing expression. Since the semantics of a function call in the meta-model is the same as in standard programming languages, we will not present any further details.

Consider, for example, the expression:

```
(x=1)+(x=2)
```

that has two sub-actions (x=1 and x=2), implying that four automata are associated with it. The following two behaviors are consistent with all four of these automata:

$$((\texttt{x=1})+(\texttt{x=2}))^+(\texttt{x=1})^+(\texttt{x=1})^-(\texttt{x=2})^+(\texttt{x=2})^-((\texttt{x=1})+(\texttt{x=2}))^- \ldots$$
$$((\texttt{x=1})+(\texttt{x=2}))^+(\texttt{x=2})^+(\texttt{x=2})^-(\texttt{x=1})^+(\texttt{x=1})^-((\texttt{x=1})+(\texttt{x=2}))^- \ldots ,$$

but the following four are not:

$$((\texttt{x=1})+(\texttt{x=2}))^+(\texttt{x=1})^+(\texttt{x=2})^+ \ldots$$
$$((\texttt{x=1})+(\texttt{x=2}))^+(\texttt{x=2})^+(\texttt{x=2})^-(\texttt{x=2})^+ \ldots$$
$$((\texttt{x=1})+(\texttt{x=2}))^+(\texttt{x=2})^+(\texttt{x=2})^-((\texttt{x=1})+(\texttt{x=2}))^- \ldots$$
$$((\texttt{x=1})+(\texttt{x=2}))^+(\texttt{x=1})^+(\texttt{x=2})^- \ldots ,$$

since they are rejected by the automata $\mathcal{A}^{\text{sub}}[\![(\texttt{x=1})+(\texttt{x=2})]\!]$, $\mathcal{A}^{\texttt{x=2}}[\![(\texttt{x=1})+(\texttt{x=2})]\!]$, $\mathcal{A}^{\texttt{x=1}}[\![(\texttt{x=1})+(\texttt{x=2})]\!]$, and $\mathcal{A}^{\texttt{x=2}}[\![(\texttt{x=1})+(\texttt{x=2})]\!]$, respectively.

3.6 Await

The action automaton for an `await` statement is shown in Figure 13. In that figure we use several concepts that we describe next.

Given an expression e, the set of global states $True(e)$ contains all states s such that evaluating e starting from s would produce a value different from zero. For example:

$$True(\texttt{x<5}) = \{s | (s(x) < 5)\} .$$

We require that expressions e_i in Figure 13 have no side-effects. More precisely, they should not contain any assignment operators, and any function calls that they may contain must be to functions of type `eval`.

Another concept used in Figure 13 is that of sets of actions $[\![T_i]\!]$ and $[\![S_i]\!]$ associated with lists T_i and S_i, respectively, in a statement:

$$\texttt{await}\{(e_1; T_1; S_1)stmt_1; \cdots (e_k; T_k; S_k)stmt_k; \} \ .$$

Recall that T_i and S_i are lists of pairs of the form $m.f$, where m is a communication medium, and f is an interface implemented by m. The set $[\![T_i]\!]$ is the union of the sets of actions associated with each pair $m.f$ in T_i. An action a is associated with $m.f$ if it is an action of a process other than the one executing the `await` statement, and one of the following holds:

- a is a call to a member function of medium m which is declared in interface f,
- a is a statement appearing in:

$$\texttt{await}\{\cdots (e_j; T_j; S_j)a \cdots\} \ ,$$

and $m.f$ appears in the list S_j.

Similarly, the set $[\![S_i]\!]$ is the union of the sets of actions associated with each pair $m.f$ in S_i, and an action a is associated with $m.f$ if it is an action of a process other than the one executing the `await` statement, and one of the following holds:

- a is a call to a member function of medium m which is declared in interface f,
- a is a statement appearing in:

$$\texttt{await}\{\cdots (e_j; T_j; S_j)a \cdots\} \ ,$$

and $m.f$ appears in the list T_j.

Now we are ready to examine the automaton in Figure 13. After the statement begins its execution, one of the statements $stmt_1, \ldots, stmt_k$, may start executing. However a statement $stmt_i$ may start execution only if the current global state is in $True(e_i)$, no action in $[\![T_i]\!]$ are currently executing and no actions in $[\![S_i]\!]$ are starting execution. Furthermore, no action in $[\![S_i]\!]$ can start executing as long as $stmt_i$ is executing.

3.7   Completing Execution Semantics

We have not shown action automata for many standard constructs, most notably function calls, but also loops and control-flow-changing statements `break`, `continue` and `return`. Semantics of all of these is standard. We also note that our approach is not applicable directly to recursive function calls. Making necessary extensions is quite possible, but they would take focus away from the special features of the meta-model, so we decided not to present them here.

Finally, we stress again that even though behaviors of action automata are defined in terms of all actions, to get the semantics of a meta-model netlist we need to hide all events that are not observable. This operation is standard in automata theory, so we will not discuss its details here.

4 Semantics of Constraints

There are three types of constraints in the meta-model, and each type is expressed in a different logic. Coordination constraints from Section 2.3 are represented by formulas of *linear temporal logic (LTL)*, quantity constraints from Section 2.4 are represented in the logic called *logic of constraints (LOC)*, and quantity axioms are represented in the LOC extension called *extended logic of constraints (ELOC)*. The choice of three different logics is driven by different requirements for three types of constraints, and our guiding principle to choose the most appropriate logic for the task at hand. We have surveyed existing, well-studied logics to find one suitable each purpose. In the case of coordination constraints, LTL fulfilled the requirements. However, in the case of quantity constraints and axioms, we could not find a logic that fits our needs, so we have proposed LOC for this purpose [1]. We will review LOC in Section 5. But first, we show how meta-model executions are transformed into structures used to interpret LTL, LOC and ELOC formulas.

4.1 Interpreting LTL Formulas

In general, LTL formulas are interpreted over sequences of objects such that for each object it is possible to determine whether it satisfies an atomic LTL formula or not. There are two types of atomic LTL formulas in the meta-model:

- meta-model expressions involving state variables, and possibly calls to interface functions of `eval` type,
- *named events*, i.e. expressions of the form `beg(p,f)` and `end(p,f)` where p is a process identifier, and f is either a function identifier (e.g. `M.writeInt` in Figure 2), or identifier of labeled statement or a block of code (e.g. `PO.Rd` in Figure 2).

Notice that p and f in the second type of atomic formulas uniquely determine a set of actions. The set can be empty if p never calls f, or it can have multiple elements, if p calls f from multiple points in the code.

Given a meta-model netlist, and its execution:

$$s_0 \xrightarrow{\sigma_1} s_1 \xrightarrow{\sigma_2} \ldots \xrightarrow{\sigma_i} s_i \xrightarrow{\sigma_{i+1}} \ldots \,,$$

we interpret LTL formulas over the sequence:

$$(s_0, \sigma_1), (s_1, \sigma_2), \ldots, (s_i, \sigma_{i+1}), \ldots \,.$$

We say that (s_i, σ_{i+1}) satisfies a meta-model expression e if s_i is in $True(e)$, (where $True$ is defined as in Section 3.6). We also say that (s_i, σ_{i+1}) satisfies `beg(p,f)` if there exists an action a associated with p and f such that $a^+ \in \sigma_{i+1}$. Similarly, we say that (s_i, σ_{i+1}) satisfies `end(p,f)` if there exists an action a associated with p and f such that $a^- \in \sigma_{i+1}$. This defines the semantics of atomic LTL formulas. The semantics of all other LTL constructs is defined in the standard way [6].

4.2   Interpreting LOC and ELOC Formulas

LOC is intended to be compatible not only with the Metropolis meta-model, but also with a wide range of functional specification formalisms. Many of these describe a system as a network of components communicating through fixed interconnections. The observed behavior of the system is usually characterized by sequences of values observed at the interconnections. In this section, we define formal structures called *annotated behaviors* intended to model such sequences, and then, in Section 5, we show how LOC and ELOC formulas are interpreted over annotated behaviors.

Formally, let E be a set of *event names*, and for each $e \in E$ let $V(e)$ be its *value domain*. Then, a *basic behavior* is a mapping $\beta : E \times \mathbb{N} \mapsto \bigcup_{e \in E} V(e)$ such that $\beta(e, n) \in V(e)$ for each $e \in E$, and each positive integer $n \in \mathbb{N}$. A *system* is specified by a set of event names, their value domains and a *set of basic behaviors*.

In the meta-model, the set of event names is exactly the set of named events that can appear in LTL formulas. However, in general they represent interconnections, e.g. wires in a hardware system, or mailboxes in a software system. The basic behavior of the system is then characterized by sequences of values on wires, or sequences of messages to mailboxes.

Basic behaviors by themselves are not sufficient to evaluate constraints. For this, we need additional information regarding performance measures. We represent this information as annotations to behaviors. Formally, given an arbitrary set T, a T-valued *annotation* is a function from $E \times \mathbb{N}$ to T. Similarly to events, if f is a T-valued annotation, then we say that T is the value domain of f. An *annotated behavior* is a pair (β, A) where β is a behavior and A is a set of annotations.

Meta-model executions, as defined Section 3, together with defined quantities, contain all the information needed to represent annotated behaviors. However, we still need to put this information in a form consistent with the definitions above. First, we define the *value* of a named event as follows:

- Beginnings and endings of labeled statements or blocks of code carry no value.
- The value of the beginning of an execution of a function is the structure containing function's arguments.
- The value of the ending of an execution of a function is the return value of the function.

In the latter two cases, the value of an event is held in memory by state variables, and thus can be easily extracted from a state in an execution.

Next, we define a transformation from sequences of event vectors (as defined by the execution semantics) to sequences of event values (as required by the definition of basic behaviors). Given a named event e, and a meta-model netlist execution:

$$s_0 \xrightarrow{\sigma_1} s_1 \xrightarrow{\sigma_2} \ldots \xrightarrow{\sigma_i} s_i \xrightarrow{\sigma_{i+1}} \ldots$$

we set $\beta(e,n)$ to be the value of e in state s_j, where j is such that e occurs in σ_{j+1} for the n'th time, i.e. the following holds:

$$e \in \sigma_{j+1}$$
$$|\{k \leq j | e \in \sigma_k\}| = n - 1 \ .$$

To ensure that this transformation incurs no loss of information, we also provide a predefined quantity GXI such that GXI.A(e,n) evaluates to $j + 1$.

Annotations to behaviors correspond to defined quantities. For each defined quantity Q of type T (including the GXI), we annotate the basic behaviors with the corresponding T-valued annotation Q such that $Q(e,i)$ and Q.A(e,i) are equal for all events e and all positive integers i.

Note that $\beta(e,n)$ is well defined for all n only if e occurs infinitely often. Not being able to consider events which occur only finitely many times might be considered a shortcoming of our approach. This shortcoming could be fixed by allowing behaviors to contain finite sequences for some events. While this modification is conceptually simple, it does introduce significant technical difficulty. To avoid tedious details, we have decided to deal only with infinite behaviors in this presentation.

5   Logic of Constraints

We have designed LOC to meet the following goals, which we believe are essential for a constraint specification formalism to gain wide acceptance:

- it must be based on a solid mathematical foundation, to remove any ambiguity in its interpretation,
- it must feel natural to the designer, so that typical constraints are easy to specify,
- it must be compatible with existing functional specification formalisms, so that language extensions for constraint specification can be easily defined,
- it must be powerful enough to express a wide range of interesting constraints,
- it must be simple enough to be analyzable, at least by simulation, and ideally by automatic formal techniques.

In case of conflicting goals (e.g. expressiveness vs. simplicity), we believe that LOC presents a reasonable compromise.

In this section we review LOC. We do so using the notation that is closer to usual mathematical notation than to actual meta-model syntax. We hope that this approach increases readability, and emphasizes the fact that LOC is applicable to other frameworks besides the meta-model.

5.1   LOC Syntax

LOC formulas are defined relative to a multi-sorted algebra $(\mathcal{A}, \mathcal{O}, \mathcal{R})$, where $\mathcal{A}$ is a set of sets (sorts), $\mathcal{O}$ is a set of operators, and $\mathcal{R}$ is a set of relations on sets in $\mathcal{A}$.

More precisely, elements of $\mathcal{O}$ are functions of the form $T_1 \times \cdots \times T_n \mapsto T_{n+1}$, where n is a natural number, and $T_1, \ldots, T_{n+1}$ are (not necessarily distinct) elements of $\mathcal{A}$. If $o \in \mathcal{O}$ is such a function, than we say that o is n-ary and T_{n+1}-valued. Similarly, an n-ary relation in $\mathcal{R}$ is a function of the form $T_1 \times \cdots \times T_n \mapsto \{true, false\}$. We require that $\mathcal{A}$ contains at least the set $\mathbb{N}$ of natural numbers, and the value domains of all event names and annotations appearing in the formula. For example, if $\mathcal{A}$ contains integers and reals, $\mathcal{O}$ could contain standard addition and multiplication, and $\mathcal{R}$ could contain usual relational operators ($=, <, >, \ldots$).

LOC formulas may contain only one variable, namely i. The domain of i is $\mathbb{N}$. Having only one variable may seem very restrictive, but so far we have not found a natural constraint that required more than one. In effect, the ability of defining annotations allows one to specify formulas that otherwise require more than one variable, as we shall see later with examples. The advantages of a single variable are simpler syntax (fewer names), and simpler simulation monitoring.

The basic building blocks of LOC formulas are *terms*. We distinguish terms by their value domains:

- i is an $\mathbb{N}$-valued term,
- for each value domain $T \in \mathcal{A}$, and each $c \in T$, c is a T-valued term,
- if τ is an $\mathbb{N}$-valued term, $e \in E$ is an event name, and f is a T-valued annotation, then val$(e[\tau])$ is a $V(e)$-valued term, and $f(e[\tau])$ is a T-valued term,[6]
- if $o \in \mathcal{O}$ is a T-valued n-ary operator, and $\tau_1, \ldots, \tau_n$ are appropriately valued terms, then $o(\tau_1, \ldots, \tau_n)$ is a T-valued term.

Terms are used to build *LOC formulas* in the standard way:

- if $r \in \mathcal{R}$ is an n-ary relation, and $\tau_1, \ldots, \tau_n$ are appropriately valued terms, then $r(\tau_1, \ldots, \tau_n)$ is an LOC formula,
- if ϕ and ψ are LOC formulas, so are $\overline{\phi}$, $\phi \wedge \psi$, and $\phi \vee \psi$.

For example, if a and b are names of $\mathbb{N}$-valued events, and f and g are $\mathbb{N}$-valued annotations, then the set of LOC formulas includes the following:

$$\text{val}(a[i]) = 5 \ \wedge \ \text{val}(a[i+1]) = 5$$
$$f(a[i+4]) + f(b[g(a[i])]) < 20$$
$$\overline{\text{val}(a[i]) = 0} \ \vee \ f(b[i]) = 0 \ .$$

When reading these formulas, it is helpful to think of i as being universally quantified, as clarified in the LOC semantics next.

In the meta-model, the multi-sorted algebra is given by the type system, including both built-in and user-defined types. The type system also defines all the operators and relations. If e is an event, i is a positive integer, and Q

---

[6] It may appear that expression $f(e[\tau])$ is in conflict with the definition of a T-valued annotation as a function from $E \times \mathbb{N}$ to T. However, when we define the semantics of $f(e[\tau])$ it will become clear that there is no conflict.

is an LOC annotation that corresponds to the user-defined quantity Q in the
meta-model, then LOC terms of the form val($e[i]$) and $Q(e[i])$ are represented
in the meta-model with expressions val.A(e,i) and Q.A(e,i), respectively. We
say that val is a *quasi-quantity*. Like an ordinary quantity, val has member
function A that takes as argument an event e and integer i, and returns the
value of the i-th occurrence of event e, but, unlike an ordinary quantity, val
has no fixed type, i.e. its type depends on the type of event e. For example, if
process P can execute function F of medium M which has the signature:

$$\text{double F(int x, char y) ,}$$

then:
$$\text{val.A(beg(P,M.F),i)}$$

has type struct{int x; char y}, and:

$$\text{val.A(end(P,M.F),i)}$$

has type double.

5.2   LOC Semantics

Informally, LOC formulas are evaluated at annotated behavior (β, A) as follows:

- the variable i evaluates to any positive integer,
- if τ evaluates to some positive integer n, then val($e[\tau]$) evaluates to $\beta(e,n)$,
  and $f(e[\tau])$ evaluates to $f(e,n)$,
- all other operators, relations and Boolean functions are evaluated in the
  standard way, and
- an annotated behavior *satisfies* an LOC formula if the formula evaluates to
  true for all possible values of i.

More formally, we first define the *value* of formulas and terms with respect
to an annotated behavior, and a value of variable i. We use $\mathcal{V}^n_{(\beta,A)}[\![\alpha]\!]$, where
α is a term or a formula, to denote the value of α evaluated at the annotated
behavior (β, A) and the value n of variable i. The value is defined recursively as
follows:

- $\mathcal{V}^n_{(\beta,A)}[\![i]\!] = n$,
- $\mathcal{V}^n_{(\beta,A)}[\![c]\!] = c$ for each element c of each value domain T,
- $\mathcal{V}^n_{(\beta,A)}[\![\text{val}(e[\tau])]\!] = \beta(e, \mathcal{V}^n_{(\beta,A)}[\![\tau]\!])$ for each event name e and each IN-valued
  term τ,
- $\mathcal{V}^n_{(\beta,A)}[\![f(e[\tau])]\!] = f(e, \mathcal{V}^n_{(\beta,A)}[\![\tau]\!])$ for each annotation $f \in A$, each event
  name e, and each IN-valued term τ,
- $\mathcal{V}^n_{(\beta,A)}[\![o(\tau_1,\ldots,\tau_k)]\!] = o(\mathcal{V}^n_{(\beta,A)}[\![\tau_1]\!],\ldots,\mathcal{V}^n_{(\beta,A)}[\![\tau_k]\!])$ for each k-ary operator o,
- $\mathcal{V}^n_{(\beta,A)}[\![r(\tau_1,\ldots,\tau_k)]\!] = r(\mathcal{V}^n_{(\beta,A)}[\![\tau_1]\!],\ldots,\mathcal{V}^n_{(\beta,A)}[\![\tau_k]\!])$ for each k-ary relation r,
- $\mathcal{V}^n_{(\beta,A)}[\![\overline{\phi}]\!] = true$ if and only if $\mathcal{V}^n_{(\beta,A)}[\![\phi]\!] = false$,

- $\mathcal{V}^n_{(\beta,A)}[\![\phi \wedge \psi]\!] = true$ if and only if $\mathcal{V}^n_{(\beta,A)}[\![\phi]\!] = true$ and $\mathcal{V}^n_{(\beta,A)}[\![\psi]\!] = true$,
- $\mathcal{V}^n_{(\beta,A)}[\![\phi \vee \psi]\!] = true$ if and only if $\mathcal{V}^n_{(\beta,A)}[\![\phi]\!] = true$ or $\mathcal{V}^n_{(\beta,A)}[\![\psi]\!] = true$.

We say that an annotated behavior (β, A) satisfies a formula ϕ, if $\mathcal{V}^n_{(\beta,A)}[\![\phi]\!] = true$ for all $n \in \mathbb{N}$.

5.3 Examples of Constraints Expressed in LOC

In the following examples, we assume that the set of event names is $E = \{in, out\}$, and that a real-valued annotation t is defined. Intuitively, we assume that $t(e[i])$ corresponds to the time of the i-th occurrence of an event e. The following common constraints are now easy to express:

rate: "a new *out* will be produced every P time units":

$$t(out[i + 1]) - t(out[i]) = P ,$$

latency: "*out* is generated no more than L time units after *in*":

$$t(out[i]) - t(in[i]) \leq L ,$$

jitter: "every *out* is no more than J time units away from the corresponding tick of the real-time clock with period P":

$$|t(out[i]) - i * P| \leq J ,$$

throughput: "at least X *out* events will be produced in any period of T time units":

$$t(out[i + X]) - t(out[i]) \leq T ,$$

burstiness: "no more than X *in* events will arrive in any period of T time units":

$$t(in[i + X]) - t(in[i]) > T .$$

Consider the latency constraint above. It is valid assuming that *in* and *out* are kept synchronized, i.e. the i-th occurrence of *in* causes the i-th occurrence of *out*. However, this is not true for all systems. In some systems, input events may be lost or intentionally ignored. In these cases, it is not obvious which occurrences of *in* and *out* should be compared for latency. Annotations provide a convenient way for a designer to add this information to the system specification. For example, assume that an $\mathbb{N}$-valued annotation named *cause* is defined for each *out* event, and that $cause(out[i])$ represents the index of the occurrence of *in* which caused $out[i]$. In this case, the latency constraint can be specified as follows:

$$t(out[i]) - t(in[cause(out[i])]) \leq L . \tag{1}$$

This example illustrates how annotations can be used to augment the design with information which is not strictly necessary for its functionality, but which helps in understanding design intentions. In general, such information could also be used by formal techniques to help prove (or disprove) the correctness of the design.

This example also illustrates how annotations can sometimes replace additional variables. Assume that *out* should be compared with the most recent *in* for latency. If LOC allowed variable j in addition to i, then this property could be expressed by:

$$(t(in[j]) < t(out[i]) \wedge t(out[i]) \leq t(in[j+1])) \implies$$
$$(t(out[i]) - t(in[j]) \leq L) \ . \tag{2}$$

If *cause* is properly defined, then (1) and (2) are equivalent. We can check that *cause* is properly defined by verifying the following LOC formula:

$$t(in[cause(out[i])]) < t(out[i]) \wedge$$
$$t(out[i]) \leq t(in[cause(out[i]) + 1]) \ .$$

5.4   Verifying LOC Constraints

At the beginning of a design cycle most annotations will likely not be defined, and LOC formula cannot be evaluated. Later on, as design details are filled in, annotations will become defined and constraints can be verified. In general, this can be done either informally by simulation, or by formal techniques such as theorem proving or automatic model checking.

Simulation Annotated behaviors are intended to be a formalization of simulation traces. However, annotated behaviors are infinite structures ($\beta(e, n)$ is defined for all positive integers n), while in reality, any simulation trace is only a final prefix of a conceptually infinite trace. By letting a simulation run longer, the trace can be extended, but it can never be completed. To check that a formula is satisfied by a trace, one needs to evaluate it for all possible values of variable i. Unfortunately, given only a finite prefix one can typically evaluate a formula only for some values of i. If any of these evaluations produces *false*, we can conclude that the formula is not satisfied. However, we can never conclude that an arbitrary formula is satisfied just from a finite simulation trace.

A simple algorithm that checks whether a given simulation trace satisfies a given LOC formula is:

1. Let the current value of i be 0.
2. Try to evaluate the formula for the current value of i.
3. If the formula evaluates to *true*, or if the given trace is too short to evaluate the formula for the current value of i, then increase i by one and go to step 2. Otherwise (i.e. if the formula evaluates to *false*), report that the formula is not satisfied and stop.

This algorithm will terminate only if the formula is not satisfied. To ensure that the algorithm always terminates, we need to extend it to either:

- conclude that the formula is satisfied for all values of i, or
- conclude that the trace is not long enough to evaluate the formula for any additional values of i.

Both of this analyses can be automated, but, unfortunately, they require complex capabilities typically found in theorem proving tools.

For example, the formula:

$$i > 5 \ \vee \ \mathrm{val}(a[i]) = 1$$

obviously evaluates to *true* for all values of i greater than 5, so if it is not violated by a finite trace with at least five occurrences of a, we can conclude that it is satisfied by all infinite extensions of that finite trace.

Similarly, given a trace in which event a occurs 18 times, the formula

$$\mathrm{val}(a[i^3 - 10i^2 + 26i]) = 1$$

can be evaluated only for five values of i (1, 3, 4, 5, 6). Unfortunately, finding this fact requires solving the following non-linear integer inequality:

$$i^3 - 10i^2 + 26i \leq 18 \ .$$

In any case, incomplete verification results are intrinsic to simulation. Systems can typically exhibit infinitely many different behaviors (prompted by different input stimuli), only few of which can be simulated with finite resources. Nevertheless, simulation is still the cornerstone of all practical verification methodologies. Therefore, it is reasonable to expect that checking LOC constraints by simulation will be valuable in increasing confidence in design performance.

Theorem Proving LOC is just a subset of a first order logic, so any theorem prover that can handle first order logic can also handle LOC, e.g. [2]. If a system behavior is also represented inside the prover, then satisfaction of LOC constraints can be formulated as theorems, and checked by the tool. How to represent system behaviors within a theorem prover is beyond the scope of this paper, but it is a topic that has attracted a lot of interest in the research community (e.g. [4]).

Even without the system specification, theorem provers can be useful in analyzing constraints. Consider for example the latency constraint:

$$t(out[i]) - t(in[i]) \leq 10 \ .$$

If we architect the system such that it consists of two subsystems, the first one taking *in* as input and producing an intermediate event x, and the second one taking x as input and producing *out*, we may decide to decompose the global latency constraint into the following two local constraints:

$$t(out[i]) - t(x[i]) \leq 5$$
$$t(x[i]) - t(in[i]) \leq 5 \ ,$$

```
interface inPort extends Port { update boolean get(); }
interface outPort extends Port { update void put(boolean value); }

process P { port inPort in; port outPort a,b;
  P(){ }

  void thread useport in,a,b {
    boolean aVal, bVal, input;

    aVal = bVal = true;
    while(true) {
      input = in.get();
      if(input) {
        a.put(aVal);
        aVal = !aVal;
      } else {
        b.put(bVal);
        bVal = aVal;
} } } }
```

Fig. 14. A simple process

and proceed with the design of subsystems based on the local constraints. Theorem provers can help ensure that local constraints indeed imply the global constraint, even before the design of subsystems is done.

Model Checking In order to use automatic model checking [5, 3] to verify LOC constraints, the following needs to be done:

1. system behaviors (including annotations) need to be represented as a finite-state automaton over some finite alphabet,
2. an LOC formula needs to be converted into a temporal logic formula over the same alphabet (or, equivalently, into a finite state automaton over the same alphabet).

Both of these steps are non-trivial, and each one may be impossible. Both are clearly impossible if value domains of some events or annotations are infinite. But even if all value domains are finite, problems may arise.

Consider the process in Figure 14. It has six observable events, three of which carry Boolean values[7] ($in.get^-$, $a.put^+$, $b.put^+$). It has many behaviors, determined by different input streams. One possible behavior with its GXI annotation is shown in Figure 15. Not all the values of GXI appear in Figure 15 because we do not show all observable events, but what is shown is sufficient to deduce temporal ordering of events in the behavior. For example, $\beta(a.put^+, 2)$ occurs between $\beta(in.get^-, 5)$ and $\beta(in.get^-, 6)$.

---

[7] Strictly speaking, values of $a.put^+$ and $b.put^+$ are structures with a single Boolean member **value**, but to simplify the notion we will ignore this extra layer.

β	1	2	3	4	5	6	7	8	$\cdots$
val($in.get^-$)	true	false	false	false	true	false	false	true	$\cdots$
val($a.put^+$)	true	false	true		$\cdots$				
val($b.put^+$)	true	false	false	false	true		$\cdots$		

GXI	1	2	3	4	5	6	7	8	$\cdots$
$in.get^-$	2	6	10	14	18	22	26	30	$\cdots$
$a.put^+$	3	19	31		$\cdots$				
$b.put^+$	7	11	15	23	27		$\cdots$		

Fig. 15. A behavior of the system in Figure 14

If we want to represent this process with a finite-state automaton, we first need to choose an alphabet. It may seem that $\{\text{true}, \text{false}\}^3$ is a good choice. In this alphabet, the behavior in Figure 15 would be represented as the sequence:

$$(\text{true}, \text{true}, \text{true}), (\text{false}, \text{false}, \text{false}), (\text{false}, \text{true}, \text{false}), \ldots$$

Unfortunately, in this representation, the system cannot be modeled with a finite number of states, because it needs to make and remember a potentially unbounded number of guesses about future $in.get^-$ values in order to determine the value of $b.put^+$ in the current "step".

A better choice of alphabet is $\{\bot, \text{true}, \text{false}\}^3$, where $\bot$ indicates that the corresponding event is not emitted in that step. In this alphabet, the behavior in Figure 15 would be represented by the following sequence:

$$(\text{true}, \text{true}, \bot), (\text{false}, \bot, \text{true}), (\text{false}, \bot, \text{false}),$$
$$(\text{false}, \bot, \text{false}), (\text{true}, \text{false}, \bot), \ldots$$

A careful reader will notice that this choice of alphabet is similar to event vectors used to define the execution semantics. A finite state representation of the process is shown in Figure 16. Transitions are labeled with values of $in.get^-$, $a.put^+$, and $b.put^+$ (in this particular order). The states are also labeled with values of aVal and bVal. These state labels are intended to ease the understanding of the automaton, but they have no formal meaning.

The choice of alphabet also affects how LOC formulas are translated into automata. For example, in the alphabet $\{\text{true}, \text{false}\}^3$, the formula

$$\text{val}(a.put^+[i]) = \text{val}(b.put^+[i])$$

is represented by a trivial one-state automaton. However, the same formula in the alphabet $\{\bot, \text{true}, \text{false}\}^3$ requires infinitely many states, because i-th occurrences of $a.put^+$ and $b.put^+$ can be separated by arbitrary many steps. On the other hand, some formulas are represented by the same automaton in both alphabets. An example is the constraint:

$$\text{val}(a.put^+[i+2]) = \text{val}(a.put^+[i])$$

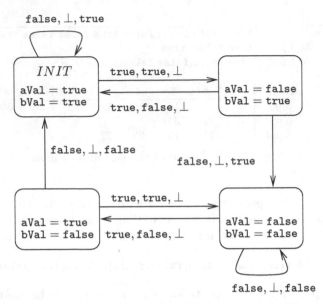

Fig. 16. A finite state automaton for the system in Figure 14

which states that $a.put^+$ is periodic with period 2. The automaton for this formula is shown in Figure 17. The transitions are labeled with the value of $a.put^+$. The state labels indicate one or two most recently seen values of $a.put^+$. As before, these state labels have no formal meaning. Automatic model checking tools can easily check that all sequences generated by the automaton in Figure 16 are accepted by the automaton in Figure 17, proving that $a.put^+$ is indeed periodic with period 2.

5.5 Extended LOC

LOC is used to specify quantity constraints, but for specifying quantity axioms we find it necessary to extend LOC. Before we propose such an extension, we first make a small syntactic change in LOC, requiring that each formula starts with explicit universal quantification of variable i. In this way, no variables occur freely in an LOC formula. This property will also be maintained by ELOC.

ELOC extends LOC in the following ways:

- in addition to integer variable i, ELOC formulas may contain additional variables of various types, including *event variables*, i.e. variables appearing in terms instead of event names,
- variables can be universally or existentially quantified.

We require that all variables are quantified. LOC semantics is extended to ELOC in straightforward manner.

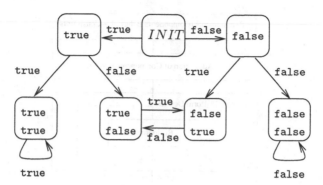

Fig. 17. A finite state automaton for the constraint $val(a.put^+[i+2]) = val(a.put^+[i])$

For example, the following are valid ELOC formulas:

$$\forall e.\forall i.t(e[i+1]) > t(e[i])$$
$$\forall e_1.\forall e_2.\forall i.\forall j.\ GXI(e_1[i]) = GXI(e_1[i]) \Longrightarrow t(e_1[i]) = t(e_2[j]) \ ,$$

where e, e_1, and e_2 are event variables, and t and GXI are annotations.

Additional capabilities over LOC give ELOC the flexibility to express more general properties which are typically required by quantity axioms. This flexibility comes at the price of verification. Verifying ELOC by simulation and finite-state model checking is much harder, if not impossible. Most theorem provers, on the other hand, can handle ELOC, as it is still only a first-order logic.

6   Design Methodology for Communication Networks

The Metropolis methodology for communication design is based on the flow shown in Figure 18. The first step consists of adapting the behavior of the communicating components and is independent from the physical resources used to implement the connection among them. This step is needed when the sender's output domain, defined as the sequence and type of the output messages, is different from the receiver's input domain, i.e. the sequence and type of messages it can accept. For example, if one process is designed to transmit packets of a certain format and size while the receiving process can accept packets of a different size, an intermediate converter between the two formats is needed [9].

The next step consists of selecting a *Network Platform (NP)* [8], i.e. the set of nodes, links and protocols that implement the communication services used by the interacting components of the system. If the type and the quality of the services offered by an existing NP do not satisfy the communication requirements, protocol layers can be introduced to derive other NPs offering more sophisticated services. For example, if a physical link only designed to transmit messages between one pair of users is to be shared by multiple pairs of communicating users,

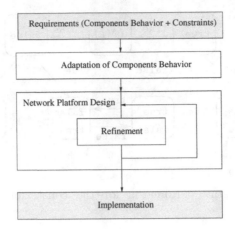

Fig. 18. Communication design flow

one must introduce a MAC protocol that schedules transmissions and avoids collisions. The components of the extended NP are the physical link initially given and the MAC protocol. Figure 19 shows three NPs: a reliable one-hop NP that supports communication among components (in the figure labeled as A and B) directly connected by a single hop link, a multi-hop NP for communication between end nodes (C and D) that are connected by a path composed of multiple nodes and links, and a reliable end-to-end NP for communication between end users (E and F).

Using the Metropolis meta-model, NPs can be represented at different levels of abstraction as netlists of processes and media. Processes represent computation units or protocol entities, media represent physical or logical links connecting processes, port interface functions are used to describe the primitives of the services implemented by a medium.

The procedure for designing an NP is called *successive refinement*: successive because it usually consists of a sequence of steps and refinement because at each step the communication is specified at a greater level of detail and at a finer granularity in time, space or data types. A typical communication refinement step requires one to define the structure of the NP, i.e. its components and topology, and to choose the behavior, i.e. the protocols used at each node. NP components can be nodes, links, protocols and NPs. If two NPs that are composed in cascade support incompatible services, it is necessary to introduce another component (called gateway, router or bridge depending on the levels of abstraction of the NPs being composed) that translates the sequence of messages from one protocol to the other [9].

While carrying out the refinement procedure, it is important to identify the appropriate levels of refinement, e.g. grouping together functions that manipulate the same type of packets, and then ensure that at each step properties

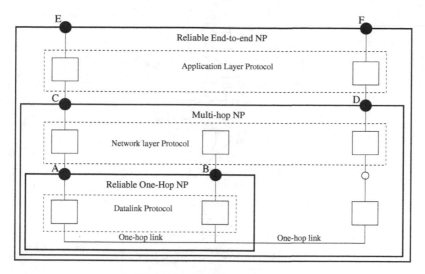

Fig. 19. Network platforms

satisfied at more abstract levels are maintained and constraints are satisfied. We identify three main phases in the communication refinement procedure:

- end-to-end: use an NP abstraction with direct links connecting sender and receiver and define the protocol between the end nodes,
- multi-hop: refine the topology so that the end-to-end connections are mapped into a sequence of one-hop links and choose the protocol that defines how messages are routed through nodes to the destination,
- link-by-link: consider pairs of adjacent nodes (i.e. connected by a physical medium) and select the protocols that handle error and interference.

The three steps are normally carried out independently. However, when the same protocol functions are used at multiple levels of abstraction (e.g. error control on an end-to-end or link-by-link basis), it is convenient either to perform some global tradeoff and avoid repetitions or do a-posteriori optimizations across layers. Each of the above phases can require multiple refinement steps and may result in multiple NP layers.

Figure 20 shows three typical kinds of refinement using the meta-model objects (rectangles and circles represent processes and media respectively). In 20a) a point-to-point one-hop link OH is refined into a multihop link composed of two one-hop links OH1 and OH2. If the nodes have multiple input and output ports, they are not simple repeaters but must include also routing protocols that take care of forwarding the messages along the route to the destination. In 20b) multiple logical point-to-point media are mapped (M1 and M2 in the figure) on the same physical media M with an arbitration scheme, modeled by processes A1, A2, A3 and A4. In 20c) a lossless connection is implemented using a lossy medium and an error correction scheme based on retransmission of unacknowledged packets.

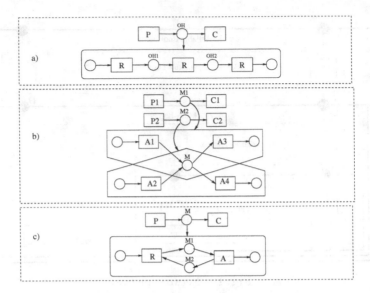

Fig. 20. Refinement examples

During each refinement step, designers refine a given abstract NP, by choosing a topology and the protocols that support communication at each node. To support this procedure, we have identified a set of common *patterns* that frequently occur in the wireless communication domain and built a library from which the designer can select and instantiate them. The library includes several patterns for each refinement step, such as: data pull and push, connection-oriented and connectionless data transfer, flow multiplexing and demultiplexing, time-division and collision-based arbitration schemes.

Below we outline the procedure followed to design the Picoradio wireless sensor network.

6.1   Picoradio System Specification

The goal of the Picoradio project [7] at the Berkeley Wireless Research Center, is to design a low power wireless network able to support a variety of distributed applications. Here we consider a specific application: the control of physical parameters in the environment, such as temperature (T), humidity (H), light (L), within predefined bounds. This must be achieved under additional constraints such as the maximum power consumption. These requirements can be declared as follows: $T \in [T_{min}, T_{max}], H \in [H_{min}, H_{max}], L \in [L_{min}, L_{max}], P \le P_{max}$.

6.2   Design of Picoradio Using Metropolis

The first step is the choice of a *control algorithm*, based on a set of sensors (S), controllers (C) and actuators (A). S and A interface the environment with

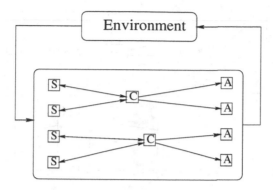

Fig. 21. Control algorithm

the control system: a sensor provides the value of a certain physical quantity in the area where it is placed, while an actuator modifies the values of a physical quantity. Controllers implement the law that determines, based on the sensed data, when actuators should be activated (Figure 21).

The design of the control algorithm is out of the scope of the paper. Hence, we assume that the control application has already been fully defined and focus on the problem of designing the communication among S, C, A components. The specification requires the following:

- the interaction between S, C, A (Figure 22a):
  (1) S - C : two use case scenarios
    - controllers request data to a set of sensors upon requests from an external user (Pull),
    - sensors send data to controllers periodically (Push),
  (2) C - A : one use case scenario
    - controllers issue command instructions to actuators,
- the number and physical location of the components of S, C and A,
- the control rate, which has been chosen to match the environment behavior, i.e. the faster the environment parameters change the higher the rate,
- a set of constraints, such as node mobility, reliability, maximum power consumption and response delay.

Figure 22b) shows the application level meta-model netlist, where S, C and A are modeled as processes. The specification of S and C is shown in Figures 23 and 24. A sensor either awaits a request issued by a controller and replies with a message carrying the requested data (pull scenario) or sends the controller the sensed data at regular intervals (push). The period between data pushes is specified using an LOC formula. The function `isDest` is called by the sensor process to check whether it is the destination of the data requests, the function `getSensedValue` returns the most updated data sample. A controller awaits requests from an external user investigating the value of physical parameters in a certain region and forwards them to the sensors in that region. It also reacts

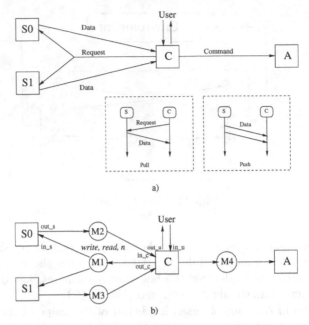

Fig. 22. a) Communication requirements, b) Application processes and media

when messages containing data samples arrive from a sensor. Then, this data is forwarded to the external user who made the initial request and is used by the control algorithm that decides whether to enable the actuators.

The behaviors of the S, C and A components are specified so that the types and size of the messages they exchange are compatible; hence, in this application there is no need for behavior adaptation. We thus proceed further to design an NP that satisfies all the given requirements. To support node mobility and maximize flexibility of deployment and use, we choose to develop a *wireless* NP, where communication occurs over RF links. Then, we apply the successive refinement procedure and choose a network topology and a stack of protocols that fully define the wireless NP.

The first step consists of choosing an end-to-end reliable NP satisfying the request-response delay constraints: we select an NP that is composed of a set of one-hop links, one for each pair of interacting S, C and A. Links are represented in Figure 22b) as communication media. Consider first medium M1 that connects a controller and the sensors from which the controller may request data. The specification of medium M1 is shown in Figure 25 and consists of a buffer that stores at most one message request and a set of functions to access the medium (**read**, **write**, **n**). The semantics of the communication over M1 is that the controller writes message requests into the buffer, while each sensor reads the buffer when there is an unread message (i.e. when the interface function **n** returns 1 for the sensor). The write is non-blocking, because message requests

```
interface SReader extends Port { eval int n(int MyID);
                                 update PacketReq read(int MyID); }
interface CWriter extends Port { update void write(int MyID,
                                 LocRange dest); }

process Sensor {
  port SReader in_s;
  port SWriter out_s;
  parameter int MyID;
  parameter int MyLocationX;
  parameter int MyLocationY;
  parameter int MyLocationZ;
  parameter double Interval;

  Sensor(int id, int x, int y, int x, double t) {
    MyID = id; MyLocationX = x; MyLocationY = y; MyLocationZ = z;
    Interval = t;
  }
  void thread() {
    PacketReq req;

    while (true)
      await {
        (in_s.n(MyID)>0; ; ) { // the pull pattern
            req = in_s.read(MyID);
            if(isDest(req))
              out_s.write(getSensedValue(), MyID)
        }
        (true; ; ) { // the push pattern
    WP:       out_s.write(getSensedValue(), MyID);
        }
      }

      constraint {
        loc GTime.A(beg(this, this.WP),i+1)-GTime.A(beg(this, this.WP),i)
          ==Interval;
      }
  }
  boolean isDest(PacketReq req){
    // check if the destination given in req designates this node.
  }
  int getSensedValue(){
    // get data from the sensor
  }
}
```

Fig. 23. Sensor process in Figure 22

```
process Controller {
port CReader in_c2;
port CReader in_c3;
port CWriter out_c2s;
port AWriter out_c2a;
port UReader in_u;
port UWriter out_u;
parameter MyID;
parameter int MyLocationX;
parameter int MyLocationY;
parameter int MyLocationZ;

  Controller(int id, int x, int y, int x, double t) {
    MyID = id; MyLocationX = x; MyLocationY = y; MyLocationZ = z;
  }
  void thread() {
    PacketUReq Ureq;
    PacketSensedData SensedValue;

    while (true)
      await {
        (in_u.n()>0; ; ) { // user request
          Ureq = in_u.read();
          out_c2s.write(MyID, Ureq.dest)
        }
        (in_c2.n()>0; ; ) { // data from the first sensor
          SensedValue = in_c.read();
          out_u.write(SensedValue);   // return data to user
          if (controlAlgorithm(SensedValue))
            out_c2a.write(command);   // command actuator
        }
        (in_c3.n()>0; ; ) { // data from the second sensor
          SensedValue = in_c.read();
          out_u.write(SensedValue);   // return data to user
          if (controlAlgorithm(SensedValue))
            out_c2a.write(command);   // command actuator
        }

      }
  }
  void controlAlgorithm (PacketSensedData SensedValue){
    // decide on enabling actuators
  }
}
```

Fig. 24. Controller process in Figure 22

```
public medium M1 implements SReader, CWriter, R, W {
PacketReq p;
int BufferSize, n[];
parameter int rsize;

  M1(int rn){
    int i;
    BufferSize=1;  n=new int[rn]; rsize=rn;
    for(i=0; i<n.length; i++) n[i]=0;
  }
  eval int n(int SensorID) {
   await { (true; this.W; this.R) return n[SensorID]; }
  }
  update void write (int ControllerID, LocRange dest) {
    int i;
    await {
      (true; this.R; this.W) {
        p.src=ControllerID; p.dest=dest;
        for(i=0; i<n.length; i++) n[i]=1;
      }
    }
  }
  update PacketReq read(int SensorID) {
    await {
      (n[SensorID]>0; this.W; this.R) { n[SensorID]=0; return p; }
    }
  }

  constraint {
    ltl G(connectionnum(this, CWriter)==1);
    loc val.A(beg(any, this.n),i).SensorID<rsize;
    loc val.A(beg(any, this.read),i).SensorID<rsize;
  }
}

interface R extends Port { }
interface W extends Port { }
```

Fig. 25. Communication medium M1 in Figure 22

that are stored can be deleted when new request arrives. While the controller
changes the medium's state in **write**, the sensors cannot access the state. Similarly, while the sensors access the medium's state, the controller cannot update
the state. However, two or more sensors may call the functions **read** and **n** concurrently. This exclusion is ensured by the **await** statements. The medium has
three constraint formulas. The first one ensures that this medium is accessed by
exactly one controller, i.e. the number of objects that connect to this medium

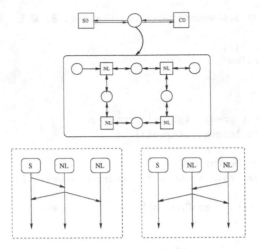

Fig. 26. Network Layer refinement

using ports with type `CWriter` is 1. `connectionnum` is a meta-model keyword that designates a built-in field of a medium for the number of connecting objects with a given interface name. The other two are LOC formulas that ensures that the ID of a sensor is within the range specified for the medium. Media M2 and M3 are similar to M1, in that they have a one-place buffer and the communication has non-blocking write semantics, since only the last data sample is used by the control algorithm.

The next step refines the reliable end-to-end NP defined above into a multi-hop NP, where any node can be used as an intermediate hop in a path from the source to destination (Figure 26). The choice of a multi-hop NP is essential to maximize reuse of resources (links) and reduce power consumption [7]. In a wireless NP the network topology is determined by the transmission power level, i.e. a node is connected to the nodes within its power range. A Network Layer protocol resides in each node and is needed to route messages from source to destination. In the meta-model representation the network layer consists of a single process with the following behavior. It receives input messages generated either by the application layer or by an adjacent node. In both scenarios (described in figure 26 using a Sequence Diagram) the Network Layer protocol first checks the destination of the message and then following a routing policy based on geographical and power-level information [7], determines to which adjacent node the message is to be forwarded.

7   Concluding Remarks

No single model of computations has shown to be well-suited for a wide range of present day heterogeneous embedded systems, and none is likely to emerge in the near future. Cognizant of this fact, we have proposed a meta-model that provides basic building blocks from which various models of computations can be constructed. The building blocks deal separately with various aspects of system design: computation of a component, communication and coordination between components, performance goals and constraints, and refinements that model design steps. Separating these concerns increases re-usability, as it allows specification not to be burdened by details that are the artifacts of a given specification formalism, and not part of the designer intent. For example, the functionality of a component can be described at a level which does not imply the implementation architecture, and thus can be re-used on many architectures. Conversely, an architecture platform that can support a range of applications can be precisely characterized and used in many designs.

References

[1] F. Balarin, Y. Watanabe J. Burch, L. Lavagno, R. Passerone, and A. Sangiovanni-Vincentelli. Constraints specification at higher levels of abstraction. In *Proceeding of the 6th Annual IEEE International Workshop on High Level Design Validation and Test - HLDVT'01*. IEEE Computer Society, November 2001. 252

[2] R. S. Boyer, M. Kaufmann, and J. S. Moore. The boyer-moore theorem prover and its interactive enhancement. *Computers & Mathematics with Applications*, pages 27–62, January 1995. 259

[3] Z. Har'El and R. P. Kurshan. Software for analysis of coordination. In *Proceedings of the International Conference on System Science*, pages 382–385, 1988. 260

[4] Warren A. Hunt Jr. and Steven D. Johnson, editors. *Formal methods in computer-aided design: third international conference FMCAD 2000*. Springer-Verlag, 2000. LNCS vol. 1954. 259

[5] Kenneth L. McMillan. *Symbolic Model Checking*. Kluwer Academic Publishers, 1993. 260

[6] A. Pnueli. The temporal logic of programs. In *Proc. 18th Annual IEEE Symposium on Foundations of Computer Sciences*, pages 46–57, 1977. 232, 252

[7] J. Rabaey, M. Ammer, J. Silva jr., D. Patel, and S. Roundy. Picoradio supports ad hoc ultra-low power wireless networking. In *IEEE Computer Magazine*, July 2000. 266, 272

[8] A. Sangiovanni-Vincentelli and A. Ferrari. System design - traditional concepts and new paradigms. In *International COnference on Computer Design, ICCD '99*, October 1999. 263

[9] A. Sangiovanni-Vincentelli, M. Sgroi, and L. Lavagno. Formal models for communication-based design. In *Proceedings of the 11-th International Conference on Concurrency Theory, Concur '00*, August 2000. 263, 264

Timed Verification of Asynchronous Circuits*

Jesper Møller, Henrik Hulgaard, and Henrik Reif Andersen

The IT University of Copenhagen, Department of Innovation
{jm,henrik,hra}@it.edu

Abstract. We describe a methodology for analyzing timed systems symbolically. Given a formula representing a set of timed states, we describe how to determine a new formula that represents the set of states reachable by taking a discrete transition or by advancing time. The symbolic representations are given as formulae expressed in a simple first-order logic over constraints of the form $x - y \leq d$ which can be combined with Boolean operators and existentially quantified. The main contribution is a way of advancing time symbolically essentially by quantifying out a special variable z which is used to represent the current zero point in time. We describe how to model asynchronous circuits using timed guarded commands and provide examples that demonstrate the potential of the symbolic analysis.

1   Introduction

Model checking [17] is today used extensively for formal verification of finite state systems such as digital circuits and embedded software. The success of the technique is primarily due to the use of a *symbolic* representation of sets of states and relations between states as predicates over Boolean variables using for instance binary decision diagrams (BDDs) [13]. By representing the set of reachable states as a predicate instead of explicitly enumerating the elements of the set, it is possible to verify systems with a very large number of states [15].

This chapter shows how to extend symbolic model checking to handle models that contain variables that range over non-countable domains. Specifically, we show how to analyze timed systems where timers are modeled using continuous variables and the behavior of a system is specified using constraints on these variables. The analysis of timed systems plays an important role in several areas:

- *Real-time systems* are a class of systems where correct behavior depends on the ability to react to external events in a predictable and timely manner. Real-time systems are found, for example, in transportation systems, aerospace, robotics, communication systems, defense systems, and industrial process control. Because real-time systems are used in time critical applications, failure to meet the required deadlines may have serious consequences as damage to property or humans. Thus, formal verification is necessary to ensure the correctness of a real-time system.

---

* Financially supported by a grant from the Danish Technical Research Council.

J. Cortadella et al. (Eds.): Concurrency and Hardware Design, LNCS 2549, pp. 274–312, 2002.
© Springer-Verlag Berlin Heidelberg 2002

- *Protocols* may rely on timing properties. Some examples are Fischer's protocol for establishing mutual exclusion, Milner's protocol for scheduling tasks, and the FDDI communication protocol used in local area networks. Analyzing the correctness of such protocols requires formal arguments involving timing properties.
- *Asynchronous circuits* consist of components that synchronize by handshake signals rather than using a global clock. Although asynchronous circuits can be designed so that they work correctly for any delay of the components (so-called speed-independent and delay-insensitive circuits), to obtain high performance and reduce the amount of circuitry, the designers need to exploit knowledge of the actual delays of the gates. As a result, the different parts of the circuit make (timing) assumptions about their inputs and work correctly only as long as these assumptions are satisfied. For circuits of non-trivial size, the circuit designer needs automated analysis methods to ensure correct behavior of the circuit, for example that the circuit is hazard-free.

We propose a simple notation called *timed guarded commands* for modeling a timed system. Timed guarded commands are similar to Dijkstra's guarded commands [22] extended with a finite number of clocks that can be tested in the guards and reset in the assignments. The notation is quite expressive: popular models of systems with time such as timed automata [2] and timed Petri nets [9] are easily encoded using timed guarded commands.

Given a system defined by a set of timed guarded commands, one may ask whether a given property is satisfied. We will focus on the basic question of whether a given combination of states is reachable, but also sketch how more general timing properties, expressed in a timed version of computation tree logic (CTL) [30], can be verified symbolically.

1.1 Current Analysis Approaches

The basic verification problem is to determine whether a given state s is reachable. The standard approach for solving this problem is to construct the set of reachable states R and then determine whether $s \in R$. To solve this reachability problem for a timed system, there are four key problems that have to be addressed:

1. How to represent the infinite state space R of a timed system?
2. How to tackle the state explosion problem for the discrete part of the state space?
3. How to perform the basic operations (resetting clocks, advancing the time of clocks, etc.) on the representation to compute the reachable part of the state space?
4. How to determine whether two representations are equivalent?

A state in a timed system is a pair (s, v) where s is a discrete state (e.g., a marking of a Petri net, or a location in a timed automaton, or the values on the wires of a circuit) and v is an assignment of values to the clocks in the system.

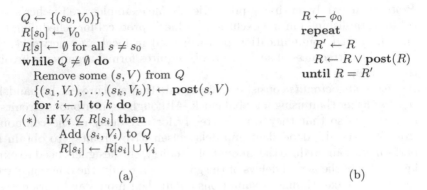

(a)   (b)

Fig. 1. Two approaches for constructing the reachable state space R. (a) Outline of the algorithm used in current tools such as KRONOS and UPPAAL, and (b) a fully symbolic algorithm

Timed systems have an infinite number of states due to the dense domains of the clocks, so clock assignments are grouped into sets when analyzing timed systems. This allows the state space to be represented as a finite set of pairs (s, V) consisting of a discrete state and the associated group of clock valuations V. The reachable states space R for a timed system can be determined by the generic algorithm in Fig. 1(a) where we view R as a mapping from discrete states s to their associated group of clock valuations V. The operator **post** fires all possible transitions and advances time from the set of states (s, V).

Current state-of-the-art techniques for verifying timed systems (e.g., [9, 35, 43, 50]) are based on representing clock assignments using a set of difference bound matrices (DBMs) [23]. Each difference bound matrix can represent a convex set of clock assignments, thus to represent V, in general, a number of matrices is needed (i.e., representing V as a union of convex sets). The operator **post** constructs the set of new states such that each V_i is a single DBM. The test in the line marked $(*)$ is performed by checking whether the DBM V_i is contained in any of the DBMs used to represent $R[s_i]$.

Although DBMs provide a compact representation of a convex set of clock configurations, there are several problems with the approaches based on DBMs:

1. The number of DBMs for representing the timing information V can become very large.
2. There is no sharing or reuse of DBMs among the different discrete states.
3. Each discrete state is represented explicitly, thus these approaches are limited by the number of reachable states of the system (the well-known state explosion problem).

1.2 A Symbolic Approach

The first two problems can be addressed by representing the set V as a propositional formula over inequalities of the form $x - y \leq d$ (x and y are clock variables and d is a constant). If we have a compact representation of such formulae and can decide valid implications (for performing the check in the line marked with (*)), we can use the algorithm in Fig. 1(a) immediately. Difference decision diagrams [38] are a candidate for such a data structure which furthermore allows reuse of sub-formula among the discrete states. Initial experiments with this approach implemented in UPPAAL [6] show a significant improvement in memory consumption, even though the discrete states are still enumerated explicitly.

In this chapter we address all three problems by constructing the set of reachable states R in a fully symbolic manner, without enumerating the discrete states and without representing the timing information as a set of DBMs. In our approach, both the discrete part of a state and the associated timing information are represented by a formula. That is, *sets* of states (s, V) are represented by a single formula ϕ, similar to how sets of discrete states are represented by a formula when performing traditional symbolic model checking of untimed systems. Using such a representation, the set of reachable states R can be computed using the standard fixpoint iteration shown in Fig. 1(b).

A core operation when performing symbolic model checking is to determine the formula $\mathbf{post}(\phi)$ representing the set of states reachable by taking any discrete transition, denoted by $\mathbf{post}_d(\phi)$, or advancing time from a state satisfying ϕ, denoted by $\mathbf{post}_t(\phi)$. Taking the transitions is straightforward, but advancing time is more involved. We introduce a variable z denoting "zero" or "current time" and express all constraints of the form $x \leq d$ as $x - z \leq d$. The use of a designated variable representing zero for eliminating absolute constraints is used both in DBMs [23] and also when solving systems of difference constraints [21].

We show how the z-variable, in addition to making the representation more uniform, also makes it possible to advance time in a set of states represented by a formula ϕ by performing an existential quantification of z: Let P_{post} denote a predicate stating whether it is legal to advance time by changing the zero point from z to z'. Thus P_{post} will require that $z' \leq z$ since advancing time by some amount δ corresponds to decreasing the reference point z by δ. Typically, P_{post} will also include constraints expressing program invariants and urgency predicates. Now, a formula representing the set of states reachable from ϕ by advancing time by δ is determined from:

$$\mathbf{post}_t(\phi, \delta) = \exists z.(\phi \wedge P_{post} \wedge z - z' = \delta)[z/z'].$$

More generally, we show that the set of states reachable from ϕ by advancing time *by an arbitrary amount* is given by:

$$\mathbf{post}_t(\phi) = \bigvee_{\delta \in \mathbb{R}} \mathbf{post}_t(\phi, \delta) = \exists z.(\phi \wedge P_{post})[z/z'].$$

Another key contribution of this chapter is that we show that performing fully symbolic model checking of timed systems amounts to representing and deciding validity of *difference constraint expressions* which are first-order propositions of the form:

$$\psi ::= x - y \le d \mid \psi_1 \wedge \psi_2 \mid \neg\psi \mid \exists x.\psi \,,$$

where x and y are real-valued variables, and $d \in \mathbb{Q}$ is a constant. A practical model checking algorithm therefore requires a compact representation of difference constraint expressions, and an efficient decision procedure to determine validity of such expressions (including a procedure for quantifier elimination).

1.3 Related Work

Model checking of timed systems (timed automata in particular; see [51] for a survey) has been extensively studied and a number of tools exist for verifying such systems. One approach is based on making the dense domains discrete by assuming that timers only can take integer or rational values. Such a discretization makes it possible to use BDDs for representing both the discrete states and the associated timing information [16, 12, 14, 3]. However, this way of representing dense domains is often inefficient; the BDD representation is very sensitive to the granularity of the discretization and to the size of the delay ranges.

The unit-cube approach [2] models time as dense but represents the timing information using a finite number of equivalence classes. Again, the number of timed states is dependent on the size of the delay ranges and easily becomes unmanageable. As mentioned above, more recent timing analysis methods use difference bound matrices (DBMs) [23] for representing the timing information [9, 35, 43, 50]. One can see the use of DBMs as expanding difference constraint expressions into disjunctive normal form and representing each conjunction of difference constraints using a difference bound matrix. Several attempts have been made to remedy the shortcoming of DBMs discussed above, for example by using partial order methods [44, 48, 8] or by using approximate methods [4, 7, 49]. Although these approaches do address the problem that the number of DBMs for representing the timing information can become very large, they are all inherently limited by the explicit enumeration of all discrete states.

Henzinger et al. [30] describe how to perform symbolic model checking of timed systems. Although apparently similar to our approach, there are a number of significant differences: First, we show that difference constraint expressions which have only one type of clock constraints ($x - y \le d$) are sufficient for representing the set of states of a timed system. This allows us to represent sets of states efficiently using an implicit representation of formulae (e.g., difference decision diagrams). Second, we show how to perform all operations needed in symbolic model checking within this logic. A core operation is advancing time which we show can be performed within the logic by introducing a designated variable z and using existential quantification.

1.4   Overview

This chapter is organized as follows: In Sect. 2 we introduce a simple model of timed systems called timed guarded commands. Section 3 shows how to analyze timed guarded commands—for example, how to compute the set of reachable states symbolically, and how to formally verify properties (e.g., check for absence of hazards in a circuit). Section 4 discusses various data structures and algorithms for implementing tools that can perform these symbolic analyses. In Sect. 5 we look at some examples of timed systems and analyze them using a data structure called difference decision diagrams. Finally, Sect. 6 is a summary of the chapter.

2   Timed Guarded Commands

We present a simple notation called timed guarded commands [39] for modeling systems with time. This notation provides the basis for modeling asynchronous circuits, and is sufficient for encoding popular notations for systems with time such as timed automata [2] and timed Petri nets [9]. First we define the syntax and semantics of timed guarded commands, and then we describe how to model asynchronous circuits in this notation. Section 3 describes how to analyze a model of an asynchronous circuit specified using timed guarded commands.

2.1   Syntax

We start with some basic definitions of the building blocks of timed guarded commands: variables, expressions, and commands.

Definition 1 (Variables). *Let C be a countable set of real-valued variables called clocks ranged over by x, and let B be a countable set of Boolean variables ranged over by b. The set of variables is $V = B \cup C$.*

Next, we define a language for expressing propositions over Boolean variables and clocks:

Definition 2 (Expressions). *Let Φ be the set of expressions of the form:*

$$\phi ::= x \sim d \mid x - y \sim d \mid b \mid \neg\phi \mid \phi_1 \wedge \phi_2 \mid \phi_1 \vee \phi_2,$$

where $x, y \in C$ are clocks, $b \in B$ is a Boolean variable, $d \in \mathbb{Q}$ is a rational constant, $\sim \; \in \{\leq, <, =, \neq, >, \geq\}$ is a relational operator, and $\phi \in \Phi$ is an expression.

We use the tokens **false** and **true** to denote false and true expressions, respectively. The symbols $\neg$ (negation), $\wedge$ (conjunction), and $\vee$ (disjunction) have their usual meaning. Other Boolean operators such as $\Rightarrow$ (implication), $\Leftrightarrow$ (bi-implication), and $\oplus$ (exclusive or) are defined the standard way.

Example 1. Let $x, y, z \in \mathcal{C}$ be clocks, and $a, b, c \in \mathcal{B}$ be Boolean variables. Then a valid expression over these variables is:

$$\phi_1 = \left(a \wedge b \wedge (x - y \neq 0) \wedge (x - z \leq 5)\right) \vee \left(c \Rightarrow (x = 0)\right).$$

The expression
$$\phi_2 = (x + y = 0) \vee (x - 2y < 3).$$

is *not* a well-formed expressions because $x + y = 0$ is not a valid atomic expression, and neither is $x - 2y < 3$.

Definition 3 (Replacement). *Let $\phi \in \Phi$ be an expression, let $v \in \mathcal{V}^n$ be an n-dimensional vector of variables, and let $r \in (\mathbb{B} \cup \mathbb{Q})^n$ be an n-dimensional vector of values. Then the replacement $\phi[r/v]$ syntactically substitutes all occurrences of v_i by r_i, $i = 1, \ldots, n$, in ϕ.*

Definition 4 (any-operator). *Let $v, v' \in \mathcal{V}^n$ be n-dimensional vectors of Boolean variables and clocks, and let $\phi' \in \Phi$ be an expression. Then the **any**-operator is written as:*

$$v := \mathbf{any}\ v'.\phi'.$$

The **any**-operator is a nondeterministic assignment operator. Intuitively, the assignment
$$(v_1, \ldots, v_n) := \mathbf{any}\ (v'_1, \ldots, v'_n).\phi'$$

has the following meaning: Assign to each clock or Boolean variable v_i ($i = 1, \ldots, n$) any value v'_i, $v'_i \neq v_i$, such that the expression ϕ' is satisfied. If ϕ' is not satisfiable then the assignment has no effect (i.e., the variables $v_1, \ldots, v_n$ remain unchanged). Typically ϕ' is an expression over $v'_1, \ldots, v'_n$ and other variables. The choice of a value for a variable v' in an assignment is made nondeterministically and independently of choices for other variables v'' made in other assignments.[1]

We will often have to perform ordinary (deterministic) assignments, so we define the following shorthands:

$$
\begin{aligned}
x &:= d & &\equiv & x &:= \mathbf{any}\ x'.x' = d \\
x &:= y + d & &\equiv & x &:= \mathbf{any}\ x'.x' - y = d \\
b &:= \phi & &\equiv & b &:= \mathbf{any}\ b'.b' \Leftrightarrow \phi
\end{aligned}
$$

Example 2. The assignment

$$(x, y) := \mathbf{any}\ (x', y').(0 \leq x' - x \leq 10) \wedge (0 \leq y' - x \leq 1)$$

has the following meaning: increment x by some value in the range $[0, 10]$, and, simultaneously, set y to some value in the range $[x, x + 1]$. For example, if $x =$

---

[1] An alternative to this independent-choice strategy is a fixed-choice strategy. In a fixed-choice strategy, if two expressions ϕ' and ϕ'' are identical then the two values bound to v' and v'' are also identical. The fixed-choice **any** operator is also known as Hilbert's ϵ-operator [31]. The independent-choice **any** operator we use is identical to Blass and Gurevich's δ-operator [10].

$y = 1$ then after the assignment we have $x \in [1, 11]$ and $y \in [1, 2]$. Notice how the primed variables x' and y' in the two expressions are used to refer to the new values for x and y, respectively.

The ability to express nondeterministic assignments using the **any**-operator is used in Sect. 3 where we describe how to analyze timed guarded commands. In this section we only consider deterministic assignments.

Definition 5 (Commands). *Let $v, v' \in V^n$ be n-dimensional vectors of clocks and Boolean variables, and let $\phi' \in \Phi$ be an expression. Then a (timed guarded) command has the form*

$$\phi \rightarrow v := \textbf{any } v'.\phi' \,,$$

where $\phi \in \Phi$ is called the guard. A command is said to be enabled if its guard evaluates to true.

A command specifies a conditional assignment: if the guard evaluates to true, then the command can be executed. Executing the command assigns a value to each variable on the left-hand side of the assignment.

Definition 6 (TGC program). *A timed guarded command (TGC) program P is a tuple (B, C, T, I, U), where $B \subseteq \mathcal{B}$ is a set of Boolean variables, $C \subseteq \mathcal{C}$ is a set of clocks, T is a set of commands over $B \cup C$, $I \in \Phi$ is the program invariant, and $U \in \Phi$ is the urgency predicate.*

In the following section we give precise semantics of a TGC program and define what it means to run a TGC program. Informally speaking, to run a program we start in some initial state and continuously either execute an enabled command or advance time by increasing the values of all clocks by some amount. The program invariant is an expression which must always be fulfilled when running a program. The urgency predicate is an expression which specifies when it is illegal to advance time. We can use this predicate to ensure that certain commands will always be executed as soon as they become enabled—that is, time is not allowed to advance if one or more of these urgent commands are enabled. As we shall see in Sect. 2.5, the program invariant and the urgency predicate are used to ensure progress of a TGC program. See [45] for a more thorough treatment of urgency in timed systems.

Example 3. An example of a TGC program is $P = (\{b\}, \{x, y\}, \{t_1, t_2\}, I, U)$, where:

$$t_1 : b \wedge (1 \leq x \leq 3) \rightarrow b \quad := \textbf{false}$$
$$t_2 : b \wedge (7 \leq x \leq 9) \rightarrow b, y := \textbf{false}, 0 \,.$$

The program invariant is given by the expression

$$I = \big(b \Rightarrow (x \leq 9)\big) \wedge \big(\neg b \Rightarrow (x \neq 5)\big) \,.$$

There are no urgent commands, so the urgency predicate is simply:

$$U = \textbf{false} \,.$$

2.2   Semantics

The semantics of a TGC program is a transition system where the set of states are value assignments of the variables, and the transitions between states correspond to either executing commands in the program or advancing time.

Definition 7 (States). *A state of a TGC program $P = (B, C, T, I, U)$ is an interpretation (i.e., a value assignment) of the Boolean variables and clocks. For each variable $v \in B \cup C$, $s(v) \in \mathbb{B} \cup \mathbb{Q}$ denotes the interpretation of v in the state s. A state s satisfies an expression ϕ, written $s \models \phi$, if ϕ evaluates to true in the state s, and we write $[\![\phi]\!]$ for the set of states that satisfy ϕ.*

We also use the notation $s(v_1, \ldots, v_n) = (r_1, \ldots, r_n)$, where $r_i \in \mathbb{B} \cup \mathbb{C}$ for $i = 1, \ldots, n$.

Example 4. Let us consider the TGC program from Example 3. The set of states $\mathcal{S}$ of this program are triples of the form (b, x, y), where b is either **true** or **false**, and x and y are real numbers. Consider the state $s(b, x, y) = (\textbf{true}, 0, 2)$, and consider the expressions $\phi_1 = b \wedge x < 9$, and $\phi_2 = \neg b \vee x = y$. Clearly, $s \models \phi_1$, but $s \not\models \phi_2$.

Definition 8 (State update). *Let $v \in \mathcal{V}^n$ be an n-dimensional vector of variables, and let $r \in (\mathbb{B} \cup \mathbb{Q})^n$ be an n-dimensional vector of values. Then the state $s' = s[v := r]$ is equivalent to s except that $s'(v_i) = r_i$ for $i = 1, \ldots, n$.*

Example 5. Consider again the state s where $s(b, x, y) = (\textbf{true}, 0, 2)$, and assume that $s' = s[(x, z) := (2, 3)]$. Then $s'(b, x, y, z) = (\textbf{true}, 2, 2, 3)$.

We now define the transitions between states. In each state, the program can either execute a command $t \in T$ if its guard is true (a discrete transition) or let time pass δ time units (a timed transition). Executing a command changes the value of the variables according to the multi-assignment, and letting time pass uniformly increases the values of all clocks by some amount δ.

Definition 9 (Discrete transition). *Let $P = (B, C, T, I, U)$ be a TGC program. Then the discrete transition $\xrightarrow{t}$ for a timed guarded command $t \in T$ of form $\phi \to v := \textbf{any}\ v'.\phi'$ is defined by the following inference rule:*

$$\frac{s \models \phi \quad s[v' := r] \models \phi' \quad s[v := r] \models I}{s \xrightarrow{t} s[v := r]}.$$

Definition 9 says that if $\phi \to v := \textbf{any}\ v'.\phi'$ is a command t in a TGC program P, then the transition system for P has a discrete transition from s to $s' = s[v := r]$ labeled t if the following conditions hold:

- the state s satisfies the guard ϕ,
- the state s updated with $v' := r$ satisfies the expression ϕ', and
- the state s' satisfies the state invariant I.

Example 6. Consider again the TGC program in Example 3, and let s be a state where $s(b, x, y) = (\textbf{true}, 2, 2)$. Then, from Definition 9, the transition system for P contains a discrete transition $\xrightarrow{t_1}$ from s to s', where $s'(b, x, y) = (\textbf{false}, 2, 2)$.

Definition 10 (Timed transition). *Let* $P = (B, C, T, I, U)$ *be a* TGC *program. The timed transition* $\xrightarrow{\delta}$ *for advancing all clocks by* δ *is defined by the following inference rule:*

$$\frac{\delta \geq 0 \quad s[\boldsymbol{c} := \boldsymbol{c} + \delta] \models I \quad \forall \delta'.0 \leq \delta' < \delta : s[\boldsymbol{c} := \boldsymbol{c} + \delta'] \models (I \wedge \neg U)}{s \xrightarrow{\delta} s[\boldsymbol{c} := \boldsymbol{c} + \delta]},$$

where $\delta, \delta' \in \mathbb{Q}$, $\boldsymbol{c}$ *denotes a vector of all clocks in* C, *and* $\boldsymbol{c} + \delta$ *denotes the vector where* δ *is added to each clock in* $\boldsymbol{c}$.

Definition 10 says when it is legal to advance time by some amount δ:

- the delay δ must be nonnegative,
- the state invariant I must hold if we advance time by δ', for any $\delta' \in [0, \delta]$, and
- the negated urgency predicate $\neg U$ must hold if we advance time by δ', for any $\delta' \in [0, \delta[$.

That is, we can advance time by δ if the state invariant holds continuously for all intermediate points in time (i.e., for $\delta' \in [0, \delta]$), and if the negation of the urgency predicate holds continuously for all intermediate points in time, except the end-point δ (i.e., for $\delta' \in [0, \delta[$).

Example 7. Consider again the TGC program in Example 3, and let s be a state where $s(b, x, y) = (\textbf{true}, 2, 2)$. Then, from Definition 10, the transition system for P contains infinitely many timed transitions $\xrightarrow{\delta}$, where $\delta \in [0, 7]$, from s to s' with $s'(b, x, y) = (\textbf{false}, 2 + \delta, 2 + \delta)$. However, there are no timed transitions $\xrightarrow{\delta}$ from s with $\delta > 7$, as this would violate the state invariant.

Definition 11 (Semantics). *The semantics of a* TGC *program is a transition system* $(\mathcal{S}, \rightarrow)$, *where* $\mathcal{S}$ *is the set of states of the program, and* $\rightarrow$ *is the transition relation as defined in Definitions 9 and 10.*

Given some initial state s_0, we can execute a program from s_0 by repeatedly either executing a command $t \in T$ if its guard is true (a discrete transition) or letting time pass δ time units (a timed transition). Executing a command changes the value of the variables according to the multi-assignment, and letting time pass uniformly increases the values of all clocks by δ. This is made precise in the following definition:

Definition 12 (Execution). *Let* $P = (B, C, T, I, U)$ *be a* TGC *program, and let* $(\mathcal{S}, \rightarrow)$ *be the corresponding transition system. An execution of* P *from the initial state* s_0 *is a (possibly) infinite sequence of state transitions*

$$s_0 \xrightarrow{\tau_0} s_1 \xrightarrow{\tau_1} s_2 \xrightarrow{\tau_2} \cdots$$

where $s_i \in \mathcal{S}$ and $s_i \xrightarrow{\tau_i} s_{i+1}$ is a discrete or timed transition of $(\mathcal{S}, \rightarrow)$.

Example 8. An example of an execution of the TGC program P in Example 3, with the initial state $s_0(b, x, y) = (\mathbf{true}, 0, 0)$, is:

$$(\mathbf{true}, 0, 0) \xrightarrow{2} (\mathbf{true}, 2, 2) \xrightarrow{6} (\mathbf{true}, 8, 8) \xrightarrow{t_2} (\mathbf{false}, 8, 0).$$

2.3 Reachability

Given a transition system $(\mathcal{S}, \rightarrow)$ for a TGC program $P = (B, C, T, I, U)$ and a set of states $S \subseteq \mathcal{S}$, we now define various sets of states reachable from S by discrete or timed transitions:

Definition 13 (Discrete successor). *Let $(\mathcal{S}, \rightarrow)$ be the transition system for a TGC program $P = (B, C, T, I, U)$, and let $S \subseteq \mathcal{S}$ be a set of states. The set of states reachable from S by executing the command $t \in T$ is given by:*

$$Post_{\mathrm{d}}(S, t) = \{s' : \exists s \in S.\ s \xrightarrow{t} s'\}.$$

The set of states reachable from S by executing any timed guarded command in T is given by:

$$Post_{\mathrm{d}}(S) = \bigcup_{t \in T} Post_{\mathrm{d}}(S, t).$$

Example 9. Let P be the TGC program from Example 3, and consider the states s_1 and s_2 where $s_1(b, x, y) = (\mathbf{true}, 0, 0)$ and $s_2(b, x, y) = (\mathbf{true}, 2, 2)$. Then

$$Post_{\mathrm{d}}(\{s_1\}) = Post_{\mathrm{d}}(\{s_1\}, t_1) \cup Post_{\mathrm{d}}(\{s_1\}, t_2) = \emptyset$$
$$Post_{\mathrm{d}}(\{s_2\}) = Post_{\mathrm{d}}(\{s_2\}, t_1) \cup Post_{\mathrm{d}}(\{s_2\}, t_2) = \{(\mathbf{false}, 2, 2)\}$$

Definition 14 (Timed successor). *Let $(\mathcal{S}, \rightarrow)$ be the transition system for a TGC program $P = (B, C, T, I, U)$, and let $S \subseteq \mathcal{S}$ be a set of states. The set of states reachable from S by advancing time by δ is given by:*

$$Post_{\mathrm{t}}(S, \delta) = \{s' : \exists s \in S.\ s \xrightarrow{\delta} s'\}.$$

The set of states reachable from S by advancing time by an arbitrary amount is given by:

$$Post_{\mathrm{t}}(S) = \bigcup_{\delta \in \mathbb{R}} Post_{\mathrm{t}}(S, \delta).$$

Example 10. Let P be the TGC program from Example 3, and consider the states s_1 and s_2 where $s_1(b, x, y) = (\mathbf{true}, 0, 0)$ and $s_2(b, x, y) = (\mathbf{true}, 2, 2)$. Then

$$Post_{\mathrm{t}}(\{s_1\}) = \bigcup_{\delta \in \mathbb{R}} Post_{\mathrm{d}}(\{s_1\}, \delta) = \{(\mathbf{true}, \delta, \delta) \mid 0 \leq \delta \leq 9\}$$
$$Post_{\mathrm{t}}(\{s_2\}) = \bigcup_{\delta \in \mathbb{R}} Post_{\mathrm{d}}(\{s_2\}, \delta) = \{(\mathbf{true}, \delta, \delta) \mid 2 \leq \delta \leq 9\}$$

Definition 15 (Reachable states). *Let $(\mathcal{S}, \rightarrow)$ be the transition system for a* TGC *program $P = (B, C, T, I, U)$, and let $S \subseteq \mathcal{S}$ be a set of states. The set of states reachable from S by executing any timed guarded command or advancing time by an arbitrary amount is given by:*

$$Post(S) = Post_d(S) \cup Post_t(S).$$

The set of states reachable from S is given by:

$$Post^*(S) = \mu X[S \cup Post(X)],$$

where $\mu X[S \cup Post(X)]$ is the least fixpoint of $S \cup Post(X)$.

The least fixpoint $\mu X[f(X)]$ of a function f is can be determined by computing a sequence of approximations

$$f(\emptyset), f(f(\emptyset)), \ldots$$

until a fixpoint is reached, that is, until $f^i(\emptyset) \equiv f^{i+1}(\emptyset)$, for some i. See also Fig. 1(b) in the introduction which shows an algorithm that computes the least fixpoint of ϕ_0. It is well known that there exists (contrived) timed systems where the computation of the fixpoint does not terminate, for example if the difference between two clocks increase ad infinitum. As in the traditional analysis of timed automata, it is possible to determine subclasses of timed guarded commands for which termination is ensured.

2.4   Modeling Timed Automata

TGC programs can be used to model popular notations for timed systems such as timed automata [2]. A timed automaton over a set of clocks consists of a set of locations, a set of events, and a set of timed transitions. Each location is associated with a location invariant over the clocks, and each timed transition from location l to location l' is labeled with an event a and has a guard g over the clocks. Furthermore, each of the timed transitions has a set of clocks $\{c_1, \ldots, c_n\}$ to be reset when the timed transition is fired:

$$l \xrightarrow{\ a,\ g,\ \{c_1,\ldots,c_n\}\ } l'.$$

A timed automaton can be encoded as a TGC program. Each location is encoded as a Boolean variable.[2] In a shared variable model as ours, the presence of an event from an alphabet Σ can be modeled by a global *event variable* e taking on any of the values in Σ. This variable can for instance be encoded using a logarithmic number of Boolean variables. Each timed transition in the automaton corresponds to a timed guarded command:

$$l \wedge e_a \wedge g \rightarrow (l, l', c_1, \ldots, c_n) := (\textbf{false}, \textbf{true}, 0, \ldots, 0).$$

---

[2] This is sometimes referred to as a "one-hot" encoding of the locations. In practice, a logarithmic encoding may be more efficient.

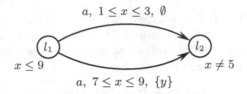

Fig. 2. The timed automaton in Example 11

The guard of the command is the guard of the timed transition g conjoined with the source location l of the timed transition and a condition e_a requiring the event variable e to have the value $a \in \Sigma$. The multi-assignment assigns **false** to the source location l and **true** to the destination location l' of the timed transition and resets the relevant clocks.

Example 11. Figure 2 shows an automaton over the clocks $\{x, y\}$ with two locations and two timed transitions. Encoding this automaton as a TGC program yields the program P from Example 3 when ignoring the event a and encoding the two locations l_1 and l_2 logarithmically using a Boolean variable b.

2.5   Modeling Asynchronous Circuits

In this section we use timed guarded commands to define a simple gate-level model of an asynchronous circuit, inspired by the approach taken in [37].

Definition 16 (Gate). *A gate G is a six-tuple $(i, o, g_\uparrow, g_\downarrow, [d_\uparrow, D_\uparrow], [d_\downarrow, D_\downarrow])$ where:*

- $i \in \mathcal{B}^n$ *is a n-dimensional vector of inputs,*
- $o \in \mathcal{B}$ *is the output,*
- $g_\uparrow : \mathcal{B}^n \to \mathcal{B}$ *is an up-guard that specifies when the output o should become true,*
- $g_\downarrow : \mathcal{B}^n \to \mathcal{B}$ *is a down-guard that specifies when the output o should become false,*
- $d_\uparrow$ *and $D_\uparrow$ denote the minimum and maximum delays from when the up-guard $g_\uparrow$ becomes true to the output o becomes true,*
- $d_\downarrow$ *and $D_\downarrow$ denote the minimum and maximum delays from when the down-guard $g_\downarrow$ becomes true to the output o becomes false.*

Example 12 (AND-gate). An AND-gate with inputs inputs a, b has $g_\uparrow = a \wedge b$, and $g_\downarrow = \neg(a \wedge b)$.

Example 13 (Muller C-element). A Muller C-element with inputs a, b has $g_\uparrow = a \wedge b$, and $g_\downarrow = \neg a \wedge \neg b$.

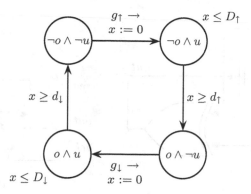

Fig. 3. Timed automaton for a gate as specified in Definition 17

Example 14 (Transistor). A transistor with gate i_1 and source i_2 has $g_\uparrow = i_1 \wedge i_2$, and $g_\downarrow = i_1 \wedge \neg i_2$.

To model the timing behavior of a gate, we introduce a clock x for measuring the time elapsed since the up-guard or down-guard has become true, and a Boolean variable u for modeling whether the gate is unstable: A gate is unstable when the up-guard is true, and the output has not yet changed to true, or, similarly, when the down-guard is true, and the output has not yet changed to false. With these definitions, we can model a gate as a TGC program as follows:

Definition 17 (Gate TGC program). *Let $(i, o, g_\uparrow, g_\downarrow, [d_\uparrow, D_\uparrow], [d_\downarrow, D_\downarrow])$ be a gate with inputs $i = (i_1, \ldots, i_n)$. Then the TGC program $P = (B, C, T, I, U)$ for G is defined as follows: $B = \{o, u, i_1, \ldots, i_n\}$, $C = \{x\}$, $T = \{t_1, t_2\}$ where:*

$$t_1 : (\neg o \wedge \neg u \wedge g_\uparrow) \vee (o \wedge \neg u \wedge g_\downarrow) \qquad \rightarrow u, x := \textbf{true}, 0$$
$$t_2 : (\neg o \wedge u \wedge x \geq d_\uparrow) \vee (o \wedge u \wedge x \geq d_\downarrow) \rightarrow u, o := \textbf{false}, \neg o$$

The program invariant is given by:

$$I = \big((o \wedge u) \Rightarrow x \leq D_\downarrow\big) \wedge \big((\neg o \wedge u) \Rightarrow x \leq D_\uparrow\big).$$

Command t_1 is urgent, thus the urgency predicate is given by:

$$U = (\neg o \wedge \neg u \wedge g_\uparrow) \vee (o \wedge \neg u \wedge g_\downarrow).$$

Let us explain the TGC program for a gate in a little more detail (see also Fig. 3 which shows a timed automaton for the program). Command t_1 models that if the output is stable false (low) and the up-guard becomes true, then the output becomes unstable false (rising) and the clock x is reset. Similarly, if the output is stable true (high) and the down-guard becomes true, then the output becomes unstable true (falling). The urgency predicate ensures that t_1 is executed as soon as it becomes enabled (i.e., time cannot advance in our model

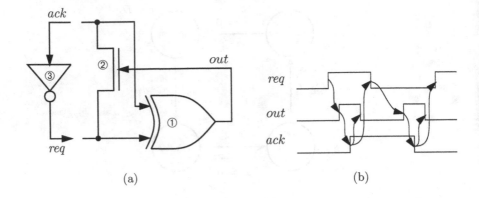

Fig. 4. (a) A pulse generator. (b) Timing diagram

if t_1 is enabled). The output then remains unstable false (rising) until $x \geq d_\uparrow$, and unstable true (falling) until $x \geq d_\downarrow$.

Command t_2 models that if the output is unstable false and $x \geq d_\uparrow$, then the output can (but does not have to) change to stable true. And similarly, if the output is unstable true and $x \geq d_\downarrow$, then the output can change to stable false. The state invariant ensures that the output must change to stable true before $D_\uparrow$, and, equally, must change to stable false before $D_\downarrow$.

Definition 17 specifies how to model a single gate as a TGC program. In the following definition we define how to model a circuit of N gates as a TGC program.

Definition 18 (Circuit TGC program). *Let $G_1, \ldots, G_N$ be the gates of a circuit, and let P_j for $j = 1, \ldots, N$ be the TGC program for G_j, where each output o_k of a gate G_k which is used as an input i_l for gate G_l is modeled using the same Boolean variable in P_k and P_l. Furthermore, the clocks of the TGC programs P_j must be distinct. Then the TGC program for the circuit is $P = (B, C, T, I, U)$, where $B = \bigcup_{j=1}^{N} B_j$, $C = \bigcup_{j=1}^{N} C_j$, $T = \bigcup_{j=1}^{N} T_j$, $I = \bigwedge_{j=1}^{N} I_j$, and $U = \bigvee_{j=1}^{N} U_j$.*

Example 15 (Pulse generator). Consider the asynchronous circuit depicted in Fig. 4(a). The circuit consists of an exclusive-or gate (labeled ①) and a transistor (labeled ②). A pulse is generated on output *out* whenever the environment (here modeled with the inverter labeled ③) changes the request signal. Figure 4(b) is a timing diagram illustrating the behavior. The up- and down-guards for the three gates are:

$$g_{out\uparrow} = (ack \oplus req)$$
$$g_{out\downarrow} = \neg(ack \oplus req)$$
$$g_{ack\uparrow} = (out \wedge req)$$
$$g_{ack\downarrow} = (out \wedge \neg req)$$
$$g_{req\uparrow} = \neg ack$$
$$g_{req\downarrow} = ack$$

Using Definition 18, the TGC program for the circuit is $P = (B, C, T, I, U)$, where the variables are $B = \{out, ack, req, out_u, ack_u, req_u\}$ (the variables $out_u, ack_u,$ and req_u are used to model unstability of the gates) and $C = \{out_x, ack_x, req_x\}$. We assume that the delay intervals for the up- and down-guards are the same for each gate; that is, $[d_{out\uparrow}, D_{out\uparrow}] = [d_{out\downarrow}, D_{out\downarrow}] = [d_{out}, D_{out}]$, and similarly for ack and req. This gives us the following set of commands T (where we have simplified the guards):

$$t_1 : \neg out_u \wedge (out \oplus ack \oplus req) \rightarrow out_u, out_x := \mathbf{true}, 0$$
$$t_2 : out_u \wedge x \geq d_{out} \qquad\qquad \rightarrow out_u, out \ := \mathbf{false}, \neg out$$
$$t_3 : \neg ack_u \wedge out \wedge (ack \oplus req) \rightarrow ack_u, ack_x := \mathbf{true}, 0$$
$$t_4 : ack_u \wedge x \geq d_{ack} \qquad\qquad \rightarrow ack_u, ack \ := \mathbf{false}, \neg ack$$
$$t_5 : \neg req_u \wedge (ack \Leftrightarrow req) \qquad \rightarrow req_u, req_x := \mathbf{true}, 0$$
$$t_6 : req_u \wedge x \geq d_{req} \qquad\qquad \rightarrow req_u, req \ := \mathbf{false}, \neg req$$

The program invariant is:

$$I = (out_u \Rightarrow out_x \leq D_{out})$$
$$\wedge\ (ack_u \Rightarrow ack_x \leq D_{ack})$$
$$\wedge\ (req_u \Rightarrow req_x \leq D_{req}).$$

Commands t_1, t_3, t_5 are urgent, thus the urgency predicate becomes:

$$U = (\neg out_u \wedge (out \oplus ack \oplus req))$$
$$\vee\ (\neg ack_u \wedge out \wedge (ack \oplus req))$$
$$\vee\ (\neg req_u \wedge (ack \Leftrightarrow req)).$$

In Sect. 3 we describe how to analyze the TGC program for a circuit, for example how to verify that the circuit is hazard-free:

Definition 19 (Hazard). *A gate G_i has a hazard if the up-guard becomes false when the output is unstable false, or the down-guard becomes false when the output is unstable true; that is, the hazard predicate for a gate is*

$$H_i = (\neg o \wedge u \wedge \neg g_\uparrow) \vee (o \wedge u \wedge \neg g_\downarrow).$$

A circuit of N gates $G_1, \ldots, G_N$ has a hazard if one of the gates has a hazard; that is, the hazard predicate for a circuit is

$$H = \bigvee_{i=1}^{N} H_i,$$

where H_i is the hazard predicate for gate G_i.

The circuit is hazard-free if and only if $\neg H$ is an invariant for the TGC program for the circuit.

Example 16. Consider again the circuit in Fig. 4. The circuit has a hazard if the environment changes too fast. For example, consider the state where *req* and *out* are high and *ack* goes up. If the exclusive-or gate is slow, the environment may lower *req before* the output of the exclusive-or gate (*out*) has fallen and thus disabling the exclusive-or gate before it has lowered *out*.

3   Symbolic Model Checking

The previous section describes how to model timed systems as TGC programs. In this section we develop the necessary theory for verifying properties of a TGC program, for example that a circuit is hazard-free. More specifically, given a set of states represented by a formula, we determine a new formula that represents the set of states reachable by executing timed guarded commands according to the inference rule in Definition 9 or by advancing time according to the inference rule in Definition 10.

3.1   Difference Constraint Expressions

Recall the definition of difference constraint expressions from the introduction:

Definition 20 (Difference Constraint Expressions). *Let Ψ be the set of difference constraint expressions of the form:*

$$\psi ::= x - y \leq d \mid \psi_1 \wedge \psi_2 \mid \neg\psi \mid \exists x.\psi \, ,$$

where $x, y \in C$ are clocks, $d \in \mathbb{Q}$ is a rational constant, and $\psi \in \Psi$ is a difference constraint expression.

The following procedure describes how to transform any expression $\phi \in \Phi$ generated by the grammar in Definition 2 to a difference constraint expression $\phi_z \in \Psi$ by introducing a new variable z (denoting "zero").

Definition 21. *Let $\phi \in \Phi$ be an expression. The corresponding difference constraint expression $\phi_z \in \Psi$ is obtained by performing the following three steps:*

1. *Replace each Boolean variable $b_i \in \mathcal{B}$ in ϕ by a difference constraint $x_i - x_i' \leq 0$, where $x_i, x_i' \in C$ are clocks only used in the encoding of b_i.*[3]
2. *Replace each constraint of the form $x \sim d$ in ϕ by the difference constraint $x - z \sim d$.*

---

[3] It turns out that when using difference decision diagrams (see Sect. 4.4) with this apparently strange encoding of Boolean variables, the Boolean manipulations can be done as efficiently as when using BDDs. See also footnote 4 on page 300.

3. *Replace each difference constraint of the form $x - y \sim d$ in ϕ by a difference constraint with $\leq$ using the equivalences:*

$$x - y > d \equiv \neg(x - y \leq d),$$
$$x - y \geq d \equiv y - x \leq -d,$$
$$x - y < d \equiv \neg(y - x \leq d),$$
$$x - y = d \equiv (x - y \leq d) \wedge (y - x \leq -d),$$
$$x - y \neq d \equiv \neg(x - y \leq d) \vee \neg(y - x \leq -d).$$

Example 17. The expression $\phi = x \geq 0 \wedge y > 0$ corresponds to the difference constraint expression $\phi_z = z - x \leq 0 \wedge \neg(y - z \leq 0)$.

We use $\lfloor\!\lfloor \psi \rfloor\!\rfloor_z$ as a shorthand for $[\![\exists z.(\psi \wedge z = 0)]\!]$; that is, $\lfloor\!\lfloor \psi \rfloor\!\rfloor_z$ is the set of states that satisfy ψ when z is equal to 0. It is easy to prove the following proposition:

Proposition 1. *Let $\phi \in \Phi$ be an expression generated from the grammar in Definition 2, and let ϕ_z be the corresponding difference constraint expression obtained as described above. Then $[\![\phi]\!] = \lfloor\!\lfloor \phi_z \rfloor\!\rfloor_z$.*

We define two useful operators on difference constraint expressions: replacement and assignment.

Definition 22 (Replacement). *Replacement of a vector $v' \in \mathcal{V}^n$ of variables by another vector $v \in \mathcal{V}^n$ of variables plus a vector $d \in \mathbb{Q}^n$ of constants, where $v_i \neq v'_i$ for each $i = 1, \ldots, n$, in an expression ψ is defined as follows:*

$$\psi[v + d/v'] = \exists v'.(\psi \wedge v' - v = d),$$

where $\exists v'.\psi$ is a shorthand for $\exists v'_1 \cdots \exists v'_n.\psi$, and $v' - v = d$ is a shorthand for $v'_1 - v_1 = d_1 \wedge \cdots \wedge v'_n - v_n = d_n$.

Definition 23 (Assignment). *Assignment of a vector $v \in \mathcal{V}^n$ of variables to a vector $v' \in \mathcal{V}^n$ of variables such that the expression ψ' holds is defined as follows:*

$$\psi[v := \mathbf{any} \; v'.\psi'] = \exists v.(\psi \wedge \psi')[v/v'].$$

Eliminating constraints of the form $x \sim d$ from the grammar in Definition 2 makes it possible to add δ to all clocks simultaneously by decreasing the common reference-point z by δ:

$$[\![\phi[c := c + \delta]]\!] = [\![\phi_z[z := z - \delta]]\!]_z.$$

Furthermore, as we shall show in the following, the set of states reachable by advancing time by any value δ can be computed by an existential quantification of z.

3.2 Forward Analysis

Given a difference constraint expression $\psi \in \Psi$ representing a set of states $[\![\psi]\!]_z \subseteq \mathcal{S}$, we now show how to determine an expression representing the set of states reachable from $[\![\psi]\!]_z$.

Definition 24 (post$_d$-operator). *Let ψ be a difference constraint expression, and let $P = (B, C, T, I, U)$ be a TGC program. Then the post$_d$-operator for (forward) execution of the command $\phi \rightarrow \boldsymbol{v} := \mathbf{any}\, \boldsymbol{v}'.\phi'$ is defined as*

$$\mathbf{post}_d(\psi, \phi \rightarrow \boldsymbol{v} := \mathbf{any}\, \boldsymbol{v}'.\phi') = (\psi \wedge \phi_z)[\boldsymbol{v} := \mathbf{any}\, \boldsymbol{v}'.\phi_z'] \wedge I_z,$$

The post$_d$-operator for execution of any command in T is defined as

$$\mathbf{post}_d(\psi) = \bigvee_{t \in T} \mathbf{post}_d(\psi, t).$$

The **post**$_d$-operator restricts ψ to the subset where the guard ϕ holds, performs the nondeterministic assignment defined in terms of the **any**-operator, and restricts the resulting set to the subset where the program invariant I holds.

The following theorems state that the **post**$_d$ operators in Definition 24 correctly construct the set of discrete successors as defined by $Post_d$ in Definition 13.

Theorem 1 (Correctness of post$_d(\psi, t)$). *Let ψ be a difference constraint expression, and let $P = (B, C, T, I, U)$ be a TGC program. Then $Post_d([\![\psi]\!]_z, t) = [\![\mathbf{post}_d(\psi, t)]\!]_z$ for any command $t \in T$.*

Proof. Let t be a timed guarded command of the form $\phi \rightarrow \boldsymbol{v} := \mathbf{any}\, \boldsymbol{v}'.\phi'$. Using Definitions 9 and 13 we get:

$$
\begin{aligned}
Post_d([\![\psi]\!]_z, t) &= \{s' : \exists s \in [\![\psi]\!]_z \wedge s \xrightarrow{t} s'\} \\
&= \{s[\boldsymbol{v} := \boldsymbol{r}] : s \in [\![\psi \wedge \phi_z]\!]_z \wedge s[\boldsymbol{v}' := \boldsymbol{r}] \in [\![\phi_z']\!]_z \wedge \\
&\qquad\qquad s[\boldsymbol{v} := \boldsymbol{r}] \in [\![I_z]\!]_z\} \\
&= \{s[\boldsymbol{v} := \boldsymbol{r}] : s \in [\![\psi \wedge \phi_z]\!]_z \wedge s \in [\![\phi_z'[\boldsymbol{r}/\boldsymbol{v}']]\!]_z \wedge \\
&\qquad\qquad s[\boldsymbol{v} := \boldsymbol{r}] \in [\![I_z]\!]_z\} \\
&= [\![(\psi \wedge \phi_z \wedge \phi_z'[\boldsymbol{r}/\boldsymbol{v}'])[\boldsymbol{v} := \mathbf{any}\, \boldsymbol{v}'.\boldsymbol{v}' = \boldsymbol{r}] \wedge I_z]\!]_z \\
&= [\![(\psi \wedge \phi_z)[\boldsymbol{v} := \mathbf{any}\, \boldsymbol{v}'.(\boldsymbol{v}' = \boldsymbol{r} \wedge \phi_z'[\boldsymbol{r}/\boldsymbol{v}'])] \wedge I_z]\!]_z \\
&= [\![(\psi \wedge \phi_z)[\boldsymbol{v} := \mathbf{any}\, \boldsymbol{v}'.\phi_z'] \wedge I_z]\!]_z \\
&= [\![\mathbf{post}_d(\psi, t)]\!]_z
\end{aligned}
$$

$\square$

Theorem 2 (Correctness of post$_d(\psi)$). *Let ψ be a difference constraint expression, and let $P = (B, C, T, I, U)$ be a TGC program. Then $Post_d([\![\psi]\!]_z) = [\![\mathbf{post}_d(\psi)]\!]_z$.*

Proof. Immediate for the definitions of $Post_d$ and **post**$_d$.

$\square$

Next, we define the operator $\mathbf{post}_t$ for advancing time symbolically from a set of states $[\![\psi]\!]_z$. The key idea is to change the reference-point from z to z' with $z' \leq z$ since decreasing the reference-point by δ corresponds to increasing the values of all clocks by δ. We require that the program invariant holds in z' and at all intermediate points in time. Also, the urgency predicate must hold at all intermediate points in time except in z'.

Definition 25 ($\mathbf{post}_t$-operator). *Let ψ be a difference constraint expression, and let $P = (B, C, T, I, U)$ be a TGC program. Then the $\mathbf{post}_t$-operator for advancing time by δ in all states $[\![\psi]\!]_z$ is defined as*

$$\mathbf{post}_t(\psi, \delta) = (\psi \wedge P_{\mathrm{post}})[z := z - \delta]$$
$$= \exists z.(\psi \wedge P_{\mathrm{post}} \wedge z - z' = \delta)[z/z']$$

where the last equality follows from the definition of assignment, and where

$$P_{\mathrm{post}} = (z' \leq z) \wedge I_{z'} \wedge \forall z''.\big((z' < z'' \leq z) \Rightarrow (I_{z''} \wedge \neg U_{z''})\big).$$

The $\mathbf{post}_t$-operator for advancing time by an arbitrary *amount in all states $[\![\psi]\!]_z$ is defined as*

$$\mathbf{post}_t(\psi) = \bigvee_{\delta \in \mathbb{R}} \mathbf{post}_t(\psi, \delta)$$

The following theorems state that the $\mathbf{post}_t$ operators in Definition 25 correctly construct the set of timed successors as defined by $Post_t$ in Definition 14.

Theorem 3 (Correctness of $\mathbf{post}_t(\psi, \delta)$). *Let ψ be a difference constraint expression, and let $P = (B, C, T, I, U)$ be a TGC program. Then $Post_t([\![\psi]\!]_z, \delta) = [\![\mathbf{post}_t(\psi, \delta)]\!]_z$ for any delay $\delta \in \mathbb{R}$.*

Proof. From Definition 14 we have

$$Post_t([\![\psi]\!]_z, \delta) = \{s' : s \in [\![\psi]\!]_z \wedge s \xrightarrow{\delta} s'\},$$

where, by Definition 10, $s' = s[c := c + \delta]$, $\delta \geq 0$, $s' \models I$, and $\forall \delta'.0 \leq \delta' < \delta : s[c := c + \delta'] \models (I \wedge \neg U)$. That is:

$$Post_t([\![\psi]\!]_z, \delta) = \{s' : s \in [\![\psi]\!]_z \wedge \delta \geq 0 \wedge s[c := c + \delta] \models I \wedge$$
$$\forall \delta'.0 \leq \delta' < \delta : s[c := c + \delta'] \models (I \wedge \neg U)\}.$$

We now introduce two new variables defined as $z' = z - \delta$ and $z'' = z - \delta'$. It is not difficult to see that with these definitions, $0 \leq \delta' < \delta$ is equivalent to $z' < z'' \leq z$. Furthermore, since

$$
\begin{aligned}
s[c := c + \delta] \models I &\equiv s[c := c + \delta] \in [\![I_z]\!]_z \\
&\equiv s \in [\![I_z[c := c - \delta]]\!]_z \\
&\equiv s \in [\![I_z[z := z + \delta]]\!]_z \\
&\equiv s \in [\![I_z[z - \delta/z]]\!]_z \\
&\equiv s \in [\![I_z[z'/z]]\!]_z \\
&\equiv s \in [\![I_{z'}]\!]_z,
\end{aligned}
$$

and, similarly:

$$s[c := c + \delta'] \models (I \wedge \neg U) \equiv s \in [\![I_{z''} \wedge \neg U_{z''}]\!]_z \,,$$

we can write $Post_t([\![\psi]\!]_z, \delta)$ as:

$$
\begin{aligned}
Post_t([\![\psi]\!]_z, \delta) &= \{s' : s \in [\![\psi]\!]_z \wedge \exists z'.((\delta = z - z') \wedge (z - z' \geq 0) \wedge s \in [\![I_{z'}]\!]_z \wedge \\
&\qquad \forall z''.z' < z'' \leq z : s \in [\![I_{z''} \wedge \neg U_{z''}]\!]_z)\} \\
&= \{s' : s \in [\![\psi \wedge \exists z'.((\delta = z - z') \wedge (z - z' \geq 0) \wedge I_{z'} \wedge \\
&\qquad \forall z''.(z' < z'' \leq z) \Rightarrow (I_{z''} \wedge U_{z''}))]\!]_z\}
\end{aligned}
$$

Using that $\{s[c := c + \delta] : s \in [\![\psi]\!]_z\}$ is equivalent to $[\![\psi[c := c + \delta]]\!]_z$, we obtain

$$Post_t([\![\psi]\!]_z, \delta) = [\![\exists z'.(\psi \wedge (\delta = z - z') \wedge P_{post})[c := c + \delta]]\!]_z \,.$$

Since $[\![\phi[c := c + \delta]]\!] = [\![\phi_z[z := z - \delta]]\!]_z = [\![\phi_z[z + \delta/z]]\!]_z$, it follows that

$$Post_t([\![\psi]\!]_z, \delta) = [\![\exists z'.(\psi \wedge (\delta = z - z') \wedge P_{post})[z + \delta/z]]\!]_z \,.$$

Using the definition of replacement, we get:

$$
\begin{aligned}
Post_t([\![\psi]\!]_z, \delta) &= [\![(\psi \wedge P_{post})[z - \delta/z'][z + \delta/z]]\!]_z \\
&= [\![(\psi \wedge P_{post})[z' + \delta/z][z/z']]\!]_z \\
&= [\![\exists z.(\psi \wedge (z - z' = \delta) \wedge P_{post})[z/z']]\!]_z \\
&= [\![\mathbf{post}_t(\psi, \delta)]\!]_z \,.
\end{aligned}
$$

$\square$

Theorem 4 (Correctness of $\mathbf{post}_t(\psi)$). *Let ψ be a difference constraint expression, and let $P = (B, C, T, I, U)$ be a TGC program. Then $Post_t([\![\psi]\!]_z) = [\![\mathbf{post}_t(\psi)]\!]_z = [\![\exists z.(\psi \wedge P_{post})[z/z']]\!]_z$.*

Proof. The first equality in the theorem follows immediately from Definitions 14 and 25. The second equality holds because existential quantification distributes over disjunction:

$$
\begin{aligned}
Post_t([\![\psi]\!]_z) &= \bigcup_{\delta \in \mathbb{R}} Post_t([\![\psi]\!]_z, \delta) \\
&= [\![\bigvee_{\delta \in \mathbb{R}} \exists z.(\psi \wedge (z - z' = \delta) \wedge P_{post})[z/z']]\!]_z \\
&= [\![\exists z.(\psi \wedge P_{post} \wedge \bigvee_{\delta \in \mathbb{R}}(z - z' = \delta))[z/z']]\!]_z \\
&= [\![\exists z.(\psi \wedge P_{post})[z/z']]\!]_z \\
&= [\![\mathbf{post}_t(\psi)]\!]_z \,.
\end{aligned}
$$

$\square$

Example 18. Consider a TGC program with the program invariant $I = x \neq 5$. Then the predicate P_{post} is given by:

$$
\begin{aligned}
P_{post} &= (z' \leq z) \wedge \forall z''.((z' \leq z'' \leq z) \Rightarrow (x - z'' \neq 5)) \\
&= (z' \leq z) \wedge ((x - z' < 5) \vee (x - z > 5)) \,.
\end{aligned}
$$

Consider the set of states satisfying $\phi = (1 \leq x \leq 3) \vee (7 \leq x \leq 9)$. The set of states obtained by advancing time from ϕ is thus given by $[\![\mathbf{post}_t(\phi_z)]\!]_z$, where:

$$\mathbf{post}_t(\phi_z) = \exists z.(\phi_z \wedge P_{\mathrm{post}})[z/z'] = (1 \leq x - z < 5) \vee (7 \leq x - z).$$

That is, advancing time from ϕ gives $(1 \leq x < 5) \vee (7 \leq x)$.

The $\mathbf{post}_d$-operator and $\mathbf{post}_t$-operator form the basis for constructing the set of reachable states symbolically. The operator $\mathbf{post}(\psi)$ determines the set of states which can be reached by taking either a discrete or a timed transition from a state in $[\![\psi]\!]_z$ and is defined as follows:

Definition 26 (post-operator). *Let ψ be a difference constraint expression, and let $P = (B, C, T, I, U)$ be a TGC program. Then the $\mathbf{post}$-operator for executing any command in T or advancing time by an arbitrary amount in all states $[\![\psi]\!]_z$ is defined as:*

$$\mathbf{post}(\psi) = \mathbf{post}_d(\psi) \vee \mathbf{post}_t(\psi).$$

The $\mathbf{post}^*$-operator is defined as:

$$\mathbf{post}^*(\psi) = \mu X[\psi \vee \mathbf{post}(X)].$$

where $\mu X[\psi \vee \mathbf{post}(X)]$ is the least fixpoint of $\psi \vee \mathbf{post}(X)$.

The difference constraint expressions constructed by the $\mathbf{post}$-operator and $\mathbf{post}^*$-operator in Definition 26 correspond exactly to the set of successors and reachable states, respectively, as defined by $Post$ and $Post^*$ in Definition 15:

Theorem 5 (Correctness of $\mathbf{post}(\psi)$ and $\mathbf{post}^*(\psi)$). *Let ψ be a difference constraint expression, and let $P = (B, C, T, I, U)$ be a TGC program. Then $Post([\![\psi]\!]_z) = [\![\mathbf{post}(\psi)]\!]_z$ and $Post^*([\![\psi]\!]_z) = [\![\mathbf{post}^*(\psi)]\!]_z$.*

Proof. Follows immediately from Definition 15 and Theorems 2 and 4.   □

Example 19. Consider again the program from Example 3. The set of states reachable from $\phi = b \wedge (x = y = 0)$ is $[\![\mathbf{post}^*(\phi_z)]\!]_z$, where:

$$\mathbf{post}^*(\phi_z) = (b \wedge x = y \wedge x - z \leq 9) \vee$$
$$(\neg b \wedge [(x = y \wedge 1 \leq x - z < 5) \vee (7 \leq x - y \leq 9 \wedge 7 \leq x - z)]).$$

3.3 Backward Analysis

Similarly to the $\mathbf{post}$ operators defined in the previous section we can define a number of $\mathbf{pre}$ operators for determining formulae for the set of states that can reach $[\![\psi]\!]_z$. These operators can for example be used to compute the set of states that satisfy a timed CTL formula.

Definition 27 (pre$_\text{d}$-operator). *Let ψ be a difference constraint expression, and let $P = (B, C, T, I, U)$ be a TGC program. Then the* **pre**$_\text{d}$*-operator for backward execution of the command* $\phi \to v := \textbf{any } v'.\phi'$ *is defined as*

$$\textbf{pre}_\text{d}(\psi, \phi \to v := \textbf{any } v'.\phi') = (\psi[v'/v] \wedge \phi_z)[v' := \textbf{any } v.\phi'_z] \wedge I_z .$$

The **pre**$_\text{d}$*-operator for backward execution of any command in T is defined as*

$$\textbf{pre}_\text{d}(\psi) = \bigvee_{t \in T} \textbf{pre}_\text{d}(\psi, t) .$$

Similar to the **post**$_\text{d}$-operator, the **pre**$_\text{d}$-operator restricts ψ to the subset where the guard ϕ_z holds before the assignment, performs the nondeterministic assignment backward, and restricts the resulting set to the subset where the program invariant I holds. Effectively, this constructs the set of states that can reach $[\![\psi]\!]_z$ by backward execution the timed guarded command $\phi \to v := \textbf{any } v'.\phi'$.

The set of states that can reach $[\![\psi]\!]_z$ by advancing time by δ is determined analogously to the forward case:

Definition 28 (pre$_\text{t}$-operator). *Let ψ be a difference constraint expression, and let $P = (B, C, T, I, U)$ be a TGC program. Then the* **pre**$_\text{t}$*-operator for decreasing time by δ in all states $[\![\psi]\!]_z$ is defined as*

$$\begin{aligned}\textbf{pre}_\text{t}(\psi, \delta) &= (\psi \wedge P_\text{pre})[z := z + \delta] \\ &= \exists z.(\psi \wedge P_\text{pre} \wedge z' - z = \delta)[z/z']\end{aligned}$$

where the last equality follows from the definition of assignment, and where P_pre is equivalent to P_post with z and z' exchanged:

$$P_\text{pre} = (z \leq z') \wedge I_z \wedge \forall z''.\big((z < z'' \leq z') \Rightarrow (I_{z''} \wedge \neg U_{z''})\big) .$$

The **pre**$_\text{t}$*-operator for decreasing time by an* arbitrary *amount in all states $[\![\psi]\!]_z$ is defined as*

$$\textbf{pre}_\text{t}(\psi) = \bigvee_{\delta \in \mathbb{R}} \textbf{pre}_\text{t}(\psi, \delta)$$

For completeness we also define the set of states that can reach $[\![\psi]\!]_z$ by executing commands or advancing time:

Definition 29 (pre-operator). *Let ψ be a difference constraint expression, and let $P = (B, C, T, I, U)$ be a TGC program. Then the* **pre**-*operator for backward execution of any command in T or decreasing time by an arbitrary amount in all states $[\![\psi]\!]_z$ is defined as:*

$$\textbf{pre}(\psi) = \textbf{pre}_\text{d}(\psi) \vee \textbf{pre}_\text{t}(\psi) .$$

The **pre****-operator is defined as:*

$$\textbf{pre}^*(\psi) = \mu X[\psi \vee \textbf{pre}(X)] .$$

where $\mu X[\psi \vee \textbf{pre}(X)]$ is the least fixpoint of $\psi \vee \textbf{pre}(X)$.

The correctness of the **pre** operators can easily be proved analogously to how we proved the correctness of the corresponding **post** operators.

3.4   Verification of Simple Properties

The **post-** and **pre**-operators can be used to verify simple propositional properties of a TGC program. There are basically two techniques for verifying that a property is an invariant for a program:

Definition 30 (Forward reachability). *Let ψ be a difference constraint expression, and let $P = (B, C, T, I, U)$ be a TGC program with the initial state $\psi_0 \in \Psi$. Then ψ holds invariantly for P if $\mathbf{post}^*(\psi_0) \Rightarrow \psi$ is a tautology.*

Definition 31 (Backward reachability). *Let ψ be a difference constraint expression, and let $P = (B, C, T, I, U)$ be a TGC program with the initial state $\psi_0 \in \Psi$. Then ψ holds invariantly for P if $\neg(\psi_0 \wedge \mathbf{pre}^*(\neg\psi))$ is a tautology.*

3.5   Verification of Timed CTL Properties

The **pre** operators can also be used to perform symbolic model checking of timed CTL [30]. Timed CTL is obtained by extending CTL [17] with an auxiliary set of clocks called *specification clocks*. These clocks do not appear in the model but are used to express timing bounds on the temporal operators. A timed CTL formula has the following form:

$$\theta ::= \phi \mid \neg\theta \mid \theta \wedge \theta \mid u.\theta \mid \theta_1 \exists\mathcal{U} \, \theta_2 \mid \theta_1 \forall\mathcal{U} \, \theta_2 \, .$$

The atomic predicates ϕ of timed CTL are expressions, see Definition 2. A specification clock u can be bound and reset by a *reset quantifier* $u.\psi$. The operators $\exists\mathcal{U}$ and $\forall\mathcal{U}$ are the existential and universal path quantifiers.

Symbolically, we can find the set of states satisfying a given timed CTL formula ψ by a backward computation using a fixpoint iteration for the temporal operators. For instance, the set of states satisfying the expression "along some execution path, ψ_1 holds until ψ_2 holds", is computed symbolically as:

$$\psi_1 \exists\mathcal{U} \, \psi_2 = \mu X [\psi_2 \vee (\psi_1 \wedge \mathbf{pre}(X))].$$

The set of states satisfying the reset quantifier is computed symbolically as:

$$u.\psi = \exists u.(\psi \wedge u - z = 0),$$

that is, the reset quantifier corresponds to restricting the value of u to zero and then remove it by existential quantification (assuming that ψ uses z as a zero point).

3.6   A Simpler Semantics

In the following, we show how to simplify the syntax and semantics of a TGC program substantially. The key idea is that a timed transition essentially is the same as a discrete transition in the sense that a guard specifies when the transition can be taken, and an assignment updates the values of clocks. This leads to a semantics with only one type of transitions. Furthermore, we can embed program invariants, urgency predicates, and guards in the expression of an assignment. We start by defining a simplified TGC program, and then show how to translate a TGC program into a simplified TGC program.

Definition 32 (STGC syntax). *A simplified timed guarded command (STGC) program P is a tuple (B, C, T), where $B \subseteq \mathcal{B}$ is a set of Boolean variables, $C \subseteq \mathcal{C}$ is a set of clocks, T is a set of commands of the form $\boldsymbol{v} := \textbf{any} \, \boldsymbol{v}'.\phi$, where $\boldsymbol{v}, \boldsymbol{v}' \in B \cup C$ are vectors of variables and $\phi \in \Phi$ is an expression.*

Definition 33 (STGC semantics). *The semantics of an STGC program $P = (B, C, T)$ is a transition system $(\mathcal{S}, \rightarrow)$ where the set of states $\mathcal{S}$ are value assignments of the variables as given in Definition 7. For each command $t \in T$ of the form $\boldsymbol{v} := \textbf{any} \, \boldsymbol{v}'.\phi$, the following inference rule defines the transition relation:*

$$\frac{s[\boldsymbol{v}' := \boldsymbol{r}] \models \phi}{s \xrightarrow{t} s[\boldsymbol{v} := \boldsymbol{r}]}$$

Analogous to Definition 24 we define the operator $\textbf{post}_{\text{STGC}}$ *as follows:*

$$\textbf{post}_{\text{STGC}}(\psi, \boldsymbol{v} := \textbf{any} \, \boldsymbol{v}'.\phi) = \psi[\boldsymbol{v} := \textbf{any} \, \boldsymbol{v}'.\phi_z].$$

Next, we show to translate a TGC program P into an equivalent STGC program P'.

Definition 34 (Induced STGC). *A TGC program $P = (B, C, T, I, U)$ induces an STGC program $P' = (B, C, T')$, such that for each timed guarded command $\phi \rightarrow \boldsymbol{v} := \textbf{any} \, \boldsymbol{v}'.\phi'$ in T there is a command $\boldsymbol{v} := \textbf{any} \, \boldsymbol{v}'.(\phi' \wedge \phi \wedge I[\boldsymbol{v}'/\boldsymbol{v}])$ in T'. Furthermore, T' contains the command $z := \textbf{any} \, z'.P_{\text{post}}$, where P_{post} is defined as in Definition 25.*

Theorem 6 (Equivalence between TGC and STGC). *Let P be a TGC program, and let P' be the induced STGC program. Then P and P' define the same transition system.*

Proof. Using Definition 23 and Theorem 2 we first show that we can embed the guard and the program invariant in the expressions of the timed guarded commands in T:

$$\begin{aligned}
\textbf{post}_{\text{d}}(\psi, \phi \rightarrow \boldsymbol{v} := \textbf{any} \, \boldsymbol{v}'.\phi') &= (\psi \wedge \phi_z)[\boldsymbol{v} := \textbf{any} \, \boldsymbol{v}'.\phi'_z] \wedge I_z \\
&= \exists \boldsymbol{v}.(\psi \wedge \phi'_z \wedge \phi_z)[\boldsymbol{v}/\boldsymbol{v}'] \wedge I_z \\
&= \exists \boldsymbol{v}.(\psi \wedge \phi'_z \wedge \phi_z \wedge I_z[\boldsymbol{v}'/\boldsymbol{v}])[\boldsymbol{v}/\boldsymbol{v}'] \\
&= \textbf{post}_{\text{STGC}}(\psi, \boldsymbol{v} := \textbf{any} \, \boldsymbol{v}'.(\phi' \wedge \phi \wedge I[\boldsymbol{v}'/\boldsymbol{v}])).
\end{aligned}$$

Next, we show that we can advance time explicitly by adding a timed guarded command of the form $\textbf{true} \rightarrow z := \textbf{any} \, z'.P_{\text{post}}$:

$$\begin{aligned}
\textbf{post}_{\text{t}}(\psi) &= \exists z.(\psi \wedge P_{\text{post}})[z/z'] \\
&= \psi[\textbf{true} \rightarrow z := \textbf{any} \, z'.P_{\text{post}}] \\
&= \textbf{post}_{\text{STGC}}(\psi, z := \textbf{any} \, z'.P_{\text{post}}).
\end{aligned}$$

$\square$

Using the symmetry between P_{pre} and P_{post}, it is not difficult to prove the following theorem:

Theorem 7. *Let ψ be a difference constraint expression, and let P be a TGC program. Then the $\mathbf{pre}_t$-operator for decreasing time in all states $[\![\psi]\!]_z$ can be defined as:*

$$\mathbf{pre}_t(\psi) = \mathbf{pre}_d(\psi, \mathbf{true} \rightarrow z := \mathbf{any}\ z'.P_{\text{post}})$$

4   Algorithms and Data Structures

The previous two sections define a notation called timed guarded commands for modeling timed systems and a technique called symbolic model checking for analyzing timed systems. To verify a property of a timed system, we start with some initial expression ψ_0 (either the initial state of the system in the forward analysis, or the negation of the property to verify in the backward analysis) and then compute a sequence of fixpoint approximations $\psi_0, \psi_1, \ldots$, until $\psi_i = \psi_{i+1}$ for some i. Two expressions ψ_i and ψ_{i+1} are equivalent if and only if the expression $\neg(\psi_i \Leftrightarrow \psi_{i+1})$ is not satisfiable.

The core operation in the fixpoint computation is thus to determine whether a difference constraint expression is satisfiable. We call this problem DCE-SAT. Interestingly, this problem has, to our best knowledge, only been studied by very few researchers; the primary focus has been on theories that are either more expressive, such as reals with addition and order, or less expressive, such as quantified Boolean formulae. An important aspect in verification of timed systems is the ability to deal with many discrete states together with the infinite nature of the real-valued variables. There are very few results on how to do this efficiently, and it remains an open problem to find algorithms and data structures that work just as well for timed systems as BDDs do for non-timed systems.

In general, the reachability problem for timed guarded commands is undecidable (i.e., the fixpoint computation might not terminate) [1, 11]. It is straightforward to model a register-machine as a TGC program using a variable for each unbounded register, and a variable for the program counter. Test, increment, and decrement are easily expressed in assignments. An interesting task would be to identify conditions on TGC programs for which questions such as reachability are decidable. This has not been done yet.

In this section we give a survey of the available algorithms and data structures for solving the DCE-SAT problem. We start by giving an overview of some of the problems (both simpler and harder) which are related to DCE-SAT. Then we briefly describe a technique called quantifier elimination, and finally we describe two algorithmic approaches for solving DCE-SAT based on matrices and graphs data structures, respectively.

4.1   Complexity Overview

Let us first look at two subsets of difference constraint expressions and see how difficult it is to determine satisfiability for these simpler theories. The first problem is DCS-SAT: determine satisfiability of conjunctions of difference inequalities (also called a difference constraint system), which is an expression of the form

$$\psi ::= x - y \le d \mid \psi_1 \wedge \psi_2.$$

This problem can be solved time $O(n^3)$ where n is the number of variables using shortest-paths algorithms such as Bellman-Ford or Floyd-Warshall [21]. Hence, DCS-SAT is in the complexity class **P**.

The second problem is QFDCE-SAT: determine satisfiability of a quantifier-free difference constraint expression, which is an expression of the form

$$\psi ::= x - y \le d \mid \psi_1 \wedge \psi_2 \mid \neg\psi.$$

Quantifier-free difference constraint expressions further allow negation, which, in combination with conjunction, also gives disjunction and strong inequality. Adding negation greatly increases the expressive power and, correspondingly, complicates the problem of determining satisfaction. The QFDCE-SAT problem is **NP**-complete, see for example [30] for a proof.

The main problem is DCE-SAT: determine satisfiability of a difference constraint expression as defined in Definition 20:

$$\psi ::= x - y \le d \mid \psi_1 \wedge \psi_2 \mid \neg\psi \mid \exists x.\psi.$$

Interestingly, it turns out that adding quantifiers "only" makes the problem **PSPACE**-complete [34]. Considering that we are working with variables over infinite domains, it is surprising that DCE-SAT is no harder than QBF-SAT (satisfiability of quantified Boolean formulae) which is also **PSPACE**-complete [41].[4]

It is also interesting to note that DCE-SAT is easier than satisfiability of slightly more general theories such as the first-order theory of reals with addition and order, which is **NEXP**-hard [32], and the theory of integers with addition and order (also called Presburger arithmetic [42]), which is **2-NEXP**-hard [20, 26, 46]. The theory of reals with addition and multiplication was shown to be decidable by Tarski [47], whereas the theory of integers with addition and multiplication (also called number theory) is undecidable—Gödel's famous Incompleteness Theorem [28].

It is of course always possible to solve each of the three satisfaction problems defined above using a decision procedure for a more general theory. For example, difference constraint systems can be decided using linear programming [33]; quantifier-free difference constraint expressions can be decided using disjunctive programming [5]; and difference constraint expressions can be decided by eliminating the quantifiers (as described in the following section) and then using the same method as for quantifier-free expressions.

4.2   Quantifier Elimination

Adding quantifiers to the vocabulary of a language greatly increases the expressive power, but also moves the satisfiability problem up in the hierarchy

---

[4] This also justifies the encoding of Boolean variables as difference inequalities.

of complexity classes. For quantifier-free difference constraint expressions, the satisfiability problem goes from **NP**-complete to **PSPACE**-complete. The same holds for (quantifier-free) Boolean expressions, cf. [19, 32]. For Presburger arithmetic the difference is even bigger: **NP**-complete for quantifier-free formulae [40], but **2-NEXP**-hard for formulae with quantifiers.

Since Tarski [47] showed that the theory of reals with addition and multiplication, which subsumes the theory of difference constraint expressions, admits quantifier elimination, there has been a substantial amount of research in developing efficient algorithms for eliminating quantifiers. Quantifier elimination consists of constructing a quantifier-free formula ψ' equivalent to a given quantified formula $\exists x.\psi$. Tarski used quantifier elimination to obtain a decision procedure for the theory of reals with addition and order. The idea is to existentially quantify out all free variables, yielding a new, variable-free formula whose truth value can be evaluated. The original formula is satisfiable if and only if this new formula evaluates to true.

There exists a number of algorithms for eliminating quantifiers in each of the different theories mentioned above. The Fourier-Motzkin method [27] eliminates quantifiers from an existentially quantified linear program, essentially by isolating the quantified variable in each inequality (which gives a set of inequalities of the form $x \leq t_i$ and $t_j \leq x$) and then adding a new inequality for each possible combination (e.g., $t_j \leq t_i$).

Cooper's algorithm [20] eliminates quantifiers from Presburger formulae, and Ferrante and Rackoff [25] give an elimination procedure for the theory of reals with addition and order. Ferrante and Geiser [24] study quantifier elimination in the theory of rationals with addition and order. Collins [18] pioneered the development of cylindrical algebraic decomposition (CAD) techniques for quantifier elimination in the theory of reals with addition and multiplication. Koubarakis [34] was the first researcher to study the complexity of quantifier elimination in the theory of difference constraint expressions.

Common for all of these quantifier elimination algorithms is that they are intended to work on the syntactic level of an expression (e.g., represented as a syntax tree). In the following we discuss two other approaches for solving DCE-SAT which are based on matrices and graphs, respectively.

4.3 Difference Bound Matrices

Any quantifier-free difference constraint expression can be written in disjunctive normal form where each disjunct is a difference constraint system. The key observation is now that a difference constraint system can be interpreted as a constraint graph: each variable x_i in the constraint system becomes a node in the graph, and for each difference constraint $x_i - x_j \leq d$ there is an edge from x_j to x_i with weight d[5]. The constraint graph can be represented as a so-called difference bound matrix (DBM) [23] M, where M_{ij} contain the least upper bound on $x_j - x_i$ or ∞ if there is no upper bound.

---

[5] If we also allow strong difference constraints of the form $x_i - x_j < d$, the weights in the graph become pairs of the form $(<, d)$ or $(\leq, d)$.

In other words, a quantifier-free difference constraint expression can be represented as a list of DBMs. Each DBM can represent a convex set of values, thus the expression is represented as a union of convex sets. Existential quantifiers can be distributed on each DBM and eliminated by running the Floyd-Warshall algorithm on the matrix and removing the rows and columns that correspond to the quantified variables. It is easy to show that the difference constraint system for the graph is satisfiable if and only if the constraint graph has a cycle with negative weight, and again the Floyd-Warshall algorithm can be used to determine whether the graph has such a negative-weight cycle. Negation and conjunction are more complicated to perform since they require that the expression is recast into disjunctive normal form.

Difference bound matrices are used in many real-time verification tools, such as KRONOS [50] and UPPAAL [36], but they suffer from a number of problems as discussed in Sect. 1.1.

4.4 Difference Decision Diagrams

Difference decision diagrams (DDDs) [38] are another candidate for a data structure for representing difference constraint expressions. Similar to how a BDD [13] represents the meaning of a Boolean formula implicitly, a DDD represents the meaning $[\![\psi]\!]$ of a difference constraint expression ψ using a decision diagram in which the vertices contain difference constraints. A DDD is a directed acyclic graph (V, E) with two terminals **0** and **1** and a set of non-terminal vertices. Each non-terminal vertex corresponds to the if-then-else operator $\alpha \to \psi_1, \psi_0$, defined as $(\alpha \wedge \psi_1) \vee (\neg\alpha \wedge \psi_0)$, where the test expression α is a difference constraint and the high-branch ψ_1 and low-branch ψ_0 are other DDD vertices. Each vertex v in a DDD denotes a difference constraint expression ψ^v given by:

$$\psi^v = \alpha(v) \to \psi^{high(v)}, \psi^{low(v)} ,$$

where $\alpha(v)$ is the difference constraint of v, and $high(v)$ and $low(v)$ are the high- and low-branches, respectively.

Example 20. As an example of a DDD consider the following expression ψ over $x, y, z \in \mathbb{R}$:

$$\psi = 1 \leq x - z \leq 3 \ \wedge \ (y - z \geq 2 \ \vee \ y - x \geq 0) .$$

Figure 5 shows $[\![\psi]\!]_z$ as an (x, y)-plot and the corresponding DDD.

As shown in [38], DDDs can be ordered and reduced making it possible to check for validity and satisfiability in constant time (as for BDDs). The DDD data structure is not canonical, however, so equivalence checking must be performed as a validity check. The operations for constructing and manipulating DDDs according to the syntactic constructions in Definition 20 are easily defined recursively on the DDD data structure, thus making it simple to specify and implement algorithms for these operations. The function APPLY(op, u, v) is used to

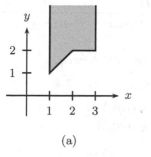
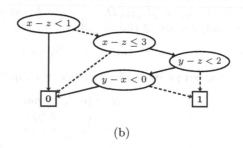

(a)   (b)

Fig. 5. The expression ψ in Example 20 as (a) an (x, y)-plot for $z = 0$, and (b) a difference decision diagram. High- and low-branches are drawn with solid and dashed lines, respectively

combine two ordered, locally reduced DDDs rooted at u and v with a Boolean operator *op*, e.g., the negation and conjunction operations in Definition 20. APPLY is a generalization of the version used for BDDs and has running time $O(|u||v|)$, where $|\cdot|$ denotes the number of vertices in a DDD.

The function EXISTS(x, u) is used to quantify out the variable x in a DDD rooted at u. The algorithm is an adoption of the Fourier-Motzkin quantifier-elimination method [27], removing all vertices reachable from u containing x, but keeping all implicit constraints induced by x among the other variables (e.g., $\exists x.(z - x < 1 \land x - y \le 0)$ is equivalent to $z - y < 1$). EXISTS computes the modified and additional constraints in polynomial time, but has an exponential worst-case running time since the resulting DDD must be ordered.

Recall that Boolean variables in Definition 21 are encoded as $x_i - x'_i \le 0$. This encoding allows us to represent and manipulate both real-valued and Boolean variables in a homogeneous manner. Furthermore, the encoding has the advantage that any Boolean expression will have a canonical DDD representation (because of the DDD reduction rules) and can be manipulated as efficiently as when represented by a BDD.

5 Examples

In this section we look at some examples: first we study the simple pulse generator from Sect. 2, and then we look at three (slightly) more realistic examples, namely Milner's Scheduler, Fischer's mutual exclusion protocol, and an RGD arbiter.

5.1 A Pulse Generator

Let us look at the asynchronous circuit from Example 15 again. We want to verify that the circuit is hazard-free using backward reachability analysis. Assume that the minimum and maximum delays are $[d_{out\uparrow}, D_{out\uparrow}] = [d_{out\downarrow}, D_{out\downarrow}] = [1,2]$, $[d_{ack\uparrow}, D_{ack\uparrow}] = [d_{ack\downarrow}, D_{ack\downarrow}] = [1,3]$ and $[d_{req\uparrow}, D_{req\uparrow}] = [d_{req\downarrow}, D_{req\downarrow}] = [3,3]$. The initial state of the circuit is:

$$\psi_0 = \neg out \wedge \neg out_u \wedge \neg ack \wedge \neg ack_u \wedge \neg req \wedge \neg req_u .$$

The hazard predicate for the circuit simplifies to:

$$
\begin{aligned}
H = &\big(out_u \wedge (out \Leftrightarrow (ack \oplus req))\big) \\
\vee\ &\big(ack_u \wedge (out \Rightarrow (ack \Leftrightarrow req))\big) \\
\vee\ &\big(req_u \wedge (ack \oplus req)\big)
\end{aligned}
$$

The circuit is hazard-free if and only if $\neg H$ is an invariant. To verify this, we compute $\mathbf{pre}^*(H)$ and check that this formula does not intersect with ψ_0 using the DDD data structure. The fixpoint $\mathbf{pre}^*(H)$ is reached after 4 iterations and does not intersect with ψ_0. Thus, the circuit has no hazards. If we change the delays for the XOR-gate (out) from $[1,2]$ to $[1,3]$, the circuit has a hazard which is reached after 12 iterations.

5.2   Milner's Scheduler

Milner's scheduler consists of N cyclers, connected in a ring, cooperating on controlling N tasks. We associate three Boolean variables c_i, h_i, and t_i with each cycler and use a clock H_i to ensure that a cycler passes the token on to the following cycler within the interval $[25, 200]$. We restrict the time a task can be executing by introducing a clock T_i that measures the execution time of each task t_i. The task t_i must terminate within $[80, 100]$ time units after it is started. The ith cycler is described by two guarded commands and the task is modeled by a third guarded command:

$$
\begin{aligned}
c_i \wedge \neg t_i \quad &\rightarrow H_i, T_i, t_i, c_i, h_i := 0, 0, \textbf{true}, \textbf{false}, \textbf{true} \\
h_i \wedge H_i \geq 25 &\rightarrow c_{(i \bmod N)+1}, h_i := \textbf{true}, \textbf{false} \\
t_i \wedge T_i \geq 80 \quad &\rightarrow t_i \qquad\qquad\qquad\qquad := \textbf{false} .
\end{aligned}
$$

The initial state is given by

$$\phi_0 = c_1 \wedge \neg t_1 \wedge \neg h_1 \wedge \bigwedge_{i=2}^{N} \neg c_i \wedge \neg t_i \wedge \neg h_i .$$

The program invariant is given by

$$I = \bigwedge_{i=1}^{N} (h_i \Rightarrow H_i \leq 200) \wedge (t_i \Rightarrow T_i \leq 100)$$

expressing that each cycler must pass on the token within 200 time units, and that each task must terminate 100 time units after it is started. Furthermore, the first guarded command is urgent, thus the urgency predicate is

$$U = \bigvee_{i=1}^{N} c_i \wedge \neg t_i .$$

We have computed the reachable state space **post**$^*(\psi_0)$ for increasing number N of cyclers. This version of Milner's scheduler has exponentially many discrete states because a task can terminate independently of the other tasks. Thus, state-space exploration based on enumerating all discrete states only succeeds for small systems. In the symbolic approach, discrete states are represented implicitly and choosing a good ordering of the variables in the DDD gives polynomial runtimes and state space representations. A system with $N = 32$ schedulers can be verified in a few seconds.

5.3 Fischer's Mutual Exclusion Protocol

Fischer's mutual exclusion protocol consists of N processes competing for a shared resource. Each process can be in one of four states modeled using two Boolean variables:

$$
\begin{aligned}
idle_i &= \neg t_i^1 \wedge \neg t_i^0 \\
rdy_i &= \neg t_i^1 \wedge t_i^0 \\
wait_i &= t_i^1 \wedge \neg t_i^0 \\
crit_i &= t_i^1 \wedge t_i^0
\end{aligned}
$$

We use the variable s_i to represent the state of a process. We write $s_i = idle_i$ for the predicate $\neg t_i^1 \wedge \neg t_i^0$, and $s_i := idle_i$ for the assignment $t_i^1, t_i^0 := \textbf{false}, \textbf{false}$, etc. Furthermore, the processes use a shared variable id, which an integer in the range $[0; N]$, for controlling the access to the shared resource. Like the state variables, this variable can be encoding using $\lceil \log_2(N+1) \rceil$ Boolean variables. The timed guarded commands for a process are:

$$
\begin{aligned}
(s_i = idle_i \vee s_i = wait_i) \wedge id = 0 &\rightarrow s_i, x_i := rdy_i, 0 \\
s_i = rdy_i \wedge x \le k &\rightarrow s_i, x_i, id := wait_i, 0, i \\
s_i = wait_i \wedge x > k \wedge id = i &\rightarrow s_i := crit_i \\
s_i = crit_i &\rightarrow s_i, id := idle_i, 0
\end{aligned}
$$

The parameter k is a constant which determines how long a process waits until entering the critical state. We use $k = 10$ in the following. The initial state is given by

$$
\phi_0 = (id = 0) \wedge \bigwedge_{i=1}^{N} (s_i = idle_i).
$$

The program invariant is given by

$$
I = \bigwedge_{i=1}^{N} (s_i = rdy_i) \Rightarrow x \le k.
$$

The following property expresses that only one process is in the critical state:

$$
M = \neg \bigvee_{i=1}^{N} \left(s_i = crit_i \wedge \bigvee_{j \neq i} s_j = crit_j \right)
$$

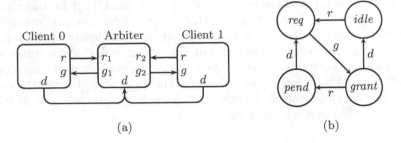

(a)   (b)

Fig. 6. RGD arbiter. (a) Abstract model. (b) State–transition diagram for one client

Fischer's protocol guarantees mutual exclusion if and only if $\mathbf{pre}^*(\neg M) \wedge \phi_0$ is **false**. We have verified Fischer's protocol for increasing number N of processes, but unlike Milner's scheduler the runtimes increase more rapidly and we could only verify systems with up to $N = 8$ processes in a few seconds.

5.4   An Arbiter

An RGD arbiter is a device that receives *requests* from two clients and issues *grants* to them such that at most one *request* is granted at a time. That is, the arbiter guarantees mutual exclusion to some resource. We say that a client is granted when its receives a *grant* for a request. When a client no longer needs the resource, it issues a *done* event to the arbiter. A client must be granted to issue a *done* event, so we need only one *done* event.

Figure 6 shows an abstract model of an RGD arbiter, and a state–transition diagram for one client. A client can be in one of four states: *idle*, *req*, *pend* or *grant*. If the client is *idle*, it can issue a request to the arbiter and move to the *req* state. When the arbiter grants the request, the client can move to the *grant* state. From this state the client can either release the resource by sending the arbiter a done event and move to the *idle* state, or it can issue another request and move to the *pend* state. The arbiter must guarantee *mutual exclusion*; that is, at most one client should be granted at a time.

In the abstract model of the arbiter we use events to model that two components (the arbiter and one of its clients) agree that something (a request, a grant, etc.) has happened, and which causes both components synchronously to perform some action. Events are good abstractions in the modeling phase of an arbiter, but in a real design of an arbiter there are no such things as events, as things do not happen synchronously. In a more realistic model, a client changes the value of some wires to indicate that it is requesting; then after some time the arbiter acquires this information; and — when the resource becomes available — the arbiter will grant the client by changing the value of some other wires, which the client will notice, and so on. There are many ways to define exactly

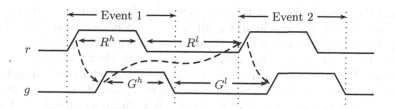

Fig. 7. Representing events as pulses

how this handshake mechanism has to work; in this example we will look at a protocol that uses *pulses* [29]. The idea is that a client sends a request (done) to the arbiter by changing the value of a wire r_i (d) from low to high, holding it high for some minimum time, and then changing it back to low again. We can think of lifting up a long rope lying on the ground and slapping it down, causing a wave to pulse from one end of the rope to the other. The arbiter issues grants similarly by firing back a pulse to the client using a wire g_i.

We can model this kind of pulse-communication in a TGC program as follows: when a client wants to request the resource, it sets a signal r high for at least R^h time units. Thereafter, the client may set r low again (but may also wait). The client must hold r low for at least R^l before it is allowed to issue a new request, see Fig. 7. Unlike a 2- or 4-phase handshake protocol, there is no ordering constraint on the falling edge of pulses. Instead, the component (a client or the arbiter) that generates a pulse must ensure that the pulse satisfies a minimum width constraint, and the component receiving the pulse must acquire it within that time. The arbiter grants requests in a similar way: When the arbiter has noticed that r is high, it will grant the request some time after (maybe infinitely long time after if the other client does not release the resource). The arbiter grants the request by setting g high for at least G^h time units. The client must acquire the grant if g is high for at least G^h time units. After G^h time units, the arbiter may set g low again (but may also wait). The arbiter must then hold g low for at least G^l time units before it is allowed to grant a new request.

To model a pulse as a set of guarded commands, we use a timer R_i to measure the time since the last r_i-transition from low-to-high or high-to-low. If r_i has been low for at least R^l time units, we can change r_i to high and reset R_i. Similarly, if r_i has been high for at least R^h time units, we can change r_i to low and reset R_i. We can model this as two guarded commands:

$$\neg r_i \wedge R_i \geq R^l \rightarrow r_i, R_i := \textbf{true}, 0$$
$$r_i \wedge R_i \geq R^h \rightarrow r_i, R_i := \textbf{false}, 0$$

As a first attempt to model the pulse arbiter, we can augment the state-transition diagram in Fig. 6(b) with the TGC program for a pulse. It turns out, however, that this it not sufficient to guarantee mutual exclusion. Consider the following scenario: A client makes a request and becomes granted; the g signal remains high and the client makes a pending request; the client sends the arbiter a done pulse, and because g still is high, the client thinks it has become granted again. Seeing the done pulse, the arbiter thinks that the first client is done with the resource, then grants the other client, and now both clients are granted at the same time. The problem is, that the clients and the arbiter need some internal variables to keep track of when they have acquired a pulse. To do so, we introduce five extra Boolean variables, r'_i, g'_i, d', for $i = 0, 1$, (initially all **false**). The idea is that a client only can move from *req* to *grant* when g_i is high and g'_i is low, and the client then sets g'_i high when taking the transition, indicating that it has acquired that grant. This gives us the following TGC program for the pulse arbiter $(i = 0, 1)$:

$$
\begin{aligned}
c_i &= idle \wedge \neg r_i \wedge R_i \geq R^l & &\rightarrow c_i, r_i, R_i & &:= req, \textbf{true}, 0 \\
c_i &= grant \wedge \neg r_i \wedge R_i \geq R^l & &\rightarrow c_i, r_i, R_i & &:= pend, \textbf{true}, 0 \\
c_i &= req \wedge g_i \wedge \neg g'_i & &\rightarrow c_i, g'_i & &:= grant, \textbf{true} \\
c_i &= grant \wedge \neg d \wedge D \geq D^l & &\rightarrow c_i, d, D & &:= idle, \textbf{true}, 0 \\
c_i &= pend \wedge \neg d \wedge D \geq D^l & &\rightarrow c_i, d, D & &:= req, \textbf{true}, 0 \\
(a_i &= idle \vee a_i = grant) \wedge r_i \wedge \neg r'_i & &\rightarrow a_i, r'_i & &:= req, \textbf{true} \\
a_i &= req \wedge \neg g_i \wedge G_i \geq G^l \wedge \neg f & &\rightarrow a_i, g_i, G_i, f & &:= grant, \textbf{true}, 0, \textbf{true} \\
(a_i &= grant \vee a_i = pend) \wedge d \wedge \neg d' & &\rightarrow a_i, d', f & &:= idle, \textbf{true}, \textbf{false} \\
r_i &\wedge R_i \geq R^h & &\rightarrow r_i, r'_i, R_i & &:= \textbf{false}, \textbf{false}, 0 \\
g_i &\wedge G_i \geq G^h & &\rightarrow g_i, g'_i, G_i & &:= \textbf{false}, \textbf{false}, 0 \\
d &\wedge D \geq D^h & &\rightarrow d, d', D & &:= \textbf{false}, \textbf{false}, 0
\end{aligned}
$$

The initial set of states ψ_0 is given by

$$
\psi_0 \equiv \neg d \wedge \neg d' \wedge \neg f \wedge \bigwedge_{i=0,1} \neg r_i \wedge \neg g_i \wedge \neg r'_i \wedge \neg g'_i \wedge c_i = idle \wedge a_i = idle .
$$

To verify that the TGC program for the pulse arbiter guarantees mutual exclusion we have used the DDD data structure to compute $\textbf{pre}^*(\bigwedge_{i=0,1} grant_i \vee pend_i)$ and check that it does not intersect with ψ_0. Thus, we have proved that the model of the arbiter guarantees mutual exclusion.

6   Summary

Analyzing timed systems is extremely difficult. Very often, current timing verification tools cannot handle systems with a complexity that occur in practice. One reason for this is that current methods enumerate the discrete states of the system, and they are thus inherently limited by the number of states in the system.

We have shown how difference constraint expressions can be used to represent and verify concurrent timed systems in a fully symbolic manner. A key idea is to avoid representing absolute constraints. Instead, these constraints are expressed relative to a special variable z, which allows us to advance all clocks synchronously by performing a single existential quantification. Programs can be analyzed fully symbolically in a forward and backward manner using the **post** and **pre** operators which construct difference constraint expressions.

This result allows us to analyze timed systems without explicitly enumerating the discrete states of the system, thus removing a key limitation of current approaches. The complexity of performing timing analysis is reduced to deciding satisfiability of constraints the form $x - y \leq d$ combined with Boolean operators and existentially quantified.

We have shortly described a new data structure called DDDs for representing and deciding validity of such expressions. DDDs attempt to obtain the compactness of BDDs, but often fail in this respect. Quantifier elimination is the core operation in real-time model checking, and a more efficient implementation of this operator is the focus of current research.

References

[1] R. Alur. *Techniques for Automatic Verication of Real-Time Systems*. PhD thesis, Department of Computer Science, Stanford University, 1991. 299

[2] R. Alur and D. Dill. The theory of timed automata. In *Proc. Real-Time: Theory in Practice*, volume 600 of *Lecture Notes in Computer Science*, pages 28–73. Springer-Verlag, 1991. 275, 278, 279, 285

[3] E. Asarin, M. Bozga, A. Kerbrat, O. Maler, M. Pnueli, and A. Rasse. Data structures for the verification of timed automata. In O. Maler, editor, *Proc. International Workshop on Hybrid and Real-Time Systems*, volume 1201 of *Lecture Notes in Computer Science*, pages 346–360, Grenoble, France, 1997. Springer-Verlag. 278

[4] F. Balarin. Approximate reachability analysis of timed automata. In *Proc. Real-Time Systems Symposium*, pages 52–61. IEEE Computer Society Press, 1996. 278

[5] E. Balas. Disjunctive programming. *Annals of Discrete Mathematics*, 5:3–51, 1979. 300

[6] G. Behrmann, K. G. Larsen, J. Pearson, C. Weise, and W. Yi. Efficient timed reachability analysis using clock difference diagrams. Technical Report 99/105, DoCS, Uppsala University, 1999. 277

[7] W. Belluomini and C. J. Myers. Efficient timing analysis algorithms for timed state space exploration. In *Proc. International Symposium on Advanced Research in Asynchronous Circuits and Systems*, pages 88–100, April 1997. 278

[8] W. Belluomini and C. J. Myers. Verification of timed systems using POSETs. In *Proc. Tenth International Conference on Computer-Aided Verification*, pages 403–415, June 1998. 278

[9] B. Berthomieu and M. Diaz. Modeling and verification of time dependent systems using time Petri nets. *IEEE Transactions on Software Engineering*, 17(3):259–273, 1991. 275, 276, 278, 279

[10] A. Blass and Y. Gurevich. Fixed-choice and independent-choice logics. Technical Report TR-369-98, University of Michigan, August 1998. 280

[11] P. Bouyer, C. Dufourd, E. Fleury, and A. Petit. Are timed automata updatable? In *Proc. 12th International Conference on Computer-Aided Verification*, volume 1855 of *Lecture Notes in Computer Science*, pages 464–479. Springer-Verlag, July 2000. 299

[12] M. Bozga, O. Maler, A. Pnueli, and S. Yovine. Some progress in the symbolic verification of timed automata. In O. Grumberg, editor, *Proc. Ninth International Conference on Computer-Aided Verification*, volume 1254 of *Lecture Notes in Computer Science*, pages 179–190, 1997. 278

[13] R. E. Bryant. Graph-based algorithms for Boolean function manipulation. *IEEE Transactions on Computers*, C-35(8):677–691, 1986. 274, 302

[14] J. R. Burch. *Trace Algebra for Automatic Verification of Real-Time Concurrent Systems*. PhD thesis, Carnegie Mellon, August 1992. 278

[15] J. R. Burch, E. M. Clarke, K. L. McMillan, D. L. Dill, and L. J. Hwang. Symbolic model checking: 10^{20} states and beyond. In *Proc. Fifth Annual IEEE Symposium on Logic in Computer Science*, pages 428–439. IEEE Computer Society Press, 1990. 274

[16] S. V. Campos, E. Clarke, W. Marrero, M. Minea, and H. Hiraishi. Computing quantitative characteristics of finite-state real-time systems. In *Proc. Real-Time Systems Symposium*, pages 266–70. IEEE Computer Society Press, December 1994. 278

[17] E. M. Clarke and E. A. Emerson. Design and synthesis of synchronization skeletons using branching time temporal logic. In *Proc. Logics of Programs*, volume 131 of *Lecture Notes in Computer Science*, pages 52–71. Springer-Verlag, May 1981. 274, 297

[18] G. E. Collins. Quantifier elimination for real closed fields by cylindrical algebraic decomposition. In *Proc. Second GI Conference*, volume 33 of *Lecture Notes in Computer Science*, pages 134–183. Springer-Verlag, 1975. 301

[19] S. A. Cook. The complexity of theorem-proving procedures. In *Proc. Third Annual ACM Symposium on Theory of Computing*, pages 151–158, Shaker Heights, Ohio, 1971. 301

[20] D. C. Cooper. Theorem proving in arithmetic without multiplication. *Machine Intelligence*, 7:91–99, 1972. 300, 301

[21] T. H. Cormen, C. E. Leiserson, and R. L. Rivest. *Introduction to Algorithms*. MIT Press, 1994. 277, 300

[22] E. W. Dijkstra. Guarded commands, nondeterminacy and formal derivation of programs. *Communications of the ACM*, 18(8):453–457, August 1975. 275

[23] D. L. Dill. Timing assumptions and verification of finite-state concurrent systems. In *Automatic Verification Methods for Finite State Systems*, volume 407 of *Lecture Notes in Computer Science*, pages 197–212. Springer-Verlag, 1989. 276, 277, 278, 301

[24] J. Ferrante and J. R. Geiser. An efficient decision procedure for the theory of rational order. *Theoretical Computer Science*, 4(2):227–233, 1977. 301

[25] J. Ferrante and C. Rackoff. A decision procedure for the first order theory of real addition with order. *SIAM Journal of Computing*, 4(1):69–76, 1975. 301

[26] M. J. Fischer and M. O. Rabin. Super-exponential complexity of presburger arithmetic. In *Proc. SIAM-AMS Symposium in Applied Mathematics*, volume 7, pages 27–41, 1974. 300

[27] J. B. J. Fourier. Second extrait. In G. Darboux, editor, *Oeuvres*, pages 325–328, Paris, 1890. Gauthiers-Villars. 301, 303

[28] K. Gödel. Über formal unentscheidbare Sätze der Principia Mathematica und verwandter System (On formal undecidable theorems in Principia Mathematica and related systems). In *Monatshefte für Mathematik und Physik*, volume 38, pages 173–198, 1931. 300

[29] M. R. Greenstreet and T. Ono-Tesfaye. A fast, ASP*, RGD arbiter. In *Proc. Fifth International Symposium on Advanced Research in Asynchronous Circuits and Systems*, pages 173–185, Barcelona, Spain, April 1999. IEEE. 307

[30] T. A. Henzinger, X. Nicollin, J. Sifakis, and S. Yovine. Symbolic model checking for real-time systems. *Information and Computation*, 111(2):193–244, 1994. 275, 278, 297, 300

[31] D. Hilbert and P. Bernays. *Grundlagen der Mathematik*, volume 2. Springer-Verlag, 1939. 280

[32] J. E. Hopcroft and J. D. Ullman. *Introduction to Automata Theory, Languages and Computation*. Addison-Wesley, 1979. 300, 301

[33] N. K. Karmarkar. A new polynomial–time algorithm for linear programming. *Proc. 16th Annual ACM Symposium on Theory of Computing*, pages 302–311, 1984. 300

[34] M. Koubarakis. Complexity results for first-order theories of temporal constraints. In J. Doyle, E. Sandewall, and P. Torasso, editors, *Proc. Fourth Internatinal Conference on Principles of Knowledge Representation and Reasoning*, pages 379–390, San Francisco, California, 1994. Morgan Kaufmann. 300, 301

[35] K. G. Larsen, P. Pettersson, and W. Yi. Model-checking for real-time systems. In *Proc. Tenth International Conference on Fundamentals of Computation Theory*, volume 965 of *Lecture Notes in Computer Science*, pages 62–88, August 1995. 276, 278

[36] K. G. Larsen, P. Pettersson, and W. Yi. UPPAAL in a nutshell. *International Journal on Software Tools for Technology Transfer*, 1(1–2):134–152, 1997. 302

[37] O. Maler and A. Pnueli. Timing analysis of asynchronous circuits using timed automata. In P. E. Camurati and H. Eveking, editors, *Proc. Eighth International Conference on Correct Hardware Design and Verification Methods*, volume 987 of *Lecture Notes in Computer Science*, pages 189–205. Springer-Verlag, 1995. 286

[38] J. Møller, J. Lichtenberg, H. R. Andersen, and H. Hulgaard. Difference decision diagrams. In *Proc. 13th International Conference on Computer Science Logic*, volume 1683 of *Lecture Notes in Computer Science*, pages 111–125, Madrid, Spain, September 1999. 277, 302

[39] J. Møller, J. Lichtenberg, H. R. Andersen, and H. Hulgaard. Fully symbolic model checking of timed systems using difference decision diagrams. In *Proc. First International Workshop on Symbolic Model Checking*, volume 23-2 of *Electronic Notes in Theoretical Computer Science*, pages 89–108, Trento, Italy, July 1999. 279

[40] D. Oppen. A $2^{2^{2^{pn}}}$ upper bound on the complexity of Presburger arithmetic. *Journal of Computer and System Sciences*, 16:323–332, 1978. 301

[41] C. H. Papadimitriou. *Computational Complexity*. Addison-Wesley, 1994. 300

[42] M. Presburger. Über die vollständigkeit eines gewissen systems der arithmetik ganzer zählen, in welchem die addition als einzige operation hervortritt. *Comptes-Rendus du I Congres de Mathematiciens des pays Slaves*, pages 92–101, 1929. 300

[43] T. G. Rokicki. *Representing and Modeling Digital Circuits*. PhD thesis, Stanford University, 1993. 276, 278

[44] T. G. Rokicki and C. J. Myers. Automatic verification of timed circuits. In D. L. Dill, editor, *Proc. Sixth International Conference on Computer-Aided Verification*, volume 818 of *Lecture Notes in Computer Science*, pages 468–480, 1994. 278

[45] S. Bornot and J. Sifakis. An algebraic framework for urgency. *Information and Computation*, 163(1):172–202, 2000. 281

[46] R. Shostak. On the SUP-INF method for proving Presburger formulas. *Journal of the ACM*, 4(24):529–543, October 1977. 300

[47] A. Tarski. *A Decision Method for Elementary Algebra and Geometry.* University of California Press, Berkeley, CA, 2nd edition, 1951. 300, 301

[48] E. Verlind, G. de Jong, and B. Lin. Efficient partial enumeration for timing analysis of asynchronous systems. In *Proc. ACM/IEEE Design Automation Conference*, pages 55–58, June 1996. 278

[49] H. Wong-Toi and D. L. Dill. Approximations for verifying timing properties. In *Theories and Experiences for Real-Time Systems Development*, chapter 7, pages 177–204. World Scientific Publishing, 1994. 278

[50] S. Yovine. KRONOS: A verification tool for real-time systems. *International Journal on Software Tools for Technology Transfer*, 1(1–2):123–133, October 1997. 276, 278, 302

[51] S. Yovine. Model checking timed automata. In *Embedded Systems*, volume 1494 of *Lecture Notes in Computer Science*, pages 114–152. Springer-Verlag, October 1998. 278

Performance Analysis of Asynchronous Circuits Using Markov Chains*

Peter A. Beerel[1] and Aiguo Xie[2]

[1] EE Department, Systems Division, University of Southern California
Los Angeles, CA 90089
pabeerel@usc.edu
[2] Fulcrum Microsystems, Calabasas Hills, CA 91301
aiguo@fulcrummicro.com

1 Introduction

In an increasing number of instances, asynchronous circuit can provide advantages in either performance, power, electromagnetic interference, and/or design time [56, 45, 5, 3]. Asynchronous circuits circumvent the limitations and somewhat rigid design framework associated with global synchronization dictated by a globally distributed clock signal. Instead, asynchronous systems generally consist of a collection of parallel computation processes that synchronize and exchange data through handshaking-based communication. This facilitates pipelining communication across long distances, optimizing for average case behavior, and integrating slow and fast processes.

Asynchronous design methodologies, however, complicate the important task of performance analysis. In synchronous design, the performance (e.g., latency and throughput) is largely governed by the period of the global clock. In asynchronous design, however, the performance is a complex function of the cycles of computation and communication between the various parallel processes, some of which may exhibit data-dependent delay and choice behavior. To reduce complexity, most performance analysis tools evaluate an abstract model in which distinct data values are abstracted away and the delays are modeled as either constants (which represent component delays averaged across data values) or random variables (which represent the distribution of component delays). These tools calculate, estimate or bound the *average* time separation of user-specified pairs of system events, or more simply, the time separation of events (TSEs). They are most often applied at the architectural/system level, estimating average latency, throughput, or response time.

For the purpose of performance analysis, random variables are more expressive than constants in modeling delays. Unfortunately, developing a technique that can analyze sufficiently general stochastic models with random delays has up to now been an elusive goal. Existing efficient techniques have been limited in either the type or size of system model they can analyze. For instance, efficient

---

* This research was funded in part by a gift from TRW, a large-scale NSF ITR Award No. CCR-00-86036, and a NSF Award No. CCR-98-12164.

J. Cortadella et al. (Eds.): Concurrency and Hardware Design, LNCS 2549, pp. 313–343, 2002.
© Springer-Verlag Berlin Heidelberg 2002

techniques to analyze both the average and extreme TSEs in models with only fixed delays and without choice (e.g., Marked graphs) are well-known [8, 26]. More complex techniques exist for analyzing the extreme and average TSEs for models with interval delays (i.e., with lower and upper bounds) but no choice [16, 25, 36]. For models with restricted form of choice (i.e., *free-choice* behavior in which decisions can be decoupled from system timing), and causality (i.e., *AND-causality*), efficient analysis techniques based on net unfoldings have been developed to analyze both extreme [24] and average TSEs [54, 53].

This paper reviews recently developed Markovian-analysis based techniques to compute average TSEs of stochastic models that are capable of specifying essentially all types causality, including both AND- and OR-causality, and all forms of choice, including free-choice and arbitration. The models approximate arbitrary delay distributions using time-discretization and are specified as a set of probabilistic communicating finite state machines which are converted into discrete-time finite state Markov chains [50]. We derive a framework using basic Markov chain theory to analyze average TSEs that represent system performance measures such as average throughput and latency [50]. We then review techniques to speed up by orders of magnitude the analysis of larger finite state Markov chains by attacking the state-explosion problem. This is achieved by developing (1) an efficient algorithm using symbolic techniques based on binary decision diagrams (BDDs) for the structural analysis (state classification) [51], and (2) a novel technique called *state compression* to accelerate the subsequent iterative stationary analysis [52]. We demonstrate both the effectiveness and the efficiency of the above techniques on a number of chip designs.

The remainder of this paper is organized as follows. Section 2 describes our stochastic models, Section 3 describes our TSE framework, Section 4 reviews efficient Markov analysis techniques to obtain TSEs on our stochastic models, and Section 5 describes the application of this methodology to several case studies.

2   Stochastic Discrete-Time Modeling

There have been developed many formalisms to specify asynchronous systems for the purposes of synthesis and verification. They include state-based models [48, 15, 37, 57], Petri-net [39] based models [13, 11, 4], and communicating sequential processes (CSP) [22] based models [17, 32]. These formalisms, however, often do not specify the delays of components and all of them do not specify delay distributions or choice probabilities, which are needed to derive key performance metrics.

An ideal performance model of an asynchronous system is a stochastic process defined by a set of random variables that probabilistically models component delays and choices. This stochastic process, however, can be very complex and often cannot be efficiently analyzed using any known method. For this reason, many proposed methods to approximate arbitrary distributions with special distributions that facilitate more efficient analysis.

One approach approximates arbitrary distributions using exponential distributions. In some limited cases, the resulting system model can be treated as a memoryless queueing network [19]. In other cases, the resulting system model is a stochastic timed Petri net [31, 35, 23]. Both types of the memoryless delay models can be analyzed as a finite state Markov chain where the states in the Markov chain have well-defined semantics [31, 35, 23]. For example, for queueing networks a state can represent the numbers of jobs in the servers while for Petri nets a state can represent a marking of places in the Petri net.

A second approach approximates an arbitrary distribution using a constant. For example, a fixed delay can be chosen as the mean of the arbitrary distribution. This type of delay models are incorporated into Generalized Timed Petri Nets (GTPNs) which can also be converted into a Markov chain by augmenting a notion of time into the semantics of a state [23]. For example, the state can be associated with a fixed time after which the Markov chain transits to some next state.

A third approach approximates the arbitrary distribution using time discretization (see e.g., [34, 35]). The result is that events can now occur only at time instants that are multiple of some unit time step. In other words, the delay interval (of reals) is discretized into an interval of integers (with a unit time step). The probability distribution function (p.d.f.) is accordingly converted into a probability mass function (p.m.f.) by interval integrations. Similar to the other two approaches, time discretization also loses some accuracy [34]. However, it is always possible to trade discretization resolution (and consequently the computational cost) with accuracy of the final performance estimates. As in the other two approximations, the time-discretized system model can be converted to a finite state Markov chain (e.g., [35]).

In this work, we adopt the discrete-time approach to approximate arbitrary delays of system components for two reasons. First, we believe it is relatively uncommon that the delay of an event can be closely modeled using an exponentially or geometrically distributed delay. A notable exception is the delay an arbiter experiences when resolving metastability [9]. Another exception may be the data inter-arrival time from the environments which sometimes may be reasonably approximated with exponential distribution. Beyond these cases, most system components (e.g., datapath components, controllers) exhibit bounded delays with arbitrary distributions which cannot be reasonably approximated as exponentially distributed random variables. Moreover, when exponential distributions do need be modeled, they can be approximated with arbitrary accuracy in discrete time using a geometric distributions. Second, we believe that it is often not adequate to model bounded delays with their mean values, as was proposed in [28].

The rest of this section details our specification approach. We first formally define the probabilistic discrete-time model and then show these models can be specified using probabilistically-annotated guarded commands.

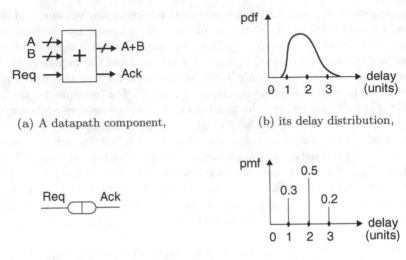

(a) A datapath component,   (b) its delay distribution,

(c) abstraction of the component,   (d) time discretization.

Fig. 1. Probabilistic modeling and time discretization

2.1   Probabilistic Discrete-Time System Models

A probabilistic finite state machine (FSM) is represented by the tuple $P = \langle I, Q, P, Q_0, O \rangle$ where Q is the state space spanned by the set of state variables V, Q_0 is the set of initial states, $P : Q \times Q \longrightarrow [0, 1]$ is the probabilistic state transition relation, and I and O are the system inputs and outputs, respectively.

Each state variable $v \in V$ has a range denoted by $R(v)$. The state space $Q = \bigotimes_{v \in V} R(v)$, where a state $s \in Q$ is the valuation of all state variables. We denote $s(v)$ the value of state variable v in state s.

The *probabilistic transition relation* P maps each state transition $(s, s') \in Q \times Q$ to a probability. We say s is the current state and s' the next state in the state transition. P is usually written as a matrix whose rows are indexed by current states and whose columns are indexed by next states. For a closed system, one with no inputs or outputs, P should be *stochastic*, which means that the sum of the probabilities of all state transitions from any state equals 1, i.e.,

$$\sum_{s' \in Q} P(s, s') = 1 \quad \text{for any } s \in Q. \tag{1}$$

The semantics of the time-discretized system model is (1) state transitions are instantaneous, and (2) once a state is entered the system makes a state transition and enters another state (possibly the same state if the state has a self-loop) after precisely one time unit. In other words, each state transition takes precisely one time unit.

As an example, consider the probabilistic FSM model of a simple time-discretized probabilistic delay element shown in Figure 1(c). This delay element

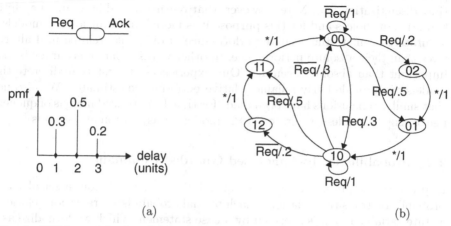

(a)   (b)

Fig. 2. FSM model of a delay element. (a) Its probabilistic delay model, (b) the corresponding state space where `state := (Ack, timer)` and `transition label := input-condition/probability`

approximates the delay of an adder shown in Figure 1(a), whose p.d.f. is shown in Figure 1(b). Notice that in this example the delay is symmetric in that the rise and fall times have the same delay. Modeling asymmetric delays is only slightly more complicated.

The delay element has a single input, `Req` and a single output `Ack`. The probabilistic FSM model for this system is the tuple $\langle \{Req\}, Q, P, Q_0, \{Ack\} \rangle$ where Q is the state space spanned shown in Figure 2(b). The model has two state variables, one representing the binary value of the output `Ack` and the other being a `timer` with range $[0, 2]$. The value of the timer is probabilistically assigned when the input `Req` changes values. It then decreases by 1 each time the system model makes a state transition until it reached 0. It remains 0 until the next time `Req` changes. The probability of each state transition are denoted with a "/" followed by a real value between 0 and 1.

Suppose the system is currently in state (00) and detects a request signal (e.g., `Req` makes a positive transition) which enables a positive transition on signal `Ack`. According to the discrete delay distribution shown in Figure 2(a), the `timer` is then randomly assigned a value at next time step. Specifically, at time instant $k + 1$, variable `timer` receives a value of 2 with probability 0.2, a value of 1 with probability 0.5 and a value of 0 with probability 0.3. We note that if `timer` is assigned a value of k ($0 \leq k \leq 2$), then the desired positive transition on `Ack` will occur $k + 1$ time steps after the positive transition on `Req`. For instance, if `timer` is set to 2 at state (00), then the model transits to state (02) after one time step. After another time step, the model transits from state (02) to state (01) with probability 1 and so forth.

Experiments show that this discrete-time model can yield high-quality system performance estimates (compared with extensive simulation) with fairly coarse time discretization [50]. Note, however, that our main goal is to guide architectural design choices and for this purpose it is more important for the models to accurately estimate the relative performance of different architectural alternatives than their absolute performance. In other words, relative accuracy is more important than absolute accuracy. Our experiences suggest that discrete-time models can provide fairly reliable relative performance estimates. We also note that similar conclusions have been made for timed-discretized models of queueing networks [30] and less accurate GTPN models of asynchronous systems [28].

2.2   Probabilistically-Annotated Guarded Commands

In practice, the probabilistic transition relation is derived from a set of partial probabilistic transition relations. Each partial probabilistic transition relation of a state variable v, P_v, is specified by a case statement which we formalize as an *ordered* set G_v of conditional assignments to v annotated with probabilities.

In particular, each conditional assignment $(g : o)$ consists of a condition (or guard) g and an associated assignment o. The condition g is a boolean predicate of current (system) state and next state values of all state variables excluding v, a domain referred to as $Q \times Q(V \setminus v)$. At least one condition in the case statement must be true for every element of $Q \times Q$ (and thus for every transition (s, s')). The first true condition and its associated assignment are said to be active. An assignment is a set of functions from $Q \times Q(V \setminus v)$ to $R(v)$ that defines the potential next state values of v (i.e., v'), referred to as $R(v)_a$.

We annotate the elements of each assignment with probabilities that add to 1. In particular, this annotation maps each value in $R(v)_a$ to a given probability. Values for v' not in $R(v)_a$ are mapped to 0 probability by default. Thus, for each state transition (s, s'), this annotation effectively defines a function *prob* : $R(v) \rightarrow [0, 1]$. Using this probability function, we define a partial probabilistic transition relation $P_v : Q \times Q \rightarrow [0, 1]$ for each variable v such that $P_v(s, s') = prob(s'(v))$.

The property that the annotated probabilities in each assignment add to 1 may be formally written as follows.

Property 1.

$$\sum_{s_1 \in R(v)} P_v(s, s_1 \otimes s_2) = 1 \tag{2}$$

for any $s \in Q$ and any $s_2 \in Q(V \setminus v)$, where $s_1 \otimes s_2$ denotes a state variable comprised of the composition of the value of v defined in s_1 and the values of all other variables defined in s_2. This property helps ensure that the specified system is Markovian.

Example: Consider the FIFO shown in Figure 3 with $n \geq 0$ stages. Each stage consists of a C-element and a delay line. All delays are discretized into time steps. The C-elements have a unit delay (i.e., one time step) and the delay lines

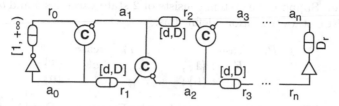

Fig. 3. An n-stage FIFO

have integer delays in the interval $[d, D]$. The left environment has an integer delay in the interval $[1, +\infty]$, while the right environment has a fixed integer delay D_r. The delay line of stage i is modeled by a timer w_i with delay range $[0, D - 1]$. To model the probabilities of delays, w_i is probabilistically set to an integer value in the interval $[d, D]$ each time the input to the corresponding delay line changes, and is decremented by one each subsequent state transition. The output of the delay line is asserted when w_i reaches 0. The probability that the delay line takes 1 unit of delay is set to 0.2, 2 units of delay 0.6, and 3 units of delay 0.2. The corresponding partial transition relation for timer variable w_i is annotated as follows:

$$P_{w_i} := \text{case}$$
$$a_{i-1}' \neq a_{i-1} : \{1'0.2, 2'0.6, 3'0.2\};$$
$$w_i > 0 \qquad : \{(w_i - 1)\};$$
$$1 \qquad\qquad : \{w_i\}; \qquad\qquad \text{for } i = 1, 2, \ldots, n.$$

The conditional assignments that have only one element in their corresponding assignment are deterministic and thus the element is, by default, assigned probability 1. Similarly, we specify the partial probabilistic transition relation of the timer variable in the delay line of the left environment as:

$$P_{w_0} := \text{case}$$
$$a_0' \neq a_0 : \{1\};$$
$$w_0 > 0 \quad : \{0'p, 1'1 - p\};$$
$$1 \qquad\quad : \{w_i\};$$

This models the delay of the left environment as having a geometric distribution with parameter p. ☐

It would be ideal if each state transition probability could be determined by simply multiplying the partial state transition probabilities of all state variables, as follows:

$$P(s, s') = \prod_{v \in V} P_v(s, s') \qquad\qquad (3)$$

for all $(s, s') \in Q \times Q$. This, however, is not guaranteed without further restriction on the model. To see this, consider the following example:

Example: Suppose the system consists of 2 state variables a and b with partial probabilistic state transitions defined as:

$$
\begin{array}{ll}
P_a := \text{case} & P_b := \text{case} \\
\quad b' \quad : \{1\}; & \quad a' \quad : \{1\}; \\
\quad 1 \quad : \{0\}; & \quad 1 \quad : \{0\};
\end{array}
$$

Both P_a and P_b satisfy the property given by Equation 2. Combined, they define two transitions from state 00, i.e., $(00, 00)$ and $(00, 11)$. Evaluating Equation 3, each state transition has probability 1 and their sum equals 2, a violation of Equation 1. Thus, the probabilistic state transition relation $P = P_a P_b$ is not stochastic. □

The violation in the above example occurs because the above probability assignment does not capture the non-determinism hidden in this model. Intuitively, this is because, for both P_a and P_b under a given current state 00, multiple conditional assignments can become active so that the choice made is between two guards, not between value assignments in one guard. More precisely, the transition of variable a depends on transition of b and vice versa. This forms a *cyclic dependence* which introduces extra non-determinism that cannot be captured by simply requiring the transition behavior of individual state variable to satisfy the property given by Equation 2.

More generally, *for every given current state*, we can draw a dependence graph for the transition behaviors of all state variables. Each state variable corresponds to a vertex of the graph and there is an edge from vertex x to vertex y if the transition of the state variable corresponding to vertex x depends on that of the state variables corresponding to vertex y. The remaining of this subsection shows that if the dependence graph is cycle-free for every possible current state then the probabilistic transition relation P is stochastic.

Let us first formalize the dependence among state variables and the required cycle-free property of the dependence graphs.

Let u and v be two state variables in V. Variable u depends on variable v in the current state $s \in Q$, denoted by, $u \xrightarrow{s} v$, if P_u is a function of v' in current state s. That is,

$$
u \xrightarrow{s} v \iff \exists s', s'' \in Q \text{ s.t. } s'(v) \neq s''(v) \wedge P_u(s, s') \neq P_u(s, s'').
$$

Let us denote by $D(s, v)$ the set of state variables that depends on v assuming the current state is s, i.e.,

$$
D(s, v) \triangleq \left\{ u \in V \mid u \xrightarrow{s} v \right\}.
$$

Because the dependency is transitive, we know that $D(s, u) \subseteq D(s, v)$ if $u, v \in V$ and $u \in D(s, v)$. Equivalently, if $w \xrightarrow{s} u$ and $u \xrightarrow{s} v$, then $w \xrightarrow{s} v$.

The *non-cyclic-dependence* property of the model can now be formally stated as follows.

Property 2. For every state variable $v \in V$ and every state $s \in Q$, $v \notin D(s, v)$.

In the previous example, one may check that $b \in D(00, a)$ and $a \in D(00, b)$. Thus, $a \in D(00, b) \subseteq D(00, a)$ due to the fact that dependency is transitive. Therefore, the model in this example has cyclic dependence among variables. In fact, since $b \in D(00, a) \subseteq D(00, b)$ for a similar reason, we have $D(00, a) = D(00, b) = \{a, b\}$. On the other hand, it can be shown that our n-stage FIFO model has no cyclic dependencies.

Below, we assume that Property 2 holds, which as stated in the next theorem, guarantees that the P matrix is stochastic [55].

Theorem 1. *Suppose the model satisfies Properties 1 and 2, then its probabilistic transition relation matrix P defined by Equation 3 is stochastic. That is, $\sum_{s' \in Q} P(s, s') = 1$ for any $s \in Q$.*

3   Markov Chain Theory and Time Separation of Events

3.1   Basics of Markov Chains

Consider a *finite state space* $Q = \{1, 2, \cdots, N\}$. In the *discrete-time* domain, a random process X on state space Q is a sequence of random variables each taking values in Q, i.e., $X = \{X_n \in Q : n \geq 0\}$. The value assumed by X_n is called the state of X at time n. Process X is a *Markov chain* (or is *Markovian*) if it satisfies the *Markov property*, i.e, its future evolution depends only on the current state. Formally, X is a Markov chain if for all $n \geq 1$ and all $j, i, x_{n-1}, \cdots, x_1, x_0 \in Q$, $Pr(X_{n+1} = j \mid X_n = i, (X_{n-1} = x_{n-1}, \cdots, X_1 = x_1, X_0 = x_0)) = Pr(X_{n+1} = j \mid X_n = i)$, where $Pr(A \mid B)$ denotes the conditional probability that A occurs given that B occurs.

If the probabilities governing the evolution of X are independent of time, X is called *time-homogeneous*. In other words, a Markov chain X is time-homogeneous if $Pr(X_{n+1} = j \mid X_n = i)$ is independent of n. In this case, we define a matrix P whose element at the i-th row and j-th column, $P_{ij} = Pr(X_{n+1} = j \mid X_n = i) = Pr(X_1 = j \mid X_0 = i)$. Clearly, we have $\sum_{j \in Q} P_{ij} = 1$ for any $i \in Q$. Matrix P is called the *1-step transition matrix* or simply the *transition matrix*. Since our Markov chains models are always time-homogeneous [50], we assume X is time-homogeneous from now on.

A *sample path* of X with length $n > 0$ is a sequence of states $(s_0, s_1, \cdots, s_{n-1})$ visited by X during a particular evolution. States s_0 and s_{n-1} are called the *head* and the *tail* state, respectively. By definition, we must have $Pr(X_{k+1} = s_{k+1} \mid X_k = s_k) > 0$ for all $0 \leq k < n - 1$. A *cycle* is a sample path of length at least 2 in which the head and tail states are identical. A *simple* cycle is one where no other two states are identical.

A state is called *recurrent* if every sample path with that state as its head may be extended to a cycle (i.e., ending in that state). Otherwise, it is called *transient*. Hence, once visited, a recurrent state is expected to be re-visited infinitely often whereas a transient state is expected to be re-visited only a finite number of times. Two states *communicate* (or are *strongly connected*) if there exists a cycle containing both states. Similarly, a subset of states communicate if any two states of the subset communicate. A *recurrent class* is a maximal communicating subset that contains only recurrent states. If Q contains transient states or it has multiple recurrent classes, X is called *reducible*. Otherwise, X is *irreducible*. Notice that all states of an irreducible Markov chain X communicate. Finally, a state is called *periodic* with a period d if d is the largest integer such that once visited the state is re-visited only after a multiple of d time steps. In the case a state has period 1, it is called *aperiodic*. States in the same recurrent class have the same period. Consequently, X is called periodic (aperiodic) if all its states are periodic (aperiodic).

Let $M = (S, P)$ be an irreducible *finite* state Markov chain in discrete time where Q is the state space and P is the 1-step transition matrix. If M is aperiodic, it tends to stabilize in the sense that the probability for M to be in any state $i \in Q$ converges as time progresses. Formally, $\lim_{n \to \infty} P\{M_n = i\}$ converges to a constant called the stationary probability of state i denoted by π_i. If M is periodic, the average probability of M being in state i over time, i.e., $\lim_{n \to \infty} \frac{1}{n} \sum_{k=0}^{n} P\{M_k = i\}$, converges to a constant. Let this constant be denoted by π_i as well. Regardless of its periodicity, M has the following nice property:

$$\pi = \pi P \tag{4}$$

where π is the row vector, $(\pi_1, \pi_2, \cdots, \pi_{|S|})$ satisfying $\sum_{i=1}^{|S|} \pi_i = 1$. π is called the *stationary distribution* of M in the sense that M_n has the same distribution for all $(n \geq 1)$ if M_0 has distribution π.

In this paper, we assume the Markov chains to be analyzed are irreducible for the following reasons. The state classification technique developed in [51] can be used to efficiently identify transient states and all recurrent classes of a Markov chain. If the original Markov chain has only one recurrent class (which is often the case [20, 51]), then all transient states can be removed, reducing the problem to finding the stationary probability distribution of an irreducible Markov chain. If the original Markov chain has multiple recurrent classes, one may first restrict the stationary analysis to each recurrent class. If necessary, one may further compute the limiting probability for each of the recurrent classes to be hit from a given initial distribution by performing a transient analysis [55].

To compute the stationary probabilities of the irreducible Markov chain we first determine its period using a symbolic version of a simple algorithm described in [29] which is very efficient in practice. For an irreducible aperiodic Markov chain $M = (S, P)$, i.e., with period equal to 1, π can be iteratively computed using the simple Power method as follows:

$$\pi^{(n+1)} = \pi^{(n)} P, \ n = 0, 1, \cdots \tag{5}$$

where $\pi^{(0)}$ is an initial distribution. The convergence of this sequence is geometric with rate determined by the absolute magnitude of the second largest eigenvalue of P. For periodic Markov chains the calculation must be a bit more complicated. Let $\{\overline{\pi}^{(n)} : n \geq 0\}$ be the sequence generated by taking the average of subsequences of $\{\pi^n : n \geq 0\}$, i.e.,

$$\overline{\pi}^{(n)} = \frac{1}{d} \sum_{r=0}^{d-1} \pi^{(nd+r)} \tag{6}$$

where $\pi^{(0)}$ is an initial distribution, and $\pi^{(k+1)} = \pi^{(k)} P$. Then, this sequence converges to π. The convergence of this iterative procedure is geometric with at least the same rate as that of the sequence $\{\pi^{(nd+r)} : n \geq 0\}$ for each fixed value $r = 0, 1, \cdots, d - 1$. Note that by setting $d = 1$, this procedure reduces to the simple Power method used in the aperiodic case. Note also that to prevent under/overflow in the presence of finite precision, normalization during the iterative procedure may be necessary.

3.2 Markovian-Based Performance Metrics

In this section, we relate several typical performance metrics to a general notion of *average time separations of events*. We show that the latter can be derived from another notion called *sojourn times* [42] of a Markov chain.

Sojourn Times Consider a irreducible Markov chain $M = \{M_n : n \geq 0\}$ with finite state space Q. Denote by A a proper subset of Q and $\overline{A} = Q - A$, the complementary subspace of A. Further, assume that both A and $\overline{A}$ have at least one state from the recurrent class of M. Clearly, both A and $\overline{A}$ will be visited infinitely often by M. Partition $(A, \overline{A})$ of the state space Q induces a decomposition of the transition probability matrix P into four sub-matrices and the stationary distribution π into two sub-vectors:

$$\begin{pmatrix} P_{AA} & P_{A\overline{A}} \\ P_{\overline{A}A} & P_{\overline{A}\overline{A}} \end{pmatrix} \text{ and } \pi = (\pi_A, \pi_{\overline{A}}).$$

The time spent by M in subset A during its $n^{th}(n > 0)$ visit to A is a random variable and called the nth *sojourn time* of M in A. More formally, a sojourn of M in subset A is a sequence $M_l, \cdots, M_{l+m}$ where $M_l, \cdots, M_{l+m-1} \in A, M_{l+m} \in \overline{A}$ and if $l > 0$ then $M_l \in \overline{A}$. This sojourn starts at time l, ends at time $l + m$, and lasts for m time steps. Let $N_{A,k}$ denote the kth sojourn time of M in A. Rubino et al. [42] show that the running average of $\{N_{A,k} : k \geq 1\}$ converges *in mean* to a constant called the sojourn time of M in A. Let it be denoted by J_A, then

$$J_A = \lim_{k \to \infty} \frac{1}{n} \sum_{l=1}^{k} \mathbf{E} N_{A,l} = \frac{\pi_A 1_A^T}{\pi_A (I - P_{AA}) 1_A^T}. \tag{7}$$

The quantity $\pi_A 1_A^T$ is the stationary probability that M is in set A, and $\pi_A(I - P_{AA})1_A^T$ is essentially the probability of the chain leaving A. In this sense, the above equation states that the sojourn time of M in A is the reciprocal of the probability of the chain leaving A given that it is in A.

The running average of the sequence $\{N_{A,k} : k \geq 0\}$ also converges *almost surely*, as formalized in the following lemma.

Lemma 1. *([55]) Let M be an irreducible finite state Markov chain. Let A be an non-empty subset of the state space of M. Then, the running average of the sequence $\{N_{A,k} : k \geq 1\}$ defined above converges almost surely to J_A given in Equation 7. That is,*

$$\frac{1}{n} \sum_{k=1}^{n} N_{A,k} \xrightarrow{a.s.} J_A. \tag{8}$$

The importance of this lemma lies in the fact that the running average of the sojourn time sequence converges to a constant for *almost all possible runs* of the Markov chain. As will be clear later that this implies the consistency of the system performance from one random run to another.

Average Cycle Time and Throughput We define an *event* as a transition of a state variable. For simplicity, this section will discuss only events of boolean state variables. Extensions to enumerate state variables are straightforward.

Denote $v(n)$ the value of variable v at time n. We say variable v makes a transition at time n if $v(n) \neq v(n-1)$. Let $Q_v^+ = \{s \mid s(v) = 1, s \in Q\}$ and $Q_v^- = \{s \mid s(v) = 1, s \in Q\}$ where $s(v)$ is the value of variable v in state s. Clearly, Q_v^+ and Q_v^- partition Q. Let us denote by $v^+(v^-)$ an event that corresponds to a state transition $t \in Q_v^- \times Q_v^+ (t \in Q_v^+ \times Q_v^-)$.

The average cycle time of event v^+, denoted by C_{v^+}, is the asymptotic time difference between two consecutive occurrences of v^+. Let the tuple (v^+, l) be the time of lth occurrence of v^+ and $\Delta_{v^+, l} = (v^+, l+1) - (v^+, l)$ be the time difference between the $(l+1)^{th}$ and l^{th} occurrences of v^+. Note that both (v^+, l) and $\Delta_{v^+, l}$ are random variables. Then, the cycle time C_{v^+} is defined to be:

$$C_{v^+} = \lim_{k \to \infty} \frac{1}{k} \sum_{l=1}^{k} \Delta_{v^+, l}. \tag{9}$$

Since the time difference of lth occurrence of $v^+(v^-)$ and its succeeding occurrence of $v^-(v^+)$ is the lth sojourn time of $Q_v^+(Q_v^-)$, we can determine C_{v^+} using sojourn times.

Theorem 2. *The running average of cycle time sequence due to event v^+ converges almost surely and in mean to a constant for which the following equation holds.*

$$C_{v^+} = \lim_{k \to \infty} \frac{1}{k} \sum_{l=1}^{k} N_{Q_v^+, l} + \lim_{k \to \infty} \frac{1}{k} \sum_{l=1}^{k} N_{Q_v^-, l} = J_{Q_v^+} + J_{Q_v^-}, \tag{10}$$

where J denotes the sojourn time of the corresponding subset of states as given in Equation 7.

Proof. By the fact that both Q_v^+ and Q_v^- are both non-empty subsets of Q plus the results of Lemma 1 and Rubino's Equation (7). □

The average cycle time of v^- is defined and can be determined similarly. In fact, we have $C_{v^-} = C_{v^+}$.

The throughput of the system is then defined to be the reciprocal of the average cycle time of some corresponding *indicating* event (such as the rising edge of a completion signal from a functional unit). Consequently, if the indicating event is v^+, then the corresponding throughput is computed as $\frac{1}{C_{v^+}}$. This naturally extends to more general indicating events.

Average Time Separation of Events (TSE) To determine other performance metrics such as latency, we need to study the average time difference between multiple events.

We define the time separations between events α and β as a sequence of time intervals, $\mathcal{I}(n) \triangleq \{I_k = [a_k, b_k] : k = 1, 2, \cdots, N_{\alpha \to \beta}(n)\}$ up to time n, where the starting and ending times of each interval are recursively defined as follows:

$$
\begin{aligned}
a_0 &= \min\{i : \alpha \in E_i\}, \\
b_k &= \min\{i : \beta \in E_i, i \geq a_k\}, \quad \text{for all } k \geq 0 \\
a_k &= \min\{i : \alpha \in E_i, i > b_{k-1}\}, \text{ for all } k \geq 1 \text{ and} \\
N_{\alpha \to \beta}(n) &= i : b_i \leq n, a_{i+1} > n,
\end{aligned}
$$

where E_i is the set of events that occur at time i.

Note that the length of time interval I_k, denoted by $\ell(I_k)$ is a random variable. In addition, I_k has zero length if $a_k = b_k$. We define the average time separation between event α and β, denoted by $\tau_{\alpha \to \beta}$, as the asymptotic behavior of $\ell(I_k)$:

$$
\tau_{\alpha \to \beta} \triangleq \lim_{n \to \infty} \frac{1}{N_{\alpha \to \beta}(n)} \sum_{k=1}^{N_{\alpha \to \beta}(n)} \ell(I_k) = \lim_{n \to \infty} \frac{1}{|\mathcal{I}(n)|} \sum_{I \in \mathcal{I}(n)} \ell(I) \quad (11)
$$

where $|\mathcal{I}(n)|$ denotes the total number of intervals in sequence $\mathcal{I}(n)$.

Theorem 3. *Let α and β are two events of an asynchronous systems that is modeled as an irreducible finite state Markov chain. Then, their average time separation $\tau_{\alpha \to \beta}$ defined in Equation 11 converges to a constant almost surely and in mean.*

Proof. The theorem is proved by similar arguments made in the proof of Theorem 2 [55]. □

Again, $\tau_{\alpha \to \beta}$ can be computed using sojourn times. The idea is to partition the time intervals into two sets: intervals that have non-zero length, $\mathcal{I}_1(n) = \{I_k \mid \ell(I_k) > 0, I_k \in \mathcal{I}(n)\}$, and those that have zero-length, $\mathcal{I}_2(n) = \{I_k \mid \ell(I_k) = 0, I_k \in \mathcal{I}(n)\}$. This can be accomplished by introducing three extra state variables into the model, say x, y and z. The behavior of x is defined such that sojourns of subspace $x = 1$ are in one-to-one correspondence with time intervals in $\mathcal{I}_1(n)$. Similarly, the behavior of z is defined such that the sojourns of subspace $z = 1$ are in one-to-one correspondence with time intervals in $\mathcal{I}_2(n)$. Finally, the behavior

P_x := case
$\quad u \neq u' \,\&\, u' = 1 \,\&\, v = v' : \{1\};$ /* if α but not β occurs */
$\quad v \neq v' \,\&\, v' = 1 \qquad\quad : \{0\};$ /* if β occurs */
$\quad 1 \qquad\qquad\qquad\qquad : \{x\};$ /* otherwise */

P_y := case
$\quad u \neq u' \,\&\, u' = 1 \,\&\, v \neq v'$
$\quad\,\&\, v' = 1 \qquad\qquad\quad : \{1\};$ /* if α and β both occur */
$\quad 1 \qquad\qquad\qquad\qquad : \{0\};$ /* otherwise */

T_z := case
$\quad x = 0 \,\&\, x' = 1 \mid z = 0$
$\quad\,\&\, z' = 1 \qquad\qquad\quad : \{1\};$ /* if x or z rises */
$\quad 1 \qquad\qquad\qquad\qquad : \{0\};$ /* otherwise */

Fig. 4. Definition of the auxiliary variables

of y is defined such that the total number of time intervals is the number of sojourns of subspace $y = 1$. Figure 4 gives the definitions of these three variables. It is important to note that the new model with these three auxiliary variables added is still Markovian because the variables can not introduce cycles in the dependency graph.

To illustrate how the auxiliary state variables track the time separation intervals, assume that both α and β are positive transitions, e.g., $\alpha = u^+$ and $\beta = v^+$. Figure 5(a) illustrates the situation where the intervals have non-zero length while Figure 5(b) shows a zero-length interval where α and β happen simultaneously. Sojourn times of $x = 1$ equal the corresponding non-zero time intervals between u^+ and v^+. Sojourns of $y = 1$ or $z = 1$ both have unit length.

It is now easy to relate the average time separation between α and β to the sojourn time of $x = 1$ by elementary probability analysis. From Equation 11, we have

$$\tau_{\alpha \to \beta} = \lim_{n \to \infty} \frac{\mathcal{I}_1(n)}{\mathcal{I}(n)} \times [\frac{1}{\mathcal{I}_1(n)} \sum_{I \in \mathcal{I}_1(n)} \ell(I)] \tag{12}$$

$$P\left\{\ell(I) > 0 \mid I \in \lim_{n \to \infty} \mathcal{I}(n)\right\} \times J_{x=1} \tag{13}$$

where $J_{x=1}$ is the average sojourn time of subspace $x = 1$.

The term $P\{\ell(I) > 0 \mid I \in \lim_{n \to \infty} \mathcal{I}(n)\}$ in Equation 13 is the limiting probability for an arbitrary time interval in $\mathcal{I}(n)$ to have non-zero length. It can be determined by the following equation:

$$P\left\{\ell(I) > 0 \mid I \in \lim_{n \to \infty} \mathcal{I}(n)\right\} = \frac{\pi_{y=1} \mathbf{1}_{y=1}^T - \pi_{z=1} \mathbf{1}_{z=1}^T}{\pi_{y=1} \mathbf{1}_{y=1}^T} \tag{14}$$

where $\pi_{y=1}$ and $\pi_{z=1}$ are the vectors representing the stationary probabilities of the states in subspace $y = 1$ and $z = 1$, respectively, and $\mathbf{1}_{y=1}$ and $\mathbf{1}_{z=1}$ are all-one vectors of proper length.

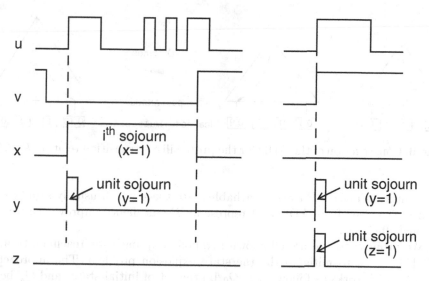

Fig. 5. The separations between u^+ and v^+ and the sojourns of the auxiliary variables when (a). u^+ and v^+ do not occur at the same time, (b). u^+ and v^+ occur at the same time

4 Symbolic Markov Analysis Techniques: A Summary

The principal difficulty with Markovian analysis is the computational challenge in dealing with the large state spaces of real systems. In particular, the most time consuming part of the analysis is the computation of the stationary distribution of the Markov chain. Once the stationary distribution is computed, the time spent in calculating the average TSEs is negligible. This section demonstrates how we address this problem by combining iterative Power method with symbolic representations using *binary decision diagrams* (BDDs) [6] and *algebraic decision diagrams* (ADDs) [2] to compute the stationary distribution. In Section 4.3, we review a more powerful approach to stationary analysis of Markov chains modeling asynchronous systems which uses a novel technique called *state compression* [52].

4.1 Symbolic Reachability Analysis

The first step in our Markovian analysis is to find all reachable states, which requires a reachability analysis. After that, we need to determine if the resulting Markov chain is irreducible. More generally, a state classification is required to determine all recurrence classes and all transient state of the Markov chain. We assume that Markov chain contains only one recurrent class so that all transient states cannot affect that stationary behavior of the systems and thus can be ignored. In [51], a powerful symbolic state classification technique is presented. The importance of finding all the reachable states is that we can then restrict

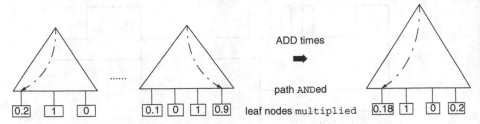

Fig. 6. Construction of the ADD for the probabilistic transition relation $\mathcal{P}(V, V')$

the transition matrix P to the reachable state space which usually significantly reduces the size of the ADD that represents P, and hence improve the computational efficiency.

We propose to use a well-known symbolic approach for reachability analysis [33, 7, 14] to mitigate the the state explosion problem. The approach is iterative and works as follows. Let Q_0 be the set of initial states and Q_k be all the states reachable from Q_0 in at most k steps from Q_0. The set Q_k can be computed iteratively as follows:

$$Q_{k+1} = Q_k \cup \{s' \mid \exists s, s \in Q_k - Q_{k-1}, (s, s') \in T\},$$

where $Q_{-1} = \emptyset$ and T is the (boolean) transition relation the system introduced in Section 2.1. The iteration continues until the *frontier set* $Q_k - Q_{k-1}$ is empty, reaching a fixed point.

This fixed point is computed using BDDs. Let $\mathcal{T}_v(V, V')$ be the BDD corresponding to the partial transition relation T_v, where V and V' denote the BDD variables for the current and the next state spaces, respectively. Then, the global (or monolithic) transition relation of a timed system $\mathcal{T}(V, V')$ is a *conjunction* of BDDs of all the partial transition relations, i.e., $\mathcal{T} = \bigwedge_{v \in V} \mathcal{T}_v$. Let $\mathcal{Q}_k(V)$ be the BDD corresponding to Q_k. Then, the set of reachable states is the fixed point of the following computation:

$$\mathcal{Q}_{k+1}(V') = \mathcal{Q}_k(V') \vee [\exists_{v \in V} \mathcal{Q}_k(V) \wedge \neg \mathcal{Q}_{k-1}(V) \wedge \mathcal{T}(V, V')].$$

4.2 Symbolic Power Method

Let $\mathcal{P}_v(V, V')$ represent the ADD for the partial probabilistic transition relation P_v. Then, the probabilistic transition relation can be represented by an ADD $\mathcal{P}(V, V')$ which is constructed using ADD `times` as follows:

$$\mathcal{P}(V, V') = \cdot_{v \in V} \mathcal{P}_v(V, V')$$

Figure 6 illustrates the construction of $\mathcal{P}$ from $\mathcal{P}_v$'s.

The symbolic calculation of the Power method is the same as the explicit one except that vector-matrix multiplication is replaced with ADD `times`. To accelerate the convergence, however, we take P^{iter}, a higher order of P to be the multiplicative. To choose a proper power number $iter$, we perform iterative squaring on $P^{2*iter} \leftarrow P^{iter} \cdot P^{iter}$ and $iter \leftarrow 2 * iter$ starting with $iter = 1$. The squaring process terminates when either the $\text{size}(P^{iter})$ exceeds a user definable constant or $\text{size}(P^{2*iter}) > 2\text{size}(P^{iter})$. This optimization yields faster convergence at the expense of more computation in each iteration step, resulting in a short run-time. Moreover, many ADD/BDD size minimization techniques [2, 43] can be used to reduce the size of $\mathcal{P}(V, V')$ with respect to all the unreachable states.

4.3   Symbolic State Compression

There are many proposed techniques to speed up iterative approaches such as Power method for large linear systems. Examples are *pre-conditioning* [40] and *orthogonal multi-vector iteration* [46]. It is unclear whether these sophisticated techniques are likely to give a significant improvements, however, because they impose significant overhead. In addition, there is an intensive ongoing research trend in probability theory on the *lumpability* of Markov chains [1, 41]. The basic idea in lumping states is to explore the *similarity* (if any) among the behavior of the Markov chain when it is in different states. Specifically, the lumpability approach partitions the state space into subsets and treats each subset as a single state such that the resulting process retains Markov property. A necessary and sufficient condition for this to be possible is all states within a subset has the same transition behavior with respect to all other subsets. However, this is a rather restrictive condition. In general, it is often not possible for a real system to satisfy this condition and get a much smaller Markov chain [21]. Therefore, this approach cannot be considered as a general method to reduce the computational complexity.

The method presented in this section takes advantage of the fact that most asynchronous systems consist mainly of components with bounded delay (i.e., it is rare that a component in an asynchronous system has unbounded delay, a notable exception being an arbiter element in metastability [9, 49]). Using time-discretization to model these systems as Markov chains leads to state spaces that have *limited feedback*. More precisely, let the (reachable) state space Q be partitioned into two subsets, B and $\overline{B}$, such that any two consecutive occurrences of any state in $\overline{B}$ is always interleaved by at least one occurrence of some state in B. In graph terminology, B is a *feedback vertex set* (FVS) of states. Time-discretization of asynchronous systems with mostly components that have bounded delays leads to models with small feedback vertex sets.

More specifically, we can use standard techniques to define a new Markov chain which has the FVS as its state space. One of the key properties of this new Markov chain is that these feedback states keep the same relative occurrence frequencies as they have in the original Markov chain. Creating this Markov chain is the first step of our method and is called *state compression*. Next, the stationary distribution of the new Markov chain is computed by the Power method or even by direct (non-iterative) methods if the new Markov chain is sufficiently

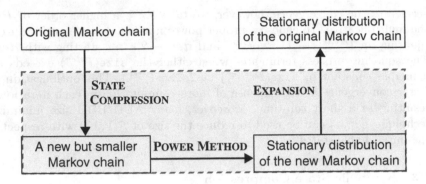

Fig. 7. Block diagram of our method

small. Finally, the stationary distribution of the original Markov chain is expanded from that of the new Markov chain just computed. This third step is called *expansion*. All these steps are implemented using symbolic techniques. Figure 7 depicts an overview of our method.

4.4   Finding Feedback Vertex Sets

It is desirable to find a minimum FVS in order to make the state space of the new Markov chain small. However, this is a well-known *NP*-complete problem [18]. Many heuristic algorithms to find a *minimal FVS* [44, 10, 38] exist, but they are all too expensive for large graphs.

We develop two simple heuristics to symbolically search for a good FVS which is not necessarily the minimum. Let us assume an irreducible Markov chain M has a state space Q and a transition matrix P. The following definitions are needed to describe the heuristics.

Definition: Given two states $i, j \in Q$ for which $P_{ij} > 0$, we say state j is a *next state* of state i and state i is a *previous state* of state j.

Definition: A state is called a *decision state* if it has multiple next states. Otherwise, it is a *non-decision state*. A state is called a *merging state* if it has multiple previous states. Otherwise, it is called a *non-merging state*.

Note that a non-decision state can reach other states only through its sole next state. Similarly, a non-merging state can be reached only through its sole previous state.

Definition: A *forward-string* is a sample path which contains only non-decision states except possibly for its tail state. A *reverse-string* is a sample path which contains only non-merging states except possibly for its head state. A *maximal forward-string* is one which is not contained in any other forward-string. A *maximal reverse-string* is defined similarly.

Note that a forward-string is maximal *iff* it starts with a next state of some decision state and ends with a decision state. Similarly, a reverse-string is maxi-

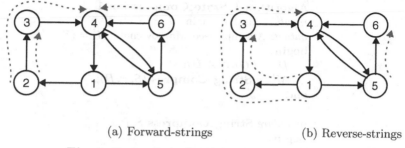

(a) Forward-strings   (b) Reverse-strings

Fig. 8. Forward- and reverse-string examples

mal *iff* it starts with a merging state and ends with a previous state of a merging state.

Example: Forward-strings and reverse-strings. Suppose the FSM model of some Markov chain is as shown in Figure 8. By definition, every single state is both a forward-string and a reverse-string. One can list several forward-strings of length more than 1. Examples are $(2,3)$, $(2,3,4)$ and $(6,4)$. The latter two are also maximal. Example reverse-strings are $(1,2,3)$, $(1,2,3,4)$, and $(5,6)$. The latter two are also maximal.   □

Finally, we define a *loop* to be a simple cycle that is both a forward-string and a reverse-string.

Our first heuristic for state compression is thus to search for all the decision states of S. If there is no decision state, any single state of S forms a FVS which must be the smallest. Otherwise, we select the set of all decision states which is also forms a FVS. The heuristics can be applied iteratively. That is, each time the heuristic is applied, a new Markov chain is created. Since a decision state in the original Markov chain may become a non-decision state in the new Markov chain, the heuristic may be applied again to get an even smaller Markov chain. This process continues until the heuristic fails to compress the Markov chain any further. Figure 9 illustrates this idea.

It is not difficult to see that the compressed Markov chain returned from Algorithm 1 does not contain any forward-string of length more than 1. In other

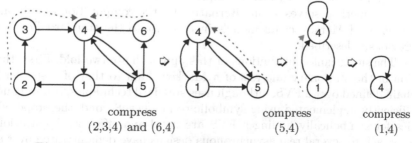

compress   compress   compress
(2,3,4) and (6,4)   (5,4)   (1,4)

Fig. 9. Forward-string-based iterative state compression

Algorithm 1 State_Compression_1
input: A Markov chain $M = (S, P)$.
output: A compressed Markov chain $M' = (S', P')$.
begin
$\quad D := FORWARD$;
$\quad M' := \textbf{String\_Compress}(S, P, D)$;
end

procedure **String_Compress**(S, P, D)
begin
$\quad$ if D = FORWARD **then**
$\qquad$ Let $S' :=$ the set of decision states in S;
$\quad$ **else**
$\qquad$ Let $S' :=$ the set of merging states in S;
$\quad$ **endif**
$\quad$ if $S' = \emptyset$ **then**
$\qquad$ Take s as an arbitrary state of S;
$\qquad$ $S' := \{s\}$; $P' := (1)$;
$\qquad$ return (S', P');
$\quad$ **endif**
$\quad$ if $S' = S$ **then**
$\qquad$ return (S, P);
$\quad$ **endif**
$\quad$ compute P' from P and S using symbolic matrix
algebra;
$\qquad$ return **String_Compress**(S', P', D);
end

Fig. 10. State compression based on forward-string concept

words, the forward-string-based heuristics compresses forward-strings down to their tail states. This same idea can be applied on the reverse-strings. That is, we may compress all reverse-strings up to their head states. These two compression ideas can also be combined.

To avoid the conflict of the two compression strategies on a forward-string that is also a reverse-string, we do not applied them concurrently but rather *sequentially.* Figure 11 shows the algorithm that adopts both forward-string-based and reverse-string-based compressions.

This method serves as an alternative for the computation of stationary distribution of Markov chain models in contrast to the standard Power method previously described.

The significant contributions of this approach are two fold. First, the reduction of the stationary analysis of a Markov chain to that of a smaller Markov chain defined over a FVS, although uses standard techniques, is novel and can be efficiently implemented using symbolic techniques. Second, the proposed heuristics for symbolically finding a FVS are novel and efficient. Application of our approach to several real asynchronous designs have demonstrated over an order

Algorithm 2 State_Compression_2
input: A Markov chain $M = (S, P)$.
output: A compressed Markov chain $M' = (S', P')$.
begin
 $S'_1 := S, P'_1 := P$;
 $D := \text{FORWARD}$;
 $Failed := 0$;
 do
  $S'_0 := S'_1; P'_0 := P'_1$;
  $(S'_1, P'_1) := \textbf{String\_Compress}(S'_0, P'_0, D)$;
  if $S'_1 = S'_0$ **then**
   $Failed := Failed + 1$;
  else
   $Failed := 0$;
  if $D = \text{FORWARD}$ **then**
   $D := \text{REVERSE}$;
  else
   $D := \text{FORWARD}$;
  endif
 while $(Failed < 2)$;
 $M' := (S'_1, P'_1)$;
end

Fig. 11. State compression based on both forward-string and reverse-string concepts

of magnitude reduction of the overall CPU time. Moreover, this method can analyze larger systems than is possible using the traditional power method.

5 Case Studies

This section gives a few performance analysis examples using the technique presented in the previous sections. The examples include analysis of a linear asynchronous pipeline (the FIFO), a differential equation solver, a pausible clock interface (PCI), and a collection of synchronized processes. Besides giving relevant performance results, each example also compares the run-time efficiencies of the technique with and without state-compression.

5.1 The FIFO

The first experiments is a FIFO with 6 stages and some trivial environments as shown in Figure 12. All stages are functionally identical. The C-element has unit delay. The delay line of each stage has a random bounded delay (3 different distributions are considered). The left-side environment (LSE) issues a new request one time unit after it is acknowledged. The right-side environment (RSE) has a fixed delay of δ. The experiment varies δ from 1 to 7. This yields a total of 21 models.

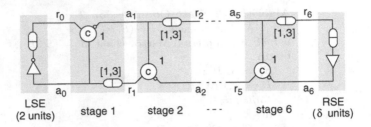

Fig. 12. A 6-stage FIFO with simple environments

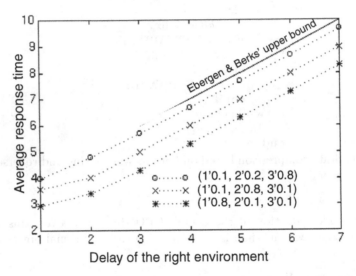

Fig. 13. Average response times

Figure 13 shows the FIFO's average response time as a function of the internal stage delay distribution and the RSE delay δ. Figure 14 shows the FIFO's throughput in the terms of its average cycle time. As we expect, the average cycle-time equals the average response time plus the LSE delay.

The models have up to 16 circuit elements and 28K reachable states. The state-compression technique speeds up the analysis by 2 to 5 times. With state-compression, all models take no more than 15 minutes to complete on a SUN SPARC20.

5.2   The Differential Equation Solver (DIFFEQ)

The asynchronous DIFFEQ ASIC [56] implements the following behavioral procedure:

```
DIFFEQ Procedure
read inputs
while (x < a) {
x1  := x + dx;
u1  := u − 3 × x × u × dx − 3 × y × dx;
y1  := y + u × x;
x  := x1;  u := u1;  y := y1;
}
output results
```

Figure 15 illustrates the structure of the ASIC. We start with an untimed RTL model used for verification of the ASIC [56]. This RTL model describes the behavior of all controllers, C1 through C4. It uses non-determinism to abstract the data-dependent delays of the functional units as well as the assignment of the *sign* signal in ALU2 that holds the result of the test $x < a$. Controller C2 examines this result to decide whether to initiate a new iteration or to terminate the procedure. We convert this model to a timed probabilistic model by assuming each state transition takes one time step and by annotating the probability distributions for the non-determinstic delays and the *sign* signal.

We focus on two performance metrics. The first is the expected delay of the entire procedure. This corresponds to the average time separation from START$^+$ to DONE$^+$. The second metric is the average delay of one loop iteration. There are two entrance points to the loop, one for the first iteration and the other for all subsequent iterations. To apply our notion of average TSEs, we introduce a new indicating variable which rises when either entrance point is reached. In addition, a second indicating variable is introduced which rises when the loop

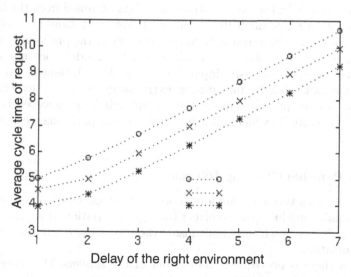

Fig. 14. Average cycle time

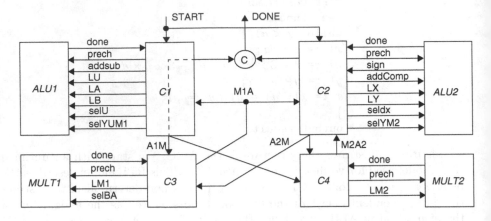

Fig. 15. A block diragram of the DIFFEQ ASIC

breaks. Then, the average TSE between the rising of the two indicating variables corresponds to the average loop delay.

We analyze both metrics on two versions of the model, one with estimated delays and the other with backannotated delays. The estimated (backannoted) model has about 20 modeled signals and 7,632 (11,036) states. Using state-compression, the estimated (backannoted) model is reduced to 614 (194) states. The run-times for both models are less than 15 minutes and are both reduced to about 1 minute using the state-compression technique.

The backannotated model yields much slower performance, primarily because the model incorporate longer wire delays that were not considered in the initial model. Interestingly, the average iteration delays obtained from the backannoted model is within 8% of the SPICE analysis. However, it should be noted that the accuracy of the results is sensitive to the accuracy of the probability distribution assigned to the ALU sign signal. Moreover, the model does not capture the correlation between successive input data to the ALU. If desired, this correlation can be approximated by introducing extra variables at the expense of larger run-time. A more practical application of our technique, however, is to compare different structures in which relative accuracy of the performance metrics is more important.

5.3   A Pausible Clocking Interface

Figure 16 shows two asynchronous modules (the senders) communicating with a synchronous module (the receiver) through a variation of a pausible clocking interface (PCI) [58] which is built inside the receiver and guarantees failure-free synchronization.

When there is no request from either of the senders, the receiver is freely clocked by the ring oscillator (formed by an inverter, two MEs and an AND gate). It continues to run freely after receiving requests from the senders if there

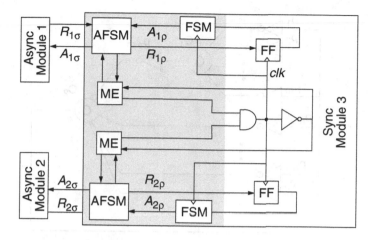

Fig. 16. A pausible clocking interface

is a clear difference between the arrival time of the requests and that of the clock edge. However, if this time difference is significantly small so that synchronization failure may occur, either the clock is *paused* by stretching its falling edge or the corresponding AFSM delays its request out (a transition of signal $R_{x\rho}$). This is done so by the corresponding ME element. The AND gate ensures that the next clock edge is delayed until all possible synchronization failures have been resolved.

The following timing assumptions are made on the model. The AND gate and the inverter have delays of 4 units and 3 units, respectively. The two senders are identical. They have a geometrically distributed delay with a parameter of 0.9. That is, the probability of a request occurring $n \geq 1$ time units after acknowledgment is $0.1^{n-1} * 0.9$. Similarly, the delay at the receiver side is also geometrically distributed with a parameter of 0.9. The mutual exclusion element *mutex* has a unit delay and is assumed to be fair with simultaneously arriving requests.

The model has 51,376 states (all recurrent) and is reduced to 8,704 states by the state-compression technique. As a result, the state-compression technique reduces the run-time (to get stationary distribution) from 12 hours (incomplete) to about 2 minutes.

5.4 Synchronized Processes

This example is a set of concurrently running processes synchronized at some special points. Figure 17 shows a simple configuration of $n + 1$ $(n > 1)$ processes from p_1 to p_{n+1} each depicted by an inverter. All processes excepted p_{n+1} start running simultaneously. Process p_{n+1} starts running only after processes p_1 through p_m $(0 < m \leq n)$ all complete and are synchronized at the C-element C_1.

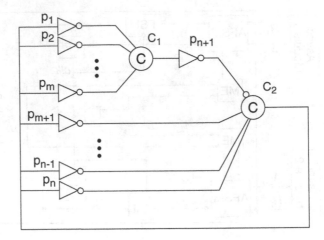

Fig. 17. Synchronized processes

The C-element C_2 waits until processes p_{m+1} through p_{n+1} terminate, and then triggers processes p_1 through p_n, making the entire procedure repeat.

We assume all processes take some independent identically distributed random processing times as follows: with probability 0.1, a process takes a delay of 1 unit, with probability 0.4, a delay of 2 units, with probability 0.4, a delay of 3 units and with probability 0.1, a delay of 4 units. Further, both C-elements take a fixed delay of 1 unit.

It might be useful to know performance metrics such as the average cycle time of the entire procedure (average time separation of any two consecutive output transitions of the element C_2), or the average waiting (idle) time for each of the processes. One might then perform a Markovian analysis in order to obtain these measures [50].

The state space of this simple configuration, unfortunately, increases roughly by a factor of 4 with each added process. For $n = 24$, we face a state space of over 10^{15} states, excluding the possibility to use any explicit approaches on currently available machines. However, due to the symmetry involved in the configuration, our symbolic technique obtain the stationary probability of each of the state using the Power method with a memory usage of fewer than 30 Mbytes. Unfortunately, it takes over 14 hours to complete on a Sparc20 (assuming the Power method starts with the initial distribution where each state is equiprobable).

With the state-compression technique, the state space is reduced to a single state for every possible configurations of the system (i.e., for every possible value of m). In fact, that single state is always one of the two global synchronization states where all processes are idle and element C_2 is about to make a transition. It is worth noticing from this simple example that high concurrency does not usually limit the state compression ratio, nor does generally the synchronization

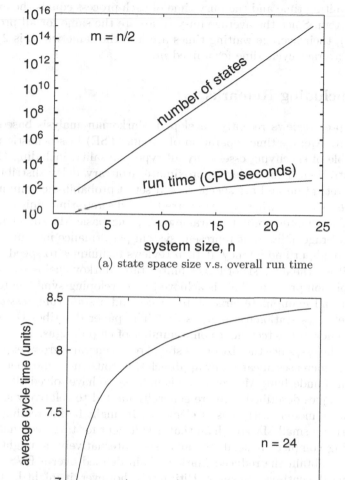

(a) state space size v.s. overall run time

(b) system performance

Fig. 18. Experimental results of synchronized processes

(e.g., at element C_1). Rather, the main reason for a high state compression ratio in the example is that there is only one feedback signal (i.e., the output of element C_2), which implies the system has a small feedback set in its state space. The Power method for the compressed chain converges immediately. For $n = 24$, the total run-time is shorter than 20 minutes for every configuration. Figure 18(a) shows that the overall run time is a small polynomial function of the system size while the number of states grows exponentially.

Figure 18 plots the average cycle time of the entire procedure computed as a function of m. Further, one can show in this example that the sum of the average waiting time and the busy time of each process equals the average cycle of the system. Since the average busy times are the same for all processes (i.e., 2.5 units), their average waiting times are also the same which is 2.5 units less than the average cycle time for a fixed m.

6 Concluding Remarks

This chapter reviews recently developed Markovian-analysis based techniques to compute average time separation of events (TSE) in stochastic models that are capable of specifying essentially all types causality, including OR-causality and arbitration. The models approximate arbitrary delay distributions using time-discretization and are specified as a set of probabilistic communicating finite state machines which are converted into discrete-time finite state Markov chains. The chapter presents a framework using basic Markov chain theory to analyze average TSEs that represent system performance measures such as average throughput and latency. It then reviews techniques to speed up by orders of magnitude the analysis of larger finite state Markov chains by attacking the state-explosion problem. This is achieved by developing symbolic techniques to represent and manipulate large state spaces and a *state compression* technique that accelerates stationary analysis [52]. The paper describes the effectiveness and efficiency of the techniques on a number of chip designs.

Nevertheless, since the size of the state space generally grows exponentially as the system increases linearly, any approach that constructs and then analyzes the *flat* (entire) underlying Markov chain is unlikely to have solved all the problems. The techniques described here are generally limited to relatively small abstract performance models with tens of elements. It might be interesting future work to construct a small Markov chain that is sufficient for targeted analysis without performing complete reachability analysis. Alternatively, it might be possible to directly obtain the reduced Markov chain defined over a FVS without ever examining the entire state space. Ultimately, however, it might be the case that the only effective analysis scheme capable of analyzing large industrial systems is a hierarchical one where all other research efforts only increase the capability of analysis at one level.

References

[1] A. M. Abdel-Moneim and F. W. Leysieffer. Weak lumpability in finite Markov chains. *Journal of Applied Probability*, 19:685–691, 1982. 329
[2] R. I. Bahar, E. A. Frohm, C. M. Gaona, and G. D. Hachtel. Algebraic decision diagrams and their applications. In *Proc. International Conf. Computer-Aided Design (ICCAD)*, pages 188–191, 1993. 327, 329
[3] Peter A. Beerel. Asynchronous circuits: An increasing practical design solution. In *Proc. of ISQED*, 2002. 313
[4] W. Belluomini and C. J. Myers. Verification of timed systems using POSETS. In *Proc. International Workshop on Computer Aided Verification*, pages 403–415, 1998. 314

[5] C. H. (Kees) van Berkel, Mark B. Josephs, and Steven M. Nowick. Scanning the technology: Applications of asynchronous circuits. *Proceedings of the IEEE*, 87(2):223–233, February 1999. 313

[6] R. E. Bryant. Graph-based algorithm for boolean function munipulation. *IEEE Transactions on Computers*, 35, August 1986. 327

[7] J. R. Burch, E. M. Clarke, D. E. Long, K. L. McMillan, and D. L. Dill. Symbolic model checking for sequential circuit verification. *IEEE Transactions on Computer-Aided Design*, 13(4):401–424, April 1994. 328

[8] S. M. Burns. *Performance Analysis and Optimization of Asynchronous Circuits*. PhD thesis, California Institute of Technology, 1991. 314

[9] T. J. Chaney and C. E. Molnar. Anomalous behavior of synchronizer and arbiter circuits. *IEEE Transactions on Computers*, C-22(4):421–422, April 1973. 315, 329

[10] K. Cheng and V. D. Agrawal. A partial scan method for sequential circuits and feedback. *IEEE Transactions on Computers*, 39(4):544–548, April 1990. 330

[11] T.-A. Chu. *Synthesis of Self-Timed VLSI Circuits from Graph-theoretic Specifications*. PhD thesis, Massachusetts Institute of Technology, 1987. 314

[12] K. L. Chung. *Markov Chains with Stationary Transition Probabilities*. Springer-Verlag, 1960.

[13] Jordi Cortadella, Michael Kishinevsky, Alex Kondratyev, Luciano Lavagno, and Alexandre Yakovlev. Petrify: a tool for manipulating concurrent specifications and synthesis of asynchronous controllers. In *XI Conference on Design of Integrated Circuits and Systems*, Barcelona, November 1996. 314

[14] O. Coudert, J. C. Madre, and C. Berthet. Verifying temporal properties of sequential machines without building their state diagrams. In E. M. Clarke and R. P. Kurshan, editors, *Computer-Aided Verification'90*, pages 75–84. American Mathematical Society, June 1990. 328

[15] Al Davis. A data-driven machine architecure suitable for VLSI implementation. In *Proceedings of the Caltech Conference on Very Large Scale Integration*, pages 479–494, 1979. 314

[16] J. Ebergen and R. Berks. Response time properties of some asynchronous circuits. In *Proc. International Symposium on Advanced Research in Asynchronous Circuits and Systems (ASYNC)*, pages 76–86. IEEE Computer Society Press, April 1997. 314

[17] J. C. Ebergen. A formal approach to designing delay-insensitive circuits. *Distributed Computing*, 3(5):107–119, 1991. 314

[18] M. R. Garey and D. S. Johnson. *Computers and Intractability: A Guide to the Theory of NP-Completeness*. W. H. Freeman and Company, 1979. 330

[19] M. R. Greenstreet and K. Steiglitz. Bubbles can make self-timed pipelines fast. *Journal of VLSI Signal Processing*, 2(3):139–148, November 1990. 315

[20] G. D. Hachtel, E. Macii, A. Pardo, and F. Somenzi. Markovian analysis of large finite state machines. *IEEE Transactions on Computer-Aided Design*, 15(12):1479–1493, December 1996. 322

[21] Y. Ho and X. Cao. *Perturbation analysis of discrete event dynamic systems*. Kluwer Academic Publishers, 1991. 329

[22] C. A. R. Hoare. *Communicating Sequential Processes*. Prentice Hall International, UK. LTD., Englewood Cliffs, New Jersey, 1985. 314

[23] M. A. Holliday and M. Y. Vernon. A generalized timed Petri net model for performance analysis. *IEEE Transactions on Software Engineering*, 13(12):1297–1310, December 1987. 315

[24] H. Hulgaard and S. M. Burns. Bounded delay timing analysis of a class of CSP programs with choice. In *Proc. International Symposium on Advanced Research in Asynchronous Circuits and Systems (ASYNC)*, pages 2–11. IEEE Computer Society Press, November 1994. 314

[25] H. Hulgaard and S. M. Burns. An algorithm for exact bounds on time separation of events in concurrent systems. *IEEE Transactions on Computers*, 44(11):1306–1317, November 1995. 314

[26] R. M. Karp. A characterization of the minimum cycle mean in a diagraph. *Discrete mathematics*, 23:309–311, 1978. 314

[27] J. G. Kemeny and J. L. Snell. *Finite Markov Chains*. Springer, 1976.

[28] P. Kudva, G. Gopalakrishnan, E. Brunvand, and V. Akella. Performance analysis and optimization of asynchronous circuits. In *Proc. International Conf. Computer Design (ICCD)*, pages 221–225, October 1994. 315, 318

[29] V. G. Kulkarni. *Modeling and Analysis of Stochastic Systems*. Chapman & Hall, 1995. 322

[30] H. J. Kushner. A control problem for a new type of public transportation system, via heavy traffic analysis. In F. P. Kelly and R. J. Williams, editors, *The IMA Volumes in Mathematics and Its Applications: Stochastic networks*, pages 139–168. Springer-Verlag, 1995. 318

[31] M. Ajmone Marsan, G. Balbo, and G. Conte. A Class of Generalized Stochastic Petri Nets. *ACM Trans. on Comput. Syst.*, 12:93–122, May 1984. 315

[32] A. J. Martin. Programming in VLSI: from communicating processes to delay-insensitive VLSI circuits. In C. A. R. Hoare, editor, *UT Year of Programming Institute on Concurrent Programming*, pages 1–64. Addison-Wesley, 1990. 314

[33] K. L. McMillan. *Symbolic Model Checking*. Kluwer Academic Publishers, 1993. 328

[34] M. K. Molloy. *On the Integration of delay and throughput measures in distributed processing models*. PhD thesis, University of California, Los Angeles, 1981. 315

[35] M. K. Molloy. Discrete Time Stochastic Petri Nets. *IEEE Transactions on Software Engineering*, 11:417–423, April 1985. 315

[36] C. J. Myers and T. H.-Y. Meng. Synthesis of timed asynchronous circuits. *IEEE Transactions on VLSI Systems*, 1(2):106–119, June 1993. 314

[37] S. M. Nowick and D. Dill. "Asynchronous State Machine Synthesis Using a Local Clock". In *International Workshop on Logic Synthesis*, 1991. 314

[38] S. Park and S. B. Akers. A graph theoretic approach to partial scan design by k-cycle elimination. In *Proc. IEEE International Test Conference*, pages 303–311, 1992. 330

[39] J. L. Peterson. *Petri Net Theory and the Modeling of Systems*. Prentice Hall, 1981. 314

[40] V. D. Ploeg. Preconditioning techniques for large sparse, non-symmetric matrices with arbitrary sparsity patterns. In *Proc. IMACS Symposium on Iterative Methods in Linear Algebra*, pages 173–179, 1991. 329

[41] G. Rubino and B. Sericola. On weak lumpability in Markov chains. *Journal of Applied Probability*, 26:446–457, 1989. 329

[42] G. Rubino and B. Sericola. Sojourn times in finite Markov process. *Journal of Applied Probability*, 27:744–756, 1989. 323

[43] T. Shiple, R. Hojati, A. Sangiovanni-Vincentelli, and R. K. Brayton. Heuristic minimization of bdds using don't cares. In *Proc. ACM/IEEE Design Automation Conference*, pages 225–231, 1994. 329

[44] G. W. Smith, Jr. and R. B. Walford. The identification of a minimal feedback vertex set of a directed graph. *IEEE Transactions on Circuits and Systems*, 22(1):9–15, January 1975. 330

[45] K. Stevens, S. Rotem, R. Ginosar, P. A. Beerel, C. Myers, K. Yun, R. Kol, C. Dike, and M. Roncken. An asynchronous instruction length decoder. *IEEE Journal of Solid-State Circuits*, 36(2):217–228, February 2001. 313

[46] G. W. Stewart. Methods of simultaneous iteration for computing invariant subspaces of non-ruminating matrices. *Numerical Mathematics*, 25:123–136, 1976. 329

[47] W. J. Stewart. *An Introduction to the Numerical Solution of Markov Chains.* Princeton University Press, 1994.

[48] S. H. Unger. *Asynchronous Sequential Switching Circuits.* New York: Wiley-Interscience, 1969. (re-issued by R. E. Krieger, Malabar, 1983). 314

[49] H. J. M. Veendrick. The behavior of flip-flops used as synchronizers and prediction of their failure. *IEEE Journal of Solid-State Circuits*, SC-15(2):169–176, April 1980. 329

[50] A. Xie and P. A. Beerel. Symbolic techniques for performance analysis of asynchronous systems based on average time separation of events. In *Proc. International Symposium on Advanced Research in Asynchronous Circuits and Systems (ASYNC)*, pages 64–75. IEEE Computer Society Press, April 1997. 314, 318, 321, 338

[51] A. Xie and P. A. Beerel. Efficient state classification of finite state Markov chains. *IEEE Transactions on Computer-Aided Design*, 17(12):1334–1338, December 1998. 314, 322, 327

[52] A. Xie and P. A. Beerel. Accelerating Markovian analysis of asynchronous systems using state compression. *IEEE Transactions on Computer-Aided Design*, 18(7):869–888, July 1999. 314, 327, 340

[53] A. Xie and P. A. Beerel. Performance analysis of asynchronous circuits and systems using stochastic timed Petri nets. In A. Yakovlev, L. Gomes, and L. Lavagno, editors, *Hardware Design and Petri Nets*, pages 239–268. Kluwer Academic Publishers, March 2000. 314

[54] A. Xie, S. Kim, and P. A. Beerel. Bounding average time separation of events in stochastic timed Petri nets with choice. In *Proc. International Symposium on Advanced Research in Asynchronous Circuits and Systems (ASYNC)*, April 1999. 314

[55] Aiguo Xie. *Performance Analysis of Asynchronous Circuits and Systems.* PhD thesis, University of Southern California, August 1999. 321, 322, 324, 325

[56] K. Y. Yun, P. A. Beerel, V. Vakilotojar, A. E. Dooply, and J. Arceo. A low-control-overhead asynchronous differential equation solver. In *Proc. International Symposium on Advanced Research in Asynchronous Circuits and Systems (ASYNC)*, pages 210–223. IEEE Computer Society Press, April 1997. 313, 334, 335

[57] K. Y. Yun, D. L. Dill, and S. M. Nowick. Synthesis of 3D asynchronous state machines. In *Proc. International Conf. Computer Design (ICCD)*, pages 346–350. IEEE Computer Society Press, October 1992. 314

[58] K. Y. Yun and R. P. Donohue. Pausible clocking: A first step toward heterogeneous systems. In *Proc. International Conf. Computer Design (ICCD)*, pages 118–123. IEEE Computer Society Press, October 1996. 336

Author Index